Presented to
the Greenville College Library
in memory of my parents,
pioneer missionaries to South Africa:
Anna Sanford Brodhead,
first head of the Art Department,
and John Pearson Brodhead,
member of the first class at G.C., 1892-
(also, on the Faculty, 1916-'18
and a B.A. graduate in 1918.)

Grace Brodhead Ward, '18.

RHODES OF AFRICA

Cecil Rhodes

RHODES OF AFRICA

by

FELIX GROSS

With frontispiece and
12 pages of half-tone illustrations

CASSELL & COMPANY LTD
LONDON

CASSELL & CO LTD
37/38 St Andrew's Hill, Queen Victoria Street
London, E.C.4

and at

31/34 George IV Bridge, Edinburgh; 210 Queen Street, Melbourne; 26/30 Clarence Street, Sydney; 24 Wyndham Street, Auckland, New Zealand; 1068 Broadview Avenue, Toronto 6; P.O. Box 275, Cape Town; P.O. Box 1119o, Johannesburg; P.O. Box 959, Accra, Gold Coast; Munsoor Building, Main Street, Colombo 11; Haroon Chambers, South Napier Road, Karachi; 13/14 Ajmeri Gate Extension, New Delhi 1; 15 Graham Road, Ballard Estate, Bombay 1; 17 Chittaranjan Avenue, Calcutta 13; Macdonald House, Orchard Road, Singapore 9; Avenida 9 de Julho 1138, São Paulo; Galeria Güemes, Escritorio 454/59 Florida 165, Buenos Aires; 25 rue Henri Barbusse, Paris 5e; 25 Ny Strandvej, Espergaerde, Denmark; Kauwlaan 17, The Hague

First Published 1956

PRINTED AND BOUND IN GREAT BRITAIN
BY JARROLD AND SONS LTD., NORWICH
F.656

In Memoriam

ELSE

AUTHOR'S NOTE

This book, the result of twelve years of research work, is based on authentic contemporary sources. The thoughts and soliloquies of Cecil Rhodes are derived from his speeches, letters and reported conversations. So as not to interrupt the continuity of the story I have refrained from giving references in footnotes.

An extensive bibliography of Rhodes and his times will be published later as it would be too bulky to be included in this volume. In order to give inquisitive scholars an opportunity to make use of this bibliography one copy will be deposited in each of the following libraries:

Public Library, Cape Town.
Library of the British Museum, London.
Bodleian Library, Oxford.
Library of Congress, Washington (D.C.).

I wish to express my gratitude to my daughter, Miss Ursula A. Gross, M.A., M.S., for her great assistance and patient collaboration. To Miss Anne Kramer, B.A., and Mr Sidney Macer-Wright, my cordial thanks for their useful help.

CONTENTS

PART I

CHAPTER		PAGE
I	TO AFRICA	3
II	DIAMONDS! DIAMONDS! DIAMONDS!	15
III	'THE HIGHEST OBJECT IN A PERFECT LIFE'	31
IV	GOD'S CHOSEN PAINTER	46
V	ELIMINATING THE IMPERIAL FACTOR	64
VI	THE SCRAMBLE FOR AFRICA	83
VII	'ALWAYS GET IN THE FIRST BLOW'	106
VIII	THE FAT OF THE LAND	126

PART II

IX	KING OF THE MATABELE	137
X	RED, BRITISH RED	160
XI	A COUNTRY FOR BREAKFAST	183
XII	ON THE PERSONAL	214
XIII	GROOTE SCHUUR	243

PART III

XIV	THE UPSET APPLECART	273
XV	A LITTLE HISTORY BEING MADE	296
XVI	'. . . ALL BUT THE BOILS'	323
XVII	UNCTUOUS RECTITUDE	341
XVIII	WAR	359
XIX	SO MANY WORLDS	386
	INDEX	421

LIST OF ILLUSTRATIONS

Cecil Rhodes (*Picture Post*) *Frontispiece*

FACING PAGE

Cecil Rhodes' birthplace at Bishop's Stortford (*Camera Press*) 22

Rhodes aged about 17 (*Rhodes Memorial Museum, Bishop's Stortford*) 22

Dry sorting for diamonds in 1872 (*Rhodes Memorial Museum*) 23

L. S. Jameson, C. F. Harrison, F. C. Selous, A. R. Colquhoun (*Rhodesia House*) 23

The diamond market at Kimberley in 1888 (*Exclusive News Agency*) 54

Alfred Beit (*Picture Post*) 54

The Kimberley Club in 1888 (*Exclusive News Agency*) 55

Charles Rudd (*Rhodes Memorial Museum*) 55

De Beers Diamond Mines at Kimberley (*Exclusive News Agency*) 118

Barney Barnato (*Elliott and Fry*) 119

The cheque drawn for the acquisition of the assets of the Central Company (*Rhodes Memorial Museum*) 119

Sir Leander Jameson (*Exclusive News Agency*) 150

The *Indaba* tree at Bulawayo (*Exclusive News Agency*) 151

Lobengula, King of the Matabele (*Exclusive News Agency*) 151

Paul Kruger and his wife (*Exclusive News Agency*) 278

Olive Schreiner (*Exclusive News Agency*) 279

Princess Radziwill (*Picture Post*) 279

Groote Schuur (*Exclusive News Agency*) 310

Parliament House, Cape Town (*Exclusive News Agency*) 310

The cottage in which Rhodes died (*Exclusive News Agency*) 311

The grave of Rhodes (*Exclusive News Agency*) 311

PART I

CHAPTER I

TO AFRICA

STRANGERS often mistook the ugly grey three-storeyed house for a boarding-school. Its cold drabness and the noise produced by the many children may have led to this assumption. To the inhabitants of Bishop's Stortford the building was familiar as the Vicarage. They did not see anything ugly in its bleak grey walls; on the contrary, it appeared to most of the few thousand people of this sleepy Hertfordshire market-town as an imposing structure with its numerous wide windows and the many little brown earthen chimneys on an almost flat shingle roof.

In front of this house there now stood often in the early mornings an elderly tall slim man. His finely-shapen head with the wide forehead of a thinker, crowned by a tuft of long white hair, and his prominent hooked nose indicated a remarkable personality. The Reverend Francis William Rhodes did not need clerical dress to stamp him as a clergyman.

Among his parishioners the Vicar's courtesy and charitable activities earned him respect rather than popularity, though people had become accustomed to his unconventional manners and eccentric ways. Everyone considered him an excellent preacher and not only because his sermons never lasted more than ten minutes. All knew of his deep and sincere religiosity. His family had to attend every church service and his children had to take turns as teachers at Sunday school. As a reward they received a pious book every year.

Watching the Vicar waiting anxiously for something or someone every morning, the townspeople at first thought that he had developed a new eccentricity. Soon they found that he was on the look-out for the postman. Was he then so deeply interested in the progress of the war between the French and the Prussians that he had to obtain his copy of *The Times* a few minutes earlier?

Others knew better: he was hoping that the postman would bring one of the rare letters from South Africa. If a man has three sons in that wild part of the world, and one of them a mere lad, it is little wonder if he is worried.

The Reverend Mr Rhodes missed his sons. It had lately become oppressively quiet in the Vicarage. At one time there had been twelve children filling the house. From his first wife, who had died two years after their marriage, there had been one daughter. His second marriage had been blessed with two daughters and nine sons. The eldest daughter had married her cousin, another Rhodes, and two of the boys had died in infancy, so that there had still been nine children to bring up.

Mr Rhodes was not a rich man but he had cherished the ambition that his seven sons, his 'Seven Angels of the Seven Churches', as he called them, should enter the church. First, of course, they had to pass through one of England's old public schools, to make gentlemen of them. He himself had succeeded, through his education at Harrow and Cambridge, in ascending on the social ladder from being the son of a simple though quite well-to-do farmer in Essex to becoming a member of the seemingly impenetrable caste of gentlefolk. About his ancestors he knew only little. In the seventeenth century they had been cow-keepers and farmers. Later one of them had also owned a brick and tile works.

Why they came to bear the name of an island in the Aegean Sea was unknown. People, judging by the outlandish name and the prominent large 'Rhodes nose', were convinced that they saw some definite Semitic traits in their features. Jewish descent of the Rhodes family was the more feasible since many Jewish inhabitants had left the island of Rhodes in the seventeenth century for Italy, whence several emigrated to London, and they may have changed their foreign name to one indicating their place of origin.

The Reverend Mr Rhodes was less concerned about the past than about the future of his family. By sending his eldest son, Herbert, to Winchester and the next two, Frank and Ernest, to Eton, he believed he had laid for them the foundation of a successful clerical career. Great had been his disappointment when all three declared that they had decided to become officers in the Army. He realized that he could not force them into taking Holy orders, but was determined not to help them financially in their purpose. His obstruction did not deter the boys. Most probably they were encouraged by their aunt, Sophia Peacock—Aunt Sophy—the wealthy spinster-sister of his wife, who had always spoilt them. Aunt Sophy financed Herbert when he entered a crack cavalry regiment, paid him a liberal monthly allowance and promised to do the same for Frank and Ernest.

None of the three eldest Rhodes boys was really suited for the pulpit. In his earliest youth the eldest boy, Herbert, had shown his unruly temperament and adventurous spirit. He did not fit into the discipline of army life either. What should be done with a young man whose only asset for the struggle of life was his education as a gentleman, who had no means and who had not learnt anything practical? There was no room in England for second sons of the nobility, much less for other young gentlemen if they could not find a niche in the Army, the Church or politics.

To emigrate? Yes, but where? To Africa? Prospects for settlers in the Cape Colony had been quite good, people said, until recently. Reports on the Natal Colony sounded more promising: a rich, almost untapped country where on luscious ground, aided by a sub-tropical climate, everything grew by itself. For the modest sum of a few hundred pounds one could buy some hundreds of acres and live the free life of a real gentleman-farmer, letting the Kaffirs do the work for a few pence. One could mix there with one's own class and would not have to fear trouble with those uncouth Boers to which one was exposed in the Cape.

Herbert left the Army and sailed for Natal. Frank, the second son, who neither possessed the easy and amiable manners of his eldest brother nor was blessed with great intelligence or initiative, also chose an army career but as his commission could not be expected for some time, he too was packed off to South Africa. The third son, a rather indifferent youngster, and later two younger boys, followed the example of the two eldest brothers. Thus five of the 'Seven Angels of the Seven Churches', to their father's bitter disappointment, had preferred the sword to the crucifix. Only two were to remain civilians.

His fourth son, Cecil John, the sixth child of the Vicar's second marriage, remained his father's last hope of seeing at least one of his boys follow his vocation. Cecil, a difficult child, was different from the others whom he outstripped by far not only in intelligence and energy, but also in stubbornness. He resembled most his elder sister Edith. Both had inherited from the Rhodes side—beside the prominent 'Rhodes nose'—their energy, imagination, shyness and a predilection for seclusion.

Cecil's temper, already in his earliest years, was unpredictable, changing suddenly from gentleness to an outburst of rage. He was a slender pale-looking child whose delicate build gave a wrong impression of frailty. His fair hair, with a golden glint, his grey-blue dreamy eyes, made him an attractive and pleasant child to look at.

Cecil was born on 5 July 1853. He grew up at a time when England was going through a bitter period of bloody wars: the Crimean War; the Indian Mutiny; the expedition to China; armed intervention in Mexico; a conflict with the United States; bombardment of Japanese ports; war in Abyssinia; uprising in Ireland.

Britannia was feeling the first pangs of imperialistic labour-pains. Manchester, Sheffield, Birmingham, the bastard children of the Industrial Revolution, were preparing themselves to act as midwives at the birth of the *Imperium Britannicum*.

Such a time of flag-waving would make an impression on any boy, even one not as sensitive as the Reverend Mr Rhodes' fourth son. And Cecil Rhodes as a boy was extremely sensitive, introvert and lonely. He could not make friends. To the boys at school, who all called each other by their Christian names, he always remained just 'Rhodes'. It was probably his proud bearing, the refinement in his speech and also perhaps a slight girlishness in him, which prevented the young ruffians from taking to him. Cecil did not even take a great interest in the school sports; only once, in his thirteenth year, did he become a member of his school's cricket eleven.

Mrs Rhodes, *née* Peacock, was already thirty years old when she became the Vicar's second wife. For almost twenty years of her life she was either pregnant or had to feed the latest baby. Besides her duties as a housewife and keeping the wild crowd of growing children under control, it could hardly have been easy to be the wife of so eccentric a man as the Reverend Mr Rhodes. She tried hard to balance the Vicar's Spartan educational methods by tender sympathy. Her charming ways, a deep understanding for the worries of her little folk, and a dreamy romanticism left their mark particularly on her most difficult children, on her second daughter Edith and on Cecil. The strong and unconventional nature and disciplinarian principles of the father, the softness and romantic nature of the mother, formed in these two children a strange duality of character which was later to ripen in each into an anomalous personality.

Mother Rhodes was particularly worried about Cecil's frequent outbursts of uncontrolled temper which seemed strange in a boy with an otherwise amiable temperament. Not that she minded his being able to use his fists well on other boys. She was less pleased, however, when his teacher reported that Cecil, believing himself to have been punished unjustly, picked up a book to throw at the master's head. At the last second he must have realized what he was doing; with a vicious bang he threw it on his desk, muttering something which might have been either an apology or a curse.

It seemed a great pity to the mother that each of her children grew up for himself without confiding in the others. Each was too strong an individuality to harmonize with the other members of the family. Yet at any threat from the outside they put up a united front.

The Rhodes boys knew most of the people in the district and as real boys always managed to ride past certain places where they would be sure to meet young girls. Cecil, however, never turned after any girl and did not even seem to see them. His critical remarks were directed rather at the farmlands through which they rode. 'This is a lazy farmer. Look, how untidy his furrows are!' . . . 'This one looks well after his stock. You can see how healthy his cattle look!'. . . . 'Lucerne should never be grown here!' . . .

Cecil never paid much attention to dress. One day he asked his brother Frank for the loan of his 'best' shirt as he was going to London. 'You can't have it,' Frank replied. 'I need it myself for tonight.' Frank knew that if Cecil wanted something, he would never give up before he obtained it. He watched him all day. Great was his surprise when on opening his drawer he found his 'best' shirt gone. When Cecil returned, Frank cornered him immediately:

'Well, Cecil, you won over that shirt of mine; but just tell me how you did it, for it wasn't on you when you left here and you had no parcel with you. What did you do with it?'

Cecil chuckled a little but his reply came coldly: 'I put it on under the old one!'

Cecil did not shine as a scholar. His father, still hoping that this one of the 'Seven Angels of the Seven Churches' would take Holy orders, supervised his progress at the local grammar school.

Young Cecil seemed to have been particularly interested in history and geography. At times he did well in the classics and even gained a distinction in this subject, whilst one year he brought home a silver medal, a prize in elocution.

Parents and teachers were once baffled when they found that thirteen-year-old Cecil had chosen as a motto for the red-plush-covered souvenir album of a class mate, the words: 'To do—or to die!' His teachers and parents probably did not realize that this precocious thought was not original. It had been taken from a bombastic poem by the Scottish poet, Thomas Campbell, *Pleasures of Hope*, which contained the words: 'Tomorrow let us do or die.'

When Cecil finished school in 1869 at the age of sixteen, the question of his future became acute. His father, eager that the boy should go either to Oxford or, preferably, to Cambridge, tutored him in the classics in preparation for the entrance examination. His future worried the boy. He was convinced that he was not suited for a career in the Army like his three elder brothers. He was also sure that he would not be able to fulfil his father's wish and enter the Church. He thought that he might become a lawyer, though he realized that it would be a hard struggle to win his father's consent, knowing his deadly hatred for lawyers and everything connected with courts of law.

Cecil confided in Aunt Sophy to whom he would have to apply for financial help in any case. She too would have preferred her nephew to become a clergyman, a much 'nicer' profession than that of a lawyer and almost equal in the social scale to that of an officer. In his dilemma Cecil tried diplomacy, using at the end of a carefully worded letter as his chief argument the religious issue, with which, as he must have known, he could easily impress an elderly English spinster:

> I cannot deny for it would only be hypocrisy to say otherwise, that I still above everything would like to be a barrister; but I agree with you it is a very precarious profession. Next to that I think a clergyman's life is the nicest; and therefore I shall most earnestly try to go to College, because I have fully determined to be one of these two, and a college education is necessary for both. I think that as a barrister a man may be just as good a Christian as in any other profession. . . .

His future career, however, was not to be decided by his father, his aunt or himself. Instead, a swarm of vivid little tubercles in his lungs were destined to shape the fate of a man, of an Empire and of a whole continent.

Shortly after he left school Cecil began to ail. The worried father took him to a London doctor who advised him to send the boy as soon as possible away from England's murderous climate to a sunnier land.

What could be more natural than that Cecil should join his eldest brother Herbert in Natal where he would surely soon regain his health with the help of the African sun? Aunt Sophy with her usual generosity provided the necessary funds for the voyage and in addition £2,000 to make him as comfortable as possible and help him settle there.

From the time when his parents had bade him farewell at Gravesend on a hot June day in 1870, he had looked forward to the day of his arrival in Durban when he would shake hands with his eldest brother Herbert. Herbert was not there.

Cecil Rhodes looked around but without losing sight of his luggage. Under his arm he had stuffed a somewhat crushed map of Africa. Ever since his journey had been decided upon, he had often studied this map until late at night. During the seventy days of his voyage the same map had helped him pass the time. For hours, when he was not busy studying his Greek and Latin grammars or translating from the classics, he would look at the two small red spots which marked the only British possessions in the vastness of the African continent, the Cape Colony and Natal.

After a long wait the unhappy boy saw a gentleman coming towards him. He introduced himself as Dr Sutherland, Surveyor-General of Natal, and a good friend of Herbert's. Herbert had asked him to look after his young brother. Herbert, he was told, was away. As a matter of fact Herbert was on an expedition to the Vaal River to look for diamonds. Herbert, if the truth be told, had left his cotton plantation in the Umkomaas Valley a few months earlier in order to join Captain Rolleston who was leading several other gentlemen of the 20th Infantry Regiment on this exciting and novel game of discovering hidden riches; Herbert, to be quite frank, should not be expected back soon; to put it altogether bluntly, Herbert had not been very successful with his cotton-growing.

Dr Sutherland took Cecil to his house near Pietermaritzburg, the capital of Natal, there to await his brother's return. Mrs Sutherland took charge of the shy sickly-looking boy who appeared much younger than his age. He gave no trouble. All day long he read, mostly in his school-books, or he leaned over his crushed map of Africa spread out on the floor.

Dr Sutherland often tried to drag him away from his books. 'What's the use of studying Roman and Greek classics in the wilds of South Africa, Cecil?'

'I promised my father, sir, to pass the 'varsity entrance exam after I come back.'

'What for, Cecil? Stay here in this country of sunshine. . . .'

'No, sir, I promised my father to become a clergyman.'

'Then I am sure, Cecil, you'll end as a village parson.'

Only when he heard the clatter of horses' hoofs or the creaking of a wagon, bringing visitors, did he come down quickly into the drawing-room. Unobtrusively he would sit in a corner. His mouth slightly open, his grey-blue eyes sparkling, rubbing his chin nervously with his forefinger, he would listen to the news and stories brought by travellers and friends.

No matter how the conversation started, it inevitably turned to the main point of interest which for two years had not only seized the whole of South Africa but had been a magnet to adventurous souls in every part of the world: Diamonds! These little pieces of crystallized carbon, for which mankind at that time had no use other than as decorations for women's hands, ears or necks, or to be encrusted in the crown-jewels of some potentate; these brilliantly shining volcanic products of the Earth's womb were to cost the lives of thousands of innocent men, to enrich a few and to change the map of a continent.

When one of the first diamonds was discovered among the paraphernalia of a Native witch-doctor, Sir Richard Southey, the Lieutenant-Governor, laid it on the Table of the Cape Parliament with the prophetic words: 'Gentlemen, this is the rock on which the future success of South Africa will be built!'

And to this rock there flocked the human ravens, the eagles, the vultures, the wolves, the jackals and the moles; they all assembled along the banks of the Orange and Vaal rivers where within a few weeks several thousand men had staked their luck. Their courage was repaid to only a very few.

One of many, Herbert Rhodes soon gave up hope and returned to his cotton plantation at the end of the year 1870. Cecil met him there and the two brothers agreed to throw their lot together. Cecil exercised his right on a free grant of 50 acres. All their land was densely covered with euphorbia. Before his unsuccessful diamond adventure Herbert had already cleared 45 of his 200 acres of this useless thorny bush.

Cecil engaged a gang of Zulus and organized their work. Within a few months he could proudly show his brother 100 acres ready for cultivation. It was no easy task to work with these Natives who had not yet had much contact with European civilization. Before he knew the small luxuries of modern life and was forced to adopt at least partly European dress, the South African Native had no use for money. Work was thus no necessity for him. All work, at home and in the fields, with the exception of hunting for meat, was done by his women-folk. It called for special enticement to lure them to the farms, and a good psychological understanding of their primitive though complicated mentality to keep them there. Cecil soon found out that many Natives needed money to pay their hut-tax. He lent them the money on their promise to work for him. And they never let him down. 'Kaffirs', he wrote home, 'are really safer than the Bank of England.'

If a seventeen-year-old boy with no experience of how to treat people, white or black, who did not know the language and had been in the country for only a few months, had achieved such success, it was only natural that settlers even from far away should come to see this miracle.

But they shook their heads disapprovingly. 'Impossible. You can't grow cotton in the Umkomaas Valley! Impossible!'

The Rhodes brothers were not disheartened when the first crop failed. Carefully Cecil reflected on what might have been the cause of this sad result. He explained it to Herbert: 'One cannot fight against grubs, boreworms, caterpillars. One has to distract these little beasts from the cotton by something more attractive—say to grow every eighty feet a bushel or two of mealies. And we did not calculate how rich this virgin soil really was. Neither did we realize what luxuriant growth this hot-house-like steamy valley would produce. We also failed to realize that the rows had been made much too close to each other thus suffocating the expanding plants. We will have to double the space between them. To make good the loss we will have to plant more. To decrease expenses we will have to use a plough. . . .'

Again the old settlers shook their heads. Cecil, once the planting was done, set about to build for himself and his brother a proper homestead. Every day he could be seen, wearing nothing but a shirt and an old pair of trousers more full of holes than patches, making mud-bricks. Within a few weeks he had finished two huts, one as a storehouse for future cotton crops and the other to live in. A new life had begun for him. He explored the neighbourhood and grew lyrical when reporting home about the mountain ravines above the valley:

> . . . It was one immense natural fernery, and there, hundreds of feet below us, stretched out the whole valley with our huts looking like specks, and in the distance hills rising one above the other with a splendid blue tint on them. . . .

Soon he could no longer spare time for such excursions. Again his ambition to go to Oxford had flared up, and with an eye on the Natives he bent over his books trying to penetrate the intricacies of Greek syntax or the refinements of Latin poetry.

The next was a bumper crop. Not only were the losses of the previous year made good, but the brothers were able to show a good profit. At the agricultural show of the district Cecil's cotton earned him a second prize of five pounds. When he returned from the platform after receiving his prize, he chuckled, jingling the five golden sovereigns in his trouser pocket and whispered to his fatherly old friend Dr Sutherland:

'Ah! yes, they told me I couldn't grow cotton!'

Cecil planned to clear many more acres for planting cotton at the end of the following year but Herbert was bored. He thirsted for adventure. His gambler's nature could only be satisfied by high stakes. After long persuasion Cecil agreed to accompany him on a trip without knowing his brother's intentions. In his casual manner Herbert informed him on the way that they were going up to the northern Transvaal, in the neighbourhood of Delagoa Bay. There lived a Native chief, Secoconi, who was said to own a big bag of diamonds. Herbert's plan was to trade guns for them. They had bought a few old breech-loaders and Herbert had even succeeded in getting hold of two brass cannons.

Unfortunately for them, the Boers on the Transvaal border kept a sharp look-out for gun-runners. The two Rhodes boys just managed to escape after dumping the two cannons in a river.

It was the first of many encounters where a lucrative Rhodes business proposition was frustrated by the diligence of the Boers of the Transvaal.

Twenty years later the two cannons were unearthed and believed to be antique pieces used in earlier times in a Portuguese fort. When they were proudly brought to a museum in Pretoria Cecil Rhodes had a good laugh. He was never ashamed to tell this story of his juvenile adventure apparently quite unaware of its moral implications. Gun-running in the whole of Africa was never considered an honest or honourable occupation; and the two brothers should have known that Secoconi's diamonds must have been originally stolen by Natives employed in the diamond river diggings.

After their return from the Transvaal, wherever they went they heard the wildest rumours about the discovery of enormous diamond fields on some farms in the Orange Free State, in a district inhabited by the Griqua tribe and not far from the banks of the rivers where thousands were still hopefully combing the sands for diamonds. What was at first believed to be just occasional small finds had proved to be a real Eldorado. One merely had to scratch the soil, and pick up diamonds like potatoes on an Irish farm. When hearing of this dreamland in the spring of 1871, Herbert Rhodes pranced like a thoroughbred behind the starter's flag. Off he was on the long trek to the new diamond fields. All the available money the two brothers could spare he took with him. Cecil remained in the broiling Umkomaas Valley, preparing his third cotton crop.

In Dr Sutherland's home he met Captain Rolleston, the great man of the river washings. He had just returned from the new diamond-fields and showed them one big and several small diamonds which he had picked up there on a claim he had bought for a few pounds. When Cecil felt the coolness of the big stone a peculiar feeling took hold of him. He had to swallow several times. And the great Rolleston talked of three 'whoppers', one worth £8,000, another £9,000 and the third £10,000 and told of the man who had found the biggest stone: 'Yes, this chap offered his claim for fifteen bob the evening before and no one would buy it.'

At night Cecil dreamt of diamonds. Should he not rather give up the struggle of taming this obstinate African soil in this soul-killing hot-house climate? He discussed it with Dr Sutherland:

> . . . Of course there is a chance of the diamonds turning up trumps; but I don't count much on them. You see, it is all chance . . . Herbert may not find one or he may find one of a hundred carats: it is a toss-up. But the cotton, the more you see of it, the more I am sure it is a reality. Not a fortune, and not attainable by everyone; but still, to one who has a good bit of land, money to start it properly, a fair road and above all a good name amongst the Kaffirs, it gives a very handsome income. . . .

He had not yet realized that farming in South Africa implicates a permanent struggle with Nature which disperses her favours and curses there in extremes. The land is either so dry that plants and animals fade away as in a desert; or, the next season, it may be floods which drown everything in their stride. Cecil Rhodes had to gain this knowledge the hard way. Everything on his plantation went wrong. After a *sluit* had dried out, his plants, through lack of water, died or became an easy prey to all the pests in the country.

In desperation he confessed to Dr Sutherland: 'It really seems an ill-fated valley. You would be surprised if I told you what a sink it has been. I believe if one only kept on, it has a capacity to absorb any amount of capital.'

In October 1871 eighteen-year-old Cecil succumbed to the lures of the diamonds in the land of the Griquas. He packed his few belongings into a Scotch cart, drawn by a span of sixteen sleek hand-picked oxen. The necessary few diggers' tools he strapped on top of the shaky vehicle. Next to his seat, wrapped in his travelling plaid, he threw his school-books, the Latin and Greek classics and a fat tome of a Greek dictionary.

And so the sixteen oxen started their slow trek, pulling the cart westwards over the blue mountains, across the green and yellow and purple veld, through the greyness of desert-like long stretches, between red-shining *kopjes* which looked like giant warts on the sun-bathed landscape, past the mushroom-like black-roofed white huts of Native kraals, through dark forest cathedrals built of giant trees, through mud and sand and grass and stones, taking a young boy to his destiny.

CHAPTER II

DIAMONDS! DIAMONDS! DIAMONDS!

HIS rickety table consisted of a turned-up packing-case. A rusty bucket served him as a seat. In an empty corner lay a pile of books topped by a Greek grammar, covered with a fine yellow sand. On his lap he held open a school-edition of Virgil's poems. Cecil Rhodes was dreaming or thinking, or, as often happened, in a state of complete absent-mindedness, his forefinger rubbing his chin in gentle rhythm. Even now, in his nineteenth year, he looked like a schoolboy who had grown too quickly out of his clothes. South Africa's sun had turned his former paleness into a healthy ruddy complexion. He wore a pair of shrunken school cricket trousers on which numerous stains of reddish-yellow sand, of oil and of rust had resisted several attempts at washing without soap and with a minimum of water. The sleeves of his school blazer went only half-way down from elbow to wrist. In spite of his clothes, with his finely-cut features, his fair longish hair blown by the wind, he could not but be taken for what he was: a typical member of the English middle-class.

At first the men around him, the rough adventurers, had tried to aim their crude jokes at him. Soon they found out their mistake: this milksop of a boy, this spoilt mother's darling, this sleepy-eyed whipper-snapper, was a damned fine reg'lar feller who knew how to dig a claim every bit as well as the oldest digger. And what he didn't know about diamonds was nobody's business. Let him stand there with mouth open and eyes half-closed, his hands deep in his pockets, dreaming away; or let him sit on his throne of a bucket reading one of those bloody learned books; he knows just the same what is going on around him. If his Kaffirs—and he has the best of them, all Zulus he brought with him from Natal—stop digging only for a minute, sixty feet below in the crater hole, if the hauling of the buckets begins to slacken, or the sifting of the yellow sand becomes slower, up he is and at them, this bastard of a mite. . . . Even if his funny voice when he is in a rage sounds like an old clarinet full of spittle, he can swear in good old English at which any sea-dog would blush like an old maid on her wedding-night. . . . And this six-foot specimen of a booby who looks as if he cannot count up to three, is a damned good businessman, beating any of the bloody Jew-boys here hollow when it comes to selling his stones. All these large-mouthed swells of diamond-merchants who just arrived from Paris, Amsterdam, and Hamburg and that crowd from London's Hatton Garden, who think themselves so awfully clever, imagining that they can pick up bargains here for next to nothing have met their match in that scraggy, spindle-legged, muzzy-looking son of a parson. It tickles one pink to see this unlicked cub put the crooked noses of the big expert swells out of joint. And Master Cecil seems to run the show on his claims and bosses his two elder brothers around as if they were his errand-boys. The eldest one, Herbert, does not care a damn any more about these claims and Frank—you know, the other Rhodes who came out here recently to help his brothers—he does just what Cecil tells him. Cecil—that boy has vim. Let the people laugh at him and his books; that boy is already worth several thousand pounds. . . .

Nobody, in this year of grace 1872, had much time even to smile in the new township of Kimberley, which, in the form of thousands of tents, wooden shacks or mere hovels covered with hessian, had suddenly sprung up on the veld in the territory of Waterboer, Chief of the Griquas, bordering on the two Boer republics of the Transvaal and the Orange Free State. More than ten thousand white men had raced to this deserted spot on the South African flat plains, where the vast emptiness, covered with a thick blue carpet of grass after the rains, appeared still more desolate for the few isolated camelthorn bushes and single mimosa trees. These men were no longer merely foreign adventurous have-nots, the down-and-out fortune-hunters of the River diggings. The diamond fever had seized respectable members of the English middle-class and with them came the human flotsam and jetsam of England's big towns: the gamblers, the publicans, the loafers, the criminals and the pimps. London's ghetto of the East End spat out its *Luftmenschen*, those who seemed to live in and of the air, and all ambitious youngsters who did not want to spend their lives in the sticky sweatshops of Mile End Road as their fathers had done before them. It seemed a strange company: the elegant young men, younger sons of England's nobility for whom no place could be found in the land of their fathers, and the big army of broken-down elements who had come into conflict with the country's laws or unwritten social tenets.

They all came to the Black Continent with only one wish, one hope, one aim: to become rich! rich! rich! Their minds turned around one single thought, one single subject, one single idea: diamonds! diamonds! diamonds!

For diamonds they endured cruel hardships. No matter if the temperature rose to well over 100° in the day or sank at night to below freezing-point. Men who were accustomed to have wholesome meals served by well-trained servants on shining china plates, sat down dirty to gulp a dish of foul-smelling stew, cooked by filthy Kaffirs, and served in a rusty tin. A ground-sheet spread under a sail-plane had taken the place of a spring-mattress and a thin cotton blanket had to serve as a cover. How could they wash when a bucket of water cost more than a gallon of beer in London's most expensive hotel? Only those lucky ones, who had already struck it rich, could afford a weekly bath of soda-water, at five shillings a bottle.

Over the whole plain, now called Kimberley, as far as the eye could see, the thousands of tents looked as if giant mushrooms had suddenly sprung out of the soil; between them the white-covered wagons appeared like monstrous caterpillars. The spiders, Scotch carts, Cape carts, landaus and coaches by which the fortune-hunters had come hundreds of miles and which now served many of them as 'homes', seemed, with their shafts pointing up to the sky, like antediluvian dragons ready to swallow their next victims with their threatening jaws. Dotted round the camps lay piles of filthy garbage and the skeletons of horses and mules, which had just been cleared by Nature's health-inspectors, the jackals and the vultures. From the other side there penetrated the stench of the Native kraals. No one had time. Not even the body of a dead man aroused anybody's interest. Sympathy? No time here for such sentimentalities. If a man was shot or stabbed to death in a brawl, murdered or robbed by a Kaffir, it was his own business. There was a tent which served as a dead-house. Who cares that the wild dogs and the jackals came at night to feast on the corpses. Have a quick one with me, brother! . . .

To find self-forgetfulness one could dope oneself by risking a week's earnings or more on a little roulette-ball or on the 'Devil's Prayer Book'. Women of course were needed for occasional happiness. Only a few unattached females—and not the youngest, the most beautiful or the most virtuous—had dared to encroach on territory reserved for rough men out to make money.

In the infernal summer heat you could work for only a few hours at a stretch. Exhausted, you flung your aching, sweating body on the ground, burying even your face in the yellow soil for coolness. You could count yourself lucky if you did not succumb to the many illnesses in the camp caused by the absence of the most primitive hygienic precautions, by the bad and scarce water, the imperfectly canned meat and fish, the absence of vegetables, the heat and the overcrowded tents. They called it camp-fever and hundreds went down with it. Today it would have been diagnosed as dysentery aggravated by malaria.

Nobody complained. They bore their burden patiently driven on by the thought of diamonds—diamonds—diamonds——

If hope dwindled, there was always at every few hundred yards a marquee where a strong drink could restore courage. Those who could not afford anything better took refuge in drowning their worries in 'Cape Smoke', a strong liquor made of the dregs of grapes.

Overnight the newly found diamonds had changed the economic structure of South Africa. Natives left their kraals in thousands. Before, when they were forced to work on the farms for a few pence a day, they had to be satisfied with earning a sheep twice a year and permission to cultivate a small stretch of land and to graze their cattle or goats. Now the Native had become a substantial component of an industrial venture and had to be coaxed to do his part. Tens of thousands of these Natives were crushed together in camps not far from that of the diggers.

Diamonds had even affected Nature. Where the veld had only a few months earlier abounded in game and birds, there were now only the vultures. The invaders had upset the balance of nature in the veld by bringing with them in their wagons the rats, mosquitoes, ticks, mice, fleas and lice as well as a good assortment of bacteria and germs.

Diamonds had upset South Africa's politics. Before the great rush nobody was interested in this treeless country. Chief Waterboer of the Griquas had lived there undisturbed. Only a very few Boers had settled in his land, and just managed to exist on what the sandy soil produced. After the first diamonds had been found, both Boer Republics, the Transvaal and the Orange Free State, claimed the territory as their own. The Orange Free State, believing it had a legal claim to the land, asserted its sovereignty by formal occupation. Waterboer did not want to fall under the dependency of either of the Boer Republics. He offered his land to the English Queen, even after a court of arbitration had decided in his favour. London, meanwhile, had already learnt from experience that to rule over African Natives led to many expensive wars. A policy of non-interference and non-expansion on the African continent outside Britain's South African possessions had therefore been adopted. However, pressed by the resident high officials in Cape Town, Mr Gladstone, Her Majesty's Prime Minister, forgetting for the time being all his usual finely worded tirades in favour of Liberalism, pocketed Waterboer's diamondiferous land for Britain, and proclaimed it as British territory under the name of Griqualand West. The Orange Free State protested vehemently. Later Britain paid as compensation the generous sum of £90,000, an amount which corresponded to one week's output in diamonds at the time.

To the two Boer governments the change on the very doorsteps of their countries was disquieting. For several decades since the Great Trek in 1836, when they had escaped from British rule in the Cape Colony, they had lived peacefully, following a strict policy of isolation. Now England was pushing forward menacingly near their borders, upsetting the peace of the veld by a new kind of civilization and sending as the apostles of a novel creed the riff-raff of Europe who preached the gospel of quick wealth and spoilt the primitive African tribes with all the vices of the White Man. Diamonds had become a factor in British politics. The Boers had to face a new problem.

When nineteen-year-old Cecil Rhodes joined the fortune-seekers, his ambition was aimed at earning sufficient money to go to Oxford. His tenacity of purpose made him overcome all the difficulties in preparing himself for the University amid the hubbub of a mining-camp, deprived of all privacy, and while forced to devote most of his time and the best part of his brain-power to his digging enterprises.

He was convinced that Oxford could not teach him anything he really wanted to learn. Not to acquire academic wisdom did he want to go there. Oxford, he hoped, would stamp him as a gentleman.

When his friends came to his sorting-table and saw him deeply buried in his school-books there would be no end to their teasing: 'Going up to Oxford soon, Cecil, to learn how to grow diamonds?'

'Very true, you chaps,' he replied, 'the educational system of Oxford seems rather unpractical but look around and everywhere in England you will find Oxford men on top!'

Left alone, he would sit for hours staring at the stones in front of him. From the beginning he had become aware of the urgent need to learn thoroughly all he could about diamonds. One had to become closely acquainted with the many qualities and faults which regulated the price of a diamond and which depended not only on its weight but on its size, shape and colour. Diamonds occur in the finest pastel shades from a deep yellow to a bluish-white, from a nutty-brown to a light bronze. You may come across green, blue, pink, bronze yellow, orange and opaque diamonds. And only twenty-five out of a hundred stones will be both clear and of a blue-white colour to pass as perfect. One had to look sharp. The keenest eye often failed to detect a flaw.

Cecil Rhodes was one of the first to use a watchmaker's magnifying glass to judge a diamond. With the glass squeezed in his eye he was easily able to discern a little black spot or a tiny white flaw inside a stone which would lower its value considerably. Sometimes great joy and the highest expectations were aroused when a perfectly shaped white and glassy stone was found. Only those familiar with the peculiarities of diamonds would be worried by the tinge of a smoky brown cloud in one corner of the stone. 'Greeners' would buy such stones at low prices or exchange them against much smaller stones in the belief that they had struck a bargain. The next day, when they went to look at their great bargain, all they would find was a fine powder. These stones, when exposed to the light, would explode internally.

To Cecil Rhodes diamonds were no longer mere pretty stones; a diamond to him was something above earthly conceptions, an aristocrat produced by Nature. Unconsciously, in his letters home, he always wrote 'Diamonds' with a capital 'D'.

He was well informed on everything concerning diamonds. Old diggers often came to consult him before they sold their stones. The *kopje wallopers*, as the itinerant diamond buyers were called, knew that they could play no tricks on him. He had already noticed that each of their testing scales showed a different weight. The slightest slant of the table might cost the seller a great deal of money. Cecil Rhodes did not trust anybody. He wrote to his friend, Dr Sutherland, to send him a water-level. The *kopje wallopers* shook their heads: 'A clever boy, that *meshuggene* longshanks!'

From his tent door Cecil Rhodes often looked down into the chasm of the big holes dug into what was once Colesberg Kopje. How was it possible that on this small round hill, the size of the garden at the Vicarage at home—not more than 180 yards broad and 220 yards long—some ten thousand people could work every day? It sounded very grand when one heard that somebody was the lucky owner of a claim, until one realized that each claim consisted of only 31 square feet and that in most cases each claim was split into four. Not even the whole claim was allowed to be worked. More than 7 feet had to be left as road.

When diggers started to go deeper, differences in the depths of neighbouring holes soon developed. Reefs collapsed and fell into the neighbour's ground. Tempers ran high. The roads, well intended, also soon broke down. Chaos reigned everywhere. Here everyone thought only for himself and let the devil take the hindmost.

Cecil Rhodes, his mouth slightly open, his hands deep in his trouser-pockets, observed each day for hours every phase of the working process. He knew that this primitive system of mining was doomed in the near future. In several mines the level of underground water had already been reached.

Something had to be done.

Cecil Rhodes had been more fortunate than many others. Through his friendship with the 'Red Caps', a group of young men owning what later became known as the Kimberley Mine, Herbert was able to peg three whole claims soon after its discovery. Cecil bought a quarter of a claim from him and he and two friends were partners in three-quarters of another claim.

Herbert soon left. Little Cecil would manage the diamond affair better alone.

And Cecil did make the three claims a complete success. The one-quarter of a claim which belonged to him alone proved to yield by far the most. Proudly he wrote to his mother:

> . . . I find on an average 30 carats a week and am working one of the few whole claims in the kopje: a claim in fact that will take me 4 years to work out at the present rate. Diamonds have only to continue a fair price and I think Herbert's fortune is made. . . . I average about hundred pounds per week.

The entire letter sounded like the report of a mine manager to his board of directors, with its cold matter-of-fact description of diamonds, their peculiarities, shapes, colours, their prices and all the details of how they are found:

> . . . There are reefs all round these Diamond mines inside which the Diamonds are found. The reef is the usual soil of the country round, red sand just at the top and then a black and white stony shale below. . . . Inside the reef is the diamondiferous soil. It works just like Stilton cheese. . . .

And so it goes on for pages. Not a single intimate note; not a word of a private nature; no endearment throughout the letter. It ends like a business communication, simply with 'Yrs. C. Rhodes.'

Mrs Rhodes must have been baffled by her son Cecil. The Vicar, probably, feared for the soul of his son who seemed to have delivered himself completely to the God Mammon. Was it a consolation to the reverend gentleman that the elder brother reported from Kimberley about people's high opinion of Cecil; that 'he is such an excellent man of business', that 'Cecil was just the contrary to most young fellows when they set up there and do well and get so very bumptious . . . that he seems to have done wonderfully well as regards the diamonds. . . .'?

The Vicar would probably have been completely downcast if he had only suspected what had become of his son.

Here was a young man, not yet twenty years of age, brought up in the well-guarded seclusion of a parsonage in a peaceful, almost dormant, little English rural town, who had suddenly been flung into the boiling cauldron of quickly made money, to

Cecil Rhodes' birthplace at Bishop's Stortford

Rhodes aged about 17 before he left for Africa

Dry sorting for diamonds in 1872 before the advent of the Hand Washing Machin
Note the sorting table in the foreground

Left to right: L. S. Jameson, C. F. Harrison, F. C. Selous, A. R. Colquhoun

fight, all by himself, with and against the excrement of mankind, the world's worst crowd of fortune-hunters and parasites.

His mental and apparently also his physical puberty was not yet completed. Lacking friends, his struggle with his ego made him retreat into himself. He had to deal exclusively with men older than himself. He became in turn moody, taciturn, excitable, impulsive, often even violent.

One of his friends noticed already at that time that 'the duality of his nature, the contemplative and the executive, had a curious counterpart in his voice, which broke, when he was excited, into a sort of falsetto, unusual in a man of his make'.

With people for whom he cared, he could at times be amiable but very often his effort to impress others became evident.

One day Rhodes had found a big diamond. He invited a few friends to celebrate with him at a picnic on the Vaal River. After lunch they all took a dip in the cool river. When Rhodes walked along the edge of the water over the broad stretch of pebbles, he suddenly bent down, shouting excitedly:

'Look here, what I just picked up . . . a diamond, a first-rater, bluish-white one . . . at least ten carat for which old Unger or any of his Hebrew brethren will gladly pay forty quid . . . exactly what this party cost me . . . exactly what this party cost me . . . Just luck, and, of course, one has to know where one's luck lies . . . to know where one's luck lies!'

His friends were sure that Rhodes had dropped the diamond there earlier.

Girls did not interest him. Frank, anxious to dispel any fears his parents might have had in that respect, assured them that it was 'quite a mistake to suppose that there are no nice girls out here'. They did not seem to exist, however, if they existed at all in Kimberley, for his brother Cecil.

'I do not believe, if a flock of the most adorable women passed through the streets, he would go across the road to see them,' Frank wrote.

Sometimes he could not evade going to dances. Much to the amusement of his friends he always chose the ugliest girls as partners. When he was chaffed about his bad taste, Rhodes, his hands defiantly in his pockets, answered:

'Leave me alone! Dancing is to me just an enjoyable exercise. and I enjoy it as such . . . just an enjoyable exercise. . . .'

And there followed a shrill falsetto laugh.

Young Cecil had no friends who inspired him spiritually. Dr Sutherland was the first to encourage him to read but great talkers are rarely ferocious readers. Rhodes already at that time found great satisfaction in talking, not in the form of give-and-take conversation but of almost exclusive monologues. Often after dinner with his friends, in his tent on Colesberg Kopje, after a long period of complete silence he would suddenly jump up and begin to talk. He argued with himself, bringing forth possible objections that the other side might raise, analysing them and setting them against his own views. In his 'home', a 16-foot by 18-foot structure, made of a flimsy wooden frame and covered with canvas, but considered luxurious by Kimberley standards at that time, he messed together with a number of other young men. There was no furniture in the tent, nor did it offer even the simplest comfort. Upon entering, the eye immediately fell on the big slightly crumpled map of the African continent which was pinned carefully against the canvas wall. Among the young men he was most attached to quiet, tall, and bearded Charles Dunell Rudd, nine years his senior, whom he had already met in Natal. They became partners in Kimberley, working a claim together, the beginning of a lifetime partnership.

Rudd had come out to South Africa for the same reason as Cecil Rhodes did two years later. His tubercular lungs had cut short a promising scholarly career at Cambridge. Upon his arrival in South Africa he had attached himself to the almost legendary English lawyer, John Dunn, whom the great Zulu King, Cetywayo, in gratitude for having acted as his counsellor, had made a Chief of a Zulu tribe with a present of 10,000 acres of the best land. Rudd acted for two years as a kind of secretary to the White Zulu Chief before he came to Kimberley.

Rudd was the very opposite of Rhodes: his quiet, settled, sharply calculating and amiable nature became a necessary complement to Rhodes' impulsiveness.

Rudd had little personal ambition. Intricate problems or a difficult situation interested him only as an opportunity for using his logical mind. Rhodes looked up to him as an ideal combination of a gentleman, a scholar and a smart business man.

Perhaps still more than to the intellectual heavyweight Rudd, Rhodes was attracted to the light-hearted wit, universal though superficial worldly wisdom, general knowledge, easy manners and winning personality of John Xavier Merriman. They had so much in common in character, their ambitions ran so closely parallel and their faults were so similar that the course of their lives offered two possibilities: to become friends or foes. They tried both—and neither made them happy.

Towards the end of the year 1872, Rhodes had become more restless, more retiring and more abrupt than before. All his friends had noticed that something must be worrying him. Yet he really should have had no worries. His claims were yielding considerable results. His personal fortune was generally estimated at far above £5,000 with ever-increasing revenues.

Dr Sutherland, whom Cecil used as his father confessor, was most worried that his young friend had lately been complaining about bad health. He was still more alarmed by a passage in one of his letters: '. . . I am afraid that life on the Diamond fields has not tended to strengthen my religious principles.'

Cecil Rhodes was saved from further mental anguish by a book.

Just at that time Darwin had stirred the world of science with his theory of evolution. Intellectual mountebanks hooked some of his ideas, adulterated them and coined them into 'popular' currency. Among the many who used and over-simplified Darwin's observations as the basis for their philosophical and religious doctrines was the writer Winwood Reade. Drugged by the mysticism of Oriental cults he tried in his book *The Martyrdom of Man* to construct a creed of atheism, taking 'Darwinism' as a basis and making it more palatable with a garnish of pseudo-scientific phrases and a piquant sauce of mystic second-hand slogans from drained Mohammedanism, Confucianism and high-sounding confusing nonsense.

For Rhodes, an innocent boy of twenty, this book solved all his doubts and scruples: Darwin became his Messiah, Reade his Apostle, and *The Martyrdom of Man* his Bible. It was not a passing phase of an intellectual evolution for him. More than twenty years later he confessed several times:

> . . . It is a creepy book. I read it the first year I was in Kimberley, fresh from my father's Parsonage, and you may imagine the impression which it produced upon me, in such a place as a mining camp. That book has made me what I am.

The hard work in a strenuous climate, the daily excitement caused by the vagaries of mining, the nerve-racking business negotiations, an irregular and insufficient diet, the unaccustomed consumption of alcoholic drinks, the late hours spent in endless discussions and in addition his spiritual anguish, lessened the resistance of a delicate body to the plodding microbes in his lungs. Cecil Rhodes fell seriously ill.

Herbert at once returned from Natal. He recognized immediately that all the boy needed was to get out as soon as possible from the dust-bowl of Kimberley. Rudd could look after the claims alone. The two brothers loaded an ox-wagon and started on a trek northwards.

Following an old missionary road their way led them leisurely through drifts over narrow mountain passes, till they came higher and higher and reached the rarefied and stimulating air of the High Veld.

This impact on Cecil Rhodes of South Africa's landscape with its wide open spaces and many contradictions, the free life on the veld with its mysterious fauna and flora, the excitement of providing the pot with food by the gun filled him for the rest of his life with a deep love of the veld.

He had become a keen observer. As much as his curiosity was caught by the new and impressive scenery, so his interest was aroused in the farmers of the Transvaal, the fabulous *Voortrekkers* and their children, who in the years 1836 to 1840 had left the Cape dissatisfied with British rule. Cecil Rhodes liked their almost Biblical mode of life, and was amazed every time by the liberal hospitality which was gladly showered upon complete strangers. A new world opened up to him. These sturdy slow-moving men with their heavy *vroue* and numerous flaxen-haired children spoke the same language, old Dutch, as had their forefathers, who had come as settlers to the 'halfway house' of the Dutch East India Company at the Cape, in the middle of the seventeenth century. As the language, their *taal,* had changed little in the last two hundred years, so there remained unchanged their strong Puritan conviction. Here were people, separated by several days' journey from their nearest neighbour, self-dependent, rulers over their thousands of acres, a law unto themselves, who were happy in their voluntary isolation though deprived of even the simplest amenities of life. Not only did these people read the Bible twice a day but they accepted literally the teachings of *Die Goeie Boek*, particularly of the Old Testament, as the guide to their lives.

Perhaps Cecil was still suffering from pangs of conscience about his newly adopted atheism that the natural religiosity of the Boers made so deep an impression on him.

Among these people, he thought, it must be good to live.

Once he had finished with diamonds, it would be ideal to retire to this land, to be near Nature, to forget all about worldly things and to regain one's health. For a few hundred pounds one could buy fertile land enough to make any English squire envious. Cecil Rhodes bought a farm of 3,000 acres. This ownership qualified him as a *burgher* of the Transvaal Republic, a fact to which he was to refer twenty years later.

The two brothers, trekking along the old 'Missionary Road', first came to the land of the Bechuanas. Already on their way north they had heard much talk about gold-prospecting in the Transvaal. When they came to the border of Bechuanaland the rumours about gold turned into fact. An English company had already begun mining in the Tati district beyond the Limpopo River.

That there was gold in the land beyond the Limpopo Herbert and Cecil Rhodes did not doubt. They must have recalled the sensation caused by an article in *The Times* about discoveries of rich gold findings in the interior beyond the Limpopo. A German geologist, Karl Mauch, in 1868, had been sure that he had found the fabulous Gold of Ophir in the land of the bellicose Matabele between the lower Zambezi and the Limpopo.

At about the same time two explorers had discovered in that very district mysterious ruins of ingeniously constructed brick-buildings and distinct traces of gold-mining activities, dating back probably to the Phoenicians. There could be no doubt that the Gold of Ophir came from these mysterious workings in the middle of darkest Africa.

But the two Rhodes brothers were not prepared for an expedition into the interior. They could go no further. 'Another time!' Herbert said resignedly. 'Another time,' said Cecil with a sigh, as he bent over his crumpled map of Africa. He could not know that this land of the Gold of Ophir would be his and bear his name within twenty years.

After seven months the brothers returned to Kimberley. Cecil's health was completely restored. Herbert, too, was much affected by their long trek. He had made up his mind never to return to a humdrum life of routine. For Herbert Rhodes the mysterious antique gold workings in the north had become an obsession. Without much ado he one day packed his ox-wagon and was off, northward bound, after he had offered his claims to Cecil. Together with Rudd, his partner, Cecil thus became owner of three of the best claims in the Kimberley Mine.

Cecil Rhodes was worried. By 1872, more than £1,600,000 worth of diamonds had been found. In consequence prices were going down. Buyers nowadays dictated their own prices. They knew only too well that most of the diggers stood on such weak legs that they had to sell immediately to keep their claims working. All buyers wanted only flawless, well-shaped and the best-coloured stones. Expenses on the other hand had increased considerably. One had to pay higher wages to the Natives if one wanted good, strong and sober men. Everybody was convinced that these rascals stole at least half of the whole production. Supervision had become very difficult the deeper the mine went. There were now in Kimberley dozens of shady characters who bought stolen diamonds from the Natives, paying a mere trifle in the form of 'Cape Smoke', old guns, beads, uniforms, watches or mouth organs.

The hauling-system in the mines had to be constantly replaced or improved. A falling reef, the biggest and an unpredictable calamity, could wither all one's hopes in the best mine overnight.

All these difficulties had to be overcome before one could make diamond-digging a sound and permanent business proposition. Moreover, one could operate successfully only on a wide basis, unhampered by neighbouring workings. The future lay in combining as many connected claims as possible. For this reason Rhodes had entered into partnership with Rudd. Costs had to be reduced by bigger production. And he had to see to it that he found claims where not only was the production high but where the finest quality of stones were yielded. In these respects his claims in the Kimberley Mine did not satisfy him fully. He could not complain about the number of diamonds found there, but very seldom were the stones flawless and pure white.

Rhodes cast his eyes on De Beers Mine, also originally owned by the 'Red Caps'. He had carefully, though unobtrusively, studied its production. There the diamonds were perhaps a little less in number but most of them were of great purity, big and of regular shape.

He began to buy claims in De Beers Mine. 'A nice little mine', he called what was to become the world's richest diamond mine.

In the short time of his activities on the diamond fields Rhodes had seen many a man fall from the height of prosperity down to complete poverty, merely by adverse conditions and through no fault of his own. Rhodes learnt from such examples. He did not want to stake his entire future on one card. The 3,000-acre farm he had bought in the Transvaal he considered as a nest-egg. But he also wanted to have a secure income. He became aware that in the terrific heat everyone was complaining about the lack of cool drinks. All clamoured for ice.

Rhodes had seen an ice-machine advertised in a Durban newspaper. Together with Rudd he bought it. Unfortunately that year it happened to be an exceptionally cool summer and the demand for ice was minimal. The next summer-season, however, brought a large enough turnover to recover the entire costs and to make a profit of £1,500 each.

Since the ice-business proved to be after all a gamble with the weather Rhodes gave it up, glad to have come out with a good profit. This money, he decided, he would not invest entirely on the diamond-fields. Some of it he would use for a secure investment. He wanted something absolutely safe, and chose an old-established railway-line connecting Durban's harbour with the town.

It was Rhodes' first deal in shares and it was symptomatic that he used his first free small capital to buy railway shares, since his later big financial schemes were mostly based on his belief in railways as a safe and lucrative investment.

Through his acquisition of several prominent claims in De Beers, people in Kimberley began to consider him as a potential factor on the diamond-market.

When his old friends, whose luck had limped far behind his own, joked about his preoccupation of late with big financial schemes, the amounts of which made them dizzy, he burst out angrily:

'I dare say you think I am keen about money. I assure you I

wouldn't care a damn, if I lost all I have tomorrow. It's the game I like . . . it's the game I like . . . the game I like!'

He had attained his aim: he now possessed the necessary funds to go to Oxford fully independent. He had passed successfully through the 'University of Life' at Kimberley. Now he was ready for another University: to become an English gentleman.

Towards the middle of 1873 Rhodes embarked for England. In his waistcoat-pocket he carried loosely a few diamonds. Nobody on board would have believed that this tall, red-faced, slim young man was the owner of several rich diamond claims whose fortune was known to be not far from £10,000. His worn-out clothes, stained and threadbare, did not give any indication of such wealth. His only pair of trousers the sail-maker of the ship had to patch up with a piece of canvas.

In October of the same year Rhodes passed the entrance examination of Oxford University.

His mother was still able to enjoy the return of her fourth son and his success in the examination. Shortly afterwards, tired, quiet and long-suffering Louisa Rhodes, a devout wife, a good mother and a patient woman, closed her eyes forever.

CHAPTER III

'THE HIGHEST OBJECT IN A PERFECT LIFE'

GREAT was the influence of Oxford over Cecil Rhodes. He first spent a year there, until 1874, when ill-health made his return to Kimberley necessary. Difficulties on the diamond market, changes in mining conditions, but especially the lack of sufficient funds prevented him from continuing his studies until 1876. Then for two years he kept all terms at Oxford though he spent the long vacation in Kimberley.

Rhodes, encouraged by his father, tried to enter University College, famed for its high standard of scholarship. But in spite of his intense cramming at Kimberley his Latin prose was not considered good enough. He had better luck at Oriel College where he was admitted as a 'passman'.

Rhodes entered Oxford with the intention of preparing himself for a profession. His father had not yet given up hope that he would enter the Church. During his first term at Oxford Cecil wrote a letter to his friend Dr Sutherland in a style on which no beneficial academic influence is as yet noticeable:

> Whether I become the village parson which you sometimes imagined me as, remains to be proved. I am afraid my constitution received rather too much of what they call the lust of the flesh at the Diamond Fields to render that result possible. . . .

His brother Frank had returned to England with Cecil to enter a crack cavalry regiment as lieutenant. Another brother had also entered the Army, as an officer in the Engineers. '. . . Whether I shall follow their example remains to be proved.'

When conditions in Kimberley had changed and Rhodes had to fight an uphill battle to retain the position which he had gained on the diamond-fields, he wanted to secure his future.

He had tasted of the sweet drug of making money. He had imagined himself on the safe way to wealth, independence and security. Now, away from Kimberley, he feared all the more the possibility of gliding back into anonymous impecuniosity. This fear of poverty became a nightmare. It impeded his clear thinking. It influenced his decisions. To such proportions did it grow that he confessed to Rudd in a letter in 1876:

> . . . On a calm review of the preceding year I find that £3,000 had been lost, because owing to my having no profession I lacked pluck on three occasions, through fearing that one might lose; and I had nothing to fall back on in the shape of a profession. . . . I am slightly too cautious now. . . . By all means try and spare me for two years; you will find I shall be twice as good a speculator with a profession at my back. . . .

He was now resolved to become a barrister. Soon, however, he was forced to realize that it was very difficult, if not impossible, to combine studies at a university with conducting financial and mining affairs from a distance of 7,000 miles, especially at a time of economic world-crisis and a slump on the diamond market.

Rudd, quiet, ever-unperturbed Rudd, seemed to have been infected with the jitters just like everybody else in Kimberley. . . . One had to buck him up with strong regular doses of one's own optimism—in the guise of conviction—that diamonds are bound to rally. . . . One knows for certain that improved methods for finding diamonds will defeat every fall in diamonds within the next two years. . . . One has to warn panicking Rudd not to sacrifice claims because of bad times. . . . And one has to stress in every letter that he should accumulate 'the ready' . . . and that now when everybody is willing to sell at any price, is the time to acquire some new claims—as bargains. . . .

One does everything in one's power to help poor Rudd. . . . Not nice for one to wake up at night sweating like a pig fancying oneself meeting various little bits of paper, called promissory notes, with one's blessed signature at the bottom. . . . Less pleasant in bright daylight to find oneself with not a blinking sixpence in one's pocket. . . . Impossible to bother one's father—going a-begging. . . . Very unpleasant being under an obligation to anyone. . . . One had to swallow one's pride and touch old Rudd's brother for a few quid. . . . Why are people in England so blastedly suspicious? . . . The blighters even charge four per cent for drafts. . . .

One should really have two heads since only one on one's neck is not enough if one has to study Aristotle's *Ethics*, read

Gibbon's *Decline and Fall*, learn the Thirty-nine Articles and at the same time escape to London and try to persuade oily Levantines in Hatton Garden, where these bastards hold their exchange on the street or in filthy little tea-rooms—try to persuade them to buy a parcel of stones at a decent price. . . . Or one has to waste hours when ordering machinery to explain to idiotic 'experts' about special winding-drums, clutch-gears, pump spare-parts, engine-valves, steel-cables—all mining requisites. . . . And one has to fight them tooth and nail when they cut you short with their perpetual 'impossible'! . . . One was also once told one couldn't grow cotton in Natal! . . . And one has to have both eyes wide open, not only so that one doesn't fall asleep over Marcus Aurelius' *Meditations*, but also to keep on the look-out for making a few quid on the side. . . .

One has to struggle through somehow. . . . One's character was so battered about at the diamond-fields that one likes to preserve the few remnants. . . . One has to work. . . . Had one not as a little boy picked as one's motto: 'To do—or to die'? . . .

Cecil Rhodes had 'sent himself up to Oxford', as he liked to put it, not only for the purpose of studying. His training to become an 'English Gentleman' he must have considered of equal importance. His boyish shyness had not left him and had with the advancing years turned him into a gauche, inhibited, and complex personality. A physical defect, small as it was, caused him constant embarrassment. The little finger of his right hand was bent at the middle knuckle and could not be straightened. He always hid it and later became very nervous if he noticed someone looking at his hands. He always kept the third and little finger doubled up when shaking hands.

A parallel is brought to mind in the withered left arm of another man, an emperor and a contemporary of Rhodes, whose crippled limb was largely responsible for the course of history between the years 1888 and 1918.

Rhodes probably also suffered under his delicate and youthful appearance which gave the impression of a rather effeminate schoolboy. It led to a defensive aggressiveness, the forceful adoption of rough manners and coarse language by which he wanted to show the tough Kimberley diggers that he was their equal.

His successes on the diamond-fields had made him a young man of means and an important though still small power on the diamond market. This prominence, however, was restricted to his capacity as a business-man. His private intercourse brought him into contact with the English nobility—even if their coat of arms were slightly smudged—with Oxford and Cambridge men, with former Public School boys and ex-army officers—with all those who belonged by birth, education or profession to the category of 'Gentlemen'. Though they mixed with everyone in Kimberley in the course of business and did not mind an occasional drinking bout with 'those fellows' for the sake of a lucrative transaction, they kept strictly to themselves. Rhodes was admitted to their circle, since his three brothers in the Army raised him almost to their caste. But he was well aware that he was only tolerated and he was intelligent enough to realize his social limitations and what a handicap his lack of polish was likely to be in the future.

When he came to Oxford he encountered that same phalanx of Gentlemen against which he had run up in Kimberley. After a short trial he gave up living in his College: 'Nasty, abominable, beastly food—pig-swill', he called the dinners served in its Hall. He thus preferred, also because it gave greater liberty, to take private lodgings, a small suite of rooms in the High.

There he met a number of other young men who became his companions for the next few years. Among them figured two lords, some younger sons of titled families and scions of the English gentry. These Oxford friends, with a few exceptions, did not strive for academic distinction. They were more interested in good living, congenial company and having their fun. Yet of this small crowd of young bon-vivants one became a judge, another an eminent historian and two, R. Rochfort Maguire, later a prominent scholar, and Charles Metcalfe, a man of many talents, became intimate collaborators of Rhodes.

Rhodes, having grown up unguided, unrestricted and unspoilt during the most important stage of a boy's development, had remained at heart an enthusiastic schoolboy. His new friends, brought up in the traditional way prescribed for young gentlemen, much younger in years than Rhodes, believed that their new dignity as Oxford undergraduates called for concealment of their discomfort amid the new surroundings. They aped their elders by putting on airs of sophistication.

This affected smugness Rhodes took as a barrier behind which the 'Gentlemen' had entrenched themselves against outsiders and he felt that it was up to his social abilities to ride it down and be accepted as an equal.

He first tried to impress them by tales of his adventures on the veld. They scarcely listened. If he had told them that he had scored a century at Lords, ridden the winner at Liverpool, lost a fortune at baccara at Brooks's, had supper with a 'Gaiety' chorus girl or at least climbed the Grand Tour over all the college roofs, they would have been interested. Only Charles Metcalfe roused himself from his lethargy; he opened his eyes, relit the cigar hanging from the corner of his mouth. He listened attentively.

Later Rhodes remarked to another friend: 'Do you know, one really can think Metcalfe honestly believed those stories were true!'

Rhodes tried other methods by which to impress his new friends. He boasted about his great business prospects and occasionally threw on the table several diamonds which he carried loose in his waistcoat pocket. 'Vulgar!' was the general opinion and an icy silence the response.

Money could not impress these young English gentlemen. One had either money, or at least credit, but one did not speak about such matters. Money did not affect one's status as a gentleman.

Rhodes now went over to displaying the cynicism of a rough and tough adventurer who enjoyed himself by shocking his audience with his views on life, his low esteem of mankind, his irreligious thoughts, all expressed in the coarsest language.

His friends were just bored. He began to work rather heavily on their nerves with his continual efforts to entangle them in arguments on political, historical or philosophical questions which had just crossed his mind or an idea which he had come across while reading. He would nettle them by storming into their common sitting-room—where they were just discussing the prospects for the next day's races at Ascot—and spluttering excitedly, fall into a falsetto:

'I have found in Aristotle the meaning of life—virtue. He says virtue is the highest activity of the soul living for the highest object in a perfect life. Now, you fellows, who among you could deny. . . .'

And he would go on and on, labouring hard to clarify his own thoughts while speaking, searching for the explanation, the solution, the answer to the problem by which his hard but slow-working brain was haunted. These monologues became Rhodes' habitual way of working out decisions. But his friends were neither willing to discuss, nor interested in listening to any such questions.

They could not know that an upheaval had taken place in the mind of this twenty-three-year-old man which for the last six years had been filled with the realistic facts of money-making in its crudest form and was now, badly prepared, suddenly confronted with the highest cultural goods of humanity.

Rhodes had to confess that the making of a gentleman needed the same patience and regular training as that of being a student. He found that there existed several clubs and societies in Oxford, through the membership of which one could acquire all those social qualities which he lacked. He joined the Bullingdon Club to which belonged the smart set of undergraduates. There one saw to the correctness in manners, dress and thought but also, at regular banquets, to the enjoyment of excellent food, the best wines and everything else that was expensive. He also became a member of the Vincent Club and was shortly afterwards admitted as a Freemason to the University Lodge.

It is usual to celebrate the initiation of a new Mason by a banquet. Was it the wine or the deep impression which the romantic symbolism of the 'Royal Art' made on him, that he nonchalantly disclosed the secrets of Masonry when not more than an hour before he had sworn a solemn oath never to reveal them? The Brethren were flabbergasted. The chairman intervened and reprimanded him severely.

Strolling along the High, or walking through the college parks, certainly in the dining-room of the Mitre Hotel, Rhodes must have often come across another undergraduate, a massive-looking six-footer, immaculately dressed according to the latest fashion. Everyone at Oxford knew him, at least by reputation, as the brilliant Irishman, Oscar Wilde. Cecil Rhodes would have met him several times at banquets of the Bullingdon Club but there is no record of any direct personal contact between the two. It may be assumed that Rhodes would not have been very interested in a young, healthy man who wrote poetry. At one time, at least, he expressed his opinion of such an occupation when a friend told him that he aspired to become a writer.

'Shouldn't do that. It is not a man's work—mere loafing.'

As different as were Rhodes and Wilde in every respect, they concurred for a short time in their great veneration of one man: John Ruskin. Together with hundreds of other students they crowded the Sheldonian Theatre, the biggest hall of the University, to listen to this strange middle-aged man with the piercing large blue eyes delivering his fanatical sermons on the beauty of Italian Art.

In the fortieth year of his life, at the same time as a bearded German refugee was sitting in the Reading Room of the British Museum working on his book *Das Kapital*, Ruskin, the hot-house-reared genius, discovered the existence of poverty, dirt and misery among England's underprivileged class. He detected the evils brought about by mechanization and found the cause of the rottenness of modern society in the existing economic system.

In the afternoons, when the students hurried from their colleges through the High to the playing-fields, they were stopped by Ruskin, who lectured to them how wrong it was that England's *élite* should waste its energy as gladiators. They should learn to honour the sanctity of manual work. They should with their own hands contribute to improving the miserable conditions of this world. There was a road badly needed through the swamps near the village of Hinksey.

Out went the Professor, in cap and gown, with his disciples. He gave them picks and shovels, wheelbarrows and heavy rollers. They broke stones, waded through mud, carried heavy rocks. Ruskin did not spare himself in setting an example. It did not matter to him that the road turned out rather crooked, and was not level except on a small stretch done by his gardener. Neither did it worry him that the work was abruptly given up after two months with only a few hundred yards completed. He left for Venice; it was the end of the experiment. A cynic like Oscar Wilde had, of course, never believed in it, but Cecil Rhodes, though unable through his illness to take part in the ethical carnival, listened to the 'Gospel of Labour' with great interest. Here was a man who had pronounced something which had occupied his own mind since his boyhood; 'To do—or to die.' The slogan struck a chord within him which was soon to grow into loud fanfares.

The man who had started as the standard-bearer of refined aestheticism and later became the prophet of a utopian socialism also supplied the philosophic jumping-board from which Cecil Rhodes was to plunge into the African continent to paint its map red with the red colour of Britain and the blood of thousands.

John Ruskin in his inaugural address to the students of Oxford proclaimed the gospel of British Imperialism:

> There is a destiny now possible for us, the highest ever set before a nation to be accepted or refused. We are still undegenerate in race; a race mingled of the best northern blood. We are not yet dissolute in temper, but have still the firmness to govern and the grace to obey. . . . Will you youths of England make your country again a royal throne of kings; a sceptred isle, for all the world a source of light, a centre of peace; mistress of learning and of the Arts, faithful guardian of time-tried principles, under temptation from fond experiments and licentious desires; and amidst the cruel and clamorous jealousies of the nations; worshipped in her strange valour, of good-will towards men? . . . This is what England must either do, or perish; she must found colonies as fast and as far as she is able, formed of her most energetic and worthiest men; seizing every piece of fruitful waste ground she can set her foot on, and there teaching these her colonists that their chief virtue is to be fidelity to their country, and that their first aim is to be to advance the power of England by land and sea: and that, though they live on a distant plot of ground, they are no more to consider themselves therefore disfranchised from their native land than the sailors of her fleet do, because they float on distant seas. . . . If we can get men, for little pay, to cast themselves against cannon-mouths for love of England, we may find men also who will plough and sow for her, who will behave kindly and righteously for her, who will bring up their children to love her, and who will gladden themselves in the brightness of her glory, more than in all the light of tropical skies. . . . You think that an impossible ideal? Be it so; refuse to accept it, if you will; but see that you form your own in its stead. All that I ask of you is to have a fixed purpose of some kind for your country and for yourselves, no matter how restricted, so that it be fixed and unselfish.

It was the language of imperialism to intoxicate the youth with the idea of belonging to a master-race destined to save the world. In Rhodes this language fell on fertile ground. He had been waiting for just such a lead. Here was his gospel. He was resolved to become its apostle and like Paul to go into foreign lands and preach it to the heathen.

He did not stand alone in his feverish dreams. The first wave of Jingoism was soon to break over the British Isles. Drunk with patriotism, cold-blooded, ever peace-loving, placid Englishmen roared with hoarse voices in 1878, demanding British intervention in the Russo-Turkish War:

We don't want to fight; but, by Jingo, if we do,
We've got the ships, we've got the men, we've got the money too.

It was all the work of that most un-English of British statesmen, Disraeli, first Earl of Beaconsfield, leader of England's Tories, Her Britannic Majesty's Prime Minister and intimate friend and counsellor.

This dandified statesman had awakened the British lion so that its fierce roar echoed over all Europe and penetrated even into the wilds of Africa from the Suez Canal—which he brought under British control at a bargain price—to Zululand and the Transvaal.

Cecil Rhodes followed all political developments closely. Much depended, he felt, on a quick recovery of the world from its prevalent economic depression. A luxury industry, such as diamonds, had been particularly affected. Rhodes regularly sent to Rudd in Kimberley detailed information about the political situation. In Lord Beaconsfield's Government he had great confidence though the pace of the British lion seemed to him still too slow.

As was his wont when an idea revolved in his mind, he had to talk about it. For several weeks his friends had to listen to Rhodes' monologues on British politics, what Lord Beaconsfield should have done, what he did do, and what he had omitted to do. 'Why don't you write and tell him?' one of his bored friends teased him.

'That's just what I am going to do.'

So Rhodes sat down in all seriousness and together with five friends, who treated the matter rather as a joke, wrote a letter to the Right Honourable Gentleman, Her Majesty's Prime Minister, full of wise advice on how to run the British Empire.

Lord Beaconsfield forestalled even Rhodes' boldest dreams and hopes: he knew that the British lion had to do more than roar to gain the world's respect. Down came the lion's claws in South Africa.

Lately gold had been found in several places in the Transvaal.

Already in *The Times* of 19 January 1874 a long letter from one David Leslie was published, in which he wrote that in the 'Transvaal, a petty Dutch Boer State established upon Native territory', gold had been discovered. On the same page Messrs. Mercer & Co., Merchants of Leadenhall Street in the City of London, 'begged to announce to their business-friends the arrival of a nugget of pure gold, weighing 18 ounces', which had been found at Lydenburg, in the Transvaal Republic.

The British Government bore these facts in mind during the years that followed. According to a report from Cape Town there was 'no reason to doubt that, if England declined to interfere, Germany would be induced to undertake the protection of the Transvaal, which would have added infinitely to our troubles in Africa'.

Britain thus simply annexed the Transvaal. Lord Beaconsfield, with his combined sense of the cunning statesman, the theatrical romantic and the flattering courtier, presented the Transvaal to his 'Faerie Queene' as a birthday present in 1877.

He was proud of the fact that the occupation of this country, in size twice as big as Britain, was made without great cost to the British tax-payer, by a detachment of twenty-five mounted police. Yet he was wise enough to conceal the strange means employed. He had been prompted into action by the false reports of his subordinates that the Transvaal was threatened to be overrun by Natives and that the Boers themselves wanted to come under the rule of Queen Victoria. It was true that the Boers in the Transvaal were at war with a Native tribe. This was nothing extraordinary to these frontiersmen. But their country, because of the great war expenses, and the small and slow incoming taxes, through internal political intrigues and long droughts, was labouring under insurmountable difficulties and was actually facing bankruptcy. The British Government, under the pretence of neighbourly friendship and for reasons of general security in South Africa against tribal aggressors, sent a Commissioner to Pretoria with a small contingent of mounted police. The Boers believed that the British wanted to help them overcome their difficulties. Through bribes and corruption within the highest quarters the British delegate met no resistance when he hoisted the Union Jack in Pretoria's Government Building on the Queen's birthday, 24 May 1877.

Lord Beaconsfield, in such matters, relied on the experts of the

Colonial Office. They had supplied him with the reports from the British Governor of the Cape Colony, urging the necessity of bringing the Transvaal under British sovereignty. The British officials in Cape Town had not forgotten that forty years before, the Boers of the Transvaal had preferred to go on the Great Trek to an uncertain destiny to staying in the Cape under the secure and civilized conditions of British rule.

Misunderstanding totally the motives of these gallant men, the short-sighted red-taped Colonial bureaucrats believed that the abolition of slavery had been the main reason for their exodus. In their political narrow-mindedness, with their proverbial lack of psychological understanding and their traditional incompetence in dealing with non-English-speaking peoples, the Cape officials searched only for materialistic reasons. They could not or would not realize that there had been other, imponderable reasons, an inborn urge for individual freedom born out of their strict Calvinistic religiosity, an almost feudal system of political independence which clashed with English Liberalism, with British power-politics and with English contempt for everything non-British. Not all Englishmen accepted in silence the rape of the Transvaal. Gladstone, the Grand Old Man of England, had already given warning to keep our hands off South Africa, 'the one great unsolved and perhaps insoluble problem of our colonial system', where nothing but confusion and embarrassment could be expected. The old man's conscience was aroused by England's blundering crime of the annexation of the Transvaal 'by means dishonourable to the character of our country'.

In Parliament there rose the tall figure of Birmingham's popular Mayor, Mr Joseph Chamberlain, a new-comer to the 'gentleman's debating club' of Westminster. A slight quivering of his longish straight nose betrayed his indignation though otherwise his ascetic pale face gave the impression of perfect calm. He screwed his monocle into his right eye, stretched himself to the full height of his six feet and without raising his voice told the Government that he considered the annexation of the Transvaal 'an act of force, fraud and folly . . . the consequence of false information supplied to the British Government'.

The English public generally was not much interested in the new acquisition to their Empire, of stretches of useless land somewhere in Africa, thousands of miles away from home, inhabited mostly by black savages and a handful of half-civilized strange white 'foreigners'. But the well-fed city merchants, the worrying owners of cotton-mills in the Midlands, the steel-manufacturers and exporters, the ship-owners and coal-mine magnates, saw in the news from Africa a bright ray of hope penetrating the darkness of the business depression which had started in 1873 and seemed now in its sixth year to have reached its climax. They had had to watch with folded hands, powerless to stop it, how British capital was leaving the country to help build up new industries in Europe and railway constructions in North America. With envy they saw how the United States had quickly recovered from the Civil War and with deep alarm they noticed there the increasing competition growing up in the cotton trade. England's wealth which had always provided the world with manufactured goods was menaced by the industrialization of Europe which could now not only satisfy her own requirements but supply export markets, a former British monopoly. Germany particularly had lately invaded the export field as a serious rival to England. She delivered the goods at lower prices and supplied them as the customer required them. German industry and trade was challenging England's monopolistic world position.

Now Africa would provide new and big markets. With this hope the patriotism of England's industrialists rose to fever pitch. Imperialism always paid high dividends, as they knew. And presently the English masses, ignorant and innocent, began to wave the Union Jack with equal fanaticism. The British Lion had recovered at least in Africa.

Thus the eyes of the British were now focused on Africa. With great interest the news was received that the land of the diamonds, Chief Waterboer's country Griqualand, which had been claimed by both the Transvaal and the Orange Free State, had now also become British territory by its official annexation to the Cape Colony. Only a very few, however, realized at the time the real importance of the acquisition of this territory, which opened for Great Britain the way to the interior of Africa.

This corridor into the heart of Africa rose in value when the result of Stanley's journey through the Dark Continent became known. The imagination of even the most placid Englishman was fanned into a state of excitement, when for two years he read in the *Daily Telegraph* Stanley's hair-raising letters about his exploits.

Stanley's dispatches were swallowed with perhaps even greater interest than they aroused in the English readers of the *Daily Telegraph* by the statesmen in most European capitals. In Berlin's Wilhelmstrasse Prince Bismarck bent his 230 lb. over the map of Africa. On the Quai d'Orsay in Paris General MacMahon pointed excitedly to places on an African map lying in front of him on a flimsy gilt Louis XV chair. In the palace of Laeken King Leopold of the Belgians stroked his silky greying beard, looked at the map of Africa and told his aides-de-camp: 'Privately I can assure you of my conviction that nations which renounce ambition are nations without a future. A people which is content with its homeland, and which dreads even the shadow of a conflict, lacks the characteristics of a superior race.'

In Lisbon, in Madrid, in Vienna, in Stamboul, diplomats conferred for hours with statesmen, and statesmen with monarchs. The scramble for Africa had begun!

Only in London's Whitehall all was quiet. It required more than what they called the uncontrolled scribblings of a penny-a-liner, to bring into motion an English Civil Servant or to fire the imagination of the honourable members in the Gothic building at Westminster. One man alone in Parliament had shown foresight: for Gladstone every political question became an academic problem which released from him beautiful though lengthy oratory in the best classical style.

His unbending ideal of Liberalism caused him to oppose colonial imperialism. But in the results of Stanley's African explorations he foresaw the opening of the African interior and he perceived possibilities already in 1877 to which Bismarck later always referred as 'the Gladstone Prophecy':

> Our first site in Egypt, be it by larceny or be it by emption, will be the most certain egg of a North African Empire that will grow and grow . . . till we finally join hands across the equator with Natal and the Cape Colony, to say nothing of the Transvaal and the Orange River on the South, or of Abyssinia and Zanzibar to be swallowed by way of *viaticum* on our journey.

It was left finally to a scientist, Sir Rutherford Alcock, President of the Royal Geographical Society, to formulate the romantic ideas of the dreamers, the vague propaganda platitudes of the politicians and the dry matter-of-fact official reports into firmly described and realistic demands:

> Whether giant strides made in the last few years by geographical discoveries . . . (are) to be followed by equally vast and rapid changes in the conditions of Central Africa and the whole continent from Egypt to the Cape depends . . . upon the means which individuals and governments may bring to bear. It is mainly a question of money and employment of capital. . . . I can only express the hope that Great Britain, so long in the foremost rank, will not be the last on the muster roll of those countries which are destined to bring the African race, the inexhaustible wealth of their fertile soil, their mineral products and free labour, within the circle of modern civilization. . . .
>
> Making practicable roads is undoubtedly the first and indispensable condition of all progress in Africa. The bullock wagon and steamboat will do the rest until the time comes, and it cannot be far distant, for the rail and telegraph to complete the work.

Another scientist, Sir Edwin Arnold, who was also a poet, took the ideas of Gladstone and Alcock and saw the future possibilities of Britain on African soil as an uninterrupted line of British possessions from the North to the South, expressed in the catching phrase 'From Cape to Cairo!'

Cecil Rhodes, deeply immersed in his studies at Oxford in the summer of 1878, in preparation for the examinations terminating his second year, was frequently observed to sit absent-mindedly at his book-covered table, his mouth slightly open and dreamily stroking his chin with his right forefinger. He had recently turned quiet and silent and kept much to himself.

Often he could be seen standing in his room in front of a crumpled map of Africa, the *Daily Telegraph* with Stanley's articles in his hand, and staring for hours at the vast mostly unmapped stretches of that mysterious continent.

He became still more taciturn.

When he left Oxford for Kimberley in the autumn of 1878 there whirled in his mind the impressions gained during these two Oxford years: Aristotle's *Ethics* had attracted him; from Marcus Aurelius the philosophizing Emperor's *Meditations* he believed to have been imbued with the foundations of a practical philosophy; Gibbon's great work on the decay of the Roman Empire had taught him the frailty of political power; Plutarch's portraits filled him with enthusiasm for 'men of action'; he worshipped with Carlyle all the heroes of this historian; he had read Loyola's writings with growing interest and regarded the Jesuits as an admirable organization.

He had not been attracted by any novels. Dickens' works were recommended to him as necessary for his education. He energetically shook his head: 'No—one is not interested in the class of people Dickens wrote about—not interested—not interested.'

More than anything that he had studied, there worked on his mind the heroic deeds of Stanley in Africa, Beaconsfield's suave oratory on the destiny of the British Empire and above all his master-stroke in seizing the Transvaal.

But overruling all his thoughts there hammered in his crowded brain day and night the words of Gladstone:

> . . . finally join hands across the equator with Natal and the Cape Colony.

The 'Cape to Cairo' idea had captivated him.

CHAPTER IV

GOD'S CHOSEN PAINTER

WITH quick nervous steps he paced the room. The red dust which had filtered through a chink in the door, through cracks in the wooden walls or through the ill-fitting corrugated-iron roof of the spacious though simple four-roomed wooden house, grated under his heavy boots. Now and then he would rush to the small window.

'If only the pumps are still working!' It sounded like a sigh. Or a prayer.

A tremble shook the whole structure of the house.

'Reefs falling in again. . . . If only not at De Beers.'

He sat down at the table, his right forefinger caressing his chin. Wild thoughts, incoherent thoughts, flashed through his mind.

Would these ghosts appear again and frighten the marrow out of one's bones? One had seen these ghosts! Why else should one barricade the doors and windows with all the furniture in the room?

That friends, as they said later, had found one's body on the floor in what they liked to call a dead faint—nervous exhaustion due to excitement—did not mean a thing. They should not have called a doctor. What did these doctors—these *quacks*, know? What nonsense to babble about a leaking heart—it was a serious coronary attack. These doctors are ridiculous . . . are ridiculous with their quick diagnosis—it's no more than guesswork. The old London doctor who had sent one to Africa was of the same type. When one wanted to visit him again last year he was already under the ground. Too funny when his successor showed one an entry in the old man's journal of 1869; 'Has only six months to live'! . . . Too funny . . . six months to live and one still lives in the year of grace 1878 . . . twenty-five years old. . . .

His heart ailment was believed to be the consequence of a complicated case of influenza to which Rhodes had fallen victim during his first term in Oxford in 1873.

From the time of this first attack the influences of a defective cardiac system showed themselves in Rhodes' behaviour, thoughts and actions. The irregular blood-circulation affected his entire nervous system: a pressure in the chest caused a subconscious feeling of anxiety leading to a permanent restlessness of mind and body.

Rhodes felt or knew now that the span of his life was limited. He would have to hurry if he wanted to see his plans realized. He had to take short-cuts and apply pressure on himself and on his collaborators. Death was waiting and knocked daily at the door.

In his haste he did not ask if the means applied to any of his projects, financial, industrial, political or personal, corresponded with the generally accepted moral code.

Mining had lately become more complicated. Some mines were already so full of water that work had to stop. Rhodes was thus looking out for an insurance against the coming slump to compensate for possible losses. It would have to be something completely independent of the fluctuations on the diamond market; something which yielded a regular steady income in ready cash; something without risks, something solid; something that everybody needed and that nobody else possessed. If he could find a steam-engine and a pump he would become the most blessed and highly paid man in Kimberley.

Rhodes had many a sleepless night thinking of how to get hold of a steam-engine. One day he heard a chance remark in a bar. Someone on a distant farm had begun to use one of those new threshing machines worked by a steam-engine. Rhodes did not ask any questions. Within a few hours he was on his way, his pockets well stuffed with sovereigns and banknotes. He did not even know where exactly to find the farm. Before he left Kimberley he entered into a contract with the boards of the big mines to take over the pumping-out of the water, and since he was without competition he succeeded in obtaining a high price.

The owner of the farm, a Mr Devenish, was surprised when a young man jumped out of a wagon drawn by eight sweating mules and, holding a bag of sovereigns and banknotes under his nose, shouted in an excited falsetto voice:

'I want to buy your steam-engine . . . I must have your engine. . . . Name me your price!'

'I don't want to sell this engine, I am sure. Just bought her and jolly glad I did.'

'I'll pay you any price. I've got the cash here.'

'Don't waste your time, young man. This engine is not for sale.'

Out of the farm-house there came Mrs Devenish. According to the custom of the country she offered the hospitality of the house to the stranger.

'I warn you, Mrs Devenish, I won't leave this place without the engine!'

Rhodes stayed as a guest for several days without succeeding in making the farmer even discuss the engine. Only once the farmer replied curtly:

'I haven't altered my mind today nor will I tomorrow or next week or any time at all. Put that into your pipe and smoke it, young man!'

Rhodes changed his tactics. Instead of following the farmer daily to the fields, he stayed with Mrs Devenish. He told her about the Vicarage, about his mother, his sisters and brothers and his sickness. Within a few days he noticed that Mr Devenish was becoming more amiable. For a few days Rhodes had stopped mentioning the engine altogether.

After dinner one day Rhodes again put the question.

Mrs Devenish took Rhodes' side fervently. Her husband was silent for a long time. Just as his wife started on a new argument, he stood up, and holding his ears in despair he exploded:

'The pair of you drive me mad. Take the blessed plant and disappear with it as quick as you can. But you'll have to pay a jolly stiff price, that much I can tell you.'

Rhodes did not bargain. He paid the price asked and immediately set out for Kimberley.

The rain had turned the road into streams of quagmire. The mules, accustomed to light and quick work, could not pull the heavy wagon through the mud. Rhodes needed a span of oxen. There was a farm nearby. The farmer declined to lend his oxen. Rhodes, afraid that he would again lose many precious days in negotiations with an obstinate farmer, bought the oxen at a fabulous price.

In the meanwhile the mining boards were becoming impatient: neither Rhodes nor a pump had appeared. Upon his arrival he had to stand up to a stormy meeting. But Rhodes knew that the owners depended on him and did not suspect how badly he needed their money. He treated them, all men much older than he, with such casualness that they were sure there must be a reason for his evident independence. In the end they changed the contract to his advantage.

One of the new provisions stipulated that the mines had to install a reservoir to receive and store the huge quantities of pumped-out water. Only a few months later, just after the last bucket of water had been pumped out of the mines, the temporary reservoir burst and all the water poured back into the mines. Rhodes immediately made a new contract at double the fee and secured for himself a monopoly for several years.

But the plant gave Rhodes and Rudd a headache for many years. The engine had to be fed with wood, and there was no fire-wood for a hundred miles around Kimberley. As soon as the farmers who brought their wagons with wood over long distances arrived at the market it was snapped up at fancy prices.

Rhodes bought a rickety cart with a shaggy horse. Before sunrise he had covered many miles and was waiting on the road outside Kimberley for the Boer farmers with their loads of wood and bought his requirements before anyone else had a chance to outbid him.

'If only the pumps. . . . If only the pumps. . . . If only the pumps. . . .'

Rhodes drummed the rhythm of these words nervously against the window-pane. With every thunderstroke his body trembled. His whole future depended on his claims in De Beers Mine not being drowned and the reef not coming down. After his return from Oxford, he and Rudd had bought several new claims adjoining the old ones. The whole of De Beers Mine had been offered to them for £6,000. They did not have the money on hand at the time to accept the offer nor could they find anyone willing to lend them such a large amount. The new claims they had bought cheaply. Most owners wanted to sell. Diamond-digging for the last few years was no longer a one-man venture; it had become an industry. When the Government had repealed an old regulation that no one might own more than ten claims, owners of neighbouring claims in all mines had thrown their property together. Amalgamations took place. Companies were formed. Mining shares became objects of speculation. On the London Stock Exchange speculators showed curiosity in 'Kaffirs', as they called these shares. The 'Kaffir-Circus' became an arena for the most foolhardy and sometimes fraudulent speculations.

Rhodes foresaw that the time would come when they would have to build a system of intricate galleries, hundreds of feet below the ground. No one knew anything about real mining, though miners from Wales and some fellows with experience in gold-mining in Australia and California had taught them a few tricks. Now they would need mining experts, engineers, new machinery, props, mechanization. Money would be needed.

Rhodes, together with Rudd, formed all his claims in De Beers into a joint-stock company, the De Beers Mining Company, Ltd., which was joined by some other claim-holders. This company owned the best sites in the mine.

A question which troubled everyone those days—and well it might—was how long the good earth would still allow them to rip up her womb and rob her of her precious riches? The yellow ground, in which the diamonds were embedded, was running out. At several places blue ground had been found beneath the yellow strata, totally different from the upper formation. Would there be diamonds in the blue ground? Sufficient diamonds? Well-coloured and sizeable stones? And how deep would the blue ground go?

A panic set in at Kimberley. Most diggers had no confidence in the blue formation. They sold their claims—if they could.

Only a very few men believed in the blue ground, among them particularly Cecil Rhodes. When experts, urgently called in by frantic owners, declared that according to the geological rules no diamonds could be expected below the yellow sand, Rhodes contradicted them sharply. To his partners, in the heat of such controversies, he remarked sarcastically:

'Yes, they also told me in Natal, that I couldn't grow any cotton there!'

This yellow ground, he argued vehemently, was only a branch of a lode of volcanic eruptions. The real bed of the diamonds was underneath the yellow layer. So firm and convincing were his pleas that his partners finally ceased their resistance to further acquisitions of claims in De Beers.

Rhodes' drumming against the window-pane now took on the rhythm of a triumphal march. How right he had been! The blue ground was yielding undreamt of-results.

Kimberley had changed during the two years of his absence. It had evolved into a town, complete with streets and a few modest brick buildings, others of corrugated-iron or wood; with churches, theatres and hotels; with saloon-bars, bar-lounges, private bars, refreshment bars and restaurant bars; with dance-halls, music-halls and brothels; with gambling saloons and roulette-rooms; with halls for baccara, chemin-de-fer and lotteries; with races, bookies and tipsters; with shops and trades-folk; with banks, stock-brokers and 'bulls and bears'; with a suburban middle-class and snobs and dandies; with unctuous churchgoers who donned black coats on Sundays; with loafers, pick-pockets, diamond-smugglers, pimps, forgers and impostors; with branches of Europe's biggest jewel-merchants who had sent their young men from London, Paris, Berlin and Vienna to open offices in one of the new buildings; with diamond-brokers, men from Amsterdam, from Hatton Garden, even from Bombay; with a town-council; with a governmental mining-board; with police and prison. Kimberley had taken on an even more cosmopolitan character: crossing Market Square one could hear people speaking in every dialect of the British Isles, in German, in the *taal* of the Boers, in French, Russian, Yiddish, broad American, and Portuguese.

Rhodes took in this picture with an expression of satisfaction. If only one's health will stand the strain.... 'To do—or to die'.... Much and hard work will have to be done.... As long as there is civilization, men will buy diamonds to put on women's fingers.... Diamonds, many diamonds—perhaps too many of the glittering stones—lie hidden in the blue ground.... We have to keep up their rarity-value and must not let the supply become bigger than the demand.... We have to keep up prices to meet the increased production expenses.... Now they dictate prices from London, Amsterdam or Paris.... We will have to make diamonds once more rare enough to be able to ask our own price.... We will have to regulate the output, regulate the sale, regulate the price.... But how? Bright Merriman has hit on the right idea: monopoly by a general amalgamation.... One has to progress slowly, unobserved and carefully not to frighten away one's chances. Connexions, alliances and combinations will have to be made to join hands with some of the big-money people, enterprising men like the Rothschilds. . . . One must have money, one must have power . . . money and power. . . .

The tapping on the glass stopped abruptly. Rhodes looked at his wrist. He became afraid when he noticed on his left hand the joining point of the raised arteries distinctly throbbing up and down. 'If only one's health. . . .'

He quickly cleared the table of its papers. His friends were coming home. Together with two other young men he was now living in a wood-and-iron house away from the diggers' quarters in what was already at that time called 'a select part of the town'. In this house he messed with eleven friends known in town as the 'Twelve Apostles'.

Rhodes needed people around him in the evenings and always tried to keep them there as long as he could. During the day he preferred to be left alone. But in the evening he dreaded solitude and in later years used to keep his visitors up half the night.

In the hour before dinner, when his friends assembled in his sitting-room for the traditional 'sun-downer', Rhodes, as usual, began and directed the conversation by bursting into a lengthy monologue.

That day he was in an extraordinarily quiet and pensive mood. In an unusually soft voice he told them:

'In Oxford I had to read a damned lot of philosophy. Once came across a passage about the importance of having an aim in life sufficiently high to justify spending one's life in trying to reach it. Made a deep impression, a deep impression on me. What should be one's aim in life? This much I know: I have not yet found it. One has still to seek it. . . .'

He stopped abruptly in the middle of the sentence. The cold atmosphere, which told him that the majority of his friends would not be able to follow him, was interrupted when someone asked Rhodes:

'Why did you come out to South Africa?'

'Why did I come to Africa—why did I come to Africa? Well, they will tell you that I came out on account of my health—or out of love of adventure—a sort of wanderlust. To some extent that may be true. But the real fact is that I could no longer stand the smell of eternal cold mutton at home . . . the eternal cold mutton at home!'

And, while rubbing his hands along his left side, there followed his usual laughter, starting with a loud chuckle and going over into a staccato of falsetto shrieks, still stammering between the fits: 'Smell of cold mutton . . . of cold mutton . . . mutton!'

There was an embarrassed silence until Rhodes, having recovered from his laughing fit, addressed a thin, rather short and insignificant-looking man across the room whose large square head showed the first signs of baldness. A drooping moustache under an amusing snub nose; two melancholic wide-set black eyes, the eyes of an affectionate dog, as a friend called them; the full-lipped mouth of an epicurean, a mouth ready to kiss, yet also capable of remaining shut for any length of time, to hurl unexpectedly a very few but bitter sarcasms into a conversation; these features constituted a face, pale, cold and reserved, yet a face of which a stranger once observed that 'one could draw at sight' on it. His hands were speaking hands, long, white and well cared-for, the hands of a sculptor, or of a violinist; nervous hands, dry, clean, strong hands, beautiful though alarming hands, like those on the portraits of decadent Renaissance princes; the hands of a skilful surgeon.

Rhodes had to repeat his question twice: 'And what made Dr Jim come to Africa?'

Even then it took some seconds until the reply came in a quiet, rather monotonous deep voice:

'A slightly mouldy lobe of the lungs to be dry-cleaned by the rays of the African sun and—to make as quickly as possible as much money as I can—be it by my skill with scalpel and knife or by luck at the card-table—that I can fulfil the dream and only ambition of my life—three acres and a cow in Sussex!'

This was one of the longest speeches which had ever come from Dr Jameson. He usually expressed his utter boredom by an outward jerk of his hands or by merely raising an eyebrow.

Dr Leander Starr Jameson could not be sized up easily. He himself was not quite clear about his own feelings, or his aims and ambitions in life. When he came to Kimberley in 1878, not quite twenty-five years old, so many different and contradictory inclinations lay dormant in him that they bewildered him and caused in him many complexities which he tried to evade by manifold diversions. He took to gambling.

He was a fine surgeon and had already distinguished himself

in London hospitals as an extraordinary young doctor who promised a brilliant career. In Kimberley Dr Jameson missed the excitement of the operating theatre. His practice, though it brought him a very good income, did not satisfy him. His tactful manners, though distant and rather haughty, made him very popular. Women of all kinds were particularly attracted by his indifference, cynicism and callousness. Easy conquests did not interest him. Without excitement there was no pleasure for him.

The only excitement that he could find in Kimberley's primitiveness was at the card-table. The same cold-blooded unimpassioned mind which he had applied to difficult operations directed his hand at poker.

He became a great gambler. No stake was too high for him. When he held cards in his hands he did not utter an unnecessary word. He never allowed his brain to become clouded by drink while playing. He only drank ginger-beer.

Even when he once lost his entire savings at poker he did not stop. He staked his house. He lost. Next came his carriage and horses. He lost. Jameson now ventured his practice. He lost. His friends gave him a small amount to try again, for the last time. He won. When he rose from his chair in the small hours of the morning he had regained all his losses and in addition won a substantial amount. He knew, he said, yawning, that he would be able to rely on his luck.

Rhodes and Jameson were immediately attracted to each other. They were of almost the same age, Rhodes being five months younger. The friendship between the two men confirmed the truth of the French proverb: *Les extrêmes se touchent*. Rhodes, at heart, was a romantic. That a financier, a ruthless, scheming, callous money-maker, should indulge in romantic ideas sounds contradictory. Have not mass murderers been known to keep canaries in their cells? Do not child-slaughterers sometimes caress a flower-pot on the window-sill? Have not habitual criminals cried like children when their pet mouse was killed by a warder? Did not Henry Ford remove his birth-place, a complete village, and rebuild it in Detroit? Romanticism always crops up.

Cecil Rhodes was never able to cast off his school-boyish romanticism. The combination of his 'two universities of life', Kimberley and Oxford, had nurtured in him a conglomerate of contradictions. In his brain insufficiently digested philosophical

he diamond market at
imberley in 1888. Alfred
eit's office is on the extreme
ft

Alfred Beit

Old Kimberley. The Club on Du Toit's Pan Road in 1888

Charles Dunell Rudd

ideas from the classics, political catch-phrases of the time, the claptrap display of British Imperialism, his freshly acquired second-hand Darwinism, his own juvenile optimism and the anxiety-neurosis caused by his defective heart, all battled against the base, the corrupt, the merciless methods which one had to apply to be successful in the world of business. The slight touch of culture he had brought to Africa from Oxford made him see a problem in everything. His restlessness prevented him from delivering himself completely to long inactive meditations. Finally his intuition, his instinct, his impulsiveness dispersed all scruples.

Dr Jameson's mind, trained on science, was never troubled by emotional entanglements but he, too, was impulsive, though it was not the nervous impulsiveness of Rhodes. It was born out of temperamental impatience.

Rhodes had the better brain, a wider vision and a stronger power of imagination. Jameson was the quicker thinker of the two. The Doctor was brilliant, a man of the world, full of convincing charm. Rhodes' brain had to labour to produce thoughts. He never lost his boyish shyness.

Rhodes was ambitious. He was permanently on the search to satisfy his ambition. He always had to have new schemes to exercise his thirst for power, to assert himself, to fight for something or against somebody.

Dr Jameson had no personal ambitions. Those which he had, had been fully satisfied during the first years of his professional life. Through his profession he had become accustomed to finding ready situations for his actions. He did not have the patience to allow conditions to mature and bring forth new situations. Just like Rhodes, he could not wait.

Neither Rhodes nor Jameson were happy men. Both demanded more from life than they received; the one because his ambitions never found an end; the other because he felt frustrated through the lack of any ambitions.

Rhodes looked up to the Doctor, probably the first scientist he had met, full of admiration for his cold-blooded logic. He was attracted by Jameson's cynicism which had its source in the Doctor's emotional poverty. Rhodes' cynicism was born out of his contempt for men.

Though Rhodes was the weaker personality of the two, Jameson immediately succumbed to him and allowed himself to become a tool in his hands and did not hesitate to venture his future fate on Rhodes. Together with Rhodes, he was sure, he would never have a dull moment. And boredom he feared far more than poverty.

The others had gone in to dinner. Rhodes and Jameson were still finishing their drinks. Rhodes' eye fell on the small figure of a young man sitting alone in a corner. He could not have been much over five feet. As compensation for his diminutive stature Nature had placed on his tiny frail body an enormous head with a conspicuously wide forehead. People were immediately struck by the lustre of his large brown eyes. They were dreamy eyes, but at the same time the penetrating eyes of a man who is accustomed to go to the bottom of things. From time to time this young man took from his pocket a small parcel carefully wrapped in tissue paper. Inside, between pads of cotton-wool, there lay a large white diamond. Carefully he took out the precious stone, held it against the light, looked at it from all angles, turning it again and again, twisting it between his fingers, toying with it all the while. One had the feeling that the touch of this beautiful stone gave him a pleasant physical sensation.

His eyes and ears did not miss anything that was going on in the room. He therefore gave no signs of surprise when he heard Rhodes address him:

'Is little Beit again up in the clouds—or calculating how much profit this little stone will fetch in Hatton Garden? We want to know what brought you from the Fatherland to Africa's inhospitable plains?'

Beit was always nervous in society. Such blunt questions embarrassed him. A quick blush spread over his face:

'Hum, if you want to know—only one reason; to make money, to make enough money to give my mother in Hamburg a thousand pounds a year and keep her a carriage and pair with a liveried coachman. . . .'

In comparison with Rhodes and Jameson he seemed dwarfed, and not only physically. By seldom taking part in general conversations he was overlooked by those who did not know him. Rhodes once declared that he was the finest listener he had ever met in his life. There was always astonishment when he was introduced as Herr Alfred Beit. No one expected Rhodes' closest collaborator, the finest financial brain in South Africa, and one of the richest men in the British Empire, to have an almost negative personality. People were still more surprised when they learnt that Herr Beit was a Jew.

It always annoyed Rhodes in the first years when, as sometimes happened, people mixed him up with Beit, thinking that he was the Jew because he looked so 'typically Jewish'.

Neither could people detect anything 'typically German' in Alfred Beit. It was said of him that he had all the good qualities and characteristics of the Germans and the Jews without showing any of their weaknesses or faults.

Alfred Beit's father had been a wealthy merchant in Hamburg. Before he died he lost his fortune and left his wife, three sons and several daughters in reduced circumstances.

Alfred Beit was born in 1853, six days after Rhodes. By a strange coincidence the three principal actors in South Africa's history were born in the same year and within a few months of each other. Relations advised the mother to send Alfred abroad to learn a trade. At the age of seventeen he was apprenticed to the well-known diamond merchants, Messrs Robinow of Amsterdam. For five hard years he learnt everything there was to be learnt about diamonds. His uncle Lippert, a wealthy merchant in Hamburg, had a branch in South Africa, and after the discovery of diamonds the house of Lippert entered into the diamond trade. It was only natural that they asked their young relative to join them there.

Beit came to Kimberley in 1875. He had a great advantage over most of the other merchants, agents and diggers in that he was thoroughly familiar with the diamond trade, was an expert in the valuation of stones and was known personally to, and trusted by, all the important diamond dealers of the world.

He was not willing to have his knowledge exploited by an employer, not even a relative, without participating in the profits. His chance came when Jules Porges of Paris, one of the world's greatest and wealthiest diamond merchants, who had acquired an interest in several Kimberley mines, needed a trustworthy agent there. He found him in young Beit and another German, Julius Wernher. These two young men became partners under the patronage of Porges. What induced Beit most to join hands with the Frenchman was the fact that Porges had excellent connections with the London and Paris houses of Rothschild, and could finance even the most expansive projects. The firm Wernher, Beit and Co., was therefore founded on a very solid basis.

Wernher, nine years older than Beit, was the son of a Prussian general. He was tall, massive and very blond. Though so different physically from his partner, he resembled Beit in everything else: in his calm, reflective and sagacious manner, his methodical, almost pedantic ways, his reliability, honesty, loyalty and outstanding business capabilities. Wernher preferred to direct their business from his office and Beit had to do the outside work. He was therefore less well known in public and once remarked: 'They think I am only Beit's Christian name!'

These men, Beit with Wernher in the background and Rhodes and Jameson, formed the best imaginable team for the conquest of South Africa. Rhodes had vision and could foresee potentialities, combinations and prospects. Jameson derobed these dreams of their romantic wrapping and translated them into the language of cold facts. He found the essentials, and with his sceptical, cynical and logical mind he diagnosed, disinfected and dissected them. Next Beit would step into action. Ideas to him meant—figures. His brain, the brain of a financial genius, was divided into double-entry ledger accounts. It could at an instant reduce any idea to a balance sheet. Rhodes found delight in juggling with big amounts like a conjurer. Beit—with the pride of a craftsman—preferred to be admired for the solidity and cleanness of his financial transactions. Beit soon became Rhodes' business conscience, his financial encyclopaedia and his ready reckoner. And there was Wernher, the Prussian Junker turned London City magnate. In the end the ball was passed to him to procure the money on the international money markets.

When Alfred Beit had arrived in Kimberley, he was amazed at the conditions on the diamond-fields. Business there was conducted by means of fraud, deceit and corruption. At least half of all the stones on the market were stolen goods and had originally been acquired from Natives by unscrupulous dealers. Later the situation had improved through the strict laws against I.D.B. (Illicit Diamond Buying) imposed by the Cape Government.

Young, unknown, and unfamiliar with the ways of Kimberley, how could one let the diggers and buyers know that Alfred Beit from Hamburg would give them a fair deal? He would, he reckoned, first have to give them proof that he trusted them. As an expert he was able to determine much better than anyone else the true quality and market price of diamonds. Thus, content with a reasonable profit, he was usually able to offer a higher price than those who were not quite so sure about the real value of the stone and who had to be careful to avoid risks. As Beit wanted to handle only the best quality and refused to deal in faulty diamonds, he soon acquired regular customers, and buyers in London and Amsterdam learnt quickly that they could rely on him.

Rhodes had first noticed Beit when he encountered him on his early morning rides. And late at night, he saw that this little man seemed to work regularly when others sat in bars or were already in bed. One night when he saw the door of the wooden hut open he stepped in and asked:

'Do you never take a rest, Mr Beit?'

'Not often.'

'Well, what's your game?'

Beit climbed off his uncomfortable high office-stool and, looking up at the six-foot Rhodes, he replied, twisting his insignificant little moustache:

'I am going to control the whole diamond output before I am much older.'

'I have made up my mind to do the same; we had better join hands.'

Thus started their friendship. It was more than a business-partnership which led these two men, so different in provenance, character, temperament, mentality and nationality to march close together for a quarter of a century. The friendship weathered even the stormy period of Rhodes' march on Africa.

Beit was—and wanted to be—only a business man. He had no other ambitions. For him business was not a means to an end but an end in itself. Money was only a second consideration. Having no interests for which he needed money, as he was not out for power in any form, with no social ambitions and indulging in no extravagances, he devoted his life to his business in the belief of fulfilling a duty, and also to help Rhodes to materialize his visions. Beit was a modest man. He left the glory and the applause to Rhodes whom he accepted as the leader. Yet, as

General Smuts, who knew both men intimately, stated: 'Without Beit, Rhodes might have been a mere political visionary, bereft of power of practical creation.'

When Rhodes was seized with an attack of loquacity nothing could stop him. That night when he went back to his sitting-room accompanied by a few of his friends, among them Rudd, Dr Jameson and Beit, he started immediately on his favourite subject, British policy.

'I tell you,' he said, 'I believe with Ruskin that all healthy men love to fight and the sensation of danger; all courageous women love to hear of such fight and how to brave this danger. And I agree with Ruskin that we Britishers have lost within the last ten years our spurs as a knightly nation; where we should not have fought, we fought purely for the sake of profit; where we should not have been disinterested we have looked on because we were frightened. . . . And I believe what Ruskin said—that we have to expect the highest destiny that was ever granted to a nation. A road of glory is opened to us as it has never been offered to a beggarly crowd of mortals. . . .

'I have read the history of other countries and I see that expansion, that imperialism, is everything. The world's surface is limited, therefore the great object should be to take as much of it as we can. . . .'

Rhodes stood up. His face had turned a dark red. He went to the wall where his old crumpled map of Africa was pinned up. With his big hand, carefully covering his crippled fifth finger with his fourth, he went over the large white spaces in Southern and Central Africa. . . . In a voice which was hoarse with emotion and which with each repetition rose into a higher pitch, he shouted:

'I want to see that all red—I want to see that all red—British red . . . I want to see that all red—British red . . . British red, British red, British red . . . red, red, red!'

At about the same time a nervous, inhibited and unhappy young man, his crippled left arm hidden under a military cape, stood in front of an antique screen on which was depicted allegorically in the form of a broad river the history of mankind from the time of the Greeks and Romans till the Napoleonic epoch. The young man, who was soon to occupy the imperial throne of Germany, had his finger on a little tributary, representing Prussia, and with a vibrating voice, lifting his hand in a threatening gesture he spoke:

'This shall be a very big river some day!'

The old crumpled map on the wall seemed to have intoxicated Rhodes. He continued to speak in an almost toneless voice as if he were frightened by the magnitude of his thoughts:

'It often strikes a man to inquire what is the chief good in life; to one the thought comes that it is a happy marriage, to another great wealth, and as each seizes on the idea, for that he more or less works for the rest of his existence. To myself, thinking over the same question, the wish came to me to render myself useful to my country. I then asked the question, how could I?

'I contend that we are the first race in the world, and that the more of the world we inhabit the better it is for the human race. I contend that every acre added to our territory means the birth of more of the English race who otherwise would not be brought into existence. Added to this, the absorption of the greater portion of the world under our rule simply means the end of all wars. The objects one should work for are first the furtherance of the British Empire, the bringing of the whole uncivilized world under British rule, the recovery of the United States, the making of the Anglo-Saxon race but one Empire.

'What a dream! but yet it is probable. It is possible.

'I once heard it argued—so low have we fallen—in my own college, I am sorry to own it, by Englishmen, that it was a good thing for us that we lost the United States. There are some subjects on which there can be no argument, and to an Englishman this is one of them. But even from an American's point of view just picture what they have lost. . . . All this we have lost and that country has lost, owing to whom? Owing to two or three ignorant, pig-headed statesmen in the last century. At their door is the blame. Do you ever feel mad, do you ever feel murderous? I think I do with these men.

'What is the highest thing in the world? Is it not the idea of Justice? I know none higher. Justice between man and man—equal, absolute, impartial, fair play to all; that surely must be the first note of a perfect society. But, secondly, there must be liberty, for without freedom there can be no justice. Slavery in any form which denies a man a right to be himself, and to use all his faculties to their best advantage, is, and must always be, unjust. And the third note of the ultimate towards which our race is bending must surely be that of peace, of the industrial commonwealth as opposed to the military clan or fighting Empire.

'Therefore, if there be a God—and I believe there is a fifty per cent chance of the existence of God Almighty—and He cares anything about what I do, I think it is clear that He would like me to do what He is doing Himself. And as He is manifestly fashioning the English-speaking race as the chosen instrument by which He will bring in a state of society based upon Justice, Liberty and Peace, He must obviously wish me to do what I can to give as much scope and power to that race as possible.

'Hence if there be a God, I think that what He would like me to do is to paint as much of the map of Africa British red as possible, and to do what I can elsewhere to promote the unity and extend the influence of the English-speaking race.'

Rhodes heaved a deep sigh. He went to his desk. From its drawer he took an envelope containing a sheaf of papers covered in his boyish handwriting.

Placing his hand on his heart, he said softly:

'I am not a healthy man. I suffer from heart attacks, because of a leaking heart-valve. One can't know when one's hour is coming. I had written it all down on this paper—my last will.'

In this paper 'Cecil John Rhodes, Esq., of Oriel College, Oxford, but presently of Kimberley in the Province of Griqualand-West', left in trust his entire estate to Lord Carnarvon, Secretary of State for the Colonies in Her Britannic Majesty's Government and to his successors in office and to Sidney Godolphin Shippard, Attorney-General of Griqualand-West:

> To and for the establishment, promotion and development of a Secret Society, the true aim and object whereof shall be the extension of British rule throughout the world, the perfecting of a system of emigration from the United Kingdom, and of colonization by British subjects of all lands where the means of livelihood are attainable by energy, labour and enterprise, and especially the occupation by British settlers of the entire Continent of Africa, the Holy Land, the Valley of the Euphrates, the Islands of Cyprus and Candia, the whole of South America, the Islands of the Pacific not heretofore possessed by Great Britain, the whole of the Malay Archipelago, the seaboard of China and Japan, the ultimate recovery

> of the United States of America as an integral part of the British Empire, the inauguration of a system of Colonial representation in the Imperial Parliament which may tend to weld together the disjointed members of the Empire, and, finally, the foundation of so great a Power as hereafter to render wars impossible and promote the best interest of humanity.

This *document humain* speaks against Rhodes not only in the schoolboy-romanticism of a twenty-five-year-old man, but by the fact that in later years, when, through his economic and political power, he was already a considerable factor in actively shaping the world's politics, he did not repudiate this puerile stolidity. When he came across it, instead of reading with frowning amusement about a juvenile irresponsible folly and then burning it, he kept it and showed it proudly to his intimates. Twenty years later he had not given up his mad idea of a secret society and many other of his childish thoughts. Some of them recur in his meditations until his last years.

It may be accepted, therefore, that this muddled romanticism of a schoolboy became the driving *motif* of Cecil Rhodes, the Empire-builder, though, as we shall see in his later life, the mercenary instinct entered into it as a mighty counterpoint. Point and counterpoint chased each other in gay pursuit until the vigorous money-leitmotiv could be covered only slightly by the mighty blast of patriotic themes.

Rhodes' testament has been called even by admiring biographers and hero-worshippers 'absurd', 'pathetic', 'childish', 'sophomoric' and 'pathetically naïve'. There is more to it than that: the 'apostolic fervour' with which he believed in his strange brand of British Imperialism was caused by his suffering for too long from a retarded puberty. Healthy normal English boys sweat out their glandular troubles on the sports fields. Less robust boys either work off their secretory overflow in active romanticism or fill pages with lyrical verses or bloody dramas. Rhodes was not strong enough for the one and no longer young enough for the other. In addition he seemed to have lacked certain constitutional properties as indicated by his high-pitched voice, his complete disinterest in girls and a rather sparse growth of beard. He tried to compensate for such lacks by delivering himself to an almost mystic imperialism based on a militant creed of racial superiority.

CHAPTER V

ELIMINATING THE IMPERIAL FACTOR

RHODES was one of the few who had weathered all the storms descending on the diamond-fields. In 1882, again under a world depression, the diamond market hit rock-bottom. Rhodes had bought still further claims in De Beers Mine. The shares of his company, the De Beers Diamond Mining Co., Ltd., now with a capital of more than £800,000, had also reached fantastic figures. By selling them at their highest prices and rebuying at a very low figure, Rhodes and his friends had made considerable profits. Every amount at their disposal was used to buy new claims. However, Rhodes had also made liberal use of bank-credits, and like everyone else he was unable to meet his obligations towards the bank. His company suffered under these unfavourable conditions.

It was not only the financial situation that gave all Kimberley sleepless nights. The reef was again falling in. The richest mines were covered overnight with thousands and thousands of tons of earth. It meant that for months it would be impossible to dig for a single diamond, and the removal of the fallen-in reef presented an expense which could bring ruin to the most solid company. A calamity like that swallowed much of De Beers big profits. The dividends were very small and De Beers shares were worth only half their nominal value.

Rhodes' belief in Kimberley's future remained unshattered. He had already made all his preparations for underground work in shafts. His aim, now no longer mere speculation but a necessity, was to own all the claims in the mine. Nothing deterred him; neither fallen reefs, nor world crises, nor impatient bank-managers.

The scramble for wealth continued in Kimberley. The four mines of Kimberley, covering altogether the small area of seventy acres, were exploited by ninety-eight individual owners.

As 'little Beit' had foreseen years before, the future of Kimberley and its diamonds depended on an amalgamation of the whole mining industry. Rhodes knew that without Beit's co-operation his own and De Beers' future was doomed. Unlike Rhodes, 'little Beit' was familiar since his apprentice days with juggling on the stock exchange.

For the time being there seemed to be little hope of interesting cautious city magnates in South African diamond mines. *The Times* wrote in 1882, twelve years after work had started on Kimberley's diamond-fields and after the yearly export had reached the spectacular figure of £12 million, that 'reports from South Africa are wicked inventions of adventurers circulated for the purpose of rigging the market'.

There was no time to be lost. Rhodes and Beit were not alone in the field. Amalgamation, with a consequent monopoly, was in the air. Others were apparently working to the same purpose, particularly Kimberley's present richest man, J. B. Robinson, the owner of valuable diamond-claims. Rhodes usually tried to overcome opposition by negotiations. He therefore wanted to join hands with Robinson; but to have dealings with Robinson without being squashed by him required superhuman talents. Among South Africa's many shrewd, cunning and ruthless financiers he was considered by far the cleverest.

His uncontrollable aggressiveness soon clashed with Rhodes' iron determination and even with Beit's diplomatic pliability. He believed that these two were out to rob him, and broke off the negotiations abruptly. From that moment onward Rhodes became his greatest enemy whom he would fight by any means, fair or foul, even after death, and who supplied him for almost twenty years with the only pleasure—an ever-increasing hatred—in his drab life. In spite of his proverbial meanness he did not mind spending large amounts when there was a chance to injure Rhodes personally, financially, politically or socially.

To characterize this man one has to use the exceptional way of starting with his death. When Robinson died in 1929, eighty-nine years old, his will, disposing of his fortune of about twelve million sterling in favour of his family—with the exception of one daughter and her two children whom he cut off cruelly with a mere trifle of two thousand pounds—without leaving a single penny to any charity or national institution, roused a storm of indignation throughout South Africa and Britain. His meanness after death corresponded with his stinginess during his lifetime. The general disgust at the will was expressed by a leading article, under the heading 'Nil nisi malum', in South Africa's most prominent newspaper, the *Cape Times*, which always prided itself rightly on its high journalistic standard. From this strange obituary can be gauged the degree of contempt in which Joseph Benjamin Robinson, whom his King had made a Baronet, was held:

> . . . His eyes were shut during his lifetime. After his death his will speaks out the almost incredible malignity of his nature.
>
> That is one way in which this will stinks to Heaven—though the mention of Heaven in this connection trenches on blasphemy—against the elementary canons of private human decency. It stinks too, against public decency. This man owed the whole of his immense fortune to the chances of life in South Africa. He has not left a penny out of all his millions to any public purpose in this country which has showered these immense gifts on him. It would have been less scandalous that he should have failed to leave anything to any public purpose if during his life he had been a public or a private benefactor, even on a scale of temperate liberality. He was not. His immunity against any impulse of generosity, private or public, was so notorious that the name of J. B. Robinson became during his lifetime proverbial for stinginess, not only in South Africa but wherever men of the world congregate together. . . . Such a will as this . . . carries a dreadful penalty. It brands the name of the man who made it with an infamy so conspicuous as far to transcend the highest pinnacle of scorn which the indignation of his contemporaries could have raised against him. The evil which the dead man thus speaks of himself is terrible to contemplate. It will live in the records of South Africa for all time; . . . the loathsomeness of the thing that is the memory of Sir Joseph Robinson.

They called him 'the Buccaneer'. There was something menacing in his appearance, like the pirates of old depicted in boys' stories, as he waddled through the streets of Kimberley, always a white sun-helmet on his head. 'Sour faced and green with spleen like a leek. . . . He had no personality, no magnetism, but resembled a mortal who had a tombstone on his soul.' Thus he was described by a contemporary.

Besides his greed Robinson was driven by a morbid ambition: he wanted to make more money than anyone else; he wanted to be a leader; he wanted to outdo everybody. With jealous eyes he watched Rhodes' rising position. Not only could he compete with Rhodes in business but he outstripped him considerably in wealth. But the English parson's son, thirteen years his junior, possessed that enviable quality which Robinson, the shopkeeper's son, would never acquire in spite of all his fabulous riches: to be accepted as a 'gentleman'.

Robinson felt his social isolation. For these reasons, his hurt pride worming him, the destruction of Rhodes became an obsession in the vain man's life. He who would not dream of throwing a penny to a starving piccaninny, who was known never to enter a bar before making sure that there was no one in it for whom he would possibly have to buy a drink, was to spend thousands of pounds in an attempt to ruin Rhodes.

Robinson was feared, hated and despised in Kimberley. Rhodes was equally unpopular but for other reasons. His eccentric manners, his moodiness and moroseness made him thoroughly disliked by people who knew him only slightly. Most of his acquaintances shrugged their shoulders at the shabbiness of his clothes. It was eccentricity carried to the point of disreputability. He seemed to take delight in shocking people by deliberate rudeness; or he would embarrass them by ignoring everybody, sitting in a corner in moody silence to break out suddenly into a strange loud jocular mood interspersed with his nerve-racking shrill falsetto laughter. All in Kimberley at that time agreed that the impression one gained of Cecil Rhodes was not that of a man of almost thirty, holding a responsible position, but of an irresponsible, spoilt, badly-brought-up boy whose head had been turned by success.

It was generally admitted that Rhodes possessed extremely high business faculties. When an important decision had to be made in Kimberley concerning the diamond industry, his advice was mostly accepted. Otherwise, if not absolutely necessary, nobody wanted to have anything to do with him.

One of his friends summarized the situation in the words: 'It is difficult to be sufficiently unconventional to shock a mining camp, but Rhodes shocked it.'

His private life contributed considerably to his unpopularity. That a healthy and rich young man should voluntarily renounce the major pleasures of life was beyond the understanding of Kimberley's easy-going crowd. Ugly rumours circulated about him. That he lived together with a young man, his secretary

Pickering, mixed only with Dr Jameson, Beit and Rudd, all bachelors, was never seen with a woman, shunned the company of all other men and seldom entered a bar, seemed unnatural to most.

One cannot expect the gossips of Kimberley to have delved into so complex a problem as a neurosis in a highly-strung young man, physically and psychologically impeded. His leaking heart-valve, even when it did not actually trouble him, must have caused the unrest and depressions that alternated with boisterous outbursts.

Rhodes at that time was passing through a serious crisis. He had staked his entire existence, as well as that of his friends, on one card—De Beers Mine. Any day falling reefs might dash all his hopes. No one could foresee with certainty how long his mines would still yield such rich results or any results at all.

It was not only a question of money. His prestige, too, was at stake; and the realization of his dreams. The boyish dreams, though still the same, were now slowly taking the shape of more realistic plans: he had to make money, to gain power. Power was necessary to execute his next step, to paint Central Africa red, British red.

Yet in making money Rhodes found no satisfaction. He had been happier in the early Kimberley days when he worked for himself and was able to give free play to his thoughts, sitting in the sun all day. Now, lately, he was incarcerated in an office. As the head of a large enterprise he was forced to receive a great number of people, many of them total strangers. He had not yet lost his shyness. To overcome this embarrassing weakness he took shelter behind a wall of cynicism, arrogance and rudeness.

With his rapidly increasing wealth and consequently growing responsibility Rhodes felt the lack of the warmth of true companionship more than ever. He had never learnt the art of making friends which consists in giving and taking, but perhaps his greatest loss was the sudden death of his eldest brother Herbert. Of all his brothers and friends none stood so near to his heart. Herbert had made a man of him in Natal and had been to him the personification of an English gentleman.

Rhodes felt lonely. The friendship with Dr Jameson, Beit and Rudd could not replace the intimate link between the two brothers.

Only sickly young Pickering possessed his full confidence. Dr Jameson was too much of a cynic, Beit too much of a double-entry calculating machine and Rudd too much of the correct and conservative cricket-playing Public School boy to follow him in his far-reaching plans of a *Pax Britannica* as visualized in his Last Will five years before. Young Pickering hung on his Master's lips.

When Rhodes' heart again caused him sleepless nights he was no longer frightened by the appearance of ghosts, though still by the thought of death and the short time probably left to him. The Last Will was taken out of the drawer. With his boyish scrawl he added to the document the words:

KIMBERLEY, 28 OCTOBER 1882.

I, C. J. Rhodes, being of sound mind, leave my worldly wealth to N. E. Pickering.

The next morning he handed the astonished young man a closed envelope containing his will, and a letter:

My dear Pickering, — Open the enclosed after my death. There is an old will of mine with Graham, whose conditions are very curious and can only be carried out by a trustworthy person, and I consider you one.

C. J. RHODES.

You fully understand you are to use interest of money as you like during your life.

While still hovering in the lofty regions of his boyish dreams the first step towards gaining power had been taken. The opportunity arose when Griqualand was formally incorporated in the Cape Colony and was to be represented in the Cape Parliament. Rhodes naturally wanted to stand for Kimberley. He soon felt a strong opposition working against him. When the Old Buccaneer learnt that Rhodes was contesting the Kimberley seat he immediately made up his mind that there was only one man entitled to represent the diamond industry in Parliament: J. B. Robinson!

Rhodes had to be satisfied with contesting a seat in a rural district near Kimberley, Barkly West, inhabited largely by Afrikaner farmers and coloured farm-hands. A certain number of Natives, 'raw' Natives fresh from their kraals as yet untouched by urban influences, though holding only nominal voting qualifications according to the still liberal Cape Colony rights, carried great weight in this thinly populated constituency. No secret ballot existed. A lively trade in buying and selling votes went on quite openly. On election day friends of Rhodes' brought a troop of about 250 well-prepared Natives to the polls to vote for Rhodes and thus secured a safe majority for him. The greatest difficulty in his electioneering campaign Rhodes found in dispelling the distrust of the Dutch farmers in his constituency. An old Dutchman gave him the reason. 'In the first place, you are too young; in the second, you look so damnably like an Englishman.'

From the preparations of this election comedy the young Parliamentarian learned the useful lesson that popularity could be bought and that 'every man has his price'. A generous method of influencing people was henceforth adopted by Rhodes as the chief instrument for paving his way. It developed into such a skilful art that he was able to apply it without danger to himself or the favoured recipient, no matter if he was of royal blood, a high statesman, an opposing financier, a whole political party or just anyone whom he happened to need at the time.

'Tell me a man's ambitions and I will tell you how to square him,' he told one of his friends. Later in life he was able to boast proudly: 'I have never met anyone in my life whom it was not as easy to deal with as to fight.'

Rhodes came to Parliament with a ready plan—the realization of his youthful dreams. All now depended on infecting the Cape Government with his enthusiasm for the urgent need to penetrate northwards into the heart of Africa and secure all the unmapped territories for Her Majesty the Queen.

That difficulties, obstacles and opposition would meet him from all sides, he did not doubt. The Cape Colony, as he soon learnt, did not offer fertile ground for imperialistic expansion. Though Britain had ruled in the Cape for almost 200 years she had not yet succeeded in 'colonizing' the country by winning the hearts of the small white population. All efforts to anglicize the people were met by growing opposition from the old Dutch settlers in the towns as well as on the *platteland*. British colonies were ruled from Whitehall, several thousand miles away. There a Colonial Secretary, guided by a Cabinet which always feared the displeasure of a strong-willed Queen, the discontent within its own ranks and censure from the Opposition, had the onerous task of combining British rule with local urgencies within the narrow frame of party politics and at the same time of bridling the red-taped permanent staff of high officials in the Colonial Office and the administrative representatives of the Government abroad. These experts had acquired their experience of colonial government through dealing with Natives or in colonies where the British element was predominant.

Psychological understanding was needed to deal with people of European descent, different in language, religion and mentality, who prided themselves in having served as pioneers of Western civilization on the African continent; and who always stood on their rights to independence as individuals. Such insight into psychological imponderabilities was not given to the British colonizers. To them the fact that they had conquered the Cape in 1806 from the Dutch and had legalized this conquest in 1814 by a payment of £6,000,000 cleared them of any moral obligations. The Dutch inhabitants of the Cape, just like the Natives in any other colony, had to accept British rule as it stood or to expect trouble. Tactlessness, chicaneries and incompetence by British officials, high and low, aggravated the position. English settlers looked down on the Dutch population and considered themselves the masters of the country.

The diamonds of Kimberley had changed the Cape Colony in its economic, political and social structure. Before, the country could scarcely eke out an existence from its agricultural products. wool, wine and maize. Now it had gained world-wide importance. Men from all nations had settled on the diamond-fields. The industry employed more Natives than the whole of the rest of the country. Trade flourished in the towns; farmers found a ready market for their products there.

With clear insight Rhodes discerned at once the necessity for a change in the sleepy, stagnant and parochial policy of the country in accordance with the changed economic, political and social conditions. He was prepared for a hard uphill fight but when in April 1881 he delivered his maiden-speech he made no great impression. His nervousness was too obvious. Lacking grace of oratory and charm of style, without control over his clumsy gestures—a disturbing twitching of his hands and an ungainly jerking of his body—he gave no cause of suspicion that he had once won at the grammar school at Bishop's Stortford a silver medal for elocution. A friend, when asked what he thought of this first parliamentary effort, replied with an audible sigh:

'Rhodes, I think you are a great parliamentary failure.'

Equally condemning were most of the Press comments. A Grahamstown paper asked bluntly:

'Who is this young man from Kimberley, come to teach us our business?'

With his contempt for formality and conventions, the dignified stiffness of parliamentary traditions did not suit him. His negligent way of dressing was immediately censured; one member asked for a motion to make the wearing of black clothes obligatory as it was in the Transvaal Volksraad. Red-faced, Rhodes rose and in his high-pitched voice, in controlled anger, he replied slowly:

'I am still in Oxford tweeds and I think I can legislate in them as well as in sable clothes.'

To sit for hours on the same spot and to have to listen, at that, to other people talking meant real torture for Rhodes, who had never been schooled in debate. Among his friends, in Kimberley and in Oxford, it had always been he who held the floor. His ideas, on the few subjects in which he was interested, were not debatable contentions but formulated results of fanatical obsessions. For these he did not require the opinions of others.

As in his younger days his speeches were mere thinking aloud. They never began with an oratorical introduction but led directly into the matter. They stopped equally abruptly. Members would realize that his speech was finished when they saw him bounce down on his seat, defiantly sinking his hands deep into his trouser-pockets.

As soon as he was in his seat, Rhodes' nervous restlessness began. Like a bored schoolboy in class, or, as a journalist said, 'as restless as a spring doll', he jumped up, flopped down again, changed his position every few minutes, sat on his hands, played with his papers. His shrill boisterous laughter often spluttered through the quietness of the small chamber.

Rhodes, elected as an Independent, did not wait long before making his weight felt in the House. The frankness of his nature, his extraordinary energy, and the impetuous fanaticism of his convictions soon made him a strong force with which Parliament knew it would have to reckon in the near future. They all realized that Rhodes had not left his well-paying work in Kimberley without a very definite purpose.

Cape Town opened Rhodes' eyes to South Africa. Though he

had now lived half his life in Kimberley, he had remained unaware of the potentialities of the country which, in the political and economic respect, began in the Cape Colony. In Kimberley people had persuaded themselves that all that counted in South Africa was their diamonds. They thought, they spoke and they dreamt diamonds. None of that cosmopolitan crowd of get-rich-quick adventurers ever worried about racial or national problems. They wanted to be left alone and not to be disturbed in their money-grabbing activities.

Rhodes had never before thought in terms of South Africa as a political factor. To him it had appeared as an inseparable part of the British Empire, one of the components of Her Majesty's possessions beyond the seas, without any national character or aspirations of its own. Like everyone else he had believed that the main task of the colonies consisted in contributing to the wealth and strength of the Motherland, thereby giving her enterprising subjects the opportunity of settling there in their younger years, making enough money, and in the autumn of their lives coming 'home' and retiring in one of Suburbia's charming cottages. Rhodes had believed that his plans of pushing North would never succeed without the machinery of Whitehall. Yet from his short political experience he learnt that 'the constant vacillation of the Home Government which never knew its own mind about us' was a weighty factor which would probably impede the success of his Northern plans. His Jingo-ardour underwent a hard probe.

In his political calculations he did not lose his sense of proportion: 'Are we a great and independent nation? No! We are only the population of a third-rate English town, spread over a vast country.' He chided all parties for the parochial aspect from which they viewed South African affairs as if 'the mist of Table Mountain covered all'.

He needed allies for his project. Looking at the English members in the House it became obvious to him that these self-satisfied and narrow-minded village-pump politicians of lawyers, wool-merchants, shopkeepers, importers and other righteous petty money-bags 'had no other policy beyond that of securing office'. Since every one of them cared only for the safe-guarding of his own material interests, the English party was split into several factions.

Rhodes' hopes turned to the other side of the House. The Dutch members, the solid, sturdy burghers and farmers with a few clergymen and teachers among them, formed a compact body welded together by their dislike and even hatred of English rule, and the consciousness of an awakened South African nationalism. This strong national spirit had developed simultaneously with a movement for using Afrikaans as a written language to form the basis of an independent national culture. Afrikaans, a patois evolved from seventeenth-century Dutch, had been used only as a colloquial language, whereas in schools and churches as well as in educated families High Dutch was spoken, until in 1875 the Reverend S. J. Du Toit of Paarl founded '*die Genootskap van Regte Afrikanders*'—the Society of true Afrikaners—with the object of 'defending our language, our nation and our people'. Later, under the name of the Afrikaner Bond, this movement developed into a revolutionary and republican party with a programme of secession from British rule and the establishment of a 'united South Africa under its own flag'—into which was to be incorporated with the Cape the two South African republics, the Transvaal Republic and the Orange Free State.

Such extreme anti-British aspirations in view of a strong British garrison and bellicose Natives threatening the rear, courted the danger of civil war. There was one man who recognized the peril into which Du Toit's fanatical Bondsmen were steering. His impassioned logic had led him to the firm conviction that the quickest and safest way to secure the independence of the Cape lay in an evolutionary process.

They called him 'the Mole' because he worked underground. Jan Hendrik Hofmeyr was more than a politician. Though he never held office, except once when for a few weeks he had been Minister without Portfolio in the Cape Government, and never accepted an official position in the Afrikaner Bond, he was a great statesman, perhaps even South Africa's greatest.

In spite of all the disappointments which England's South African policy caused him and notwithstanding his critical attitude towards certain characteristic weaknesses of the English people, Hofmeyr always cherished in his heart a quiet admiration for Britain, especially for her culture, her historical tradition and—English sport.

A man who for twenty years was the most prominent protagonist of England's national games, football and cricket, and who for twenty years was the president of leading sports clubs, could hardly have been such a dangerous Anglophobe as the London authorities and English Press believed Hofmeyr to be. Bitterly he complained that in England he was held up as 'a Nihilist and a Red Republican' and that as a member of the Afrikaner Bond he was believed to pray every night for England's flag in the Cape to be hauled down and the Colony's own flag to be hoisted.

Such accusations offended Hofmeyr's susceptibilities. He prided himself on political honesty. His honesty had caused him to renounce a clerical career as he could not accept the official orthodox views of his superiors. As a political journalist—he had started at the age of seventeen as the editor of an influential Afrikaans paper—he was cruelly and honestly outspoken. Through his frankness he had won the respect, if not the love, of his fellow-countrymen. And only his blunt and undemagogic candour had allowed him to succeed in ousting Du Toit from the Bond and in forging this party into a strong and weighty instrument for a constructive South African policy of independence. Its aim was federation with the help of Britain instead of a futile anti-British republicanism with revolutionary operetta-methods. Du Toit left the field and accepted a governmental position in the Transvaal.

Hofmeyr now had the Bond under his thumb. 'The Mole' was looking out for allies. The Bond, though the strongest single party, needed a coalition to break the English block in power. Rhodes felt that Hofmeyr, a man eight years his senior, well versed in parliamentary jugglery, and with a strong party behind him, was the only man in a House full of nonentities and mediocrities who would understand his plans for expansion. British Imperialism and South African Nationalism, in his opinion, should be able to co-operate for a higher aim, the unification of a Greater South Africa.

Much to Hofmeyr's surprise Rhodes came to his side to overthrow the Cabinet of the time. He distrusted Rhodes, who had been described to him as 'a regular Beefsteak John Bull Englishman full of the exclusive traditions of Oxford'.

Rhodes had never yet met an Afrikaner of his own social and educational standard. His opinion of the Dutch people of the

Cape was based mainly on casual encounters with farmers and diggers in and around Kimberley. Hofmeyr asked him to his home. When his carriage had driven him from the centre of the town over less than a mile to Camp Street, Rhodes thought that he was in the country. His eyes, well-trained in taking in the beauties of Nature as well as the noble dignity of old Dutch architecture, feasted on the shining whiteness of 'Welgemeend', the eighteenth-century ancestral homestead of the Hofmeyr family. It led him to think of its owner not as the irresponsible agitator described by the English Press, but as the head of an old-established family of landowners, an important component of the country, who had every right to have a say in its government. Looking out from the wide *stoep* Rhodes was fascinated by the almost overwhelming view of the majestic mountains, the sea and the green plains of the north over which was spread the dark blue roof of the sky. Still more he rejoiced in the noble beauty inside. This country possessed a highly artistic tradition of beautiful workmanship as was shown by the exquisitely shaped chest of drawers, the massive wardrobes, the elegant glass show cases all made of the native finely grained stinkwood darkened almost to black in the course of centuries, the graceful old Cape silver candlesticks and bowls, the shining copper vessels filled with the flowers of the mountains—proteas in all shapes and colours, heaths of various shades, arum-lilies, and the red blooms of the aloe.

Rhodes now began to feel that the Cape was more than an English colony; it was a country with an individuality, a pronounced tradition and a culture of its own.

The two politicians felt their ground carefully and they soon discovered the similarity in their ultimate aims: the inevitable unification of South Africa. They agreed that the evolutionary process could be instigated, led and accomplished by the Cape and only by working together with Britain. Hofmeyr had no objections to Rhodes' plan of northern expansion of the Cape provided that he would assist the Bond in the protection of the Cape farmers.

Unfortunately the plans for close collaboration between these two men had to rest for a few years when the blundering policy of the English Government and the staggering stupidity of the military and administrative authorities in the Cape brought the relations between the Dutch and English elements to breaking-point.

In 1877 Britain had annexed the Transvaal, carrying out a threat uttered forty years before when some ten thousand Boers began their Great Trek from the Cape. The causes of their exodus were the insurmountable divergence from the British in all political and religious questions, the enforced exercise of liberal tendencies towards the Natives and Coloureds at their expense, the exclusion of the Dutch in the government of the land of their birth and the difference in their mode of living.

In their new lands, behind the Vaal and behind the Orange River, they had started their republics on a patriarchal system. Inexperience, their strong individualism and love of independence, their hatred for authoritative coercion, made the consolidation of their governments difficult. Costly permanent warfare against neighbouring Native tribes, the impossibility of collecting taxes, the lack of trade-communications and internal political squabbles had brought the Transvaal to the verge of bankruptcy and the threat of being overrun by the Zulus.

There remained only one remedy: help from outside. President Burgers took up secret negotiations for an alliance with the Germans, Belgians and Portuguese. But no European power showed any interest. Only Britain was anxiously waiting to step in:

> Should the people of the Transvaal Republic consider it advisable . . . to invite H.M. Government to undertake the government of that territory . . . the request could not properly or prudently be declined.

The Boers had understood from previous negotiations that British help would consist of confederation, with the government remaining in their hands. This belief rested on a proclamation in the name of the Queen:

> The Transvaal will remain a separate Government with its own laws and legislation. It is the wish of Her Most Gracious Majesty that it shall enjoy the fullest legislative privileges compatible with the circumstances of the country and the intelligence of its people.

Notwithstanding all promises, the Transvaal was annexed by England, in April 1877, its administration was taken over and the State was deprived of its sovereignty. An Act was passed in the Imperial Parliament at the same time 'for the union under one Government of the South African Colonies and States as may agree thereto'. Britain had started to swallow the African continent!

Rhodes in later years attributed all subsequent difficulties with the Transvaal to the 'shocking misgovernment by the Imperial Commissioner who conducted business on lines of a second-rate line regiment'. The position of the Boers became untenable. All negotiations concerning the sovereignty of the Transvaal were declined by the British Government. The hearts of the Boers were filled with hope by the election speeches of Gladstone, condemning the oppressive policy of the Tories. Then Gladstone took over the government in April 1880. The Boers believed that England's Grand Old Man of liberalism would bring them justice, freedom and help, but how could they know that promises in election speeches and the finest oratory from the opposition benches are forgotten when the exigencies of office demand it?

In their desperation, the Boers were now driven to open revolt. They had nothing to lose but their lives. In December 1880 they declared their independence and proclaimed the South African Republic with a provisional government by a Triumvirate headed by an elderly farmer, Paul Kruger.

With almost criminal levity high English officers in command of the occupation troops neglected military precautions as if they were conducting manœuvres at Aldershot. Within the first weeks they had to admit that they were dealing with a formidable enemy who was far superior to them in mobility, in tactics on a hilly territory, in marksmanship and in endurance. In the first two encounters British detachments were ambushed and almost annihilated by the Boers. Mr Gladstone ordered peace negotiations to be begun immediately.

For the period of the negotiations a truce was declared. It was broken by an English general. The Boers avenged this breach of faith by inflicting a great defeat on the British on Majuba Hill which cost the lives of many brave English soldiers, including their commander. Such a disaster to her arms and prestige compelled Britain to conclude an immediate peace even under unfavourable conditions.

In August 1881, by the Pretoria Convention, complete self-government was restored to the Transvaal, though Britain succeeded in keeping her thumb on the throat by adding to the preamble the harmless-sounding phrase: 'Subject to the suzerainty of Her Majesty.' This little clause was to serve for the next twenty years as England's noose round the Transvaal's neck. Britain also reserved for herself 'the control of the external relations of the said State, including the conclusion of treaties'.

A shout of rage echoed throughout Britain: Avenge Majuba! And in the Cape Colony, among the English population, the shout gathered force until it became a wild roar.

Rhodes remained comparatively calm. Some years before he had said:

'The Dutch are the coming race in South Africa and they must have their share in running the country.'

To accomplish this a reconciliation between the English and Afrikaners would have to take place. They all, the Boers in the Transvaal and the Afrikaners in the Cape, dreamt, as he did, of a united South Africa. So did Mr Gladstone and his Liberals in England, but the South African confederation would be something different from what he, Cecil Rhodes, had in mind. In the blunders of high British officers in the Transvaal, in the ridiculous interference of Whitehall's black-coated politicians, one had seen where ignorance over a distance of 6,000 miles could lead and one would not be able to expect any understanding, much less assistance, when one went to open the road to the North. 'One has to eliminate the "Imperial factor"', mused the man who had entered the Cape Parliament only a short time before as a fiery Jingo.

Within this short time, strengthened by the events in the Transvaal and under the charm of the Cape landscape and people, Rhodes, the Englishman, the British Imperialist, suddenly felt himself to be a South African. His claim of regarding himself as a son of the country was met with scorn by the English side who looked upon his alliance with the Bond as something akin to treason. The Afrikaners considered this turn-about of so rabid a Jingo as a clever political somersault by which Rhodes probably hoped to land on the Presidential chair of a future South African Federation. Only Hofmeyr believed in Rhodes' honest conversion after Rhodes, on being taxed in Parliament, had declared openly:

'. . . By the accident of birth I was not born in this country, but that is nothing. I have adopted the Colony as my home.'

Rhodes was now completely convinced that the narrowness of the English mind would not allow their following him in his flight into the heart of Africa. Only the Afrikaners would understand him.

Thus after Majuba, he found his way back to Hofmeyr. Through a link with the Bond his political independence would be preserved. This freedom from party fetters was essential for his political agility if he was to unlock the North.

He did not plunge entirely into the nationalistic mentality of the Bond extremists. Britain remained for him the Mother of the Empire and South Africa her daughter who would set up house as soon as she was old enough but without tearing the family bonds. When a republican journalist interviewed Rhodes and pointed out that they wanted him as the leader of a United South Africa provided he agreed that they must be independent of the rest of the British Empire, he replied:

> No! You take me for a rogue or a fool. I should be a rogue to forfeit my history and traditions, and a fool because I should be hated by my own countrymen and distrusted by yours.

In spite of events in the Transvaal, Hofmeyr still believed that South Africa's future depended on a welding of the English and Afrikaner people into a nation as part of the British Empire. He was convinced that Rhodes did not join in the Englishmen's cries of 'Avenge Majuba', though he was afraid that, like other Englishmen, he had looked upon the first defeat of the English by the Boers as a humiliation.

Both men looked forward with some apprehension to their first talk after the end of the Transvaal war. Without preliminaries Hofmeyr began to sound Rhodes:

'It is an awful pity that the war broke out,' he remarked.

For a few moments Rhodes looked at him in silence, rubbing his chin vehemently with his forefinger. Then he burst out in his shrillest descant:

'No, it is not. . . . No, it is not, it's not. One has quite changed one's opinion . . . quite changed one's opinion. It's a good thing . . . a good thing. . . . Has made Englishmen respect Dutchmen and made them respect one another. . . . Quite changed one's opinion. . .'

Hofmeyr's eyes sparkled behind his spectacles. Slowly he replied:

'Well, when an Englishman can speak like that to a Dutchman, they are not far from making common cause with one another.'

Rhodes was certain of Hofmeyr's reliability. Now he could proceed to action. It almost happened that his activities took place at the other end of Africa, in Egypt, and that he perished in the Sudan at the hands of the 'Mad Mahdi' together with General Gordon, at the fall of Khartoum in 1885.

Rhodes, as a member of a governmental Commission, met General Gordon after he had been called to South Africa in 1882 to pacify and later to administrate rebellious Basutoland. The fifty-year-old general, as 'Chinese Gordon', enjoyed great popularity in England. His gallant exploits in quelling the Chinese Revolution (1860–64), his fearless fight against slave-traders and his consolidation of England's power in the Sudan as its Governor-General, had aroused the admiration of the English people and made him a national hero.

Here was a 'man of action' according to Rhodes' liking: a 'hero of nerves', an empire-builder, unconventional, full of contempt for 'solemn plausibilities', driven by his own initiative to spread the gospel of Britain's greatness, hard and unyielding towards Whitehall's bureaucratic despotism and audacious in opposing his own government. He looked up to the general with awe. Though a difference of twenty years in age stood between them and they were completely opposed in their social and mental make-up, a deep friendship linked them immediately. Even their differences did nothing to slacken their intimacy. At the end of one heated argument Gordon burst out:

'You always contradict me. I never met such a man for his own opinion. You think your views are always right and every one else wrong. You are the sort of man who never approves of anything unless you have the organizing of it yourself.'

They could not agree on the importance of material goods. Gordon was absolutely disinterested in worldly possessions. After the successful ending of the Rebellion the Chinese Government wished to express its gratitude. They took him to the Peking

Palace, led him to a large strong-room filled to the ceiling with gold and jewelled treasures, and invited him to take it all.

'What did you do?' Rhodes inquired, his eyes shining.

'Refused it, of course. What would you have done?'

'I would have taken it and as many more roomfuls as they would give me. It is no use for us to have big ideas if we have not got the money to carry them out.'

Nevertheless Rhodes was a man after Gordon's own heart. Rhodes, though he admired Gordon as the personification of British Imperialism, doubted whether he would be able to work in close co-ordination with him. One of the hindrances, he felt, was Gordon's strange belief in spiritual influences. Thus he needed scarcely any reflection when Gordon one day asked him:

'What are you going to do after your work is finished here in Basutoland?'

'I have to go back to Kimberley and look after my diamond mines.'

'Stay with me. We can work together.'

'I have to execute my own plans.'

'There are very few men in the world to whom I would make such an offer . . . very few men, I can tell you; but, of course, you *will* have your own way.'

Two years later Gordon had repeated the offer to Rhodes to come with him to the Sudan. When Rhodes learnt of the tragic end of this brave general who had been captured and beheaded by the Mahdi at Khartoum, he sighed: '. . . I wish I had gone with Gordon. I would willingly have died with him.'

Someone asked him if he could possibly have extricated poor Gordon from his hopeless position in besieged Khartoum. Rhodes smiled. 'Very simple: by "squaring" the Mahdi.'

CHAPTER VI

THE SCRAMBLE FOR AFRICA

THE hoofs of eight mules stamped a syncopated rhythm on the sun-baked road one summer day in the year 1885. Road? Roaming herds of elephants in search of water during droughts centuries ago, trod out a path. Later missionaries had travelled over it on their way north. Traders had used it to reach the land of the Bechuana, where they exchanged their shabby products of Western civilization for ivory and pelts. This primitive path was the only direct link between the Cape Colony and the heart of Africa. The hunters called it the 'Missionary Road'.

The carriage was jolted, shaken and tossed and often threatened to overturn. But the ruddy face of its occupant, under a big slouch hat, radiated contentment and happiness.

Cecil John Rhodes, once more, for the third time within three years, on his way to Bechuanaland as Her Majesty's Deputy Commissioner on a special mission for the Government of the Cape Colony, had every reason to be satisfied with himself. At the age of thirty-two he had succeeded in all the preliminary plans for his great scheme. As chairman of De Beers, a company with a capital of a million pounds, he represented a mighty financial factor in South Africa's business world. Politically, he possessed the coveted instrument on which he could play his own tune.

Between two parliamentary sessions he had been able to hurry to Oxford and perform the unique feat for a Member of Parliament of concluding his studies and obtaining the degree of a Bachelor of Arts and so fulfil one of the ambitions of his youth.

Cecil Rhodes smiled as he leaned back on the hard padding of the coach as it rolled across the plains of Bechuanaland. Well might he smile. He, Cecil Rhodes, Esq., B.A. (Oxon), M.P., former Treasurer of Her Majesty's Government of the Cape Colony, now Leader of the Opposition, charged by the Colonial Office to act as Her Majesty's Assistant Commissioner, was on his way to engrave his name in the book of the great English Empire-builders. . . .

The scramble for Africa had begun. Everything now depended on developments in the Cape and the adjoining territories whether his plans would be realized within a short time. Cecil Rhodes was in a hurry. The beat of his leaking heart, the metronome of his actions, drove him to greater speed. Lately his thoughts had turned more than ever to the vast unexplored countries in the North. Rumours of gold-findings in the land of the Bechuana and the Matabele persisted. Was this Ophir, the Land of Gold, whence was brought to King Solomon the gold, rare wood, precious stones, silver, ivory, spices and apes and peacocks as was written in the Book of Kings?

Suddenly there had appeared a threat that the jumping-board for his dive into the vastness of Africa's interior would be drawn from under his very feet. Bechuanaland, the door to the North, from where he had dreamt to start painting the land red, British red; Bechuanaland, the gate which could shut off the Cape from the riches lying in wait for him; Bechuanaland, the 'Suez Canal of the trade of the Cape', was now in danger of being lost for ever.

Since 1881 a state of anarchy had existed in the border strip of Bechuanaland along the western frontier of the Transvaal. The way to the interior, along the 'Missionary Road', lay through this fertile land. Already in Livingstone's time, the Boers had claimed control over this road. Because the greater part of Bechuanaland consisted of the Kalahari desert and other wide arid stretches, this fertile, well-watered area had always been the battle-ground of land-hungry tribes. Two groups of chiefs had been on the war-path since 1881. The one part appealed in vain for British protection and was ousted by its opponents with the help of Boer farmers who had recently settled in the territory. Volunteers streamed in from the Transvaal as well as from the diamond fields, who, attracted by the promise, given by the chief, of generously sized farms conquered from his enemy, fought side by side with the Boers. Among these volunteers there figured a great number of shady elements, lawless fellows under the leadership of 'Scotty' Smith, an almost legendary figure of the Robin Hood type, supposed to have been an officer in the Guards and descended from a noble family.

The British Government had not yet fully digested the 'shame of Majuba' or the expenses of the Zulu wars and thus declined intervention unless the Cape Colony was willing to participate in the costs and provide actual military assistance. Whitehall was not in the least perturbed when the 'ruffianly freebooters' proclaimed the conquered territory as independent states, the Republics of Stellaland and Goshenland.

Rhodes immediately scented the danger that the Transvaal was hiding behind these freebooter republics, with the intention of barring the Cape Colony's access to the North. He succeeded in 1882 in having a commission sent to Bechuanaland, including himself as one of its members. He was able to persuade one of the fighting big chiefs to cede the whole country to the Cape by the promise of help against the Boer freebooters. Having just finished a campaign against the Basutos at the cost of £3 million, the Cape Government, however, could not be persuaded to such expensive adventures, especially since unfavourable conditions in the Colony had caused a 'retrenchment mania'. A bank crisis had followed a slump on the diamond market; phylloxera had ruined the Cape wine export; smallpox, particularly in the Kimberley district, obstinately diagnosed by Dr Jameson as harmless skin-trouble in order to please the mine-owners, had decimated the Natives.

Disgusted, Rhodes returned to Kimberley from his first mission to Bechuanaland. His own affairs were in urgent need of his presence. His bank was becoming worried about his high overdraft. Rhodes did not care. His thoughts were concerned only with saving Bechuanaland and providing free access to the North for the Cape. He was sick. This time something more than his old heart-trouble and the usual camp-fever gnawed at his system Dr Jameson advised him to stay at home. But he must, even if he had to crawl, go to Cape Town and tell those blockheads of Parliamentarians that the whole future of the Cape was at stake in Bechuanaland. Could they not see, those pothouse politicians, that one was standing before the most momentous question ever faced by this country: whether the Cape Colony was to be limited to its present boundaries or whether it was to become the dominant power on which the future Federation of South Africa would be built and from where civilization would spread over the entire interior?

There was Paul Kruger behind those filibustering republicans, and nobody saw that he was out to strangle the Cape by barring her way to the open spaces of the North. . . . Those clever Boers knew full well why they had chosen that sly, tenacious, shrewd old mule of a zealot as President. He was showing an admirable master hand in his daring policy. . . . If one looked in comparison at Whitehall's blindfold passiveness and negative parochialism one could scream, one could. . . . They could not see in Cape Town through the haze over Table Mountain that this narrow strip with the Missionary Road to the North was the bottle-neck of South Africa. Whoever possessed Bechuanaland would be master in South Africa. . . . Some of those mealy-mouthed old women of politicians who object to bringing the Natives under our control by taking their land, will probably say: 'How improper! How immoral!' I do not have these scruples. . . . I believe that the Natives are bound gradually to come under the control of the white man. . . .

Still suffering from his indisposition, Rhodes, once in Parliament, immediately caught Mr Speaker's eye. He had felt too sick to prepare his speech and thus spoke without notes. His words spluttered out in cascades.

When he noticed that his speech was meeting with an icy reception, Rhodes gave warning, in order to please the Bond members, of a threatening Imperial interference in Bechuanaland. No sign of any emotion showed on Hofmeyr's poker face. His followers lolled in their seats, bored. Suddenly life came into them. Attentively they leaned forward. Were they hearing right? Was this indeed the Member for Barkly West speaking, that arch-Jingo? They had never really trusted his assertion of friendship for the Dutch. But '*Onse Jan*' had told them that his friend Rhodes was a *ware en opregte vriend van Afrikanerdom*. And their *leier*, such a learned man, ought to know better than they, simple ignorant farmers from the *platteland*. They straightened themselves in their seats, and some held their cupped hands to their ears. Not a word did they want to miss.

Rhodes braced himself for an ultimate effort. He stepped back a few paces to lean against the wall. Defiantly he sank both fists deep into the pockets of his jacket. His face was flushed crimson. His faltering falsetto voice indicated that though his emotions were carrying him away, he was choosing his words carefully:

'We know that all sorts of "fuel" are said to be in Bechuanaland and Imperial interference in Bechuanaland would be one source of fuel. . . . We want to get rid of the "Imperial Factor" in this question, and to deal with it ourselves. . . .'

The English members of the House looked stunned. Almost open treachery to Her Majesty's flag, they thought. What a peculiar fellow, this Rhodes! Hofmeyr shook his head. No! Bechuanaland belonged by rights to the Boers. The English were surely not interested in being involved in a probably expensive squabble with filibusters and Natives for the sake of a sandy waste. What nonsense was this fellow talking: hundreds of thousands of pounds of trade from the Cape to the Interior via the 'Missionary Road'! Rubbish! Probably a few Jewish *smousers* (hawkers) went there occasionally, cheating the Kaffirs with rusty Napoleonic muskets, beads and Manchester goods and bringing home some ivory, pelts and similar odds and ends.

Rhodes became aware that the English in Cape Town were ostracizing him. In several towns of the Colony he was burnt in effigy.

Now he stood alone. He did not give up hope. Perhaps, he mused, Bechuanaland could only be saved by 'Grandma', and one would have, after all, to rely on the 'Imperial Factor'. In a letter to Whitehall he implored the British Government to annex Bechuanaland. It was decided to follow his advice provided that the Cape Colony bore half of the expenses involved. The Cape Government declined the offer and from Whitehall there came a short note to Rhodes that they considered the incident closed.

The year 1884 saw a complete change in the whole situation. Germany unwittingly came to Rhodes' aid. The black-white-and-red flag was suddenly, and much to Britain's consternation, hoisted on the African continent.

Bismarck had misjudged colonial possessions as expensive hobbies, but with Germany's progressing industrialization and a large population increasing menacingly, the question of absorption of her surplus in men and manufactured goods became acute. He now realized that other countries kept colonies as dumping-places for just such a purpose.

Another lesson the German Chancellor learnt from his own private estate: he had erected a large paper mill and a distillery on his Varzin farm. For ten years, in the boom after the Franco-Prussian War, business flourished. Then the world-slump of the eighties affected the sale of his paper and *Schnaps*. Herr Luederitz, a merchant of Bremen, advised him to try to export. Africa was a good market. With cheap liquor one could buy the whole of the continent, but, of course, *die verdammten Engländer* would not let German competitors even pick crumbs from under their table. How different it would be if Germany had colonies of her own. There was a tremendous stretch of land, for instance, reaching from the south-west coast of Africa inland for thousands of miles right into the heart of the continent. Britain had occupied only a tiny spot on this south-west coast. Here was a place to start with German colonies. If the Government stood behind him, Herr Luederitz would himself hoist the flag of the Fatherland there.

Bismarck gave his blessings and along with it a shipload of his Varzin *Schnaps*. He had caught Gladstone, the Foreign Office, the Colonial Office and the British Ambassador not only napping but sound asleep. Hoping still to hook England into his net of alliances, he did not want to cause any discord over some sun-baked African sand-dunes. His inquiries through the British Ambassador whether Britain objected to a German settlement on the African south-west coast remained unanswered. Whitehall's inquiry in Cape Town of what should be done was accidentally pigeon-holed and did not come up for discussion for months. They were busy once again in Cape Town forming a new Cabinet. Rhodes became Treasurer in the new Ministry. Thus he, just as the entire British and Cape Governments, can be held responsible for having missed this chance of stopping Germany from obtaining a foot-hold on African soil.

When they finally woke up it was too late. Luederitz had settled on the Bay of Angra Pequena and this land, only 150 miles from the frontier of the Cape Colony, was declared German territory. Rhodes realized fully that only the quickest action could forestall further damage. 'We must have Damaraland,' became his daily prayer. His colleagues, occupied with ridiculous petty party matters, did not show the slightest interest.

Since it seemed so easy to acquire colonies, Bismarck's appetite for 'a place in the sun' grew. A few months later Germany formally annexed Damaraland and Namaqualand with a coast-line of 930 miles and a total area of 320,000 square miles, a territory larger than Germany itself. Before Britain had time to recover from the shock the Germans also acquired territory in the Cameroons and Togoland, and established themselves in Zanzibar in East Africa. The French, the Belgians and the Portuguese were also pushing forward, each nation driving on in a mad race to cut for themselves as large a chunk of the African body as they could. They had no use for these swampy, fever-invested lands. No one else should have them—that was the only aim in their colonizing plans.

In Downing Street they were immediately worried by German penetration into the South African sphere and the threat of their joining hands with the Boers. Only Bechuanaland separated the German colony from the Transvaal.

Rhodes used the German bogy with great skill. Knowing how deeply Hofmeyr hated the Germans, he emphasized that Germany would no doubt employ her Bismarckian *Machtpolitik* by absorbing the Transvaal. And what barred Germany's way? Bechuanaland!

England was now wide awake to the danger of an attempted strangulation by Germany in Africa. Gladstone was no colonial enthusiast. But the Grand Old Man, always with his ear to the ground, heard the voices of the voters protesting against his 'policy of scuttling'. This time he would have to be firm. A torpedo-boat sent to the Zulu coast drove away the Germans, who were just engaged in hoisting their flag there.

Gladstone was not entirely free to act. The year 1884 was bringing the British Government galling humiliations at home and abroad. Gladstone and his colleagues were accused almost of murder by having delayed the relief expedition to Khartoum to save Gordon. The German successes in Africa; the failure of an Anglo-Portuguese treaty by a combined German-French opposition; the danger of war with Russia over her encroachment in Afghanistan; Germany's blackmail tactics of threatening to take France's side against Britain in the Egyptian dispute; all these failures had made the external position of Britain extremely difficult.

In order to pacify Germany, Gladstone had to agree to a congress in Berlin to settle all colonial questions.

Something new in diplomatic terminology and consequently in practical appliance was introduced with the elastic phrase 'zones of influence' which in the near future Colonial Powers were to use for the exploitation of Africa. One could not—in consideration of the Liberal voters and, of course, one's own Christian conscience—leave the Natives out altogether in a document of about 60,000 words. Two hundred words of hypocrisy, bigotry and lies were devoted to them, such as 'watch over the preservation of the native races, and the amelioration of the moral and material conditions of their existence . . . to educate the Natives, and lead them to understand and appreciate the advantages of civilization'.

King Leopold of the Belgians, Cecil Rhodes, Dr Peters, Herr von Wissmann and Major Pinto must have had a good laugh when they read this document.

Gladstone, certainly, was not in a hilarious mood. This Bechuanaland affair which he had hoped would settle itself somehow was a heavy load on his mind. The German encirclement of Britain's African possessions was aggravated by an increased unrest among the Boers who were agitating for a complete alteration of the Pretoria Convention of 1881. With displeasure the gentlemen at Whitehall saw among the Boer delegation in London Commandant Smit, the victor of Majuba, and the Reverend S. J. Du Toit, the militant Republican agitator from the Cape, now in the service of the Transvaal.

The Boers succeeded in obtaining a few amendments to the treaty. Some boundaries were corrected; they were now allowed to call their state 'The South African Republic'; its internal administration was to be free of British supervision. But they were not given the freedom to expand. Treaties with Native tribes were still to require approval from London.

In their main demand, the abolition of British suzerainty as laid down in the preamble of the Pretoria Convention, the Boers did not succeed. True, in the new agreement the word suzerainty was not mentioned at all. With diplomatic shrewdness the British Government circumnavigated the delicate subject with the simple-sounding statement in a new preamble that 'the following Articles of a new Convention . . . shall . . . be substituted for the articles embodied in the Convention of 3 August 1881'.

The Boers did not learn until later to their consternation that they had been duped by legal trickery: the old preamble with the suzerainty clause was not suspended by the new Convention.

At Downing Street they were highly satisfied with this achievement. Yet their peace of mind was to be seriously disturbed during the next few weeks. President Kruger and his delegation, before returning home, had toured the European capitals. In Holland he had concluded contracts for a railway-line from Delagoa Bay in Portuguese East Africa to Pretoria. Was he out to eliminate the British ports in South Africa and the railway planned from there to Pretoria for the transport of all Transvaal shipments? It would mean a considerable loss in harbour dues, customs fees and later in railway costs, besides having to forgo control of what was going into and coming out of the country.

Still more disheartening was the news of Kruger's reception in Berlin. There Bismarck, speaking at a banquet in honour of Kruger, emphasized Germanic kinship between the two nations and Germany's interest in the welfare of their kinsfolk in Africa. He ended with the assurance that Germany 'will take no steps in Africa except hand in hand with the Boer people'.

It did not need further incentive to drive Britain to action. Bechuanaland had to be saved from serving Germany's advance to join hands with the Transvaal. The filibuster republics would have to disappear and the whole territory be declared British. To execute this delicate mission Whitehall chose the Reverend John Mackenzie, a missionary and successor to Livingstone. A worse selection could hardly have been made. The reverend gentleman believed that his ability in dealing with Boers and Natives alike, after his many years in Africa, was infallible. In his heart there burnt with equal strength the aggressive love of a Jingo for Britain and a contemptuous hatred of the Boers. His tactics were dictated by the Aborigines Protection Society in London. This society, with all its well-intentioned members of pious old dowagers, ambitious social climbers, liberal-minded citizens, fiery gospel propagandists, bazaar-organizing busy-bodies and clergymen full of self-importance, had lately become a political instrument intent on influencing the government in its colonial policy. Propaganda from their headquarters in Exeter Hall had persuaded Downing Street not to let the Natives in Bechuanaland be enslaved either by the Transvaal Boers or by the Afrikaner Bond in the Cape Colony who had as little to recommend them.

As the main requisite for his mission, the Reverend Mr Mackenzie packed a good stock of Union Jacks into his trunk. At first his work seemed to go smoothly. He came to an understanding with Van Niekerk, the 'President of the United States of Stellaland', who was willing to accept Her Majesty's protection for his burghers. Out of gratitude for such docility Mackenzie nominated him Assistant Commissioner and agreed that the existing government in Stellaland should continue. Behind Van Niekerk's back he obtained from the Native chiefs the cession to Britain of the entire Bechuanaland territory, including also Stellaland. Van Niekerk protested vehemently. Mackenzie threw the 'President' into jail. When complete anarchy followed, the reverend gentleman went to his trunk, unfurled the biggest Union Jack, hoisted it and declared the territory annexed by Her Britannic Majesty.

In Goshenland, Mackenzie received a still less cordial welcome. The President, Gey van Pittius, took no notice of the Queen's emissary though his attitude left little doubt but that he would resist by force any attempt at British interference. Mackenzie was not given a chance even to unlock his trunk to take out one of his flags. Frantically he implored the Governor in Cape Town to send him at least 200 mounted police. The Government of the Cape, encouraged by the Governor, Sir Hercules Robinson, and the majority of the English parties, had come to the conclusion that perhaps Rhodes had after all been right in his warning against bringing in the 'Imperial Factor'. The combination of Downing Street and Exeter Hall was bound to fail and would probably result finally in the seizure of Bechuanaland by the Germans or the Boers. Hofmeyr was still adamant in his contention that this territory belonged to the Transvaal.

Rhodes did not tire of trying to convince everyone that the Cape Colony should take Bechuanaland under its protection. Mackenzie was recalled. It was rather strange, many thought, that the Governor should ask Mr Rhodes, now Leader of the Opposition, to go to Bechuanaland as Commissioner to replace Mackenzie. Sir Hercules Robinson had warned him:

'Oh, you can go up, but I can give you no force to back you up. You must use your own judgments.'

'Will you allow me to do what I like?'

'Yes, but if you make a mess of it, I shan't back you up.'

'That is good enough for me.'

Within a few days Rhodes was on his way. It had become

obvious to him that the Stellalanders were not playing at politics, revolutions or wars out of a love for adventure. They were harmless Boer farmers whose only interest lay in gaining security for their property. After Mackenzie had threatened them with expropriation of their farms, they felt that they could no longer trust any Englishman.

Rhodes had learnt from mixing with the Cape Dutch farmers of the Bond how to overcome their racial prejudice by the sheer vehemence of his personality. Whenever his friends heard that Rhodes had made a new conquest of an opponent, their first question was always 'How much?' Lately Rhodes had been able to answer several times:

'No, not "squared", you're quite wrong—just on the personal!'

Rhodes was determined to put the whole force of his formidable personality into play in Stellaland. Van Niekerk, who had been set free just before Rhodes' arrival, received him full of distrust and was not at all disposed to enter into negotiations. Yet, like all the Stellalanders, he was much impressed by Rhodes' personal courage in coming to their camp alone and unarmed. He referred him to de la Rey, another of their leaders. With wild eyes, fumbling with his gun, de la Rey refused even to listen to Rhodes and shouted 'Blood must flow!'

Rhodes, without blinking, looked at the excited man with a smile, his natural boyish smile, and answered calmly:

'No, give me my breakfast first, and then we can talk about blood.'

De la Rey was embarrassed at having to be reminded by a *verdomde Engelsman* of the traditional Boer duties of a host. He took Rhodes to his farm-house. Rhodes stayed there for a week and became godfather to his grandchild.

After that the negotiations with the Stellalanders went easily enough. Rhodes promised them that their land-titles would be recognized if they agreed that Stellaland remained a British Protectorate until it was finally annexed by the Cape Colony. Rhodes pocketed this agreement with relief and set out for Goshenland.

There he found an atmosphere of even greater and more bellicose animosity than in Stellaland. The Goshenites, again at war with the Natives, had just occupied a large slice of land belonging to a tribe protected by Britain. Van Pittius, calling himself 'Administrator of Goshenland', gave Rhodes to understand that he considered him a nuisance. After Rhodes had refused to recognize him in any official capacity he paid back in the same coin by referring to 'Mr C. J. Rhodes, calling himself Commissioner for Bechuanaland'.

'A pretty kettle of fish,' muttered Rhodes. This hardened Boer, he had to confess, was immune to treatment 'on the personal'. Van Pittius ignored Rhodes. He was not moved in the least when Rhodes pointed out that by fighting against Natives who stood under British protection they were waging war against the Queen.

Such obstinacy could easily be traced to outside influence. As Rhodes had feared, Kruger was the force behind it, by his nomination of General Piet Joubert, the Boer Commandant-General, as 'Commissioner of the Western Border' with the function of 'preserving order'. Before Rhodes had an opportunity to approach him, there appeared on the scene the Reverend Mr Du Toit, freshly returned with Kruger from London and the European capitals.

He hated Rhodes with all the fervour of a man whose ambitions had been shattered. He held Rhodes responsible for his having been ousted by Hofmeyr from the leadership of the Bond—he who had been its founder, the apostle of an Afrikaans renaissance and the herald of Afrikaner republicanism in the Cape.

Rhodes must not succeed. Rhodes must be humiliated; and with him the whole crowd of Cape intriguers and the whole English race. Up went the Vierkleur flag of the Transvaal in Goshenland.

President Kruger knew nothing of this temperamental outburst of his Inspector of Education. He had been waiting for several days for a reply from Whitehall to his telegraphed suggestion that the Transvaal should take over Britain's responsibilities in Goshenland. When no answer came on the tenth day, seeing that Du Toit's hoisting of the Vierkleur had presented him with a *fait accompli*, Kruger proclaimed the provisional annexation of Stellaland and Goshenland by the Transvaal 'in the interest of humanity and for the protection of order and safety, subject to the consent of the British Government according to the London convention'.

Rhodes found this territory much too hot for him and left quickly for the Cape, the second time within two years that he returned from Bechuanaland in despair. His scheme of operating without the 'Imperial Factor' had failed utterly. Only one possibility remained: Bechuanaland would have to be saved by 'Grandma'; by her armed forces if necessary.

Though still a novice at the game, Rhodes showed a master hand in creating in the Cape a popular storm of wild wrath against the scheming Transvaalers who, as an instrument of Bismarck, wanted to throttle the Cape. Hofmeyr and the Bond were caught by the bogy of Germany. Patriotic fervour in the Cape's summer heat, cleverly fanned by Rhodes, reached the boiling-point of wild chauvinism.

In England the wave of indignation splashed high in the columns of the Tory papers, who reminded their readers that Majuba had not yet been avenged. Mr Joseph Chamberlain pleaded vehemently in the Cabinet for an expeditionary force to end the Bechuanaland trouble once and for all. Gladstone was anxious to avoid war if possible. At last, however, the Governor of the Cape, Sir Hercules Robinson, declared that military interference was absolutely necessary. Whitehall decided to send out to Bechuanaland General Sir Charles Warren and a force of about 4,000 men with orders to clear Bechuanaland and, in case of interference from the Transvaal, to go to war.

At the end of December 1884 General Warren and his army, including Cape volunteers and, to the great disgust of all Afrikaners, a contingent of Cape Coloureds, set out on the war-path.

Kruger in his sagacity withdrew his proclamation. Thus there no longer existed a reason for armed interference.

Hofmeyr dropped a confidential warning to Rhodes about the certainty of open armed revolt of the Cape Dutch to aid the Boers in the case of British aggression. London, however, remained adamant in her decision.

Rhodes, now that the assistance by an armed force was no longer needed and would only cause new trouble, cursed the moment when he had called for the 'Imperial Factor'.

Warren was undoubtedly a good and gallant soldier. His mission, however, required political and diplomatic aptitude and tact. These civilian qualities the General did not possess.

After his arrival he had asked Rhodes to collaborate with him by going to Stellaland and keeping Van Niekerk in good humour during the operation of ejecting the Goshenites. Since Warren had confirmed Rhodes' agreement with Stellaland, Van Niekerk's men remained quiet and declared that they would not interfere with Warren's mission.

As soon as Warren came to Stellaland, however, he repealed Rhodes' agreement by pretending that he had signed the telegram of confirmation without reading it. Rhodes, during his stay in Stellaland, had assured the Stellalanders by a solemn promise in his capacity as Her Majesty's Assistant Commissioner that their land-titles would be recognized. Warren, ignoring this binding agreement, ordered the restitution to the Natives of their land.

When Rhodes remonstrated about such breach of faith and the flat abnegation of his authority, Warren mounted the high horse and asked for strict subordination to his orders. When Rhodes offered to resign, Sir Hercules Robinson implored him to remain at his post as his confidential representative. Rhodes, fearing that Warren would commit further blunders, agreed to stay. To 'restore the General's *amour-propre*' Rhodes declared himself ready to 'act in direct subordination to him' instead of to Sir Hercules. Rhodes even swallowed the bitter pill of having to endure the sight of Mackenzie who had just published in a widely read English magazine heavy personal attacks against him. Warren had parried the thrust of the 'Colonial' against the 'Imperial Factor' by calling back Mackenzie as his Assistant Commissioner. There was now a close union between the bellicose martinet, the exponent of Jingoism, and the pious Boer-hater whom Exeter Hall provided with all the moral ammunition of chauvinistic fervour he needed for combating the Boers, the Bond, the Colonials and, particularly, Cecil Rhodes.

Warren had arrived in South Africa with a closed mind of animosity against Rhodes, the result of official and public slandering of Rhodes as an anti-British and pro-Boer opportunist who for his own political and financial benefit had stepped down to the lowest form of disloyalty by taking the side of filibustering enemies of Her Majesty.

Lord Randolph Churchill had expressed the general contempt in which Rhodes was held in England when he inquired in a debate in the House of Commons after Rhodes' nomination as Assistant Commissioner, why 'some cipher' had been chosen to replace the Reverend Mr Mackenzie in Bechuanaland. From the

Ministerial benches came the lukewarm reply in defence of Rhodes that he was 'a gentleman of some distinction who had always shown himself to be a great sympathizer with the native races'.

These opinions about his disloyalty and the fact that he was 'regarded as a most horrid individual' at home, affected Rhodes deeply. He felt himself misunderstood. When he had demanded the 'elimination of the Imperial Factor' he had not referred to the British flag or, in other words, to the idea of the British Empire about which his romantic ideas had changed but little since his early Oxford days. His scruples concerned only the unelastic, red-taped stubbornness with which the Colonial Office conducted its policy, scruples shared in the Cape by English and Dutch alike.

Warren set out from England with the intention of strengthening the 'Imperial Factor' in South Africa by eliminating Kruger's attempt at a hegemony of the Boers in South Africa and by breaking the spirit of colonialism as defined by Rhodes.

Besides his political bias against Rhodes, Warren was jealous of the more gifted man. As an ambitious soldier, Warren had set himself to gain political successes which might lead to his nomination for the governorship of Bechuanaland or even, perhaps, to sit one day in Cape Town as Governor of the Cape Colony and Her Majesty's High Commissioner for South Africa. He saw in Rhodes a danger which would rob him of the fame he expected as saviour of Bechuanaland.

Before Warren could set his military machine into motion, President Kruger, in order to remove even the faintest reason for armed interference, went to Goshenland and warned the people of the futility of resisting Warren's expedition by force. He invited Warren to a friendly talk in an unofficial conference on the border of the Transvaal and the Cape.

Though it had been agreed that both parties should be accompanied only by a personal escort, Warren proceeded to the meeting with a military detachment. Kruger felt hurt by this tactless demonstration of distrust. The President's anger increased when he learnt of the presence of the Reverend Mr Mackenzie, whom he held responsible more than Rhodes for cutting him off from the North. The inclusion of a forceful antagonist of the Boers was countered by Kruger when he set before his English guests the Reverend Mr Du Toit. There faced each other these two professed heralds of Christian love as documented in the Sermon on the Mount, yet both ever ready in their blind chauvinistic hatred to unfold the flag of war against whosoever opposed their ideas of nationalism.

Many people came away from their first meeting with Kruger with the impression of having looked upon the stone-monument of a prehistoric man. The monumentality of his appearance made one forget his grotesque ugliness. Each single feature of his face seemed too small in proportion to his bulky body, six feet in height and more than 200 pounds in weight.

One could not help being reminded of the Prophets of the Old Testament. People have compared him to a composite picture of Abraham Lincoln and Oliver Cromwell, with something of John Bright around the eyes and Benjamin Franklin's mouth. Others were reminded of Ulysses, General Blücher, Bismarck. One visitor confessed that his first thought on seeing Kruger was, without blasphemy, 'That's Jehovah Himself!'

The cartoonists enjoyed themselves in making fun of the long fringe of grey beard framing the dark-skinned face, with the clean-shaven upper lip; the thick irregular brows above a pair of dark, almost black eyes, flashing fearless eyes, whose smallness and the sagacity which spoke from them recalled those of an elephant; the large broad nose from which a system of deep furrows spread criss-cross over the whole face; the crude flat ears in contrast to the finely shapen mouth which was mostly closed tightly and opened only occasionally for a short benevolent smile warming up the ugly granite face with the beautifying rays of human sympathy. The cartoonists could not indicate in their distorted portraits the commanding power over men of his sonorous bass voice. This voice captivated friend and foe. Simple Boers admitted that to hear Oom Paul scold an audience terrified them as if the Lord were speaking through his mouth.

No one who came in contact with him could fail to recognize the dignity and nobility of his personality. There emanated from him an almost hypnotic influence, making strangers and old friends alike feel his magnetic power and strength.

The moral code of his life did not come to him by the easy way of taking it over from father, teacher or preacher. As a mature married man, more than thirty years old, he retired for many days into the solitude of the mountains and there battled with his God for the purification of his conscience and the peace of his soul. He came back a new man, blindly devoted to the tenets of the strict Puritan Calvinistic doctrines of the Dopper Church.

In his faith he refused to compromise or exercise tolerance. Since his religiosity directed his private and public life with equal severity, his political views often contrasted amazingly with the modern outlook. His adversaries maintained that he looked upon conditions of the nineteenth century through slits; that he represented the anachronism of a seventeenth-century Calvinist in the machine-age; that he applied the intolerant Mosaic eye-for-an-eye-tooth-for-a-tooth laws as his policy against the Machiavellian diplomacy of *fin-de-siècle* politics; that he adhered too strictly to his self-chosen motto '*Wees getrou, maar vertrou niemand*'—be trustworthy but trust no one.

Among the pioneers who, after having conquered the perils of a three-year trek, had settled in the country beyond the River Vaal was the father of eleven-year-old Paul Kruger, and his family. As a boy of twelve Paul had already had to take his stand, with a rifle in his hand, fighting with his elders against the Natives and shooting lions and elephants. There remained no time for learning out of books. What he had to know in order to read the Bible, as well as a little writing, was taught to him by his mother. These pious people believed that all human knowledge was contained in the Good Book. Further knowledge would only lead to disbelief.

Next to the duty to his God came Kruger's determination to preserve the personal independence of his people and the freedom of their country. The ardent nationalism of the Boers was not an artificial political instrument of chauvinistic imperialism like its European version. The Boers considered themselves the masters of the land for which they had paid with their own sweat and blood, from which they had wrested every single corn-cob, for which they still had to endure cruel hardships and privations.

Their patriotism had nothing in common with the abstract nationalism with which governments intoxicate the masses in order to make them forget that their country really belongs to the privileged few and that they are only tenants there. Every single Boer realized that he and his brothers were the owners of their country; that the soil on which he worked was his own, his indisputable property, and that the whole country was owned in the same way by other free burghers and by no one else. His patriotism was concrete; his own soil was his fatherland. When he was called upon to defend his country, he took his own rifle, mounted his own horse and fought for the sanctity of his own home, the safety of his own family, the protection of his own property. The State to him was not a political conception enforced on him, but a practical co-operative society for mutual benefit. His nationalism was not directed against any other country but was the expression of his pride in his freedom, pride in his soil, pride in his personal achievements against odds.

Boers always had large families. Kruger's children numbered sixteen. To perpetuate the feudal system a father had to provide sufficient land to be divided among his numerous sons. The time had come when their own country no longer had sufficient fertile land for their rapidly increasing numbers. Expansion beyond their border became a necessity. There they would find sufficient and good pastures. That it belonged to the Natives caused them no scruples. They did not consider the Natives the lawful owners of this land since most of the tribes had come down from Central Africa and had taken it from the original inhabitants, the Hottentots. They identified the Native as the 'Son of Ham' who according to the Bible was cursed: 'a servant of servants shall he be unto his brethren'. Thus the Boers felt themselves justified in considering these Sons of Ham as their 'hewers of wood and carriers of water'.

Kruger's policy of trying to expand the Transvaal was thus founded on the conceptions traditional to the Boers. Opposition to this necessity of expansion was considered as wilfully aimed at the extinction of the Boers. Britain had tried once already to strangle them. Now, by cutting them off from access to the rich pastures of the North and encircling them from all sides, the death-sentence had been pronounced.

Sitting at the conference table, his eyes closed, Kruger was playing with a ring. With difficulty he removed it from his finger, passed it to Warren and pointed to the inscription: 'Take courage, your cause is just and must triumph in the end.' The inner side bore the figures 6,591: 587, indicating the results of a plebiscite in the Transvaal against British rule in 1877. The ring had been presented to Kruger anonymously by 'an English friend of the Boers' during his visit to London in 1878.

Gesticulating menacingly with his pipe, Kruger shouted at the stiff English general opposite him, 'You are putting a ring fence round me!' And referring to the London Convention he said with a bitter smile, 'The Boers feel like a man whose clothing has been taken away from him and then restored to him without his watch and purse.'

Warren was scarcely listening to Kruger's complaints. When Kruger continued to plead, he hissed at him, 'To find people standing on the ground and insisting on their claims is to me simply an act of rebellion.'

Warren, though he did not take a very active part in the negotiations, took care to prevent Rhodes from usurping the leadership. Rhodes kept in the background as he first wanted to study the old man. Kruger appealed to him as a 'man of action'. Were they not both filled with the same ideas, driving at the same aim, though each for his own country? His 'greatness in simplicity and simplicity in greatness' made a deep impression on Rhodes. The longer he watched the old man struggling to find justice for his Boers by crushing the icy indifference of this haughty Englishman Warren, the more his sympathy grew for Kruger.

> I began to acquire my admiration for Oom Paul, for had he not conceived the noble scheme from his point of view, of seizing the interior, of stretching his Republic across to Walfish Bay, of making the Cape Colony hidebound, and of ultimately seizing Delagoa Bay, and all this without sixpence in his Treasury?
>
> I regard him as one of the most remarkable men in South Africa, who has been singularly unfortunate. When I see him in Pretoria with Bechuanaland gone and other lands around him gone from his grasp; and last of all, when he with his whole idea of a pastoral republic, finds that idea vanishing, I pity that man, I cannot help pitying him.

Rhodes considered it opportune to come to terms with the President. He resorted to his new technique of approaching him 'on the personal'. It had no effect on Kruger. He now tried to come to his aid in small matters against Warren. Kruger ignored these overtures. It was obvious that he detested Rhodes whom he knew to be responsible for all the trouble in Bechuanaland.

Having been informed by Du Toit, Rhodes' severest enemy in South Africa, about Rhodes' political development, Kruger looked upon him as the personification of Jingoism. Feeling that the final round between Britain and his country had now begun, with Rhodes as its driving force, he described Rhodes as 'the curse of South Africa'. Asked for an explanation, he said:

> This young man I like not; he goes too fast for me; he has robbed me of the North. I cannot understand how he manages it, but he never sleeps and he does not smoke. That young man will cause me trouble if he does not leave politics alone and turn to something else. Well, the racehorse is swifter than the ox, but the ox can draw the greater loads. We shall see.

The freebooters had given up all resistance. Their former republics were now under British administration. The boundaries had been freshly fixed by an agreement between Warren and Kruger. No reason remained for military action. The High Commissioner, the Cape Government, and particularly Cecil Rhodes believed that Warren's mission had ended. Warren, however, wanted to earn cheap military glory and a hitting political success so as to make himself commendable for high honours as the great South African statesman and military genius.

Warren set out to occupy Stellaland and Goshenland. He cancelled all agreements made by Rhodes. Van Niekerk was imprisoned. The boundaries were altered. All previously acknowledged land-titles were declared null and void. 'All Dutch Boers and non-teetotallers' were excluded from acquiring land in Bechuanaland. Martial law was declared and the fighting chiefs and their tribes reinstated in their former domains.

Rhodes saw all his work undone by an ambitious soldier who had succumbed to the promptings of the militant parson, mouthpiece of Exeter Hall, the Reverend Mr Mackenzie. Foaming with fury, Rhodes asked for the recall of Mackenzie who had no official status. He accused Warren of having deliberately broken faith with the Stellalanders and Goshenites by not keeping the solemn promise given by Rhodes with Warren's consent. Furiously Rhodes wrote in his report to the High Commissioner:

> . . . I remember, when a youngster, reading in my English History of the supremacy of my country and its annexations, and that there

were two cardinal axioms—that the word of the nation, when once pledged, was never broken, and that when a man accepted the citizenship of the British Empire there was no distinction between races. It has been my misfortune in one year to meet with the breach of one and the proposed breach of the other.

Rhodes worked feverishly to avert further damage. The General, feeling himself safe in his position under the blessings and praises of Whitehall, now set out for his final stroke: to remove the man who through his criticism and accusations was impeding his actions and who might eventually rob him of his glory. He demanded the recall of Rhodes on the grounds that he was 'dangerous to the peace of the country' and that, until he was removed, it was 'not considered safe to move on'.

Rhodes resigned. He felt a loathing for the whole Bechuanaland affair. . . . He had, without reward, wasted a whole year out of his costly life over it; a period which he could have used more profitably by looking after his business. He had fought for this job at the risk of his political position and personal relationship with all sections of the country because he thought it would be for the best interest of the country and of South Africa that the territory should be British. . . . And all he had got was the offer of a little brass medal which he had naturally to refuse . . . all he had got was to be told by a crotchety, irritable General, the representative of Her Majesty, that he was dangerous to the peace of the country . . . dangerous to the peace of the country! . . . He should really not worry but let them stew in their own juice. . . . The best would be to go on a trip round the world; perhaps it would be better, as he had discussed it with Gordon . . . poor Gordon now dead—he could wish to have been with him there —discussed it with Gordon and later with Warren. Perhaps really better to go home into politics and be elected to the House of Commons. . . .

But Rhodes decided to continue. After all he had attained his goal. The way into the heart of Africa was open, and in addition the aspirations of the Transvaal for supremacy in South Africa were broken for ever. However, Warren had antagonized the Transvaal more than was necessary. Rhodes considered himself completely innocent, having forgotten that he was the originator of the Northern scheme. For what had happened now he blamed

Warren and Warren alone. He needed the goodwill of the Transvaal, as he expressed in a speech after his return:

> . . . The only possibility of the union [of South Africa], is our being able to regard the inhabitants of the Transvaal just as we regard our own fellow-colonists. . . . It is with this idea that I went into politics. This is what I have steadily advocated throughout my political life . . . I have kept this end steadily in view as the ultimate goal of my politics.

In Sir Hercules Robinson he still had a strong ally. By writing privately to a junior member of the British Cabinet to whom he introduced himself as the brother of Frank who had been at Eton with the recipient, he tried to influence Whitehall, particularly for the removal of Warren:

> Do not be led away by the assertion that I am pro-Dutch in my sympathies. I had to consider the best mode of permanently checking the expansion of the Boer republics into the interior. The only solution I can see is to enclose them by the Cape Colony . . . and my instructions have been that after asserting British supremacy the course desired was Colonial annexation, against which Warren has agitated ever since he went into the country. . . . Conduct such as Warren's is just heaping up future trouble in this country and destroying all chance of success for those who are working to cement the two nationalities on the basis of true loyalty to the British flag.

At last he succeeded. Warren was recalled.

Under the final solution southern Bechuanaland came under British administration for future transfer to the Cape, for which Rhodes had to wait ten years. The North of Bechuanaland was declared a British protectorate to be governed by its Native chiefs.

Rhodes continued to attack Warren after the General's return to England. In a heated controversy between them in letters to *The Times* Rhodes did not aim at the General so much for the sake of revenge as to whitewash himself in British eyes from the widely spread taint of being anti-British and pro-Boer, disloyal to the Queen and an instrument of the Bond. Already at this stage he bore in mind that for the fulfilment of his plans he would have to go to England for support and—money. He thus needed an unblemished name in Whitehall. At the same time he had to keep English as well as Dutch voters in the Cape in good humour.

Diplomatically he therefore declared in Parliament that by 'elimination of the Imperial Factor' he had really meant his belief in 'Colonialism', but of course under the British flag.

At the same time he confessed:

'I came down to the House in 1881 a most rabid Jingo, but I have since passed through the fire of Bechuanaland.'

To President Kruger, sitting on the *stoep* of his house in Pretoria, his new State Secretary, young Dr Leyds, freshly imported from Holland, read the strangely contradictory news of Rhodes' oscillations between Imperialism and Colonialism. The President drew heavily on his long-stemmed pipe. Interrupting the reader he said slowly:

'Only four people I fear: God, the Devil, de la Rey for his enormous strength and his quick tongue and—*daardie Engelsman* Rhodes!'

CHAPTER VII

'ALWAYS GET IN THE FIRST BLOW'

EVERYONE in Kimberley knew Barney Barnato. Anywhere else people would have stopped to look twice at the short chubby man with the pink baby cheeks and the large black piercing eyes which seemed never to be still; eyes which betrayed an overflowing wealth of humour. The thin upper lip, partly covered by a waxed and pointed reddish-brown moustache, the massive protruding lower lip and a chin stretched forward menacingly, gave warning of stapled energy and alertness. Longish yellow-brown hair, carefully parted in the middle, accentuated the chubbiness of the face to which a long broad nose and fleshy projecting ears stood in grotesque contrast.

His clothes, one could see, came from an expensive tailor. The loudness of the large-check tweed jacket and trousers, with the low-cut red waistcoat and an enormous silk four-in-hand cravat in all colours of the rainbow and held together by a large diamond pin, gave evidence of great wealth rather than of good taste.

Strangers would take him for a 'bookie'. Here in Kimberley not only was he known to everybody but they were all aware that he, Barney Barnato, of the firm of Barnato Brothers, lord over the Kimberley Mine, biggest property-owner in town, biggest diamond merchant in the world, master of the 'Kaffir Circus' on the London Stock Exchange, was the richest man in South Africa.

By the smile of self-satisfaction, by the heavy pompous walk with which he idled along Market Square, one could easily surmise that he enjoyed his importance.

Whoever passed him would take time at least to greet him with a 'Hullo, Barney!' '*Goeie more*, Barney!' '*Schener tog for eich*, Barney!' Many would stop, merely to shake hands. For everyone Barnato had a friendly word. People in need knew that they could always appeal to him successfully. Barney Barnato understood the language of poverty. Out of his waistcoat-pocket would come a sovereign. Once he explained: 'I always carry a stock of quids in that pocket for the benefit of stony-brokes.'

One March day in 1888 Barnato was in a less jocular mood than usual. He smiled vacantly when greeting his friends in the street. Anything wrong, perhaps, with 'Central'? How could anything possibly be wrong with Kimberley's richest mining company, the Kimberley Central Company, to which now belonged the whole of the Kimberley Mine, when the shares had soared within the last few weeks from £14 to £49? Barney's company was worth £8 million. Something wrong? Ridiculous!

But Barney would not let himself be buttonholed. 'Sorry, old chap, I'm in a hurry. Having lunch with Rhodes at the Kimberley Club.'

Just like Barney! It was only early morning but it seemed he had to let them know that he had at last succeeded in crashing those doors which had always been closed to him.

Barney Barnato was seized by an attack of stage-fright which had already caused him a sleepless night. Today his future would be decided. Tomorrow he would again be good old Barney, liberally treating his old cronies to drinks in the bars, freely distributing from his pocket big cigars which bore on their labels his portrait with the Kimberley Mine in the background and the words 'La Flor de Barney Barnato'.

Petticoat Lane, the centre of London's East End ghetto for the petty Jewish traders, had been his home. There, after leaving school at fourteen, he had passed through the high school of smartness in the commercial battle of life, selling every week-day from a little hand-barrow all that a Jewish housewife needed for her home and kitchen. But on Sundays, the great day in the 'Lane' when the *Yoks*—the sailors from the nearby East India Docks, workmen from the neighbourhood hunting for a bargain and even, out of curiosity, stolid citizens from the West End—came to market, Barnato acted as one of the *spielers* who with exuberant glibness could sell almost anything at a good price no matter if it was a headache powder, insecticide, toys, worthless 'gold' watches or bird-seed.

His father, Isaac Isaacs, had trained his two sons, Henry and Barnett, well for early independence, and Harry and Barney soon felt that life in the ghetto atmosphere of Whitechapel was too boring and slow for them. Harry found a job as barman in the 'King of Prussia', the rendezvous of music-hall artistes. Since their earliest youth both boys had been enthusiastic about the theatre. Acquaintances at the 'King of Prussia' encouraged the two boys to try their luck on the stage. They appeared in little East End music-halls, as the 'Barnato Brothers', Harry as 'gentleman' in evening dress, as strong man, acrobat, juggler and teller of smutty stories and Barney as his stooge in the make-up of a clown, presenting a pathetic figure in his clumsiness and helplessness, due mostly to his short-sightedness.

When rumours of diamond finds were whispered in 'The Lane', Harry was among the first who went to South Africa and Barney followed soon afterwards. All that was left of his savings after paying for his passage was less than fifty pounds. Barney arrived at a bad time. His brother, like everyone else, had suffered under the many slumps on the diamond market. Barney's training in 'The Lane' stood him in good stead. He bought and sold whatever came his way. And when there was nothing to be sold Barney earned money as a prize-fighter and once even appeared as a circus clown.

When times improved, Barney associated himself with another young man, Louis Cohen, whose only asset, like his own, consisted of tenacity, hope and good humour. With a few pounds of their savings Barney and Louis Cohen established themselves as *kopje wallopers*, wandering from one digging to another, trying to find diggers who would entrust them with the sale of their diamonds. Sometimes they even dared to buy on their own account.

Barney Barnato, watching, listening and questioning, had not wasted a minute since he came to Kimberley, learning everything there was to be known about diamonds. His first big success came through a horse. To the horror of his partner he paid £27 10*s*. for a half-starved shabby pony and a rickety old buggy which he obtained from a diamond buyer who had 'made his pile' and was going back home.

'I tell you, Louis, this blooming gee-gee, bless its panting little heart, is a *mezzia*—a bargain!'

He was right: without waiting for any directions from the reins this equine caricature took him on its own from one digging to the other, where he was made welcome as the successor to the former buyer and obtained all his business. Now Barney could move more freely. He took a tiny shop, a mere cubby-hole, in Maloney's Bar. It cost a pound a day. Louis Cohen scolded him:

'You are *meshugge*—totally mad, Barney. You're ruining us!' Barney replied: '*Schweig stumm*—shut up, you *schlemiel*. I'm tired of hoof-padding. Let the fellers come to us, for a change.' Again Barney was right. Maloney's was the first bar on coming to town from the claims. No digger would pass there without 'lifting his elbow'.

The partnership did not last long. After a year Barney joined his brother Harry.

Yet Barney, always a restless man, could not sit still in the office and left that part of the work to Harry. He seemed never to tire of making the rounds of the claims and having a friendly chat with the diggers. They did not mind the interruption in their work. It always meant a quarter of an hour of hearty laughter. Cleverly he combined his humorous talents with business acumen to profitable results. He knew, too, how to make everyone understand that no liberties could be taken with him. As he once told a friend:

> Never let a feller wrong you without getting square, no matter how long you wait; and never wrong a man if you can help it, because he will wait his time to get back on you, and at the worst possible moment. . . . If you are going to fight, always get in the first blow. If a man is going to hit you, hit him first and say: 'If you try that, I'll hit you again!' It is no use your standing off and saying: 'If you hit me, I'll hit you back.' D'ye follow? D'ye understand?

His great moment came in 1876. Desperate nervousness had seized Kimberley when the yellow ground became exhausted and the blue soil yielded almost no results. Barnato had heard that the Kimberley mines were old volcanoes. Knowing every turn of the reef and every claim on the fields, he was convinced that the diamonds came from deep below and that the deeper one went, to where the pressure must have been greatest, the larger, richer and better would be the finds. Barnato was 'determined to go on until it broke me'. And, like Rhodes, he was prophetic when he said that 'the blue ground was the true home of the diamond'.

Barnato bought four claims in the best part of the Kimberley Mine at a price of £3,000. Within a few weeks they yielded him a weekly income of £1,800. Barnato's star was rising. Such meteoric ascent to wealth had to bring jealousy in its trail.

Rumours went through town that these claims had only been bought by Barnato as an artful dodge to screen his nefarious dealings in I.D.B., Illicit Diamond Buying.

No longer was he cheered in the bars as 'Jolly old Barney'. People ignored his friendly greetings. Old cronies avoided him.

Instead of being able to enjoy his rapidly increasing wealth Barnato grew morose. Often these days he would repeat to himself and to others, 'If you are going to fight, always get in the first blow. . . .' He bought more claims. He had come to the conclusion that he would have to buy the six centre claims in the Kimberley Mine in order to gain control over the whole. The future, he realized, pointed to the industrialization of diamond mining which would only be achieved through amalgamation. With a capital of £115,000 he founded his own company; he bought new claims; he increased the capital of his company which paid 36 per cent in dividends. He amalgamated all the other companies working in the Kimberley Mine into the Kimberley Central Company. Only one company, the French Diamond Mining Company, of which most of the shares were in French hands, still remained outside. In the 'Central', as his company was generally called, he was holder of the majority. It was admittedly the richest mine in Kimberley, and Barnato the wealthiest man, having made several millions in his financial transactions. With the dexterity of a financial acrobat he operated on the world's stock exchanges. If the London market was saturated he offloaded his new issues in Vienna, Amsterdam or Paris.

Gradually, and with the help of men of straw, he bought up the shares of two companies, De Beers Central and Oriental, which owned the best claims, right in the heart of De Beers Mine. Without these two mines Rhodes would never be able to expand or amalgamate. Rhodes had already cast his eyes on the two mines, but not having the money on hand he thought that they would no doubt one day fall into his lap. When in 1883 he was ready to take them over, Rhodes was surprised to find that Barnato owned them.

Though they lived a stone's throw from each other, the two had never met. 'Funny little fellow, that Whitechapel prancer,' said Rhodes. 'Impossible person,' remarked Beit. 'I hate the sight of that scoundrel,' was Dr Jameson's comment.

'Send a message round to him to come and see me,' Rhodes

said. 'But in the office only, mind you. Don't want to be seen in public with him, otherwise people will think we too have come down to I.D.B. No doubt at a reasonable profit, he'll be glad to sell these parcels.'

Barnato replied that if there was something Mr Rhodes wanted, would Mr Rhodes kindly come to see him.

Rhodes was amused. 'This little blighter means business. Will be a hard nut to crack.' Yet, to his amazement, Barnato offered no resistance. He agreed with Rhodes that amalgamation was essential at De Beers, just as in his Kimberley Mine. He stated his price. Rhodes tried to bargain. With pointed politeness Barnato answered that ever since he had left 'The Lane' he had stuck firmly to his prices. Within a few minutes the deal was concluded. 'Cunning fellow, this Barnato,' Rhodes said when he came home.

Barnato, though he could certainly have obtained a still higher price, was determined to oblige Rhodes in helping him to amalgamate the remaining companies in De Beers Mine. Only Rhodes and he himself would then be left as the big *machers* on the Fields and they would have to come to an understanding to prevent over-production and stop the fall in prices on the diamond market.

Rhodes had come to a similar conclusion. The diamond market would have to be cleaned of irresponsible elements. He felt, however, that an understanding between Barnato's group and his own would be insufficient. The only solution was a diamond monopoly through a complete amalgamation of the two groups which would later easily absorb the few outsiders. It was no doubt in his mind that he, Cecil Rhodes, would become the leader of this monopolistic centralization of the diamond industry and the diamond market which, when completed, would become the biggest and most powerful private institution in South Africa, a strong force influencing the future of the entire African continent. It would give him the social, political and financial standing necessary for his future plans: to open up the North, to paint Africa's map red. He wanted to secure the Diamond Fields only as a 'jumping-off place'.

Rhodes was worried about over-production. Since the introduction of underground mining and mechanization De Beers was able to produce up to one million carats a year. Barnato, whose Kimberley Mine had always produced bigger yields, would perhaps double De Beers' output. Prices were sinking rapidly. He had asked 'little Beit who had a flair for figures' how many men in England and the United States were married per year. On the basis of these figures and those of the average export of diamonds over the last years, Rhodes discovered that regardless of the economic position men would never spend more than £4 million annually on diamonds—on small stones when prices were high, on bigger ones when low, but never exceeding that amount. Only a monopoly would save the industry, by restoring high prices and limiting production.

Rhodes lived, slept and worked with only the one thought of a gigantic diamond monopoly corporation. In the middle of the night he would come, half-dressed, drive Beit or Rudd out of bed, throw himself into a chair and, stroking his chin nervously with his right forefinger, shout in an excited, high-pitched voice: 'I have just hit on an idea that has been worrying me for weeks...' And for hours he would talk about his plans.

Once a friend, Dr Sauer, found him sitting on a rock on the edge of De Beers Mine, as if in a trance, staring into the deep hole in which the workmen appeared like ants. What was he thinking about? Pronouncing each word distinctly, Rhodes replied:

'I was calculating the amount of blue ground in sight and the power that this blue ground would confer on the man who obtained control of it all.'

Only one man stood in his way, 'that cunning little Jew, Barnato'. He was the only man in South Africa whom he feared. Barnato's path ran along the same lines as his own. One day they would clash. Either they would have to go along the road together or one of them would have to step aside.

How was he to approach Barnato? To 'take him on the personal' would perhaps flatter one in whom, in spite of all his millions, there certainly remained enough of Whitechapel to lap up any kindness bestowed on him. At their first dealings he had fallen for it. An invitation was sent to Barnato to meet Rhodes in Dr Jameson's house. Barnato knew of Jameson's raving dislike for him and had tried several times unsuccessfully to be on friendly terms with the doctor.

The meeting went off contrary to Rhodes' expectations. It was a very determined Barnato, obviously fully aware of his strong position, who sat opposite him, smiling benignly and completely obdurate. He would not even enter into discussions on the value of the Kimberley Mine or on the price of Central shares. He replied calmly: 'Mr Rhodes knows as well as I do that Kimberley Mine can produce yearly, even under the worst management, twice as many diamonds as the whole world would be able to buy.'

Rhodes saw the threat in his words. Barnato could bring down the price still further and would still be making a profit. He tried again. Finally, as if bored with Rhodes' repeated pressure to name a price, Barnato exclaimed: 'The value of the Kimberley Mine, why it's worth three times what De Beers is worth.'

Only with difficulty could Rhodes restrain himself from showing his disappointment. It would mean war now, battle to the knife. Though different in many respects from himself, he had a liking for Barnato, and at the same time he was afraid of him, because he felt Barnato's superiority when it came to financial operations. Rhodes was never a financier and had never learnt the art of building up a sound financial structure for his various big enterprises. He was by nature a speculator, a financial adventurer, an imaginative punter. For an idea Rhodes would venture everything: his fortune, his whole personality, his future. He did not ask about and was not at all concerned with such 'details' as whether his actions corresponded with the accepted moral and legal standards. He felt himself above good or evil. Rhodes believed in his visions, his instincts, his mission. He took everyone who stood between him and his aims as a personal enemy. Soon he imagined that he was surrounded by enemies. It was true that Rhodes' unpopularity increased in proportion to his success. His ruthlessness, his abruptness, his overbearing haughtiness, his cynicism expressed in acid sarcasms and his proverbial tactlessness and apparently inhuman indifference, gave people a low opinion of Rhodes as a man. Some admired him as an outstanding expert on all questions concerning diamonds. The larger number envied him for his success and said that he had merely been luckier than others. Those who hated him for having 'pushed them out of their luck' or for 'letting nobody else make a living in Kimberley' were at that time in the majority.

Rhodes' vanity was hurt by the antagonism displayed towards him. He now saw an enemy in everyone. Though his unpopularity was in most cases due to his voluntary seclusion from the outside world, he avoided people still more. His shyness, born out of a feeling of insecurity and inferiority, the fear that one wrong step could hurl him back into the abyss of anonymity, caused him to live in a friendless vacuum. His ideas, his plans, his future, was all that counted and everything for which he was striving could be summed up in the one word, Power; the instrument with which to obtain it, Money. To General Gordon he had explained:

> If one has ideas, one cannot carry them out without wealth to back them. I have therefore tried to combine the commercial with the imaginative, and up to the present I've not failed.

It was certainly no pose when he indicated that money, even great wealth, in itself never satisfied him. To him money was equivalent to power, as he repeatedly expressed it in his naïve, primitive way:

> Money is power, and what can one accomplish without power? That is why I must have money. Ideas are no good without money. . . . For its own sake I do not care for money. I never tried it for its own sake but it is a power and I like power. . . . I want the power—let who will wear the peacock's feathers.

Most of Rhodes' business decisions were dictated by intuition, unlike Barnato, who relied exclusively on knowledge.

Rhodes came to Kimberley to gain wealth; Barnato to find security and social improvement. The fact that Rhodes was aware of his social superiority became evident during the meeting with Barnato, though he tried hard to conceal it by an enforced amiability. Barnato had no illusions about Rhodes' low opinion of him, Beit's badly disguised contempt, or Dr Jameson's obvious disgust.

When he returned from the meeting he first swallowed a large gulp of brandy, before telling his nephew and junior partner, Woolf Joel, what had happened: they had 'grovelled' before him, with their 'sweet talky-talk' had given him champagne with porter, their favourite booze, in the belief that they would easily be able to 'take a rise' out of him who in their eyes was still a nobody, an outcast—a bloody East End Jew-boy—but for all their 'soft sawder' they weren't able to pull wool over his short-sighted 'peepers'. They just gave him a 'sickener'.

Deep in thought he added, more seriously:

'Rhodes looks down on me because I have no education—never been to college like him. . . . If I had received the education of Cecil Rhodes, there would not have been a Cecil Rhodes.'

Rhodes had not impressed him when he tried to show off by quoting Greek poetry. There was, however, something undefinable about Rhodes which attracted him. He felt a kindred spirit in Rhodes whose existence, he thought, was animated by the same desire to reach the top, to let the world feel the pull of his money. And in this typically English *goy*, just as in himself, this aim pulsated so strongly that he pursued his schemes ruthlessly and forcibly. Only, where in Rhodes one spoke of 'financial ingenuity' and 'unavoidable hardships necessitated by economic exigencies', the same methods in his own case were labelled 'dirty tricks' or the 'pettifogging sharp practices of Whitechapel'. Barnato could not help liking Rhodes. He was at least an opponent with whom the battle became an exciting game. Rhodes had made some allusions to his plans in the North. He still had to laugh when he thought of Rhodes' 'crack-pot schemes'. Was Rhodes *meshugge* that he wanted to waste his *kosher* money taming savage Natives in a country where a lion waits for you at every corner to serve for its breakfast? Without doubt, Rhodes was a bit 'dotty'. Those staring blue eyes could sometimes give you the creeps. . . .

The fight was on. Rhodes had told Barnato that he would push him out of the Kimberley Mine by acquiring the majority of Central shares. Beit was shocked at this method of letting one's opponents in on one's future plans, but Rhodes believed in playing with open cards. He explained:

'I find in life it is far better to tell the town-crier exactly what you are going to do and then you have no trouble.'

The trouble, however, soon started. Rhodes raised his arm to strike his first blow. Like a general he had planned his campaign. He was not yet able to aim at Barnato's Central, but he could harass him by curbing his further expansion. Still one independent mine, adjoining Barnato's mines, remained in the Kimberley Mine. Rhodes negotiated with the proprietor but in the last minute he was outbid by Sir Donald Currie, a wealthy shipowner, who also had the intention to amalgamate. Rhodes did not give up easily. He sent two of his friends to Cape Town to offer Currie a reasonable profit on these shares. Currie was on the point of embarking for England. 'Follow him on the same ship,' was Rhodes' order. Currie was not disinclined to accept the offer and buoyed up Rhodes' agents. When the ship stopped in Madeira, Currie received by cable from Kimberley the latest share prices, which were much higher than those offered by Rhodes. He told the agents in not too parliamentary language what he thought of Mr Rhodes' business methods. When informed of the reason for the breakdown of the negotiations Rhodes manipulated the market so as to bring these shares down to a price below his original offer. Now, he thought, old Currie would be only too glad to get rid of them at the old price. Currie, however, was informed simultaneously of Rhodes' market manœuvres. His language once again was very outspoken when he declined to have any further dealings with Rhodes.

Rhodes was beaten. He had learnt one more lesson: it was easier to pick up diamonds in Kimberley than to pick the pockets of millionaires. He consulted 'Little Beit'. He negotiated once more, secretly, with Barnato. But Barney had become even more obdurate, laughing at all offers and continually making dark allusions to a very big stock of 'beauties of diamonds' kept in reserve for the 'psychological moment'. Rhodes' nerves snapped. He shouted at Beit: 'One can never deal with obstinate people until one gets the whip-hand of them. The only thing we have to do to secure success for our industry is to get control of Kimberley Mine. . . .'

Barnato had announced his decision to introduce Central shares on the London Stock Exchange. Quick action was necessary. Rhodes had already acquired one-fifth of the issued Central shares by pledging his own De Beers shares. Now his own means were exhausted. He explained to Beit that in order to buy sufficient Central shares they would have to have at their disposal £2–3 million:

> A big undertaking! If one can only have the pluck to undertake it, one must succeed. Don't let us go to the shareholders. If we fail, they can only make us personally liable. . . . But where's the money to come from—where's the money to come from—the money to come from?

After a dramatic pause Beit turned to Rhodes and, swaying

nervously from side to side in his easy-chair, from which his crossed legs did not quite reach the ground, said:

'Oh, we'll get the money if we can only buy the shares.'

Beit had good connections with the London House of Rothschild. He discussed the matter with their representative in Kimberley, an expert mining engineer, suggesting that he would first buy the French company, thus encroaching on the Kimberley Mine. Rhodes, with freshly awakened optimism, had no doubt that the Rothschilds would jump at the plan, and took their help so much for granted that he set out for London without waiting for Rothschild's reply.

In August 1887, in high spirits, he opened the door to New Court in London City, where a simple plate indicated the premises of N. M. Rothschild & Sons, Merchants. He lost a good deal of his courage when he found that it was not as easy as he had expected to see His Lordship Nathaniel Mayer, first Baron Rothschild, even if one was Cecil J. Rhodes from Kimberley. He was received with icy politeness by one of His Lordship's managers in the drab atmosphere of dusty solidity which ruled in these dark offices where everyone whispered as if in the House of the Lord. Rhodes was told that the matter was under consideration by the House's experts. This cold shower did not unnerve him entirely. He would have to have their decision soon, no, immediately, and so he told the almost flattened Stock Exchange high priest in trembling descant:

'Sir, I'll call again in half an hour. If you are not ready with your answer then, I shall go elsewhere.'

Rhodes had nowhere else to go, of course. But his crude bluff was effective. Lord Rothschild was interested in having a look at a digger from South Africa who had dared to threaten with raised voice the House of Rothschild and had set it a time-limit. But he would have to wait until the matter had been thoroughly investigated by the experts of the firm. Rothschild regarded this business not as an investment but as a preliminary step towards amalgamation and monopoly. After a short time Rothschild asked Rhodes to visit him again in order to clear a few points and when Rhodes was at the door he heard Lord Rothschild say to his assistant:

'You may tell Mr Rhodes, that if he can buy the French Company, I think I can raise the million pounds sterling.'

Rhodes left New Court in triumph: the House of Rothschild, 'the Bankers of Kings and the Kings of Bankers', had become his ally—a 'sometimes puzzled and anxious ally', as Lord Rothschild later described the connection.

Losing no time, Rhodes made a substantial offer to the directors of the French Company to acquire all shares, which, after long bargaining, they accepted with the provision that an extraordinary meeting of shareholders should agree to it. Before the meeting was convened Barnato, as one of the principal shareholders, having learnt of Rhodes' offer, bid £300,000 more for the company. Barney Barnato would not allow himself to be pushed aside as easily as all that. 'If you are going to fight, always get in the first blow. . . .' He indicated to Rhodes that he would pay even more and intended to outbid him to the last.

For Rhodes there was more at stake than the French Company: his reputation with the Rothschilds. They were already anxiously inquiring about the delay.

Since it was Rhodes' belief that there was no one in the world with whom it was not 'as easy to deal with as to fight', there was no reason why it should not be possible with Barney Barnato. One would have to try it again, either 'on the personal' or simply by 'squaring' him.

They met once more. Barnato came well prepared. In a suitcase he had brought with him a large selection of the finest diamonds which the Central Company kept in reserve. When he saw them, Rhodes would understand what great power Barnato could wield if he were to sell them on the market cheaply. He spread them out—a collection worth well over a million pounds.

Talking like a Sunday School teacher to a sulky schoolboy, Rhodes poured forth tirades about cutting each other's throats through Barnato's obstinate interest in the French Company.

Barnato, however, could not be taken 'on the personal'. Rhodes took out his cheque-book:

'Now, Barnato, you just tell me how much it is worth for you to give up your obstruction against the French Company coming under my control. Name your figure, man!'

'No, Mr Rhodes. If I could see your scheme would be for the benefit of the shareholders in the French Company I would never have objected to it.'

'Well, if you will withdraw your opposition I will give you

Kimberley. A very early picture of the De Beers Diamond Mines

Barney Barnato

The cheque drawn by De Beers for the acquisition o the assets of the Centra Company in liquidation

De Beers Consolidated Mines, Limited.

No. 5050 Kimberley 18th July 188

The Cape of Good Hope Bank Limite

KIMBERLEY BRANCH

Pay Liquidators Kimberley Central D. Mg. Co. Ld or Order

Five millions three hundred & thirty eight thousand six hundred & fifty po

£5.338.650

Secretary.

This Cheque must be endorsed by the party to whom it is Payable

THE CAPE OF GOOD HOPE BANK, LIMITED.

a cheque to cover all that you think you lose by allowing my offer to pass.'

'No, that won't do. It would put me all right, but what about the shareholders in the French Company?'

Should one shout at him to stop that bloody nonsense of silly talk or burst out laughing in his face? Imagine that cunning little fellow all of a sudden discovering a conscience in his bosom! Rhodes, however, soon realized that Barnato was quite serious in his attitude. A break with Barnato had to be avoided. He squinted at the side-table where Barnato's numerous parcels of diamonds lay. Barnato could and would upset the whole market for years by their sale.

Rhodes made another suggestion. Seeing that Barnato was not willing to withdraw his protest against Rhodes' taking over the French Company, Rhodes was prepared to pass all his shares in that company to Barnato at the original price and would not even ask for cash but accept payment in Central shares.

Barnato, of course, saw the trap. Rhodes, however, was not the *macher* in this game but only the dummy of the Rothschilds. With the Rothschilds one would have to keep on good terms—and what was wrong with having the House of Rothschild as shareholders in one's company? Then nothing would ever go wrong—the Rothschilds are like guardian angels in time of need. The French Company in his possession would remove the last outsider from the Kimberley Mine. Now he would be able to work more economically through mechanization and produce diamonds at a cost of less than six shillings. If he wished, he might sell a carat at the price of even fifteen shillings and still make a good profit. He must mention that to Rhodes and show him his diamonds. But first let this deal be finished with. That he would not have to pay cash for the French Company suited him very well. A real godsend. He would need all his money, every single *stiver* very soon. Gold was being found in the Transvaal, he had heard. One must be prepared for such a case. All right, let Lord Rothschild come and buy some of his Central shares. He will be welcome.

Rhodes was surprised at Barnato's quick acceptance and naïvely believed that he had tricked Barnato. Barnato, on the other hand, was convinced that he had made the better bargain. In one point, however, he was mistaken: the Rothschilds were not interested in his shares and were acting merely as financing agents for Rhodes and his partners.

After the deal was signed, Barnato showed Rhodes his diamonds. 'Only a part of our reserve stock,' he said proudly and with obvious malice. Rhodes opened one parcel after the other and looked silently at the stones. With expert eyes it did not take him long to realize that these diamonds represented the acme of quality that the Fields could produce.

'Have you ever seen a bucketful of diamonds, Barney?' (The 'cunning little Jew' had suddenly become 'Barney' to him.) 'It has always been a dream of mine to see a bucketful of diamonds. . . . I'm sure that's a bucketful lying here on the table . . . certainly . . . a bucketful here on the table. . . . Shall we try, Barney? Think of it, a bucketful of diamonds. . . . One is really tempted to try. . . .'

And before Barnato realized what was happening, Rhodes had brought a bucket and quickly poured the diamonds from their tissue wrappings into the vessel, filling it almost to the brim. With flushed face, his eyes half closed in rapture, he buried his hands in the precious stones and let them glide through his fingers.

He seemed to have been completely carried away and almost started when he heard Barnato's voice:

'A good show, isn't it? Could De Beers do as much?'

'No, De Beers could never have done it.'

This time Rhodes scored over Barnato: he knew that to sort and value these stones anew would take several weeks. Only to gain time had Rhodes staged this little comedy.

Every day now counted. A battue-hunt for Central shares had been started by Rhodes. In Kimberley, London, Paris, Berlin, Vienna and Amsterdam, Beit had instructed his brokers to buy up every single Central share coming on the market, no matter at what cost. Rhodes had scraped together every single penny. Beit contributed £250,000 to the battle-fund and the Rothschilds were willing to put £2–3 million at their disposal. Now he was starting to get the whip-hand of 'that obstinate little donkey'.

Rhodes enjoyed the drive whole-heartedly. There were 176,592 Central shares of a nominal value of £10 each which constituted the original capital of Central. The shares were quoted at £14 when Rhodes began to buy. More than half of the issued capital was in the hands of Barnato and his friends. Rhodes at the beginning owned one-fifth. His stock increased from day to day though at rapidly mounting prices.

Barnato now also started to buy in order to ward off Rhodes' attack. Soon he noticed that he was buying shares secretly sold by his friends who were tempted by the dizzy offers. Rhodes observed the same thing: several of his friends thought it wiser to cash in on a quick profit before it became too late. Ever-correct Wernher, Beit's partner, who was acting as Rhodes' agent, was becoming worried about the big engagements of his firm in Central shares. When Beit one day reported the purchase of another large amount of Centrals he feared that his partner would reproach him. But Wernher reassured him: 'Oh, that's all right. I found the firm was more involved in these shares than I liked, so I have sold a lot at excellent prices.'

Barnato went on buying but when the shares reached a quotation of £40 per share, four times their original price, he was convinced that they had exceeded their true value. He now began slowly to sell himself, at the same time driving the price up to £45. If these *chochems*—these wise chaps—he thought, want to have my Kimberley Mine let them pay through the nose for the pleasure. . . . He kept quite a large number so that he would still have a say when it came to the funeral. And, besides, he had been clever enough to retain his Founders' Preference shares without which they could do nothing.

When Rhodes had more than 100,000 out of the 170,000 odd shares at his command, he thought the time had come to sound the gong, though Barnato had by no means been knocked out.

To flatter Barnato's vanity, who, he knew, suffered under his 'bubble reputation', Rhodes had invited him to the Kimberley Club. It was not easy to become a member there. Jews were generally excluded.

They retired to a private room. Everything seemed to go smoothly. Barnato had given up all resistance, and the financial side was settled to their mutual satisfaction. There was only one point, about which they could not come to an agreement. Rhodes insisted on bringing into the deed of trust of the future company, which was to amalgamate the Kimberley and De Beers companies, his 'cranky ideas' as Barnato called them. 'What has a diamond-mining company,' he asked excitedly, 'to do with . . . now listen:

"anywhere in the world construct, maintain and operate tramways, railways, roads, tunnels, canals, gasworks, electric works, etc.?" . . . and now listen: "acquire tracts of country in Africa or elsewhere . . . and expend thereon any sums deemed requisite for the maintenance and good government." . . . No, no, I'm not interested in Mr Rhodes' painting the map of Africa red with our money, the only purpose of which was and is—and for which it was entrusted to me by the shareholders—to dig for diamonds. . . .'

They went on to Dr Jameson's house, where they could speak more freely. Midnight had passed. Rhodes put his hand on Barnato's shoulder, looked him straight in the eye and said: 'Listen, Barney, I want to make a gentleman of you. I'll see—and I can guarantee you almost that I'll have you elected to Parliament for Kimberley as the representative of the Diamond Industry. I'll back you personally. . . . And I'll have you made a member of the Kimberley Club. . . .'

Barnato softened. He willingly agreed to a clause 'to guard against the adoption of any unwise policy,' that he and Rhodes as well as Beit and a representative of the Rothschilds be nominated Life Governors and Directors of the company, which was to be styled De Beers Consolidated Mines with a capital of over £2½ million. It was a profitable position, as Life Governors received 15 per cent of the profits of the company, which was to bring them each a yearly income of £300,000 to £400,000 for many years, until this royalty was abolished by a payment in De Beers' shares worth several million pounds.

In the morning, after fifteen hours' discussion, Barnato declared:

'Well, Rhodes, some people have a fancy to one thing, some to another. You want the means to go North, if possible, and I suppose we must give them to you.'

When Barnato came home, exhausted, he sat up with his nephew Joel to review the events of the previous hours. As if to render account to himself, he said almost in a whisper:

'There is no other man who lives in the world who could have induced me to have gone in with him in the amalgamation; but Rhodes has an extraordinary ascendancy over men, and he gets men to do almost anything he likes. No one would believe it at first, but he roped me in as he ropes in everyone else. Of course,

I don't mean to say I did not make good terms with him, but I had always been so much opposed to the amalgamation that I was surprised myself at being able to come to terms at all. But that's Rhodes' way. Somehow or other you find it impossible to stand out against him, and so you come in with him and find it to your profit to do so. You can't resist him: you must be with him!'

Difficulties arose when some minority shareholders of Central objected to the amalgamation on the grounds that De Beers had in its deed of trust so many strange propositions that did not correspond with the tasks of a mining company. The case was fought out at the Supreme Court. In a judgment against amalgamation it was declared of the new company that it 'can do anything and everything and since the time of the East India Company no company had had such power as this. . . .'

Rhodes in consequence had to place the Central Company in liquidation and acquire its assets. It was a loss merely of time and concerned only a small minority of shareholders. Upon amalgamation the owners of Central who agreed had received for one of their £10 Central shares two £5 De Beers shares plus £2 10*s.* in cash. De Beers shares at that time had reached a maximum price of £49 after they had changed hands at only £15 four months before.

Rhodes had predicted on the day of amalgamation that the price would soon go down:

'And tonight they'll talk it all over with their wives and tomorrow they'll all sell like hell.' And in fact, the following week the shares were down to £38.

One of the shareholders buttonholed Rhodes with the words: 'I hear, Mr Rhodes, you have settled Central on the basis of two De Beers shares for one Central. May God forgive you, Mr Rhodes, but I never can.'

The Kimberley Central shares had cost De Beers more than £3 million to acquire. For the poorer mines, formerly described by Rhodes as 'those mines that are too rich to leave and too poor to pay, which were once to me what I might call spectres of the night', he had to pay more than £2 million before he had full control over the entire Kimberley diamond industry and 90 per cent of the world's diamond production.

In order to control the sale of diamonds Rhodes, with some of the biggest diamond merchants, had founded the Diamond Syndicate in London. The first contract for five years amounted to £25 million. When negotiations became difficult over a difference concerning £5,000, Rhodes cabled: 'I thought I was dealing with diamond merchants, not retail grocers.'

The price of diamonds, after amalgamation, went up to thirty shillings per carat. De Beers had to watch that supply and demand should balance. In the De Beers office a wooden box measuring two feet by nine inches was kept in a heavy safe. As soon as this box was filled production was stopped immediately. The little wooden box yielded the shareholders a yearly dividend of at least £2 million and up to £4 million.

Rhodes' financial position improved proportionately. From De Beers alone he received in dividends and fees an annual income of £300,000, later mounting to half a million. With the various share dealings and the foundation of the new company, and the Diamond Syndicate, he had made a large fortune. Counting the shares in his possession alone, he was worth several million pounds.

Neither the Board of Directors nor the auditors and his colleagues could prevent Rhodes from considering himself lord and master over De Beers. Board meetings were to him nothing but a nuisance of a formality. He would always arrive late, glance at the agenda and in a few sentences give his opinion, ending with these words addressed to the secretary: 'I think we are all agreed about that. . . .' And so he would hurry through point after point until at the end of the last item he would jump up from his chair and, already at the door, would murmur: 'That's all for this morning, I think. Good morning, gentlemen.' Before anyone could open his mouth, he was out of the room.

After amalgamation Rhodes introduced the compound system in order to break I.D.B., the only leak in his otherwise watertight monopoly. The Natives, employed on the 'floors', where the dried diamondiferous soil was washed, carried away, undetected by even the most careful supervision, more diamonds than they left behind. Rhodes considered it better to buy these diamonds at a low price from the Natives than to let them fall into the claws of the I.D.B. vultures. Thus De Beers was buying through agents the bulk of their own diamonds from their own Natives.

The white workmen, though well paid, soon became dissatisfied with the changed conditions after amalgamation. After most of the smaller mines had closed and mechanization had replaced a great number of hands, it became more difficult to find work and employers were less easily amenable to their demands. Demonstrations, instigated by a kind of trade union, the 'Knights of Labour', at which several window-panes were smashed, were directed against Rhodes. They blamed for the loss of their jobs and their present misery 'the existence and domination of one greed, Monopoly, one giant Corporation, as well as the overweening greed and ambition of one wealthy, overestimated, disappointed politician'.

Among many employees as well as among the inhabitants of Kimberley a deep hatred was fermenting against Rhodes. The dissatisfaction was aggravated by a feeling of being constantly watched in their jobs as well as in their private lives by De Beers' secret agents. These agents had not only to prevent I.D.B. but also to report on the political activities of the staff.

Very often Rhodes was blamed for measures against the workmen of De Beers of which he did not even know. He had given instructions to the managers to exercise the greatest economy. Once a deputation of miners complained about a reduction in their wages. Among them were many men whom Rhodes had known in his earliest Kimberley days. He told them that they would in future be paid at the old rate and that their reduction would be refunded to them. Rhodes was furious. He stormed into the board-room where the managers were just assembled. Without a word of greeting he shouted:

'If we are going to cut, begin at the top. I'm paying you people a thousand a year, and for what? Cut by all means, but begin at the top . . . and begin now. And my picture is hanging on the wall of this room gazing down on you bastards. . . . Give me a knife . . . give me a knife. . . .'

And, in a towering rage, Rhodes cut the painting to pieces.

CHAPTER VIII

THE FAT OF THE LAND

TOWARDS the middle of 1886 gold was found in the district of the Witwatersrand, the Ridge of the White Waters, thirty miles from the Transvaal capital, Pretoria. An exodus took place from Kimberley.

Scenes of the early Kimberley days were repeated. A town of tents, tin-shanties and wooden boxes grew up overnight. It was called Johannesburg.

It immediately became obvious, however, that mining gold on the Rand confronted diggers with a proposition different from early conditions in Kimberley. For dealing with the hard rock of the Rand a miner had to know something about blasting and had to have a crushing plant and stamp batteries. Gold-mining demanded considerable financial resources.

The Kimberley magnates at first found that they would have to finance this new venture on the Rand by themselves. London City bankers and speculators considered all gold finds with the utmost suspicion. *The Times* opened its columns to warnings that '*bona fide* investors should be very cautious . . . as fully 75 per cent of the properties . . . may be accurately described as "bubbles"'.

Among the first who had received information about the gold finds was J. B. Robinson. Unfortunately he happened at the moment to be 'stony-broke' and, much to his disgust, had to ask Alfred Beit for financial assistance for partnership in the new venture. Out of loyalty Beit offered Rhodes half his share. Rhodes showed no interest. Only after long persuasion did he agree to send one of his friends, Hans Sauer, a young medical practitioner, to the Rand. Sauer, like many other doctors in South Africa, knew something about geology.

Dr Sauer went to the Rand in the same coach as Robinson. Robinson assured the doctor that he was on his way to Pretoria to buy wool. Dr Sauer retaliated by telling him that he was on his way to spend a holiday with an aunt.

The young doctor carried in his pocket-book a cheque from

Rhodes for £200. This trifling amount, reluctantly handed over, turned out to be the best investment Rhodes ever made. Sauer secured options on several farms situated on the most promising side of the suspected run of the Reef.

Upon Sauer's return to Kimberley his impassioned report was received with little enthusiasm by Rhodes. Rhodes reproached him for the 'extravagance of having wasted twenty to thirty pounds on some options' and refused to refund him for the outlay. Beit's offer to enter into partnership with him and Robinson, Rhodes refused point-blank. Anything connected with the 'Buccaneer' he would not touch.

Beit's vivid interest and activities on the gold-fields alarmed him. He told Rudd: 'It will never do to let Beit forget that his diamond interests are calling him. If Beit becomes too deeply involved in this gold business I may risk losing his support, which I absolutely need, for the fulfilment of my dreams in the North and the acquisition of the political power that I must have behind me when the moment arrives. . . .'

Being in the middle of his battle of amalgamation, Rhodes resisted with might and main being dragged into a new venture. Kimberley and its diamonds had become part of himself. De Beers was his creation. He was attached to it like a mother to her child whose birth had almost killed her. Gold, in contrast, had no meaning for Rhodes. Each diamond possessed a life in itself, an individuality, a personal destiny. Gold—cold metal—could not inspire his imagination.

In these days Rhodes stood for hours staring at his old crumpled map of Africa, now almost faded in the piercing African sun. He did dream of gold but of Africa's real source of gold, the Gold of Ophir, the Queen of Sheba's gold-mines. He was convinced that the reef on the Rand was only a branch of a lode, an offshoot of the true goldfields in Mashonaland and Matabeleland.

That these gold-fields of the Rand should be situated in the Transvaal, in Paul Kruger's domain, only thirty miles from the old President's residence, vexed Rhodes considerably. Overnight, the Transvaal had been reborn as an important factor in South Africa. Should he, Rhodes, invest money and become dependent on *Meneer* Kruger and his Boers' goodwill?

Only reluctantly, and after two days' persuasion, did Rhodes set out for Johannesburg together with Dr Sauer and Rudd. His humour did not improve when he saw that Beit, Robinson, Barnato, and many others who had made money in Kimberley, had invested large amounts in buying claims or whole farms all round the new township.

Rhodes became still more sceptical when Gardner Williams, the able and shrewd expert whom the Rothschilds had charged with the investigations, told him: 'If I rode over these reefs in the States, I would not get off my horse to look at them.'

Sauer had procured for the sum of £250 an option on a large portion of the main reef which would have made him the biggest and richest gold-producer in the world. Rhodes hesitated. To buy this rocky land would mean a speculation which might, perhaps, endanger the fulfilment of his plans in the North.

Rhodes was in a bad mood. He was tired from the uncomfortable ride in the express coach. He looked at the grey rock, stroking his chin nervously with his right forefinger. His eyes roamed slowly over the hills. As if speaking to himself, he told Dr Sauer:

'It is all very well; but I cannot see or calculate the power in these claims. . . . When I am in Kimberley and have nothing much to do, I often go and sit on the edge of De Beers mine, and I look at the blue diamondiferous ground . . . and I reckon up the value of diamonds in the blue and the power conferred by them. In fact, every foot of blue ground means so much power. This I cannot do with these gold-reefs.'

Therein lay the contrast between the aims, mentality and purpose of Rhodes and those of all the other fortune-hunters engaged in disembowelling the African soil. They all desired only to make money to satisfy their greed. Money to them meant an elevated social position, luxury, escape from a cloudy past, a confirmation to themselves and to the outside world of their superiority. Rhodes did not aspire to any of these primitive ambitions. Such desires were marketable commodities within easy reach of any money-bag. He wanted to turn his money into power; power over entire countries and their inhabitants; power over the destiny of masses; to be a supreme law unto himself and to others . . . to be like the great Roman emperors who set out as simple generals to conquer new lands and came back a Caesar, a God. . . . Money had first to be condensed into power before it was of use to Cecil Rhodes. And for this purpose money had to flow in without the fear of outside interference. To dig for gold would mean to fight.

Before he was able to come to a definite decision, a telegram brought him news of a crisis in the illness of his young friend and secretary Neville Pickering who had been bed-ridden for some time. Pickering had been Rhodes' constant companion and on whom he had bestowed more confidences than on anyone else.

Rhodes' face turned grey when he read the message. He interrupted a discussion about the various options procured through Sauer:

'I am off with tonight's coach. Pickering is dying.'

'What about the options?' Sauer intervened. 'You cannot go now. You must wait.'

'I must go to my friend. Get me a seat quickly.'

There were no seats left. After a generous tip a small space was made for him on top of the coach, amid the mail-bags and the passengers' luggage. Only by holding tightly to the rope strung across could Rhodes get through the 300-mile trip, which, with short stops, lasted for more than fifteen hours. He came only just in time for his young friend to expire in his arms and to hear his last whispered words:

'Thank you, Mr Rhodes. You were everything to me—father, mother, brother, sister and friend.... Thank you, Mr Rhodes!...'

At the funeral Rhodes appeared in his usual outfit of crumpled stained flannel trousers, Norfolk jacket and grey slouch hat. He was observed to hide his tears behind a large handkerchief.

Rhodes now took quarters in Dr Jameson's house. Coming home from the cemetery he collapsed into a chair. He raised the glass proffered to him and said to Jameson:

'Well, I must go on with my work. After all, a thing like this is only a big detail . . . only a big detail . . . a big detail.'

Telegram after telegram arrived from Sauer in Johannesburg frantically asking Rhodes to return or at least to wire his decision as most of the best options had already expired. Rhodes did not answer. Only after the negotiations with Barnato had been brought to a successful end was he disposed to look again at the possibilities on the Rand. His resources were all firmly invested in his diamond venture. Rudd was thus sent to London to find financial backing. Lately English investors had been pricking up their ears whenever they heard of new gold shares to which they might subscribe. The mania of 'entering on the ground floor' was once again being exploited by unscrupulous financiers.

All the money needed by South Africa to build up her gold industry was at her disposal. Thousands streamed to the Rand, the pockets of many well padded with big capital, while others carried only letters of recommendation. Even big banks and private bankers in England, France and Germany, were now sending out envoys to Johannesburg. Official and unofficial observers of governments sneaked around the Rand and tried to build up contacts with the Transvaal Government in Pretoria.

Rhodes was no longer able to resist the magnetic attraction of money-making on the Rand. His optimism had been restored by the new connection with the Rothschilds, though his finances still remained precarious, with all his worldly possessions set on diamond amalgamation. Since others had found it so easy to have their more or less honest prospects financed from the pockets of grasping, maddened gamblers, Rudd was to raise the necessary capital in London. Rhodes paid his second visit to the Rand from where he wrote to his partner in London:

> The opinion is steadily growing that the Rand is the biggest thing the world has seen, owing to its wonderful climate, its facilities for work and its enormous auriferous deposits; it has plenty of good things awaiting hard work and development.

First he tried to amalgamate the existing important claims. No one, however, had need of Rhodes. Gold, unlike diamonds, was not a speculative commodity. The price of gold was almost rigid, and there was no danger of under-selling. All the big producers were already linked with international financial institutions or private financiers so that fresh funds for expansion were always easily found.

His pockets empty and his credit exhausted to the last penny, Rhodes, with the genius of a 'superb adventurer', as a colleague later described him, founded in the most grandiose style a new company, The Gold Fields of South Africa, later called The Amalgamated Gold Fields of South Africa. The modest capital of £125,000 Rudd procured in London. Within a short time the capital was raised to well over £1 million.

Rhodes on his second visit started to buy land. He made his

purchases mostly on the West Rand and went farther afield than any other speculators had done.

The farmers had now learnt to ask high prices. At the sale of one property, the farmer, after the price had been fixed, came with several flower-pots of miserable geraniums. The man insisted that they were the property of his *vrou* and would have to be paid for separately. Rhodes had to pay several thousand pounds—'the most expensive flowers in the world, worth a place in Kew Gardens'.

A few thousand pounds more, what did it matter and who cared! The mugs of shareholders would have to pay for it! Each of the newly-acquired properties was formed into a separate company. Having thus financed the purchase of several large gold-bearing properties, or at least where optimistically he thought gold ought to be found—an assumption later proved in many cases to have been fallacious—Rhodes now topped his financial ingenuity. After the model of De Beers, he converted Amalgamated Gold Fields into a 'holding company' which bought the shares of all his other gold holdings. Again, as in Kimberley, Rhodes and Rudd received founders' shares reserving for themselves one-third of all profits. His gold-fields, by acquiring from time to time share majorities in other companies, soon ranked second among the Big Ten of the Rand.

The court's objections to the deed of trust of De Beers on the grounds that the company could 'do anything and everything . . .' were even more tenable in the case of Rhodes' Goldfields Company. Here he alone was master and no Lord Rothschild could raise a warning hand and quote to him some paragraphs from the Company Laws.

The formation of two such formidable corporations had made Rhodes a rich man, whose exact fortune it was already difficult to gauge because of the many holdings in his various companies and their subsidiaries. His income of several hundred thousand pounds, of which he did not use more than £3,000 a year, increased from year to year.

Rhodes considered this fortunate turn in his affairs as a natural step towards his final aim, and regarded all the money which flowed into his hands as the necessary ammunition for conquering the North. There was only one obstacle in his way: Paul Kruger, the President of the South African Republic.

Kruger was extremely alarmed about the influx into his territory of foreigners in such large numbers. These Uitlanders could easily endanger the whole structure of the thinly populated republic whose white population of not more than 12,000 voters would soon be exceeded by the increasing number of *rooineks*—'red necks'—the name given to foreigners, not yet acclimatized to the South African sun. To him it meant more than the political consequences: he feared the moral infection of his burghers through the infiltration of foreign elements. Johannesburg in the third year of its existence already had a population of over 10,000.

In his predicament Kruger asked President Brand of the Orange Free State for advice, who told him: 'Make friends with your Uitlanders!' As far as the needs of the gold-mining industry were concerned, the Transvaal Government granted all possible facilities. *The Times* in 1888, in a dispatch from its Johannesburg correspondent, spoke of 'President Kruger's remarkable common sense and whose dealings with the crowd of newcomers to the gold-fields are both wise and liberal'. Another article, from a different source, said that the English on the Rand would rather live under the Transvaal authority, in spite of rising taxes, than under the restored rule of the British Crown, remembering with bitterness the 'faithless desertion by Gladsone in 1881'.

The mine-owners, however, continued to grumble and were always bringing forward new demands. Kruger suspected, and his suspicions were well founded, that Rhodes stood behind these malcontents. He had not forgotten the humiliation he had suffered at the conference at Fourteen Streams. He grew alarmed when Rhodes suddenly came to him and asked him about an extension of the Cape Railways to the Transvaal and a rail link between the Rand and Delagoa Bay. Kruger feared a new device for throttling the Transvaal's freedom of movement. He also warned everyone in his capital against the serious consequences of selling property to Rhodes, whose agents, authorized to invest more than £100,000 for this purpose, were trying their best to buy land and house property in Pretoria. No one dared to transgress the President's warning.

Kruger had acceded to the demands of the mining industry as much as he could but refused categorically to consider their political grievances, particularly their claims to a franchise for which a few had asked. At a banquet in Johannesburg he said with his eyes on Rhodes:

> . . . Wealth cannot break laws. Though a man has a million pounds he cannot alter the law. . . . Is it a good man who wants to be master of the country, when others have been suffering for twenty years to conduct its affairs? . . . It is the unthankful people to whom I have given protection who are always dissatisfied, and, what is more, they actually want me to alter my laws to suit them. . . .

Rhodes understood that this warning was directed against him. He made a scornful and tactless reply in the Cape Parliament. Speaking about the extension of railways, he said:

> . . . We can extend fifty miles to the Vaal River, but by doing so at present we shall probably excite the animosity of an individual, for one of the most extraordinary things in that republican state is the extraordinary influence of that one man—I refer to Paul Kruger. I say it with all respect, that man is the dictator of the Transvaal. . . . I regard him as one of the most remarkable men in South Africa, who has been singularly unfortunate. When I remember that Paul Kruger had not a sixpence in his Treasury when his object was to extend his country over the whole Northern interior, when I see him sitting in Pretoria with Bechuanaland gone, and other lands around him gone from his grasp . . . I pity the man. When I see a man starting and continuing with one object and utterly failing in that object, I cannot help pitying him.

Kruger sat on his *stoep* in the early morning, listening with closed eyes while his secretary read to him the translation of this speech. He took the heavy vellum-bound Bible from the table and thumbed through its pages until he came to Psalm 3, which he read aloud:

> Lord, how are they increased that trouble me!
> many are they that rise up against me. . . .

When he had finished, he leaned over the book and for many a minute he did not speak. His inflamed wise little eyes looked over the emptiness of the square in front of his house, and he thought he saw the land, the heavy obstinate holy soil of the Transvaal, the beloved land which his father, his brothers and he himself had conquered step by step under tortuous privations and sacrifices; the blessed fertile soil which had to be defended continually against the ragings of the elements; the blissful soil sanctified by the blood of his brethren. . . .

Without changing his position he said to his secretary: '*Ons Voortrekkers het die land skoongemaak; ons is geregtig tot die vet van die land. . . .*' ('Our pioneers cleared the land; we are entitled to the fat of the land.') And falling again into silent meditation he finally stretched his enormous torso to its full length. Tears ran down his cheeks as he spoke with thunderous voice as if addressing the entire assembled nation. The truth of his wise words of prophecy were soon to become evident to the whole world and to show the tragedy of a great, simple man and his heroic freedom-loving people:

> Do not talk to me of gold, the element which brings more dissension, misfortune and unexpected plagues in its trail than benefits. Pray to God, as I am doing, that the curse connected with its coming may not overshadow our dear land just after it has come again to us and our children; pray and implore Him who has stood by us, that He will continue to do so, for I tell you today that *every ounce of gold taken from the bowels of our soil will yet have to be weighed up with rivers of tears, with the life-blood of thousands of our best people in the defence of that same soil from the lust of others yearning for it solely because it has the yellow metal in abundance. . . .*

PART II

CHAPTER IX

KING OF THE MATABELE

'WA *duba, wa duba sebele!*—they give me trouble; they truly give me trouble.' The words come from the depth of a burdened heart. The King closes his eyes. The King's counsellors, the *indunas*, all elderly men, nod their heads in confirmation.

From the back of the assembly the King's official praisers strike up their song of adulation: '*ye*, *hay*, *hay*, oh Lobengula, King of the Matabele and Master of the Mashona, Son of Umziligazi, the Drinker of Blood, child of the Great House of Kumalo, the House of Dingaan, King of the Zulus, Calf of a Black Cow, Man Eater, Lion, thou art as great as the world. . . .'

'*Hamba guhle*—depart in peace,' said the King, and he dismissed the crowd around him.

'*Sala guhle, kumalo*—stay in peace, oh King! *Bayete, bayete*—salute to the King!'

Only three old men, his chief counsellors, Lotje, Babyaan and Umsheti, remained. They shook their heads. Was it possible, as the King had told them, that these big white chiefs were waiting in the kraal for many moons to obtain the King's permission to dig for gold in his lands?

'*Mai babo, yo, yo gho*—Mother of Angels, listen to this madness!' cried the eldest of the three counsellors as he helped his master from his usual seat for state occasions—the coachman's box of a big wagon, a present from one of the traders.

The King slept inside this wagon although he owned several large huts and a roomy red-brick house. In one of his huts there hung a large oleograph in a fly-spotted gilt ornamental frame, showing the Great White Queen bedecked with pearls, diamonds and orders and with the royal crown on her head. In one corner stood two large battered rusty biscuit-tins, loosely covered by their lids. 'Those silly glass-pebbles' with which the tins were filled to the brim were often brought to the women's kraal for the children to play with. Every Matabele whom the

King allowed to go and work in the Big Hole of the white men had to bring him back a big diamond stone on his return. No white man ever saw this treasure, but it is estimated that the King must have owned diamonds worth more than £5 million.

It took some time until the King had descended from the wagon-box to the ground. His enormous weight of almost 300 pounds was less evident when he stood upright. His height of six feet four inches and his erect carriage made the enormity of his figure appear proportionate. Upon this heavy, gigantic body, which was naked except for a short breech-cloth of blue monkey-skin, rested a finely modelled head with the features of a remarkable man, whose eyes indicated a vivid intelligence, iron energy and a forceful character.

Lobengula was a monarch in every respect. Even his white adversaries, missionaries, unsuccessful concession-hunters, disappointed speculators or hunters and traders whom he had refused to 'give the road' through his country, admitted it.

Lobengula had been made king against his own will. When his father died, the eldest son who had been brought up by missionaries in Natal was unwilling to return to become king. He feared for his life because the majority of the Matabele objected to him as their ruler: 'Why bring him back? Will a baboon reared in the domesticity of the white man ever be rid of the smell of the white man?' They clamoured for Lobengula who vehemently refused to reign. He would have preferred to rear cattle, a love which remained with him to the end. As king he spent much of his time supervising his stock. Lobengula was probably the greatest cattle-owner of his time. For his stock which was calculated to amount to 500,000 beasts he used his whole country as grazing ground. He would rather have remained with his cattle than be disturbed by the heavy royal duties. He foresaw the difficulties awaiting him among his own people and he also knew that the White Man was pushing farther north. He felt that the time was near when the Matabele would have to defend their country against a white invasion.

His father already had had to learn that the Transvaal Boers had cast their eyes on the fat pastures of Matabeleland. He had been a general in the Zulu King Chaka's army. Chaka, jealous of Umziligazi's victories and popularity among the troops, had quarrelled with him and Umziligazi had left Zululand together with his warriors. His aim had been to settle peacefully in the Marico valley after he had beaten all opposition of local tribes along his way. The Boers came and drove him farther north until, in 1838, he settled between the Limpopo and the Zambezi. Umziligazi and his warriors had had to beat their way yard by yard until they reached the airy plateau of Matabeleland with its endless green cattle-thronged stretches of land, blessed with a rich virgin soil, many streams and good rains. Before the Matabele had been able to settle, the neighbouring tribes, the Mashonas, Malakas and Maholi, had to be taught 'to get up and let them sit down'. The Barotse too had to learn that just as the House of Kumalo was the indisputable ruler of Zululand, so its branch under Umziligazi was determined to become and to remain the dominant power between the Limpopo and the Zambezi. The annual raids into the neighbouring districts served as a reminder of this resolution to the tribes around them. Though the Matabele had established themselves as what in European diplomatic language would have been styled the 'paramount power' among the Native states north of the Limpopo, Lobengula feared clashes with the Boers. His father had hoped that after the Matabele had retreated beyond the Limpopo they would be allowed to remain in the new country in peace. He therefore in 1853 gladly concluded a treaty of friendship with the Transvaal. Lobengula, with an instinctive political sense, surmised that the land-hungry Boers would sooner or later, in spite of the still-existing treaty, seize Mashonaland which, though not incorporated in their country, belonged to the Matabele as a conquered and occupied territory. Another grave cause for anxiety was the discovery of gold in the rocks of his country.

Already in his father's time Matabeleland had attracted many white men who crawled in the royal kraal 'like locusts'. In the first years of his rule Lobengula categorically refused permission to many white people to prospect for gold in his territories. Only in 1876, upon the recommendation of the missionary Robert Moffat—the only faithful friend the Matabele nation ever had among all the many white men with whom they came into contact, a man of sterling qualities, a true Christian, a real friend of Umziligazi's for 23 years—did Lobengula grant a concession to one Tom Baines, an explorer and artist who had accompanied

Livingstone at the time of his discovery of the Victoria Falls. In this document Lobengula took the greatest care to safeguard his sovereign rights:

> In making this grant I, Lobengula, do not alienate from my kingdom this or any other portion of it; but reserve intact the sovereignty of my dominion. . . .

Lobengula declined to name an amount to be paid for the rights granted but left it to the judgment of Mr Baines, 'the good white man, to make me annually . . . such present as might seem proper to him and acceptable to me'.

The concession was never used.

All Lobengula's fears turned to fact and much worse and much sooner even than he had expected. It had started in 1882 when the Transvaal Boers, prompted by President Kruger's prophetic forebodings of a coming British push north, tried unsuccessfully to persuade Lobengula to enter into a new treaty with them. At his instigation P. J. Joubert, his Commandant-General, wrote to Lobengula warning him of the danger to his country from Britain, thus trying to entice him into renewing the treaty of thirty-two years before. This letter was a masterpiece of psychological understanding of the primitive yet shrewd political mentality of a Native ruler:

> . . . Now, you must have heard that the English . . . took away our country, the Transvaal, or as they say, annexed it. We then talked nicely for four years and begged for our country. But no; when an Englishman once has your property in his hand, then he is like a monkey that has its hands full of pumpkin seeds—if you don't beat him to death, he will never let go. . . . Now they are gone, and our country is free, and we will now once more live in friendship with Lobengula, as we lived in friendship with Umziligazi, and such must be our friendship, that so long as there is one Boer and one Matabele living these two must remain friends. . . .

And at the end there came an indirect warning against any raids which Lobengula might be planning against the Transvaal, referring to what happened to another Native chief who tried to fight the Boers and had to pay a fine of 5,000 cattle and 4,000 sheep and goats 'for his wickedness'. Lobengula assured the Boers of a renewal of their old friendship and told them that if hunters wanted to kill elephants or any Boer wished to graze his cattle for a short time on his pastures, they should ask him for permission and he would 'give them the road'. But never, never, would he allow a Boer to enter his country accompanied by a woman or permit anyone to build a hut there.

Three years later Lobengula was again keeping a wary eye on the Boers for Kruger had now cast his eyes, as Lobengula had predicted, on Mashonaland, and was plotting with the Germans and Portuguese to 'eat up' his territory.

The climax to all his fears came when he heard that an *impi* of the Great White Queen consisting of many thousands of her men, led by one of her great *indunas*, General Warren, and under the guidance of her counsellor, the 'Man who made the Big Hole at Kimberley', had subdued the Bechuanas and was standing on the borders of Matabeleland. When would the time come for his country to be eaten up by the Great White Queen whose insatiable greed had already devoured the land of the Zulus—the home of his noble ancestors—and of the Swazis, the Griquas, the Xosas, the Basutos and the Tongas. . . ?

Lobengula's fears were well founded. From Bechuanaland General Warren had sent emissaries into Matabeleland who reported about the great wealth and trade possibilities offered by this commercially virginal country. When this report was published in *The Times*, City merchants pricked up their ears.

Lobengula's information about a conspiracy between the Boers, the Germans and the Portuguese to gain a footing in his territories also proved to be true. Warren, in his dispatch to Whitehall, enclosed a communication from his agent in Bechuanaland, dated May 1885.

> The Boers are determined to get a footing in Mashonaland . . . by thus taking the Matabele on the flank, and gradually acquiring their territory by conquest, thence overspreading all the independent tribes to the west and south of here. I have also good proof that the Germans and Portuguese are working quietly but slowly to acquire as much of these lands and the Transvaal under their protection as occasion will allow of, and believe that they, as well as the Boers and other nations, are only waiting to hear what action the British Government will take to settle on their own.

News of these Northern ambitions of the Boers had not come as a surprise to London's Colonial Office. At the conference preceding the London Convention of 1884 Paul Kruger had made no secret of the fact that the Transvaal would now be forced to look to the North for expansion, and no objection had been raised from the British side.

Lobengula, realizing his impotence in the face of aggression, had to sit and wait for further developments for two years, expecting any day that his and his nation's last hour was about to strike.

From visiting missionaries, hunters and traders he learnt of the happenings in southern Africa and was able to gain a fairly accurate picture of the African political scene.

The defeat of the British army at Majuba at the hands of the Boers and the long and brave resistance of the Zulus against the British led Lobengula to believe that the Great White Queen was perhaps after all not so powerful as the missionaries had always led him to believe. Under this delusion, and principally to safeguard himself from an attack by the Transvaal in the rear, he thought that a consolidation of friendship with the Boers would avert the catastrophe looming over his country.

President Kruger was enthusiastic and without losing time drafted a treaty which would make Lobengula an ally of the Transvaal and would oblige him, if requested, to put his *impis* under the command of the Boers. It also made provision for a Transvaal official to be permanently stationed at the royal kraal as consul with extra-territorial rights.

As the first occupant of this post President Kruger immediately dispatched to Bulawayo to obtain Lobengula's signature to the treaty one of his confidantes, Pieter Grobler.

If ever Kruger's treaty was translated to Lobengula it must have been in such a way as to make him believe that it contained nothing more than a confirmation of the old treaty of friendship which he himself had renewed in 1882. Had he known the real and far-reaching obligations to which this document committed him, he would never have put his great elephant-seal to it.

It was said at the time that if President Kruger sneezed in Pretoria, Cecil Rhodes heard it in his office in Kimberley. Rhodes very soon knew about the negotiations with Lobengula: Kruger was entering the North by a back door! It would have to be prevented at all costs. And when Rhodes said 'all' that was just what he meant.

'You must do something!' he implored Sir Hercules Robinson, without yet knowing what it was that he wanted to be done.

Sir Hercules had received strict instructions from Whitehall not to involve Her Majesty's Government in any new African adventures or experiments. The trouble and money squandered on waging war in the Transvaal, in Bechuanaland, in Zululand and on other smaller expeditions had for the time being cured both parties in Parliament of colonial imperialism. No cabinet, whether sailing under the Tory or the Whig flag, would risk exposing itself to a censure of its colonial policy. British intervention in Matabeleland was thus out of the question. The Transvaal, as Robinson pointed out, had so far acted perfectly within the frame of the London Convention according to which she was at liberty to conclude treaties with Native tribes in the North without having to ask Britain's consent.

Sir Hercules declared that all he could do to help Rhodes in shutting out the Boers from the North was to block their last remaining entry into Matabeland. The boundary between Bechuanaland and the Transvaal had not yet been fixed. The High Commissioner could declare that part of Bechuanaland through which ran the direct road from Pretoria to Bulawayo as 'exclusively within the sphere of British influence'. This small geographical correction would complete the lock-out of the Transvaal from the North. But Rhodes did not consider this sufficient since it left the possibility of an alliance between Lobengula and Germany or Portugal.

Sir Hercules had become more cautious since Lord Salisbury had replaced Gladstone as tenant of No. 10 Downing Street. He told Rhodes:

'To have secured Bechuanaland, well, I think that's enough.'

Rhodes gave Robinson a glassy look, then took him by the arm and led him to the window.

'Do come with me and look at the blockhouse at Table Mountain,' he spluttered excitedly in his high-pitched voice. 'Those good old people, 200 years ago, thought that blockhouse at Table Mountain was the limit of their ideas, but now let us face it today. Where are we? We are considerably beyond the Vaal River, and supposing that those good people were to come to life again today, what would they think of it and their blockhouse? . . . Sir, will you consider, during the period you have been the representative of Her Majesty in this colony, what have you done? We are now on latitude 22°.'

'And what a trouble it has been! But where will you stop?'

'I will stop where the country has not been claimed.'

'Let us look at the map.'

Rhodes, with trembling finger, pointed at the southern border of Tanganyika. Before Sir Hercules could express his disapproval Rhodes cut in:

'The Great Powers at home mark the map but do nothing to add to it. . . . Let *us* try to mark the map, and we know that we shall do something.'

'Well, I think, you should be satisfied with the Zambezi as a boundary.'

'Let us take a piece of note-paper, and let us measure from the blockhouse to the Vaal River; that is the individual effort of the people. Now let us measure what you have done in your temporary existence, and then we shall finish by measuring up my imaginations.'

'I shall leave you alone! No one can resist you.'

Sir Hercules' only stipulation referred to any expenses arising from a treaty with Lobengula, which would have to be borne by Rhodes.

In many offices of the colonial administration in South Africa key positions were in the hands of intimate friends of Rhodes' from his Oxford days. The most useful of them at that moment was his friend Sir Sidney Shippard, the Administrator of the new Crown Colony of Bechuanaland. He would have to deal officially with matters concerning Matabeleland. Another of his Oxford pals was Captain Francis Newton, who held the important position of Private Secretary to the Governor and High Commissioner. In Pretoria, as Her Majesty's Agent accredited to the South African Republic, another Oxford friend, Ralph Williams, kept him well posted about everything going on there. With Captain Graham Bower, the Imperial Secretary and Sir Hercules' right hand, he was on the best of terms since they had combined in intriguing against General Warren during the Bechuanaland affair. And Sir Hercules Robinson was a shareholder in De Beers!

For the negotiations with Lobengula, Rhodes hit on the idea

of winning over the Reverend J. S. Moffat, son of the friend of the Matabele, the famous missionary Robert Moffat. Moffat had grown up in Matabeleland and since his boyhood 'Joni' had been Lobengula's friend. The king was very fond of 'Joni' and looked upon him as one of his own.

Sir Sidney Shippard agreed with Rhodes' suggestion to entrust Moffat with the negotiations with Lobengula so as to counteract Kruger's clever ruse of planting a consul at Bulawayo. Shippard suggested that the reverend gentleman stay there in a permanent capacity as Her Majesty's Deputy Commissioner. From a humble servant of the Lord, preaching the gospel of brotherly love to the heathen, Moffat thus underwent a metamorphosis and turned into a civil servant of Her Majesty the Queen, with orders to bring to an unsuspecting black-skinned ruler the blessings of European civilization. One cannot help doubting whether the ex-reverend gentleman informed his black royal friend about his professional change when he came to see him. His first task, that of nullifying the Grobler Treaty by convincing Lobengula that he had been deceived by the Boers, met with no great difficulties. But after that experience of the falsehood of the white man it was small wonder that Lobengula refused point-blank to sign any other treaty.

For many days Moffat talked, as Lobengula called it, 'like a hungry dog barking at the meat on a high table'. After one such long *indaba*, doubts about 'Joni's' honesty began to rise in Lobengula's mind.

He ended their discussion with the proverb:

'*Akuqili lazikhoth' emblana*—there is no clever person who ever licked himself on the back.'

With his knowledge of Zulu, Moffat understood the meaning: if a cunning fellow attempted too much he would in the end be found out when trying the impossible.

Moffat could not return with empty hands. His official reputation, his future, was at stake. He again went to see the king and told him that politeness between monarchs on being offered a treaty required at least an answer by letter and that the king should have one written to the Great White Queen, stating his reasons for the refusal of her offer. When, on the next day, 11 Feburary 1888, Lobengula fixed his great elephant-seal to a sheet of paper brought to him by Moffat, he was firmly convinced that he was signing a letter merely expressing his regrets that he was unable to enter into a treaty with the Queen's Government.

The document, brought proudly back to Cape Town by the ex-missionary, enchanted his masters beyond all expectations. It contained what was naïvely described by the authorities as 'a compact of perpetual amity with the Great White Queen'. Its final sentence robbed a free country of its sovereignty for ever:

> ... It is hereby further agreed by Lobengula ... on behalf of himself and his people, that he will refrain from entering into any correspondence or treaty with any foreign State or Power to sell, alienate or cede, or permit, or countenance any sale, alienation, or cession of the whole or any part of the said Matabele country under his chieftainship, or upon any other subject without the previous knowledge and sanction of Her Majesty's High Commissioner for South Africa. ...

Mr Moffat knew what he had done. When presenting this ominous document to his chief, he thrust out his chest and said with obvious satisfaction:

'The days of the Matabele are now numbered!'

President Kruger had been officially informed by the High Commissioner of the agreement with Lobengula, and immediately protested verbally to the British Agent that the British Treaty was void as it was contradictory to his own earlier agreement with Lobengula. Reserving all his rights he promised a written reply in due course. Probably he wanted to wait for a report from Consul Grobler, who was just leaving for Bulawayo, the Matabele King's royal kraal.

On his previous journey to and from Lobengula, Grobler had, with the King's permission, used the old direct road from Pretoria to Bulawayo. Through the High Commissioner's suddenly imposed frontier regulations, this road had in the meanwhile fallen for the greater part to the Bechuanaland Protectorate in the territory of the Paramount Chief Khama. Moffat, under instructions from Cape Town, impressed on Khama the importance of safeguarding his right of way to the whole road and of allowing no one to pass without his, Khama's, permission.

When Grobler, with Lobengula's permission to 'take the road' as before, travelled with his party along this road, he was ambushed and mortally wounded. As President Kruger could not make investigations in the territory of a British Protectorate he had to content himself with the British explanation that the incident had been caused by a petty chief and that Khama would pay Grobler's widow an annual pension of £200.

It was clear to everyone in Pretoria, in Bulawayo and in the neighbouring German and Portuguese territories that the only party who would benefit by preventing Grobler from taking up his appointment was one man: Cecil J. Rhodes.

The murder on his territory of a white man, an *induna* of the Boers, whom he had assured only recently of the friendship of the Matabele upset Lobengula. He liked white men and as long as they complied with his rule and did not interfere with the ways and customs of his people, he did not object to their coming to hunt or trade in his country. Some of them, like the Scotsman James Dawson, possessed his full confidence and were often consulted by him. He even gave his Great Seal into Dawson's custody. Besides the welcome residents, the traders and hunters, Lobengula's kraal also served as a haven to a great number of shady elements, white, black and brown fugitives escaping from the law of the Cape, Natal or the two Boer Republics. Lobengula described these white hangers-on as 'my white dogs' or as *umfagozana*—'low fellows who are no gentlemen'. He knew how to handle them.

All his experience came to naught however, when his kraal became crowded with a type of white man new to him: the concession-hunters. The worries arising out of the treaty which his false friend 'Joni' Moffat had wormed out of him in February 1888 were still rotating in his tortured brain when fresh trouble started with the arrival of white men who asked for something which his simple mind could not grasp: concessions of land, his land; concessions to dig for gold; concessions of roads; concessions . . . concessions . . . concessions. . . .

To a tribal Native the idea of private ownership of land was as inconceivable as the idea that someone owned the sun, the rain or the water in a well. None of the white men who came to Lobengula with the intention of exploiting Matabeleland—least of all Rhodes—realized that their request for land to dig for gold appeared to the Matabele mind as nonsensical as would to us a Tibetan monk asking the Queen of England for permission to buy the moon and offering to pay for it with cowrie shells. But who bothered to investigate the Matabele mind?

'*Ngihlezi phezu kwegeja lishisa*—I am sitting upon the hot iron of a hoe,' the King said, and sighed deeply as he descended from his wagon after an *indaba* on that summer day in 1888. As was the wont of his people, he clad his thoughts in an old Zulu proverb. Old Babyaan replied with another:

'*Aku langa lishona lingenandabo zalo*—no sun sets without its troubles.'

Again the King sighed.

'*Ukufa kwenhliziyo ngumzwangedwa*—death of the heart is felt only by oneself.'

The King and his three counsellors recapitulated the events which had led to the present climacteric position in the seventeenth year of Lobengula's reign.

When Lobengula came to speak of the negotiations about the gold concessions, repeating the arguments over and over again while pouring down big calabashes full of beer, he could find no way out and could only chime in with the sighs of his advisers and cry out again and again, parrot-like:

'*Mai babo, yo, yo gho*—Mother of Ghosts, listen to this madness!'

For him there was no choice, he knew. What he would not give, would be taken from him by force. They did not need to tell him what a strong man Rhodes was. Yet his last representative, Mr John Fry, had not much impressed him as the emissary of a great chief.

Fry had not seen much of the king. Soon he had had to leave Bulawayo because of ill-health and shortly after his return to Kimberley he died. He had to be replaced immediately. The greatest haste was imperative. Rhodes was not, he knew, alone in the race. The royal kraal swarmed with concession-hunters.

'I must not leave a vacuum there—I must not leave a vacuum,' Rhodes squeaked repeatedly. The word 'vacuum' became his favourite expression for the next few weeks. If he could only go himself to Bulawayo to conclude the deal with Lobengula. Because of the importance and urgency of the mission it was decided that his partner Rudd should go though Rhodes knew that he was not really suited for this sort of business. Rudd was too honest, too correct, too hidebound for the job and would need the assistance of someone with more push. Rhodes' choice fell on Frank R. Thompson, whom he already knew as an exceptionally capable young man who had accompanied Warren on his expedition and had on that occasion spent some time in Matabeleland where he had quickly become popular with Lobengula. As the third member of the party Rhodes selected an old friend of his university days, the learned, dapper Irishman Thomas R. Maguire, a Fellow of All Souls College, who had won fame at Oxford as an athlete, a double-first scholar, a dandy, and a great debater.

In September 1888 the triumvirate of Rhodes' envoys arrived in Bulawayo. It did not take them long to find out that they had the entire royal kraal, from Lobengula down to the lowest slave, against them.

The greatest resistance, working from underground, came from their numerous competitors, Englishmen, Cape Colonials, Boers, Portuguese and Germans, who all had their tents pitched or their wagons stationed around Rudd's camp. Among them there figured prominently E. A. Maund, the agent of the Exploring Company, a syndicate of wealthy London merchants backed by a few titled people and with excellent connexions in parliamentary and governmental circles. No new-comer to Matabeleland, 'Maundy' was a favourite of Lobengula's, their friendship dating back to the days of the Warren expedition to Bechuanaland. During that time there also was born Maund's hatred for Rhodes, which he dutifully had to share with his commander. Here now was Maund's opportunity: if he himself could not wrest a gold concession from the King, he could at least bring all his influence to bear upon 'Lob' to frustrate Rhodes.

An opponent of no less strength and burning with an equal hatred for Rhodes was Mr E. R. Renny-Tailyour, the representative of Edward A. Lippert, a cousin of Beit's. Renny-Tailyour's antagonism came to Rhodes by proxy: Lippert had fallen out with cousin Beit whom he had cheated in some business deal. Later Beit had refused help when Lippert had come into financial difficulties. Whenever there was an opportunity Lippert delighted in annoying his cousin, and this family squabble he extended with the same intensity to Rhodes. Behind Lippert there stood a group of German banks.

Including these, the most important competitors, there were all told the representatives of eleven different groups in the field racing for Lobengula's favour. Just after the arrival of Rudd's party there appeared on the scene the Anglican Bishop of Bloemfontein. In the bishop's company travelled a mysterious German, Count Pfeil. It was not difficult to notice that the monocled count would have been more at ease in the uniform of a Potsdam guards officer. He emphasized rather too loudly his civilian status and the fact that he was there only on a hunting-trip. It seemed strange that the count had spent many weeks in Pretoria where he must have bagged less trophies than intrigues. He had preferred to travel over longer routes rather than pass through British territory. All this seemed very suspicious and the more so when Thompson found out that the count was well equipped with all the utensils for prospecting, assessing and surveying.

Lobengula now began to enjoy the presence of the many white men in his kraal because their homage flattered his vanity. Their presents he welcomed greedily and had no wish to stop their flow. He therefore kept up all their hopes, so that they all became convinced that they had almost reached their goal.

It was no easy life to attend Lobengula's court as a petitioner. Rudd and Thompson, accustomed to roughing it after their many years of camp life, did not suffer as much as did Maguire, who hated the discomforts of outdoor life. Lobengula took delight in humiliating all foreigners by insisting on their strict adherence to his court etiquette. His audiences took place in the big dung-covered buck-kraal; his guests had to approach him crawling on their stomachs and had then to squat for many hours, unprotected from the full glare of an almost tropical sun.

At every audience they had to go through the ordeal of eating each two big platters of half-roasted meat covered with myriads of fat flies and of swallowing two calabashes full of lukewarm Native beer. Then there came the nerve-racking tribulations of endless heckling and arguing with Lobengula, of being exposed for hours on end to his cross-examination.

At every interview Lobengula would come out with the same question:

'You are sure you are not coming after grass and land?' And every time Thompson would reply:

'No, King! No; it is minerals we want. We are not Boers; we have no cattle to feed.'

Sir Leander Starr Jameson

Bulawayo. The famous *Indaba* tree under which Lobengula dispensed justice
From an old photograph

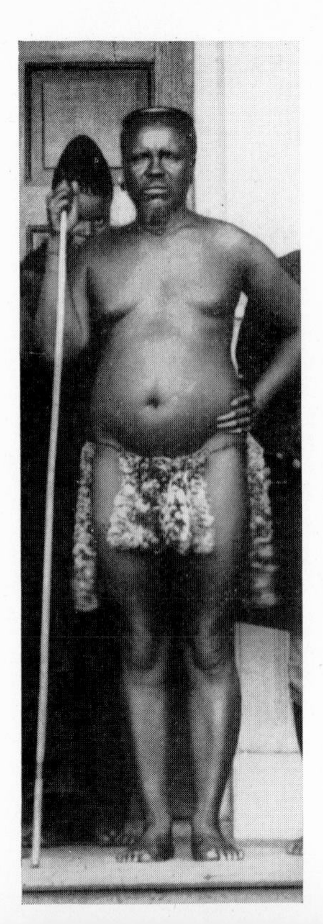

Lobengula, King of the Matabele. One of the few extant photographs, as he was suspicious of the 'Evil Eye' of the camera

Lobengula preferred Thompson, who spoke his language and whom he trusted to a certain extent, to the other applicants. 'Tomosi' was in his eyes the perfect gentleman, the only one who had never told a lie, in contrast to all the others who 'had spoken with two tongues in their mouth'.

To destroy his doubts Thompson gave the King an affidavit on oath in his capacity as Justice of the Peace of Her Majesty the Queen that Rhodes did not aspire to Lobengula's land.

This sworn declaration was given by Thompson in the best of faith, relying on Rhodes' repeated assurances and his written instructions on that point.

The negotiations went on for more than a month. Rudd did not despair. He was not deceived when he placed his hopes on Rhodes finally supplying him with the sword to cut the Gordian knot. Excitement mounted in the royal kraal when it was announced that Sir Sidney Shippard, the Commissioner for Bechuanaland, would be arriving together with his deputy, the ex-missionary John Moffat. Tension increased when reports arrived from the frontier that Shippard was escorted by an *impi* of the Great White Queen's soldiers, led by a very big *induna*. The Queen's envoy seemed in such a hurry that he travelled even through the night, 'when', as Lobengula observed bitterly, 'only beasts and ghosts should be abroad'. Lobengula detested Shippard, who was known among some Native tribes as *Marana maka*, Father of Lies.

Though the sudden arrival of the Queen's representative brought all the fears he had accumulated during the last few years to a state of panic, the King exercised the greatest self-control and received his guest with all the honours due to so high a personality. Although the mercury had almost reached the top of the thermometer, Sir Sidney, conscious of the importance of his mission, appeared at the ceremonial reception strictly according to Whitehall etiquette in striped trousers, frock-coat and stiffly starched collar and shirt. When he later took off his suffocating official dress and changed into the cooler colonial garb, he also changed, unknown to Lobengula, from the representative of Her Majesty the Queen to the secret agent and accomplice of Cecil Rhodes.

Shippard quickly came to the point: he had heard that the King was much molested by concession-hunters and he wanted to let

Lobengula know that 'they were not in any way connected or authorized by Her Majesty's Government'.

Rhodes must have briefed Shippard carefully. In this way they would take the wind out of Maund's sails, who, Rhodes feared, was trying to beat him at his own game, having led Lobengula to believe that the Colonial Office favoured Maund's syndicate. 'Great Britain', Shippard continued, 'is not in any way concerned with either mining schemes or trading ventures and you may be quite certain that any private concession-seeker who professes to represent the British Government is trying to deceive you.' After a week Shippard left. To Lobengula's astonishment Moffat also went a few days later.

Activity in the royal kraal now became feverish. Every day for hours Lobengula sat in council with his *indunas*. Rudd and his party were summoned to the buck-kraal several times a day. In the camps of the concession-hunters and in the trading stations many people wondered why Lobengula sent for the Reverend C. D. Helm, Moffat's successor as the Senior Missionary of the London Missionary Society, to act as his interpreter.

The work of this reverend gentleman was not to be restricted to mere translation. The King, who had full faith in the honesty and fairness of the missionaries, had asked Helm to advise him in the matter of the concessions. Helm told Lobengula that it would be in his interest to come to an arrangement with a strong group like Rhodes' to work the Mashonaland gold-fields. Otherwise, he warned, 'there will be a rush there soon and things will come to a climax'.

Unfortunately Mr Helm concealed from Lobengula the important and rather strange fact that he who had been sent out to spread the gospel had just been engaged by Rudd on behalf of Rhodes at a salary of £200 per annum 'to help them a little'.

Rudd was therefore glad when one day he and Maguire were called to the King and found with him only Thompson, Helm and Lotje, the only one of Lobengula's counsellors who was on the side of the white men. The day before Rudd had let the King know that he would have to leave for home on urgent business. Helm at the same time had tried to goad Lobengula into agreeing to sign a concession by insisting that he had to return urgently to his mission station. Again Lobengula dallied. Again Thompson had to assure him that Rhodes did not want land but only gold, and to give him a verbal promise—which was not put in the concession agreement—that 'they would not bring more than ten white men to work in his country, that they would not dig near any kraals and that they and their people would abide by the laws of his country and in fact be as his people'. All this Helm translated and explained.

Lobengula was now convinced that all that 'Ulodzi', the Man of the Big Hole, as he called Rhodes, wanted to do in his country was to dig another big hole there as he had done in Kimberley.

But no, he said, he would not sign. He never signed his name. This went on for half an hour. New arguments. Suddenly the King turned to Helm:

'*Hellem lete lapa*—Helm, give it to me!'

And so on 30 October 1888 Lobengula signed what was to become his death-warrant. He sold the freedom of his people, unwittingly, for a consideration of £100 monthly, 1,000 Martini-Henry rifles, 100,000 rounds of ammunition and a gun-boat (a special suggestion of Rhodes' in a letter to Rudd: 'same as Stanley put on the Upper Congo'). For this blood-money he granted to Rudd 'the complete and exclusive charge over all metals and minerals situated and contained in my Kingdoms Principalities and Dominions. . . . I do hereby authorize the said grantees . . . to take all necessary and lawful steps to exclude from my Kingdoms Principalities and Dominions all persons seeking land metals minerals or mining rights therein . . . and I do hereby undertake . . . to grant no concessions of land or mining rights from and after this date without their consent and concurrence. . . .'

When Rhodes had discussed with Thompson the planned mission to Bulawayo, he had said: 'Thompson, if you can get Lobengula's seal to a concession, I'll go crazy!' Now this moment had come.

By a stroke of genius the document was not only witnessed by the Reverend Mr Helm but the reverend gentleman obliged his new master by endorsing it with the words:

> I hereby certify that the accompanying document has been fully interpreted and explained by me to the Chief Lobengula and his full council of Indunas and that all the constitutional usages of the Matabele Nation had been complied with prior to his executing same.

Rhodes and his friends realized the need for counteracting any possible insinuations that the concession had been squeezed out of Lobengula by high pressure from official quarters, previously administered to him by Shippard and Moffat. Shippard, who for several weeks had been a few yards from the very spot where the negotiations between the Rhodes-group and Lobengula took place, therefore had the unabashed audacity to report to his superiors that 'no Governmental officer or representative had anything to do with the Concession; and my knowledge of what took place is limited to hearsay and to the contents of the document'.

'*Marana maka*—Father of Lies' had merited his nickname once more. But as is often the case with such jugglers with truth, his memory was apt to slip at times. A few years later he boasted:

> From my first arrival in Mafeking in 1885 I was in correspondence with Lobengula with a view to ultimately securing his territory for England in accordance with the plan decided on between Rhodes and myself in 1878.

The Governor and High Commissioner Sir Hercules Robinson frowned at the grant of modern firearms to the Matabele. Rhodes lightly brushed aside these scruples: 'Quite harmless, these rifles in the Kaffir's hands; they are always pushing the sights on the gun as high as they will go because they believe the bullets then hit harder. Of course with the sight fully pushed out, all the shots go far over the aim!'

The old man was satisfied with this evasive reply. But Lord Knutsford, the Colonial Secretary in Salisbury's Cabinet, could not be put off so easily, and Robinson was informed that the paragraph about guns in the Rudd concession was unacceptable to the Government. This difficulty could not deter Rhodes from proceeding with his plans. That much he had learnt about handling red-taped officialdom. Let them face a *fait accompli* and they will joyfully succumb to an offered compromise. One must not leave a vacuum there . . . no vacuum there . . . no vacuum, Rhodes repeated innumerable times.

Some pressure would have to be brought to bear on fat old 'Lob' to make this savage realize that Rhodes meant business when he made an agreement. Sir Hercules, naturally, gave in when approached by Shippard on Rhodes' instructions to ask Whitehall for an increase in the number of Bechuanaland police by 200 or 300 men in order to safeguard the life and property of the British residents against possible unrest in Matabeleland. Lord Knutsford tried to bargain but finally 200 men were added to Shippard's—or should one say to Rhodes'—private army.

None of these highly placed Colonial officials seems to have shown any scruples in deceiving their Government in misusing the taxpayer's money to aid and abet the rape of a country. They knew perfectly well that all these expenses were not intended for the benefit of their own country or for the glory of their Queen but for the enrichment of one man. One does not like to believe that men in their position, particularly not an old Civil Servant with an immaculate past and as generally esteemed for his wisdom, efficiency and impartiality as was Robinson, nor such ambitious, highly talented and seemingly correct younger men as Shippard, Bower and Newton, would have been open to corruption in the form of expectations of gratitude from the omnipotent Rhodes or that they would have risked their good name, their career and the bloody consequences for even a very high stake. Though much circumstantial evidence points in this unsavoury direction —Robinson after his retirement became a director of De Beers, and his wife at a farewell-party received a costly diamond-necklace from the same company; Shippard later turned from a Civil Servant into the well-paid chairman of the Chartered Company, and Newton after his retirement was given a high position in that company—yet one would rather like to blame their weakness of character, their blind obedience to Rhodes' orders and their lack of sound judgment when confronted by Rhodes' overwhelming persuasive power, and his cleverly administered poison of Jingoism.

Up to that stage Rhodes had still been able to give out as his ulterior motive his patriotic aims of acquiring the North for Britain—'to paint all this red'. Now, having obtained the Rudd concession, he began to convert his 'hobby', his 'imagination', into a dividend-paying business proposition. Even the most innocent Civil Servant could hardly have failed to observe that all his former patriotic catch-phrases were turning into the lingo of the Stock Exchange.

Rhodes now parted with the rest of his conscience. The Empire-builder became the company promoter. He inserted a declaration in the newspapers that Lobengula had granted an exclusive concession to Messrs Rudd, Thompson and Maguire and that in consequence no one—under the threat of arrest—was allowed to enter Matabeleland. Such high-handed action by private monopoly-holders had, of course, no legal backing, but Rhodes still had his friends in the right places. Shippard obligingly arrested the agents of a competing concern when they tried to cross the border.

The Cape Town papers strongly criticized this strange governmental policy of protecting a concession monopoly. Rhodes did not care. He was burning to leave for London. His concession had to be put into working order. At the last minute there occurred an unexpected hitch. Thompson's reports from Bulawayo sounded alarming. Shippard and Moffat sent a warning that Maund was causing serious trouble. At first Rhodes treated the news lightly. He was far more concerned that no vacuum should occur. What he had not expected was that Lobengula was about to create just such a vacuum.

Thompson had scarcely left the royal kraal with the precious document well secured under his shirt when Lobengula became conscious of the possible meaning of the concession document which he had signed for Rudd. They had cleverly left no copy for him, and he was thus unable to have it translated independently. His suspicions increased when Helm, in spite of repeated requests, would not send him his own copy. At last after weeks of waiting he held this copy in his hands. So strong was still his faith in the honesty of missionaries that he summoned two other missionaries besides Helm to his kraal. He had to act quickly. Not much longer would he be able to control the growing ferment amongst his *impi*. They whispered in the kraals that the King had sold a great part of their country to Rhodes.

Lobengula first put the most important question to the two missionaries, after they had read the concession document: had he given away any of the land of the Matabele? After the two men had studied the paper again they told the king that in their opinion the white men could not very well dig for gold without land.

A deathly silence settled over the assembly. Lobengula's expression did not alter.

'If gold is found anywhere in the country can the white men occupy the land and dig for it?' he asked.

'Yes, King!'

'If gold is in my garden, can they come and dig it?'

'Yes, King!'

'If gold is in my royal kraal, can they enter and dig?'

'Yes, King!'

The King dropped his head. He gave the impression of having been completely crushed and beaten. Suddenly a convulsive twist ran like a flash through his colossal body. He turned slightly towards his chief counsellor, and fixed him with a mad stare, his eyeballs protruding:

'Lotje, this was your doing! You've blinded my eyes; you've closed my ears; you've betrayed me!'

The old man bent his head. He rose, full of dignity, and walked slowly through the rows of *indunas* towards the gate. Before leaving he turned towards the King and gave him the royal salute: *Bayete!* He knew his fate. Shortly afterwards he was killed and with him his wives, his children, his grandchildren, his cattle, even his fowls and dogs. Of his kraal only an ash-heap remained.

The King now turned to Helm, who during the proceedings had sat, uncomfortable and sweating profusely, behind his two missionary brethren. With scalding words the King accused him of falseness, of betrayal, of fraud, of double-crossing, of perfidy. He dismissed the embarrassed evangelist with the words:

'Hellem, you call yourself a man of God? You are no better than a trader.'

When the King saw Thompson in the crowd he beckoned to him and said in a voice which did not conceal his rage:

'Tomosi, all the killing is not yet over.'

Lobengula had finally seen through the tricks of Shippard, Moffat and Helm. If he could only approach the Great White Queen directly and explain to her the misery into which Rhodes had plunged him!

There remained only one man in his kraal who, having once been an officer of the Queen and the eye and hand of that great *induna* Warren, would be able to help him. That man was Maund. He would buy Maund's allegiance by granting him a new concession.

Maund suggested that Lobengula should write a letter to the

Queen which would be brought to London by two Matabele *indunas*, with Maund acting as their guide and interpreter. Lobengula chose the seventy-five-year-old Babyaan, a relative of his, and Umsheti, a small, gouty, bad-tempered man of sixty-five. Maund on behalf of the Exploring Company received a concession for a large part of Mashonaland and was made an *induna* of that district.

Rhodes was warned in time. His friends at Government House in Cape Town were on their guard. Moffat protested that Lobengula's delegates could not leave the country without the High Commissioner's permission. Shippard had them arrested on the Bechuanaland border for entering the Protectorate unlawfully. But Maund merely had to indicate that a cable to the Colonial Office would easily clarify the existence of this unknown regulation. Maund now got his two *indunas* as far as Cape Town. Next Robinson and Rhodes' friend, Captain Bower, and Rhodes' old Oxford pal, Newton, stepped in to thwart Lobengula's and Maund's plans. The two *indunas* were again arrested upon their arrival in Cape Town and brought to Government House where they had to undergo a lengthy cross-examination. Seeing that they had no plausible legal reason for stopping the two *indunas* from proceeding to London, Bower and Newton questioned their credentials. They accused Maund of having picked up two vagrant Natives whose nakedness he had only recently covered with ornamental Native garb.

Maund was not the man to be deterred by such brow-beating. After all machinations had been unsuccessful, Rhodes asked his accomplices at least to retard the departure of Maund's delegation for as long as possible, so as to give him time to arrive in England before them.

Before Rhodes could leave South Africa he had to provide against another threatening vacuum in Bulawayo. Rudd, through illness, had been unable to return there. Thompson, it seemed, had the jitters. Helm was clearly bowled out through Lobengula's loss of confidence in him. Moffat, too, had apparently lost his grip on Lobengula. Someone energetic, someone cunning and yet tactful and with a winning personality, was required for the difficult task of keeping that fat savage humoured so that he would keep to the terms of the concession. The only man with these rare qualities was Dr Jameson.

As soon as Lobengula met Dr Jameson he took to him. His cool, sarcastic and light-hearted manner fascinated the King. At the time of the doctor's arrival Lobengula, in addition to his other troubles, was plagued by the gout. Dr Jameson quickly freed the King of his agonizing pains with the aid of morphine.

For the time being, however, Lobengula did not weaken in his determination to deny the validity of the Rudd concession. He refused point-blank to accept the arms brought by Dr Jameson according to the concession. All Dr Jameson succeeded in doing was to persuade him to store the guns and arms in a provisional shelter quickly erected by Jameson's men. Lobengula did, however, accept the monthly payment of one hundred sovereigns, which seemed a strange contradiction of his denial of the agreement. Was it greed or did he want to avoid a complete break with Rhodes before his *indunas* arrived in London? Or had Dr Jameson, perhaps, dosed him so generously with morphine that he had actually blocked the royal brain system?

The dreaded vacuum had been averted. Rhodes, his mind at rest and full of hope, sailed for England in April 1889.

CHAPTER X

RED, BRITISH RED

ROBERT A. T. G. CECIL, third Marquis of Salisbury, Her Majesty's Prime Minister, sat at his mahogany desk at 10 Downing Street one day in April 1889 studying a file just sent over from the Colonial Office. His lordship yawned over the documents in his hands and asked his secretary in his usual abrupt way: 'And who may be this Mr Rhodes? Rather a pro-Boer M.P. in South Africa, I fancy.' Before long Lord Salisbury was to know only too well who Cecil Rhodes was.

From his simple room in the noisy Westminster Palace Hotel, Rhodes was busy trying to burrow his way through Downing Street into Matabeleland. He had started with his preparations for obtaining a Charter from the British Government even before he had the Rudd concession in his possession. At first he thought that he could best foster his plans in South Africa by entering politics in England. Rhodes was keenly interested in the Irish Home Rule problem which in 1886 had reached its climax. Paralleling Ireland's position within the British Empire with that of South Africa, Rhodes, still at times dreaming of a British World Federation, believed in federation within the British Empire and therefore considered Irish representation in the English Parliament imperative.

During his previous voyage to England Rhodes had met Mr Swift MacNeill, one of Parnell's closest friends. They had many and long discussions which culminated in Rhodes' offer of a gift of £10,000 to the funds of the Irish party. In a lengthy letter to Parnell, dated June 1888, Rhodes stipulated as a condition for his gift that the Irish party must accept Home Rule not in the form of Separation but only of Federation with full representation in the English Parliament. Parnell accepted this condition.

Parnell and Rhodes became good friends. The Irish leader had just passed through the agony of his sensational law suit against *The Times*, and at the time of Rhodes' visit was still busy fighting tooth and nail to retain the leadership of his party. Sadly he told Rhodes: 'I'll lose: the priests are against me.'

Rhodes was pacing up and down the room as usual, his hands deep in his trouser-pockets. Suddenly he stopped, and looking Parnell straight in the eye he asked him:

'Can't we square the Pope?'

Parnell was never able to make out whether Rhodes had meant it seriously. In spite of such *faux pas* Parnell liked Rhodes. He once remarked to his friend MacNeill:

'What a pity that Rhodes is not in the Imperial Parliament. As it is, he will not live in history.'

Rhodes had a very high opinion of Parnell whom he esteemed as 'the most reasonable and sensible man I ever met'.

Since Rhodes' gift of £10,000 had not been given secretly or bound Parnell to discretion, it immediately became known in all political circles. It was therefore understood when Rhodes in the spring of 1889 came to London with the concession in one hand and his hat in the other to dance attendance on the political mighties, that he had 'squared' the Irish party. The English Press knew all about his previous skill in 'squaring'. Nobody could believe such a generous donation to have been given without an ulterior motive. He was accused of being either a sincere Home Ruler and an insincere Imperialist or a sincere Imperialist and an insincere Home Ruler. To these reproaches Rhodes replied:

'I gave Mr Parnell's cause £10,000 because in it I believe lies the key of the Federal system, on the basis of perfect Home Rule in every part of the Empire, and in it also the Imperial tie begins.'

To friends, however, Rhodes cynically said that 'his intention at the time was merely to keep the Irish party in the House of Commons from opposing his Charter when he chose to apply for it'.

Already at the beginning of his parliamentary career Rhodes had valued highly the importance of 'having a good Press'. When he had seen his first speeches reported in only a few lines in the Cape Town papers he had bought a large interest in one of them.

In England at the time W. T. Stead, a minister's son a few years older than Rhodes, was the most outstanding journalistic personality. As its editor he had modernized the *Pall Mall Gazette* by his revolutionary and individualistic way of presenting the news. Through his example he had forced the other papers to come down from their pedestals from where they spoke above the heads of the masses. Stead can be called the father of modern journalism.

He did not regard the task of his paper as completed by broadcasting the news and commenting upon it. He wanted the Press to exercise an ethical influence for the improvement of morals, to further the educational standard of the people and to spread faith in the future of the British Empire as the bastion of world peace and advancement of mankind.

W. T. Stead represented a mighty factor in English public life. His printed words weighed heavily in the council of England's leaders, and they studied his opinions in the *Pall Mall Gazette* as 'though it were the organ of Fate itself'.

Such a man, Rhodes judged, would be useful to have as a friend. He must meet Stead!

At the beginning Stead was not at all impressed by the young South African millionaire. Rhodes broke the ice by telling Stead that he had wanted to meet him four years ago to express his admiration for the courage he had shown in fighting social evils. There followed Rhodes' impressive recital of his romantic ideas of the *Pax Britannica*; of the Federation of the Germanic countries led by England; of the conquest of Africa to maintain the supremacy of the Anglo-Saxon race by finding new unoccupied land in which to settle English colonists and to create new markets; of the founding of a secret society organized in the style of Loyola's Society of Jesus. In his desultory way, jumping from one point to another, starting to expound one idea without having come to the kernel of the last, Rhodes continued by confiding to the stranger opposite him his most intimate thoughts on God, the world and himself. Money, he said, he regarded only as a means to work out his ideas.

Stead listened intently. What he heard was music to his ears. One Romantic was getting drunk on the sweet drug of romantic reveries administered to him by another. Rhodes rejoiced at having found at last a congenial soul who would share with him his 'dreams' for which he had never found an echo. Here was the man for whom he had been waiting, the man who would help him realize the 'dreams'. And besides, this man would certainly be of tremendous value to him in London in helping him to settle quickly all those tiresome formalities concerning his 'little hobby in Matabeleland'.

As was his custom, Rhodes' next step was to take out his cheque-book, and offer Stead 'as a free gift £20,000 to buy a share in the *Pall Mall Gazette* as a beginning' with a promise of more to come the following year.

When Stead declined Rhodes showed genuine astonishment. The next day £2,000 damages were awarded against Stead in a libel case. He had to ask Rhodes for that amount.

Rhodes did not restrict himself to Stead and his paper in preparing the English Press for a good reception. *The St James Gazette* had shown a strongly critical attitude towards him. He took its editor, Sir Sidney Low, an eminent journalist of great political influence, into his confidence and changed his animosity into sympathy with his projects. He also succeeded in establishing friendly relations with Moberly Bell, the manager of *The Times*, and the Reverend John Verschoyle, assistant editor of the ponderous *Fortnightly Review*, became his helpful and admiring friend.

The field was now prepared in as far as publicity was concerned. The first step on the political scene had been taken through Parnell. Making prominent members of the two main parties of Parliament acquainted with his schemes and finding contacts among present and future Ministers was to be the next task.

Lord 'Natty' Rothschild assisted Rhodes in meeting politically and financially influential men, though he himself as well as his firm showed little enthusiasm for Rhodes' exploration schemes.

Rhodes realized that such conservative bankers as the Rothschilds could not be expected to be elevated from the grooves of double entry into the realms of his 'dreams'. They had no 'imagination', Rhodes said to his friend Stead:

> Look at the criminal in his cell and at Lord Rothschild! It is hard to say which has the harder lot. The prisoner has some fun, at least, with the spiders and the mice, but look at Rothschild! Out of 365 days, he spends 300 in turning over bits of paper and marking them. Look at the two men far enough off, so as not to see any difference in clothing, and it will be hard to see any difference between them. Think of that man and his millions—what could he not do with them!

Something which could and had been done with such a fortune was the palatial mansion which Lord 'Natty' had built for himself at Tring Park. Rhodes, though unaccustomed to such splendour and to the number of prominent names which he encountered at Tring, did not feel out of place there as he would have done only a few years before. His success and his wealth had given him the necessary self-assurance to meet on equal terms the leading politicians whom Lord Rothschild invited for him.

Of the people whom he met there he felt most attracted to Lord Rothschild's son-in-law, Lord Rosebery. His attention was also drawn to the tall and extremely thin figure of Mr Joseph Chamberlain, whose ascetic face never seemed to move or register any signs of inner perturbance and which appeared still more mask-like with the monocle screwed into his right eye. His was a cold and an almost cruel face, in which there burnt, under the ice of frozen emotions, a frantic ambition, tireless energy and morbid vanity.

Meeting Chamberlain was an important event for Rhodes, who knew that he was a member, and the most interested member, of the South African Committee of the House of Commons which would have the fate of his scheme in its hands.

When after dinner the ladies retired, Rhodes managed to place himself next to Chamberlain. At first there was a long silence. Chamberlain, his arms folded and his legs stretched out, had that vague look which had earned him the sobriquet of 'The Sphinx'. Rhodes fixed his eyes on him questioningly and when he found that the other was going to make no attempt at starting a conversation, he began, as usual, by plunging straight into a question which had worried him:

'Mr Chamberlain, I am told you do not like me?'

Chamberlain did not change his relaxed position. His answer came in the chilling voice that he used successfully in the House when wishing to chastise a backbencher:

'I am not aware, Mr Rhodes, that I have given anyone the right to tell you that. But if you put it to me, why should I? I only know three things about you. The first is that you are reported to have said that every man has his price. It is not true, and I do not like the man who says it. The second is that you have talked of "eliminating the Imperial Factor" in South Africa. The third is that you gave £10,000 to Parnell, and that is not exactly a claim on my gratitude.'

After this freezing rebuke Rhodes realized that he would have to do more spade-work than he had anticipated. His own dislike of Chamberlain dated back to 1877, when the same man who today played himself up as a great imperialist had protested against the annexation of the Transvaal as 'an act of force, fraud and folly'.

Rhodes had to give vent to his fury. All the way home in the carriage he sat without speaking, but when he arrived at his hotel he said to the amazement of a young man unknown to him whom he had taken with him:

'Some people spend their time in growing orchids, others spend their time in making empires!'

His next disappointment came when he called at the Colonial Office and was told by Lord Knutsford, the Colonial Secretary of State, that Lord Gifford and George Cawston of the Exploring Company represented in Africa by Maund, had come to apply for a Charter with a similar concession from Lobengula in their hands. Knutsford also mentioned that, according to the latest reports, it seemed that Lobengula was making difficulties about these concessions. The Government, so Rhodes was told, did not want to be involved in a private dispute between two opposing groups and it would be in the interest of Mr Rhodes as well as of the gentlemen of the Exploring Company if they would come to an agreement about their claims and join hands in the exploitation of the mineral wealth of Mashonaland which, under certain conditions, would find the approval of Her Majesty's Government.

Rhodes at first was not so sure whether he should not fight, but he finally saw that he had no choice. He had just decided to try and amalgamate his interests with those of his opponents when Maund and Lobengula's two delegates arrived in London. In the Colonial Office Lobengula's letter to the Queen had the effect of a bombshell. This letter read:

> Lobengula desires to know that there is a Queen. Some of the people who come into this land tell him there is a Queen, some of them tell him there is not.
>
> Lobengula can only find out the truth by sending eyes to see whether there is a Queen.
>
> The *Indunas* are his eyes.
>
> Lobengula desires, if there is a Queen, to ask her to advise and help him, as he is much troubled by white men who come into his country and ask to dig gold. They asked me for a place to dig for gold, and said they would give me certain things for the right to do

> so. I told them to bring what they would give, and I would show them what I would give. A document was written and presented to me for signature. I asked what it contained and was told that in it were my words and the words of those men. I put my hand to it. About three months afterwards I heard from other sources that I had given by this document the right to all the minerals in my country. . . . I have since had a meeting of my *indunas*, and they will not recognize the paper, as it contains neither my words nor the words of those who got it. . . . I write to you that you may know the truth about this thing and may not be deceived.

As soon as the letter was delivered Rhodes came forward with a declaration that it was a forgery. His argument was that it had not been witnessed by any missionary, though Rhodes could have had no doubts why Lobengula, after his recent experiences with the reverend gentlemen, had found a flaw in their honesty. As far as the Great Elephant Seal was concerned—simply ridiculous, said Rhodes, to consider it as proof of Lobengula's hand. This seal was always kept in the cash-box of one of the traders, and the King did not know its meaning at that. And why, pray, had Lobengula accepted his monthly payments if he seriously denied having granted Rudd the concession?

Lord Knutsford accepted this flimsy explanation without asking for further proof. The Rothschilds and Lord Rosebery had convinced him that Rhodes, with the enormous capital of De Beers and the Goldfields behind him, would be preferable to the Exploring Company in exploiting Lobengula's country.

Maund in the meanwhile, having become aware of the fact that Rhodes was the stronger party, was already reflecting whether it would not after all be wiser, as Rudd had already hinted at Bulawayo, to come to terms with Rhodes. They met in London accidentally. Rhodes tackled Maund bluntly:

'Listen, Maund, if it comes to a fight, money will be no object—but there may be means of accommodation.'

As a direct result of this meeting, Maund immediately flagged in his zeal. He advised his friends of the Exploring Company to march with Rhodes rather than lose all chances. Since they were not willing, however, to sell out to Rhodes at his price, a fight for the best possible terms continued.

The Colonial Office had to remain neutral, or at least to appear neutral, in this squabble over alleged concessions, the more so after some indiscreet questions had already been asked in the House. First Mr Chamberlain had inquired 'whether in view of the character of the concession . . . H.M. Government will take any steps to call the attention of the Chief to the disadvantages and dangers to the peace of the country incident to such a monopoly; and whether, in event of H.M. Government extending at any future time a protectorate over the Colony, now under the sphere of British influence, they will refuse to recognize the concession in question or any similar concession that may be contrary to the interests of the Chief and people of Matabeleland, and likely to lead to complications and to the breach of peace?'

Baron de Worms, the young Under-Secretary of State, replied evasively that the Government had so far abstained from interfering but that Lobengula had now asked for advice, and that someone would be sent to him by the Queen. He emphasized the Government's disapproval of the gifts of arms and ammunition. And it was certainly not the intention of the Government, he said, to countenance such concessions if a Protectorate was to be declared.

Such questions by the Member for Birmingham were greatly disliked by the Right Honourable gentlemen on the Treasury bench. However, one could discuss such matters with Mr Joseph Chamberlain in Committee or tackle him privately in the Lobby. It was a different matter, and far more disturbing and dangerous to members of the Government, when the Radical Member for Northampton, Mr Henry du Pré Labouchere, rose and poured forth one of his mud-slinging, impudent and libellous attacks, as his enemies called them, but which his friends described as his audacious campaigns against evils and defects in public life.

'Labby' wanted to know 'whether it is a fact that Lobengula denies having knowingly signed a concession . . . and asserts that a Missionary, acting as interpreter, erroneously interpreted the document to Lobengula', and 'whether the Secretary of State for the Colonies can see his way to put an end to all exclusive concessions granted to British subjects within South Africa'.

The greatest precautions would now have to be taken by the Colonial Office not to supply Labouchere with material for another of his biting vituperations not only in Parliament but also in his widely circulated weekly paper, *Truth*.

Lord Knutsford, realizing the danger arising out of Chamberlain's sudden curiosity in Lobengula and from 'Labby's' apparent preparation for a disclosure in *Truth*, sent a message to Lobengula which would make it clear that the Colonial Office was washing its hands of the matter in innocence:

> The Queen advises Lobengula not to grant hastily concessions of land or leave to dig, but to consider all applications very carefully. It is not wise to put too much power in the hands of the men who come first, and to exclude other deserving men. A king gives a stranger an ox, and not his whole herd of cattle, otherwise what would other strangers arriving have to eat?

Rhodes fumed with rage. Again a vacuum was threatening to undo the work of the past months. Rhodes now saw clearly that what he needed was a more convincing title to the mineral rights in Matabeleland than the vague Rudd concession. Did they not call him on the London Stock Exchange 'the great amalgamator' after the wonders he had performed with De Beers? He would show once again that, even though that Birmingham big stiff denied it, everybody had his price.

Much more easily than he had expected, Rhodes came to an agreement with Cawston and Lord Gifford by which the Exploring Company, possessor of Maund's comprehensive concession, together with its sister enterprise, the Bechuanaland Exploration Company, was amalgamated with Rhodes' company, the Central Search Association, holder of the Rudd concession. A new concern comprising all these companies was founded, the United Concession Company, with Rhodes, Beit, Rudd, Cawston and Lord Gifford on the Board.

The acquisition of the Bechuanaland Exploration Company was particularly welcomed by Rhodes, though this Company's only asset was a promise given by Lord Knutsford in 1888 'that no offer from any other party for a Railway Company in British Bechuanaland should be entertained during the period required for making a survey of the route and consideration of their proposals'. The Colonial Office had further consented to exercise a 'fair influence on Native chiefs of the territories in question'. Though the project had been well favoured by the Colonial Office, Sir Hercules Robinson, when the surveying party of the Company arrived in Cape Town, had made difficulties in every respect, as did Sir Sidney Shippard in Bechuanaland. These two

Colonial administrators, just like their friend Rhodes, did not like this interference of the 'Imperial Factor' in a matter concerning a vital Cape Colony problem of policy which, they thought, ought to be handled from Cape Town. Apart from this, there had been a silent understanding that the way to the North and the territories beyond the Limpopo were the exclusive concern of Rhodes!

Rhodes at the time showed the greatest interest in the railway project which coincided with his own plans. The engineer in charge of the surveying party, Charles Metcalfe, was one of his Oxford pals. So well must he have beguiled old Metcalfe at Oxford with his stories of South Africa, that this good lad still believed in them and was actually dreaming of a railway across the whole African continent, stretching from the Cape to Cairo. Such a gigantic scheme, surpassing even Rhodes' 'dreams'—which did not go farther than the Zambezi at the time—fired his imagination with a new and stronger impetus. His mind so far had been principally occupied with the exploitation of the mineral resources of the North. Metcalfe, however, had not only conceived the idea of linking South Africa by rail with Egypt and the British possessions in the Sudan but already had plans in his pocket showing their feasibility. Moreover, his group of the Bechuanaland Exploration Company had the blessing of Whitehall for the project. The negotiations with Metcalfe had broken down when Cawston and Lord Gifford found Rhodes competing against them in Bulawayo for a gold concession.

Much still remained to be done. Others came with more or less genuine concessions from Lobengula. Without much investigation as to their legal merits Rhodes acquired, sometimes at exhorbitant prices, a number of the strangest documents for all sorts of rights granted by Lobengula.

The concession companies Rhodes had acquired were united into the British South Africa Co. (B.S.A.C.) with a capital of £1 million in £1 shares of which De Beers, Goldfields, Rhodes and his friends (among them Dr Jameson with 4,500 shares) subscribed more than three-quarters while the rest was to be reserved for friends in South Africa. Rhodes, Beit and Rudd, as well as Cawston and Lord Gifford, became the directors.

Rhodes knew the history of his country. He had learnt that Britain's wealth and the might of her Empire were founded on her old possessions abroad which had been acquired as a result of the spirit of enterprise of a few daring men of action with no help from their Government other than receiving a piece of vellum containing a beautifully written 'Royal Charter'.

Rhodes set out to apply for a Charter and sent his associate, Lord Gifford, to approach Lord Knutsford. Though he was well received and the Secretary of State expressed the interest of the Colonial Office in the scheme, it was hinted politely that 'much would depend on the personal directorate'—or, in other words, that men 'without background' like Rhodes, Beit, Rudd and Cawston would not be acceptable to the Government as sufficiently reliable contractors.

Lord Salisbury was anything but enthusiastic about the project as in his opinion 'such far-reaching objects fell properly within the province of the Government'.

The lukewarm reception of his plans by the authorities infuriated Rhodes. He understood that he was expected to present for his Board a list of titled nobodies whose names were popular or a few immaculate men with reliable political affiliations in order to make his scheme palatable to the cliques of Whitehall. Rhodes began to look round for men with big names. He first asked Arthur Balfour, Lord Salisbury's nephew, who, however, declined with a visible shudder.

Just as once before, the German Government came to Rhodes' aid, even if only indirectly. H. M. Stanley had just returned from a two-year expedition by which he had acquired almost the entire Lake district of Equatoral East Africa. Bismarck heard of Stanley's negotiations with England for the annexation of this territory. Wilhelmstrasse immediately reminded Downing Street of the agreement of 1886, according to which spheres of influence should be respected by both sides. Salisbury did not want to have new difficulties with Prince Bismarck. He seemed blind to the fact that Germany, by seizing the territory between German East Africa and the Belgian Congo, would cut off the direct connection between South Africa and the British possessions in East and Central Africa.

Germany seemed to have decided on further colonial expansion in Africa, and Portugal too had shown signs of an ambition to annex territories in Central Africa.

In South Africa the Transvaal and the Orange Free State had

entered into an alliance. Paul Kruger had not abandoned his desire for expansion and was threatening to 'burst his kraal'. Disquieting reports of Boer activities came from Matabeleland. The brother of the murdered Transvaal consul, Piet Grobler, had brought to Pretoria a solemn declaration sworn before a Justice of the Peace in Bulawayo that Lobengula had never signed the Moffat Treaty. President Kruger therefore declined to recognize this treaty and claimed Matabeleland in accordance with the London Convention which stated that the territory to the north of the Republic should remain open to the Boers.

With the isolation of Britain in Europe where she had to face Bismarck's solid Triple-Entente, a frightened Russia eager to appease an alternately threatening or flirting Germany, and an estranged France, Lord Salisbury found the general political situation difficult enough without inviting clashes with the Great Powers in the colonial field, which might upset Britain's recently recovered prosperity. On the other hand, he was determined not to renounce any of Britain's colonial rights, since he did not want to be numbered among the 'Little Englanders'. Yet Lord Goschen, the tight-fisted Chancellor of the Exchequer, would never consent to any tax-money being used for what he called 'Imperial adventures north of the Zambezi'.

The Prime Minister was fortified in his resolution not to allow any African soil to slip through his fingers after he had listened to a young consul who had spent twelve out of his thirty years in Central and East Africa. He reported to him about the valuable territory of Nyasaland, including the fertile Shire Highlands and all the land stretching from north of Lake Tanganyika as far as Uganda, bordering on the Belgian Congo and linking up with the Sudan. All this land on which the Germans, and to some extent also the Portuguese, had cast their eyes could be brought under the British flag if immediate action were taken.

Salisbury went to the map on the wall and let his finger slide slowly from the Cape over Bechuanaland, Matabeleland and Mashonaland, crossing over the Zambezi to Nyasaland, along Lake Tanganyika, over Uganda and the Sudan, until he stopped at Cairo. In a hushed voice he said: 'Cape to Cairo—Cape to Cairo . . . and all British!'

Eleven years had passed since 'the Gladstone Prophecy', as Bismarck had called it, which had predicted the linking of the

British possessions north of the Equator with those in South Africa ('be it by larceny or be it by emption') and since Sir Edwin Arnold had coined the catching phrase 'From Cape to Cairo.' The slogan had only recently, in August 1888, been reintroduced through an article by the same young man who was now standing at his side.

He was rather young, but Lord Salisbury was convinced that he would be able to rely on the sound judgment of Harry Hamilton Johnston, a former art student at the Royal Academy who had recently been appointed British Consul for Portuguese East Africa. Here was a serious and enthusiastic young official of the consular service whose great knowledge of Africa, as a result of his leadership of a scientific expedition, had been recognized by several British scientific societies. He had done most valuable work as British Vice-Consul in the Cameroons, where he had brought the land of several chiefs under British influence, thus laying the foundation for a protectorate in the Niger delta.

Lord Salisbury, at the end of the interview, saw clearly all the advantages of bringing such precious territories under the British flag. But what could be done to materialize Johnston's suggestion with no funds available for such an expedition?

Johnston in a very despondent mood went to a dinner-party for a meeting with Rhodes arranged by John Verschoyle of the *Fortnightly Review*. They sat talking about their African plans and dreams until daylight, Rhodes repeating again and again Johnston's phrase which he had now heard for the first time, 'Cape to Cairo'. . . . He was captivated by it. It expressed all he had ever dreamt of. These three words would serve him well to fire the imagination of the masses in South Africa and England and to drag the people with him to the conquest of the African interior.

This rare opportunity must not be allowed to pass. He had made up his mind: 'You are to see Lord Salisbury at once, tell him who I am and give Lord Rothschild as my reference. . . . Say that if money is the only hindrance to our striking north from the Zambezi to the headwaters of the Nile, I will find the money! . . . What was attempted by Alexander, Cambyses and Napoleon, we practical people are going to finish.'

With trembling hand Rhodes wrote out a cheque for £2,000 as a first instalment with which Johnston was to equip his expedition, and a declaration to the British Government promising

£10,000 annually for the administration of Nyasaland. The only condition was that Johnston left for Nyasaland within four weeks.

These amounts Rhodes considered a good investment also from the point of view of ingratiating himself with Lord Salisbury. Rhodes was right in his assumption: Lord Salisbury declared himself very satisfied with this solution to the question of acquiring new colonial possessions cheaply with private aid. It would give that arrogant young Kaiser no reason for complaint against the British Government since they could always deny knowledge of this private expedition.

'Quite a smart fellow, this man—what do you call him . . . Rhodes,' was Salisbury's impression after he had had a talk with him. He now looked with greater sympathy at the application for a Charter by Rhodes' company.

At the end of the conversation Rhodes asked how far north he should go. Salisbury shrugged his shoulders and pointing to the map answered: 'Take all you can get and ask me afterwards!'

Rhodes was prepared for opposition. Through the efforts of his new friend Johnston, Chamberlain was persuaded to abstain from asking indiscreet questions in Parliament. In order to protect himself and his scheme from further attacks Rhodes needed a bulwark of personalities so high in standing that his company would be above criticism. Such people could not be lured by the prospects of money alone. They would have to be baited by some patriotic motives in addition. Two incentives would have to be used by Rhodes to stir the patriotic sentiments also of the masses: the one based on hatred and fear, the other dependent on a melodious catch-phrase. Both were at his disposal: Germany was feared and hated by the English for threatening the peace of the world and for unfair trade competition through her 'cheap and nasty' products. Now she was trying to oust Britain in the colonial field!

Rhodes yoked in his friends to spread the propaganda along these lines. To Metcalfe he wrote: 'It will come better from you, as I am looked on with some distrust at home.'

Promptly there appeared in the *Fortnightly Review* an article by Metcalfe in which he gave warning that the path of Britain into the interior was imperilled by Germany's rivalry for the heart of Africa. In one of the following issues of this journal was published another article in the same vein by another friend of Rhodes', the famous hunter and author, Frederick Courteney Selous. To have acquired the co-operation of a man of Selous' reputation was to be of great advantage to Rhodes. The opinions of an authority such as this were willingly accepted in official circles as well as by the English Press. The idea of 'Cape to Cairo' had gained impetus and was taking root. Even an austere scientific assembly like the Royal Geographical Society joined the propaganda campaign for Rhodes' scheme.

After the careful instigation of this preliminary publicity campaign, Rhodes began to worry about finding men of sufficiently high rank to be considered 'acceptable' to Whitehall. The Rothschilds were still very reluctant to be involved in Rhodes' 'hobby'. Rhodes knew of only one other person in England in the same social position as the Rothschilds: the old Baroness Burdett-Coutts.

The beautiful mansion in classical Georgian style of No. 1 Stratton Street, Piccadilly, was the centre of London's social life, and the mistress of the house was Angela Georgina Burdett-Coutts, first Baroness, of Highgate and Brookfield in the County of Middlesex. She compelled attention not only by the millions which she owned and the huge amounts she constantly gave away to charity, but by her grace, her wit and the fine intellect and inexhaustible energy with which she managed her business affairs and manifold charitable enterprises.

Rhodes had met this remarkable old lady, now seventy-five years old, through an introduction by the Reverend Mr Helm, from Bulawayo. Well informed about Lady Burdett-Coutts' deep interest in missionary work, he told her about his future plans, stressing particularly the great advantages the missionaries would have in spreading the gospel and the benefits to be gained by the savage Natives if their countries came under the civilizing influence of Britain. At the end Rhodes approached her with the blunt request to provide him with high-ranking patrons for his schemes. Rhodes' wildest expectations were surpassed when Lady Burdett-Coutts arranged a party for him with the Prince of Wales as guest of honour.

When Rhodes explained his scheme to His Royal Highness, he found not only a willing ear but also the understanding of a man sufficiently schooled in business affairs to be able to judge the soundness of a financial proposition. The Prince became infected with Rhodes' enthusiasm and promised to submit the plan to the

Queen, who, after consulting with Lord Salisbury, gave her consent to grant Rhodes a Royal Charter. Since it was not considered advisable, for political reasons, that the Prince should accept the leading position in the Chartered Company, he recommended instead his son-in-law, the Duke of Fife. Also for political reasons, the Duke was to take the position only of vice-chairman and thus the Prince of Wales chose for the chairmanship his good old friend the Duke of Abercorn. Both dukes had very close political connections, Fife with the Liberals, and Abercorn with the Tories.

With the royal blessing and two dukes on his Board it was easy for Rhodes to fill the other seats on the British South Africa Company before applying for the Charter. Lord Gifford and Cawston of the Exploring Company had to be on it according to the terms of the merger, and it was natural that Rhodes should be nominated managing director with Maguire representing him on the London Board. Beit and Rudd were also included. The Duke of Fife brought in a senior partner in his banking firm, Sir Horace B. Farquhar, and also, on his friend Stead's recommendation, Lord Albert H. G. Grey, nephew and heir to Earl Grey, an acquisition described as Rhodes' greatest achievement.

Rhodes now felt that he needed a background more adequate than the Vicarage of Bishop's Stortford to lift himself to the same social level as his new associates. If he could not boast of noble birth he would at least show a descent from old gentry stock. He acquired from a distant relative an estate at Dalston, once owned by his grandfather, Samuel Rhodes. In the churchyard the new squire had some gravestones of the family restored and had others brought there from various places, in order to establish a 'family vault'. Dalston now became 'the old family seat'.

Through his new connections and through Beit, Rhodes became friendly with a number of city bankers who were to be very useful in the future, such as Baron d'Erlanger, in later years a director of the Chartered Company. He much admired Rhodes' talent for publicity, declaring that 'Rhodes fired the imagination of that most conservative class of human beings, the British investor, by christening his route the Cape to Cairo'. Of still greater advantage were Rhodes' business dealings with the bankers G. & A. de Worms, who took a great financial interest in the Chartered Company.

The Times, formerly sceptical about the plans and personality of Rhodes, now waxed almost enthusiastic in a leader which heralded 'the formation of a new company of British capitalists and philanthropists . . . opening up to trade and civilization certain territories in central Zambezi'.—'It is rich,' it continued, 'fabulously rich, we are told, in precious metals and half a dozen others besides. . . . Whether the Company finds the wealth of Ophir in the mountains and rivers of Mashonaland or not, we cannot doubt that it will lay the basis of a great English-speaking colony in what appears to be the fairest region in Africa. . . .'

One can almost see Rhodes and his intimates smile as they read the passage about 'British capitalists and philanthropists'. Perhaps it was at this opportunity that there first escaped his lips the ugly words which he later used repeatedly: 'Pure philanthropy is all very well in its way, but philanthropy plus five per cent is a good deal better.' The Liberal papers, however, showed their scepticism in as blunt a form as they could without tempting the English libel laws, and encouraged by their condemning criticism the Reverend Mr Mackenzie raised his arm to give what he thought would be the death-blow to Rhodes' plans by an attack in his pamphlets against 'a Cape colonist who is believed to have received very influential support . . . from persons in authority at the Cape. . . . A single speculator who buys for an old song the most valuable territory in South Africa. . . .' Fortified by royal backing, Rhodes was not much disturbed by his old opponent's vendetta. He was far more worried by the hostility displayed towards him in Parliament, which came not only from the side of the 'Little Englanders' but also from staunch imperialists.

Labouchere again asked some embarrassing questions in the House, his curiosity this time being directed at the relationship between the High Commissioner, Sir Hercules Robinson, and Rhodes, and the official help received in attaining the Rudd concession.

Feeling against Robinson ran high in the House because of a speech he had delivered on his departure from South Africa and his retirement from office. He had said that '. . . there is no permanent place in the future of South Africa for direct Imperial rule on a large scale! . . .' Such variations on Rhodes' theme of the 'elimination of the Imperial Factor', which he was trying to live down, turned many politicians against the Charter. They argued that Rhodes was a double-tongued anti-Imperialist flirting with the Boer-friendly and anglophobian Bond in South Africa and at the same time playing up to the Jingo spirit at home.

The revival of 'John Company', in the form of Rhodes' Chartered Company, met with opposition on both sides of the House. As chief speaker and most ardent opponent there rose Sir John Swinburne who had a special axe to grind with Rhodes for having encroached on a territory to which he believed himself to have a prior claim as the founder of the Tati gold-mines. Though the Tati district was expressly excluded from the Rudd concession, Sir John saw his prospering company dwarfed by Rhodes'. He complained that the treatment of the Charter in Parliament was 'a hole-and-corner affair . . . being railroaded through the House of Commons at an outrageous speed'. Pleading for adjournment, he concluded with the words:

'The fact is, this Charter will give to a syndicate of private adventurers as much power as the old East India Company possessed. . . . The whole pith of the Charter is really to confer all these powers on one person, Mr Cecil Rhodes.'

Following his principle of preferring negotiation to fighting, Rhodes offered Sir John Swinburne a price far above its true value and successfully persuaded him to sell him his Tati concession and merge his company with the Rhodes' group.

To suppress any arguments that Rhodes, by the terms of the Charter, would be at the receiving end without any compensatory obligations, while the Government was forced into the rôle of a goddess bestowing on him far-reaching favours without expectations of any returns, Rhodes offered to extend the railways and telegraph lines in the North and to begin to build immediately a telegraph line between Mafeking and Tati. He also offered an annual amount of £4,000 for the salaries and expenses of a suggested Imperial Resident at Bulawayo.

Finally, on 10 July, Lord Knutsford informed Cecil Rhodes that the Cabinet had decided to recommend to Her Majesty to grant the British South Africa Company a Royal Charter. It was only by dint of the greatest exertion by Rhodes assisted by Sir Hercules Robinson that the resistance of the Colonial Office was broken down and all Rhodes' demands were met. The hardest fight occurred right at the beginning when the future boundaries of the Chartered Company were fixed. The Colonial Office made no difficulties about the other frontiers but insisted obstinately that the Zambezi should be the boundary in the North. Rhodes remained adamant in demanding full freedom to go as far north as he wished, skilfully using the 'Cape to Cairo' leitmotiv in his plea. In the end Lord Knutsford gave way and the Charter contained no mention of the northern boundaries in regard to the extension of the Company's territory.

As a matter of fact, the Government could not and did not grant land in a country over which it possessed no claim to jurisdiction in any form. Only much later, by a Report of the Lords of the Judicial Commission of the Privy Council of 29 July 1918, was a legal interpretation of the purport of the Charter given:

> The Charter simply gave capacity to own and to grant land, but in itself it granted none. It used, indeed, the expression 'the Company's territories', but this referred to the area within which those capacities might be exercised, and did not amount to an anticipatory grant by the Crown of land which in 1889 was not the Crown's to bestow. . . .

After the Charter had already gone through, Lord Salisbury felt that it had been granted for something which did not exist. In a note to the Colonial Office he pointed out that Rhodes possessed no claim to land:

> . . . that the British South Africa Company has found itself hitherto somewhat embarrassed by the fact, on which those opposed to it were not disinclined to dwell, that the 'Rudd concession' obtained from Lobengula in 1888 did not in terms purport to grant more than mining rights in his territories, and that therefore it had but an imperfect right, if any right at all, to grant such titles to immovable property as were necessary for the development of a civilized community and of operations other than mining in its field of operations South of the Zambezi.

Translating from the official lingo, it becomes evident that the Charter was granted to the Company only for the exploitation of mining rights derived from the Rudd concession, the only asset, in the opinion of the British Government, that the Company possessed. However, Rhodes and his associates had purposely concealed the fact that the Company did not even own the Rudd concession! The Rudd concession, just like the Maund concession, the Tati concession, the Bains concession and the Nyasaland agreement, had been acquired and were held by the United Concessions Company, the private company founded and owned by Rhodes, Rudd and Beit together with Lord Gifford and George Cawston.

Only after the Government had confirmed its decision of granting the Charter did Rhodes make a contract between the British South Africa Company and his United Concessions Company, conferring on the former the rights (but not the title!) connected with the Rudd and other concessions against a payment of 50 per cent of all profits deriving therefrom. Rhodes, behind the back of the Government and of his shareholders, and without paying a penny for this valuable claim, thus made himself a secret half-share partner of the British South Africa Company. What enormous value this clandestine partnership represented was to become evident in 1890 when the Company was forced to buy from Rhodes—that is, from his United Concessions Company—the Rudd and other concessions in his hands for one million fully paid £1 shares of the Chartered Company of which the market value was then already between £3 and £4 each and which were to climb within the next few years to £7. Lord Gifford and Cawston received 75,000 shares while the bulk went to Rhodes, Rudd and Beit, each of whom therefore made a profit of over a million on this deal!

The British Government, just as much as the shareholders, was completely taken in by this nefarious trick. It took the Colonial Office more than three years and then only by a change in Government to discover the fraudulent manipulations which had been kept secret from them in 1889. The Secretary for the Colonies, Lord Ripon, informing the Chartered Company in 1892 that he had just received official report of the arrangement between the two companies, stated:

> . . . it is clear that Her Majesty's late Government [Salisbury's] was unaware of it when they advised the grant of the Charter. Whether knowledge of the arrangement would have influenced their action is a question which they alone could answer, but Lord Ripon thinks it important to place on record a statement of the state of their information at the time when alone their knowledge or want of knowledge of the arrangement was material.

Contrary to general belief at the time, the Charter did not give any great political powers to Rhodes. On the other hand, it also did not put him under any great obligations. The obligations which it did impose on him concerned the rights of the Natives and were formulated in vague terms. The Charter granted by the Queen on 15 October 1889 stated that the Chartered Company, on the prescribed field of operation, could exercise full benefit of its concessions 'so far as they are valid'; that the Company might, with the approval of the Government, acquire other concessions and rights 'including powers necessary for the purposes of government'; that the Company 'preserve peace and order . . . and may establish and maintain a force of police', that the Company 'shall consider carefully native laws and customs, particularly land-property rights'; and that the Company make regulations for the preservation of elephants and other game. One paragraph was inserted, suggested by Rhodes' legal friends, which made the Charter completely incontestable, even by the shrewdest lawyers: 'Her Majesty do further will, ordain and declare that this Our Charter shall be taken, construed and adjudged in the most favourable and beneficial sense for, and the best advantage of, the Company . . . notwithstanding that there may appear to be in this Our Charter any non-recital, mis-recital, uncertainty or imperfection.' Paragraph 30—'Our Naval and Military officers and Our Consuls and Our other Officers in Our Colonies and Possessions, and on the high seas, . . . be in all things aiding to the Company and its officers'—meant that the Company could call upon the help of the British Army and Navy in its tasks.

As a result of pressure from Exeter Hall the Colonial Office insisted on the prohibition of intoxicating drinks in the Company's territories, but the final formulation of Paragraph 12 of the Charter perplexed all those who knew about the abominable though very profitable trade in spirits in Native territories and its effects on the aborigines:

> The Company shall regulate the traffic in spirits and other intoxicating liquors within the territories aforesaid, so as, *as far as practicable*,[1] to prevent the sale of any spirits or other intoxicating liquor to any Natives.

[1] *Italics by the Author*

There was a general outburst of abhorrence about a paragraph which dealt with slavery. Paragraph 11 of the Charter stated that:

> The Company shall to the best of its ability discourage and, *so far as may be practicable*,[1] abolish by degrees, any system of slave trade or domestic servitude in the territories aforesaid.

Rhodes was now faced for the first time with translating his 'dreams' into realities. At this point he was concerned only with the problem of financing his march to the North. 'Our concession is so gigantic, it is like giving a man the whole of Australia,' he told Rudd. For its exploitation enormous sums would have to be handy. For the time being, and as long as these amounts did not have to be shown in cash, he manipulated the financing of the Chartered Company by using the money of De Beers and the Goldfields. The Rothschilds had already remonstrated about the unorthodox use of the capital of these two concerns. Generous and helpful as they had been at the foundation of his diamond amalgamation and of the Goldfields, they still held coldly aloof from helping to finance the Chartered Company. He thus had to find the means on the money market and induce speculators, investors and savers to take up on the Stock Exchange the one million shares of £1 each of the Chartered Company.

Invulnerable against criticism through his high connections, he could unload his shares on an unsuspecting public. Carefully he directed the market so that the shares were taken up in large quantities at double and treble the price of their nominal value until they rose to a maximum of more than £7 for the £1 shares. The publicity slogan of 'Cape to Cairo' had worked wonders. The most absurd paradox was the fact that the majority of the shares of this company, meant by its founder to become the bastion of British supremacy in southern Africa and the basis of the realization of his imperialistic dreams, were bought by French and German speculators. This fact was of course not revealed to the public, just as the shareholders were kept in the dark about all matters concerning the Company. And what little they were told when offered its shares was painted to them in glowing colours. Actually the assets of the Chartered Company were nil. Its future was built on hopes. The main hope, described in terms of a certainty, lay in finding gold in the concessioned territories. The

[1] *Italics by the Author*

only authorities for such expectations were certain passages in the Old Testament which referred to the Land of Ophir, the tales of some ancient travellers and a few pieces of auriferous rock found twenty years before by an amateur explorer and painter. But the names of the high-ranking personalities on the Board dispersed all scruples, suspicion and caution.

Serious criticism was raised about the methods employed in forming the Company. It was stated openly that its shares were 'used by Rhodes to conciliate the influence of influential people'. Rhodes doled out liberally to those who had assisted him in promoting the Company options on £1 shares which could be sold, even before they were paid for, at £2 or £3. Rhodes' friends defended him against such reproaches with the astonishing explanation that he 'looked at the matter in a broad way and recognized all those who had helped him secure the Charter and given requisite financial guarantees as entitled to the first chance of profit by the enterprise which they had helped to bring into existence'. He was taxed with the same offence in South Africa —that he used a large parcel of these shares to 'square' his local influential friends.

Rhodes was beginning to become impatient. Africa was calling him. Thompson's latest reports from Bulawayo carried the alarming tidings that Lobengula was once more falling under the influence of his 'white dogs'. Thompson seemed again to be suffering from the jitters.

Before the Charter was officially proclaimed Rhodes set out for South Africa to gather the harvest from the seeds of his 'dreams'.

CHAPTER XI

A COUNTRY FOR BREAKFAST

DARK, silent clouds were hanging over the royal kraal of Bulawayo. No one dared to speak aloud. Not even the highest *induna* would have dared to criticize Lobengula. Rather they pitied him. They whispered that since he had had Lotje and his whole clan killed the King often did not touch food or beer for days. Not that the King repented of having put to death his chief counsellor; but he felt that he could no longer rely on the advice of any of his *indunas*. They said that the King was robbed of his sleep at night by *madhlozi*—ghosts. He could be seen wandering through his kraal in the dark or sitting in his goat-kraal fully robed in his regal war-dress, brewing medicines with the help of the chief witch-doctor. What worried the people most were the rumours that for several moons the King had called none of his wives nor any of his concubines to the brick house to share his mat with him.

Even the highest *indunas* were kept in the dark about their royal master's plans, let alone his thoughts, worries and fears. Very seldom now were they called to the royal kraal for an *indaba*. It was whispered in Bulawayo that the King seemed to have been cured for ever of his former partiality towards white men. His great friend whom he calls 'Tomosi', the mouth of the Man who made the Big Hole, the gossipers said, seems to have fallen into disgrace. Even the Queen's *induna* 'Joni' Moffat has been waiting already for weeks to see the King.

The fact was that Lobengula felt like a trapped animal robbed of its freedom and left no choice but to wait for the death-blow. The only *indunas* admitted to the royal presence were his emissaries, Babyaan and Umsheti. Again and again they had to tell the King their tales about the land of the Great White Queen. During one such discussion he opened the old biscuit-box, and dug under his diamonds. Out came the cursed piece of paper by which he was supposed to have given away his land to the white men. He ordered Thompson, the traders and the white hangers-on of the kraal to appear before him. Everyone had told him that Thompson had blinded his eyes by magic and that the concession was not valid. Let them now tell him how to rid himself and his country of the danger of being eaten by the big-mouthed guns of the white devils:

'What have you got to say? There is the paper!'

The white men looked uncomfortable. None of them seemed willing to talk. Finally one found the courage to step forward and say:

'King, we have read the paper again and we must say that this document is all right. What we said about Mr Thompson we know now was wrong.'

Lobengula's face expressed such contempt that the man quickly stepped back into the crowd. The King rubbed his hands across his lips: 'Tomosi has smeared fat on your mouths,' he said. 'Oh, what liars all you white men are! Tomosi, you've lied the least. —Tomosi, have you not got a brother named Rhodes who eats a whole country for breakfast?' With these words the King, his eyes flashing fire, dismissed them.

Lobengula had guessed correctly that the sudden change in attitude of the resident white men in Bulawayo was brought about by corruption. Rhodes had bombarded Thompson with letters for weeks, always fearing that the last of his envoys would, as Rudd and Maguire had done, become nervous and quit his post, thus creating the abhorred vacuum. He persuaded the brave Thompson not to give up, tempting him with prospects of the future:

> . . . I ask you plainly: do you believe you could have a grander chance in the world if the thing succeeds. . . ? When I tell you that the Rand is selling today for £30 millions what may I ask is the value of our Concession if we get settled in harness. . . ?

Rhodes was equally worried about the opposition to his concession from the influential traders and about their claims based on previous grants from Lobengula. He therefore advised Thompson:

> I think you underrate your opponents. Could you not gradually employ them? Napoleon was prepared to share the world as long as he got Europe. Work on these lines. Can't you give the whites who are in the country something. . . ?

Thompson followed Rhodes' suggestion and distributed freely among the traders and the 'white dogs' several thousand pounds. They pocketed the money with satisfaction but Thompson won their full loyalty only after he had shown them a letter from Rhodes which contained the passage:

> . . . I am arranging with the Colonial Office to withdraw any chance of action against any of the whites, so you can assure them they are safe. . . .

By this clever stroke of promising them immunity—though Rhodes' interference as a private individual with the course of British Justice is amazing—Rhodes removed their main cause for opposition. As fugitives from the British police, most of the white men in Bulawayo had had very good reason for trying to prevent British infiltration into Matabeleland.

Feeling that the noose around his neck was tightening, Lobengula in his desperation again wrote a letter to the Queen:

> The white people are troubling me much about gold. If the Queen hears that I have given away the whole country it is not so. I have no one in my country who knows how to write. I do not know where the dispute is as I have no knowledge of writing.

Having learnt from his previous experience, Lobengula this time adhered strictly to prescribed procedure and went to the Reverend Mr Moffat as the representative of the Queen to have his signature witnessed and the letter forwarded through official routes. The letter caused great dismay to Rhodes' friends in South Africa—Sir Sidney Shippard, J. S. Moffat and Captain Bower—all of whom served their Queen as high colonial officers with the same devotion with which they looked after the interests of their other master, Cecil Rhodes.

Rhodes had just returned from London with the Cabinet's confirmation of the Charter. The royal proclamation of the Charter was expected towards the end of October. It was now the middle of August. A letter from Bulawayo to London usually took about seven weeks. This meant that Lobengula's letter would arrive before the Charter was officially announced and could thus easily, if not upset, at least delay all Rhodes' plans. The letter would have to be kept back, Rhodes suggested, until there was no longer any danger of a collision. His friends obligingly kept back the letter which was dispatched to London four days before the Charter was gazetted and arrived there exactly 110 days after Moffat had received it from Lobengula.

When no answer arrived from the Queen, Lobengula's fears turned to panic. His régime of terror in the royal kraal had worked on his young warriors to such an extent that they openly voiced their demand to 'wash their assegais in blood'. Much as Lobengula, in normal times, had welcomed the eagerness which drove his *matjaha*—young recruits—into battle to win the right to marry, he did not even dare to send them on harmless raids beyond the border. He had learnt about the increase of the Bechuanaland Police which Sir Hercules Robinson, at Rhodes' request, had so cleverly squeezed out of the Colonial Office. These police-*impis*, Lobengula was told, were suspiciously busy on the Matabele frontiers. He feared that if he allowed his young bloods to go for *gubagubo*—to rattle their shields—it might lead to clashes with the Queen's *impis*.

The high spirits of Lobengula's *matjaha* found an outlet in insulting and threatening Thompson. He was a brave man who had never shirked the greatest perils of the veld and had never shown fear of even the wildest Natives. But what he had to suffer in Bulawayo, where he was no longer safe by day or night, went even beyond his power of endurance. He had now wasted his time and health in Bulawayo, without a break, for more than a year. Why could not Rudd or Maguire come to replace him or better still Rhodes himself for whom Lobengula was clamouring all the time?

Rhodes replied from Kimberley that he should stay in Bulawayo until the concession was ratified by Lobengula. While praising him for his work Rhodes warned him sternly that he would lose his credit and rewards 'which would be hard for your own future' if he did not see the matter through to the finish 'which is now so near'. Rhodes must have realized that this was somewhat harsh on an associate who for over a year had risked his life for him almost daily and therefore added:

> Please do not view this as a threat but look at it practically. If we lose the Concession we have nothing for the Charter. . . . If I were to isolate myself in the interior at this moment the whole of the base would go wrong.

Rhodes did, however, announce that he might send Dr Jameson to help Thompson in Bulawayo. The doctor had already proved that he was the only one among Rhodes' friends, who, by his strong nerves, his energy and no less by a never-failing personal fascination, could manage Lobengula. Rhodes knew him for a passionate hazarder who gambled not so much for the sake of money as for the thrill of outwitting an opponent. Here was a gamble! Dr Jim would certainly jump at the opportunity of out-trumping an opponent like Lobengula. Dr Jameson's answer to Rhodes' inquiry when he would be willing to start arrived promptly: 'By tomorrow's mail-coach.'

While Dr Jameson was being jolted in the coach to Bulawayo, Rhodes was on his way to Pretoria to settle with President Kruger the Transvaal's still ardent and vociferous aspirations to the North.

Upon his arrival Rhodes was told that the President could not see him that day, Saturday, as the town was full of burghers who had come from near and far for the *nagmaal*—Holy Communion—and many of whom would call on the President and leave him no time to see anyone else. 'And tomorrow?' asked Rhodes, already irritated by this cool reception. The President's secretary looked at the visitor with an expression of incredulity: '*Tomorrow is Sunday*.' 'I know,' said Rhodes, 'but I have to leave.' 'The President does not see any visitors on Sundays.' 'Tell him Cecil Rhodes wants to see him.'

The secretary came back quickly with the President's answer: 'Tell him that I do not do business on *die dag van die Here*. So Mr Rhodes can wait or go.'

Rhodes turned purple. Picking up his hat, he hissed: 'The old devil! I meant to work with him, but I am not going on my knees to him. I've got my concession, though, and he can do nothing.' He left for Kimberley by the next coach.

Historians have agreed that this interview, which did not take place because of the obstinacy of two strong-willed men, might have changed the entire course of South African history.

Rhodes was in a hurry to return to Cape Town in order to ask the help of his friends in Government House against a fresh attempt by Edward Lippert and Renny-Tailyour to obtain a new concession from Lobengula on behalf of a German syndicate. Rhodes' men had reported that Renny-Tailyour was in Johannesburg, where he was observed to hold long conferences with

Lippert, both frequently visiting the agents of a German bank. When Rhodes heard that Renny-Tailyour was buying a travel wagon and engaging several Matabele boys as servants for a journey to the North and had asked all to keep the matter secret, he became determined to prevent him or Lippert from crossing the border into Matabeleland. It seemed evident that one of them wanted to take the concession document to Bulawayo for Lobengula's signature. Government House, as always, was obliging without asking any questions about the legality of their friend's demands. Shippard immediately issued an order to the Bechuanaland Police to arrest Lippert and Renny-Tailyour if either of them should try to enter Matabeleland. The incredible occurrence, contrary to all concepts of law and justice, of a British subject being put under arrest on British territory without a legal warrant and for the only reason that he was about to enter a foreign country outside British jurisdiction, took place when Renny-Tailyour arrived at Tuli, the frontier-station in Bechuanaland. Renny-Tailyour calmly told the officer that he would launch a complaint with the High Commissioner and would wait as his prisoner for the reply. A few days after his arrest a Native runner was seen racing along the road, wildly swinging a cleft stick to which was fixed a heavily sealed letter. Already from afar, as was the custom of royal runners, he shouted: 'A royal message from my lord, King Lobengula, to his slave Renny . . . Renny. . . !'

Nonchalantly Renny-Tailyour put the letter in his pocket. He went to the camp-commander to tell him that there was now no longer any need for him to go to Bulawayo.

To the officer's question he replied with well-simulated indifference: 'Really, nothing of importance, but this letter here saves me a lot of bother, as it contains a concession just signed by Lobengula and his council of *indunas* by which all land-rights of Matabeleland are transferred to me and Lippert.'

This time Rhodes had been outwitted. Lippert had not given up hope of getting the better of Rhodes and particularly of his hated cousin Beit, even after they had obtained the Rudd concession. He consulted Th. ('Offy') Shepstone, a barrister recognized as the greatest authority on concessions in South Africa. 'Offy' was the son of a famous British Colonial official, Sir Theophilus Shepstone, who was known throughout southern Africa as 'Somtseu'—the Mighty Hunter—and esteemed as a great friend of the Zulus. This friendship was extended to his son 'Offy' not only by the Zulus, among whom he had grown up, but by many other tribes, especially the Matabele. Lobengula was very fond of 'Offy' and regarded him as his best friend among the white men. He therefore accepted Shepstone's advice to give Lippert a land-concession by which the Rudd concession would become valueless because it did not cover sufficiently the right to take possession of land. If Lippert was nominally the owner of all land, how would Rhodes be able to dig for gold? Lobengula, in the hope of forestalling Rhodes' further onslaughts by having Rudd's gold concession disputed by another white man, willingly signed the Lippert concession.

Rhodes was furious. His anger changed to fear when he learnt the full contents of the Lippert concession. It contained exactly those rights which he needed so as to legalize his own concession and make the Charter workable. These land-rights had worried Rhodes a good deal and he had discussed this point in London. Chamberlain had advised him: 'Well, you have got the gold of the whole country, which in itself is nine points of possession, so I should say that even if you have it not in theory, you have it in practice. But I should like you to get some territorial acknowledgment from Lobengula, further strengthening your claim as a whole.'

Knowing full well the value to the Chartered Company of their concession, Lippert and his group asked a stiff price for it which Rhodes declined to pay. Negotiations dragged on for a long time until Rhodes had to swallow the bitter pill of paying Lippert his exorbitant sum. Thirty years later the highest English law-court decided that the Lippert concession did not really offer any legality as a title to the ownership of land.

Thompson, in the meanwhile, could no longer bear to stay at Bulawayo with the now certain prospect of being murdered by the excited Matabele. He decided to flee as quickly as he could. Just on the border he met Dr Jameson, who persuaded him to return with him to Lobengula.

The King, however, refused 'to give him the road', saying: 'No—I do not want to see that man who has spoken to me with two tongues. Lobengula chases liars away like mangy dogs.' It took Dr Jameson's persuasive influence eventually to obtain permission for Thompson to enter Bulawayo with him. Jameson was warmly received by Lobengula, who was still very fond of 'U'Dogetele'. The doctor used all his charm in executing Rhodes' order 'to keep Lobengula sweet'. Again he treated him successfully for his gout and cured his inflamed eyes. By his humour, his presents and his captivating amiability, Dr Jameson helped considerably to improve the mood of the King and also to dispel some of his fears.

One day, when Jameson had started to prepare Lobengula for the impending occupation of Mashonaland by the Chartered Company, the King, turning to his interpreter, had burst out:

'"Ulodzi" has sent me many emissaries and among them "U'Dogetele", whom I like, who is "Ulodzi's" mouth; but I am Lobengula and I want to see the big white chief himself; I am tired of talking with his messengers and the bearers of his words; their stories don't all agree.'

Progress was slow. Whenever the subject of Mashonaland was broached Lobengula broke up the interview. The prospect of persuading him to consent to the Chartered Company's entry into Mashonaland deteriorated rapidly. The Colonial Office, persistently egged on by Rhodes' ducal associates in London, had prepared a theatrical coup by which Lobengula should be left in no doubt that behind Rhodes and the Chartered Company stood H.M. the Queen and the British Government and that they were resolved to back the gold concession if necessary by the might of their army. The occasion of notifying him officially of the granting of the Charter was chosen as the right moment.

On a hot summer day at the beginning of 1890, there jogged along the rugged road to the royal kraal a heavy coach on the doors of which, below a large golden crown, was inscribed the royal monogram V.R. The cumbersome vehicle, drawn by eight fat and shiny mules in silver-coated harness, was followed by many riders in scarlet uniform, with glittering silver breast-plates and shiny silver helmets from which costly feathers fluttered in the wind. Each of these uncanny appearances rode a wonderful charger covered with costly material and most of them carried drawn swords. The cattle in the kraal became restless. The dogs howled and crept away with tails between their legs. Chickens fluttered in terror into the bushes. Women cried hysterically and pulled away their children to hide in the huts.

A contingent of the Royal Horse Guards, together with the

regiment's band, and led by three officers, had arrived to announce the Charter to Lobengula in the name of the Queen and to express her approval of the concession. Before the letter could be handed over to Lobengula it was shown to Dr Jameson who angrily tore 'this unintelligible rubbish' to pieces, not in the least concerned that it came from a Minister of the Crown and was thus a State document. He sat down immediately and wrote another letter, more suited to Rhodes' purpose, which was presented to Lobengula as coming from the Queen.

Lobengula received the delegation with dignity and closely inspected the escorting Guardsmen. He tapped their breast-plates with his fingers and remarked to Jameson: 'Now I know that Babyaan was not telling me a lie when he said that the Great White Queen clothed her soldiers in iron.'

Dr Jameson declared himself satisfied with the 'excellent results' of his falsified letter on Lobengula, who was evidently deeply impressed. Nevertheless Lobengula still refused to discuss the question of 'giving the road' to Rhodes' men in his country through which ran the direct route to Mashonaland. The festival of the First Fruit was approaching. On that occasion the King would have to throw the sacred assegai to indicate to his *impis* the direction of their next raid. His unruly young warriors were pulling at the leash more than ever. They had already threatened loudly to kill all white men in Bulawayo. Where should he send them? He could not possibly let them loose on Mashonaland. There they would without doubt clash with Rhodes' men. In the east, as he had learnt, Portuguese *impis* were massing, waiting for a reason to make an inroad on his territory. To the north? He knew that the King of Barotseland had just asked the Great White Queen to give him protection. To the west? There stood Shippard's Bechuanaland Police. To the south? Should he provoke a repetition of history and have his men decimated by the Boers? . . . There was nowhere to go! . . .

Tens of thousands of eyes were focused on the King. The men stood lined up, breathless from the intoxicating wildness of their war-dance. Their deafening shouts rose still higher when Lobengula slowly raised himself from his seat, a lion-kaross slung over his shoulders, with long monkey tails dangling from the leopard-skin around his waist and on his head the royal rubber-ring with a long single heron-feather. His head held high and stretching himself to his full height, he walked with ceremonious steps to the centre. '*Nanku*! *Nanku*! There he is!'

Lobengula received the sacred spear from an old *induna*. He grasped it with firm hands and whirled it round and round in an ecstatic dance. Breathlessly they waited to see in which direction the spear would be thrown. Suddenly the King stopped and with the utmost vehemence drove the spear into the ground. Bitter silence settled on the crowd. In the silence the King walked slowly, leaning on the sacred spear, towards his hut.

Many months passed. According to Rhodes' latest reports to Dr Jameson, it seemed that Selous had indicated a possibility of entering Mashonaland by another direct route for which a road would first have to be made. The vexatious passage through Matabeleland and the consequent possibility of a clash with Lobengula's *impis* would thus be avoided. Lobengula would merely be required to close his eyes to Rhodes' march into Mashonaland. The King, however, justly claimed Mashonaland as an integral part of his kingdom. His father's *impis* had conquered it and the Mashonas accepted the Matabele as their masters. To Lobengula Mashonaland represented a valuable asset from where he collected considerable taxes and drew his supply of slaves. Tens of thousands of head of cattle, forming a great part of his wealth, were permanently put there to graze.

In May 1890 after Dr Jameson had been at the royal kraal for four months he thought that it was time he returned to civilization. He felt that Lobengula's evasiveness might continue for ever if he did not put him under the pressure of an ultimatum. He prepared his departure, and went to take his leave of Lobengula. He saw the King lying on his sleeping-mat stark naked, staring into space and apparently deep in thought. When he refused to listen to him, Dr Jameson broke off abruptly with the words: 'Good-bye, King, you've given me your promise about the road. On the strength of that promise, I'll bring in my *impi* to Mashonaland. Otherwise—there will be war!'

When he had returned to South Africa in August 1889, with the Charter concluded and only still to be officially proclaimed by the Queen, Rhodes had felt that he was the ruler of a country twice the size of the United Kingdom, but which still had to be conquered. The long months of negotiations had played havoc with his nerves. In South Africa it was Cecil Rhodes who set the pace. Now he wanted to start out immediately on his march to the North, or, as he now preferred to say, 'up yonder'. He wanted to begin with the railway and telegraph lines which he was obliged to build according to the terms of the Charter. The Colonial Office made no move to supply him with the required material. Perhaps they first wanted cash? He cabled to them asking to whom he should make the payment. After a week he received their reply: 'No so fast; you must wait until the Charter is granted.'

He was kept busy. De Beers and the Goldfields needed his attention. The mines in Kimberley were running smoothly, but in Johannesburg the gold-boom which had started in 1887 had been in its fullest bloom until the latter half of 1889 when prices suddenly collapsed and the get-rich-quick brotherhood had to interrupt its dance around the golden calf.

Rhodes encountered great difficulties in Johannesburg. The Rothschilds were not satisfied with his liberal jockeying of funds out of De Beers and the Goldfields into the Chartered Company. At a shareholders' meeting of Goldfields, they, together with other shareholders, refused to allow an increase of its capital by £120,000 for investing in Chartered shares and also demanded that the Company sell all its stock of De Beers' shares.

Any interference by shareholders, even by members of the board of directors, Rhodes regarded as an insult which he would not stand. In his anger he wrote to Rudd:

> Goldfields have behaved disgracefully and I am thinking of resigning, but shall await your decision. I have no intention of working for these fellows for the balance of my life.

The threat, of course, was not meant seriously, but as usual Rhodes had employed the right tactics: Goldfields subscribed heavily to the Chartered shares.

As a result of a few lucky incidents the position on the Rand changed overnight. Rich coal-fields were discovered in the Transvaal, and consequently the exorbitant price of coal dropped to a point where also the poorer gold-mines could be worked on a profitable basis. Fears that the reef would pass out at a greater depth proved to be unfounded. The greatest innovation, which brought about the salvation of the industry, consisted of a cyanide process by means of which gold could be extracted from the ore up to 95 per cent.

The hectic days of boom, this time in a form wilder than ever before, descended once more on Johannesburg, and seemed to settle there as a permanent condition, spreading also to the share markets of London and the Continent. Into Johannesburg there now streamed a fresh crowd from all parts of the world.

The birth of this cosmopolitan town of 50,000 inhabitants, three-quarters of whom were British, only forty-odd miles from his country's capital, was regarded by President Kruger and his government with divided feelings. Uitlanders—foreigners—in Johannesburg already outnumbered the Boers considerably, and were asking for the franchise.

In England the growth of a British enclave in the heart of the Transvaal did not pass unnoticed. The *Saturday Review* predicted prophetically that 'the actual owners of the soil' in Kruger's country would soon dwindle into 'an insignificant minority'. *The Times* considered it necessary to point out that 'the subject is assuming proportions that must soon engage the attention of the Imperial Government . . . the transformation which has only just begun, must be carried further until the political power now monopolized by the Boers is shared with the preponderating mass of new citizens mainly of British descent'. It was also the first but not by far the last time that *The Times* expressed the hope that the ticklish question of the Uitlander franchise would be easier to settle when the sixty-six-year-old President Kruger would 'pay the debt of nature'.

Wishing to find a means of meeting this precarious situation which would be just to his own people as well as to the Uitlanders, President Kruger went to Johannesburg to gain his own impressions. He was to address a mass meeting of local residents and also hear their opinions. When the President appeared on the platform and was about to begin his speech, a few young hooligans thought it a good opportunity for expressing their patriotism in musical form by singing 'Rule Britannia'. President Kruger, having waited in the expectation that someone would restore order, began to show signs of anger. With a contemptuous look he shouted at the gleeful singers: '*bly stil*—keep quiet.' They burst into roars of laughter. The President turned his back on them, took his hat and walked with dignity out of the hall. He returned immediately to Pretoria. Later he heard that on the same night two ruffians of Uitlanders had climbed on the roof of the *landrost's* building, the seat of the district administrator, and had pulled down the *Vierkleur*—the flag of the Transvaal—and trampled on it.

Judging by these two incidents, one can understand why President Kruger did not consider the Johannesburg rabble worthy of becoming burghers of the Transvaal. By the weight of their numbers they might soon push his Boers against the wall.

Rhodes did not take great interest in the Rand at all. The Goldfields merely had to help supply him with the means to materialize his 'dreams'. In Kimberley he was the master and dictator. On the Rand he was only one among many, and his old opponent, J. B. Robinson, saw to it that Rhodes should not repeat his Kimberley manœuvres of obtaining a monopoly. In Rhodes' mind there existed nothing but the North. Though he was duly re-elected in his old constituency of Barkly West in 1888 he could not spare the time to attend the session in 1889. He felt that he would first have to consolidate his political position in South Africa in order to win over the Cape Parliament for his drive 'up yonder'. By his alliance with the Colonial Office and with British capital and by seeking and accepting a Royal Charter for the exploration of the North, Rhodes had sinned against his own much-publicized demand of 'eliminating the Imperial Factor'. It was now up to him to make this contradiction plausible to Hofmeyr and the Bond and also to make his approaching conquest of Mashonaland sufficiently palatable to them, since the 'Mole' still maintained that the North really fell within the sphere of interest of the Transvaal. He needed the Bond's collaboration in order to win over the Cape Parliament for his northern railway projects. He could not 'square' a man like Hofmeyr with Chartered shares, though these shares, with a guaranteed immediate profit of £2 to £3 each, had appeased the conscience of several other Bondsmen. Hofmeyr remained sceptical. When he met Rhodes after his return from London with the Charter he taxed him:

'You have got hold of the Interior, now be generous. Let us down gently.'

Rhodes shook his hand and said: 'I'll take you with me!'

Now that it could no longer do him any harm to be reported in England as a dangerous anti-Imperialist ready to 'cut the painter', he let himself go in condemning a British Colonial policy which allowed Africa to be mapped out in Berlin. He told his voters in Barkly West:

> . . . My belief is that the development of South Africa should fall to that country or countries which by their progress shall show that they are best entitled to it; and I have faith that, remote as our starting point is, the development will occur through the Cape Colony; that . . . we shall be able to obtain the dominant position throughout the interior . . . and I have confidence that the people of the Cape Colony have the will, and the pluck, and the energy to adopt this as their inheritance.

In spite of these pompous words, Rhodes preferred to have his conquest of the North organized by English dukes, financed by international stock exchange gamblers, sanctioned by the British Crown and directed by the Colonial Office. There was certainly nothing South African about the British South Africa Chartered Company, the head office of which was in London and on the Board of which was not to be found a single South African. Only when it came to pulling the hot chestnuts out of the fire and when he needed courageous young men to do the dirty work connected with the annexation, did he want South Africans. In return he gave them only words, high-sounding phrases and empty slogans such as:

> When we commenced that policy of taking over the North—and you must not give me the sole credit—the thought that guided me in my ideas was that the world was limited, and that the country to which we all belong should have as much of it as it could possibly get. This was a consideration which affected, not only the people at home, but the people here, including not only English but Dutch. If we are a great people, it is because we are an amalgamation of races. . . .

Such words were meant principally to flatter the Bond and to destroy any suspicions of his imperialistic aspirations. Hofmeyr could not be so easily deceived. Facts and figures of stock exchange transactions with Chartered shares spoke too loudly against Rhodes' sincerity. At one time, at the beginning of 1890, Rhodes was seriously contemplating whether it would not be better for him to do without political fetters and drop his Parliamentary activities. He had already decided to resign from Parliament but friends, especially Merriman and some young Liberals, men like Sauer, Molteno and Schreiner, persuaded him to remain. They had appealed to him previously to 'give his time and attention to other things than mining . . . to the politics of this Colony and the States adjoining—in fact the whole of South Africa'. The suggestion that he should aspire to the Premiership of the Cape and that they would gladly serve under him received from him a willing ear. Master of Kimberley—Dictator of the North—Prime Minister of the Cape . . . was not this the road towards the Presidency of a Federated Greater South Africa? As Prime Minister, Rhodes predicted, quite accurately, he would get on much better with the newly appointed Governor, Robinson's successor, than if he came to him as a representative of the Chartered Company to ask for favours. Hofmeyr and the Bond, however, would have the last word, since every Cabinet depended on their grace.

He was now determined to throw in his lot fully with the Bond. He needed the Afrikaners in order to fight 'Krugerism', which, with its racial, nationalistic and religious insularity, and its aim of hegemony in South Africa under the Transvaal *Vierkleur*, threatened the success of a federation of South Africa. This danger could only be fought hand in hand with the Bond. Hofmeyr was also striving for a South African federation and believed that out of a complete amalgamation of Dutch and British there should grow a South African nation as an independent part of the British Empire, endowed with complete home rule.

Rhodes played up to the Bondsmen, most of whom were farmers, by referring to his ancestors as simple British yeomen, though only a few months previously in London, in order to impress his new feudal connections, he had promoted the ancestral cattle-dealers to the status of gentry. He went on a 'daring raid' to Paarl, the idyllic little town where the Bond had been founded and which was venerated as the citadel of *ware Afrikanerdom*, and showed the Bondsmen a heart throbbing with anxiety for the welfare of the Afrikaner *boer*: 'We must protect our grain and our wine and whatever the country can produce. . . . First of all let us see that when the farmer puts his plough into the soil, he reaps a profitable harvest. . . .'

He went to Stellenbosch, the seat of Afrikaner learning, to address the young Afrikaner students at the Victoria College on graduation day. When Rhodes had finished his speech the head student, a slender youth, stepped on the platform. There was something arrogant in his bearing, yet his face, too serious in contrast to his youthful appearance, expressed the humility of a scholar. His personality impressed more than it attracted. It seemed to lack the warmth of emotional power.

His words, in spite of an initial shyness, came forth in well-formed phrases; his deeply reflected thoughts were expressed in a sonorous and flexible voice cleverly employed to bring out intended oratorical effects. He spoke of Pan-Africanism. Rhodes immediately ceased to look bored and listened with interest to what was a pleasing tune to his ears. Afterwards he inquired after the name of this youngster: Jan Christiaan Smuts, he was told, aged twenty, the son of a Cape farmer. Later he told Hofmeyr: 'Keep your eye on that young fellow Smuts!'

In order to please Hofmeyr, Rhodes gave way to many of his demands. He consented to religious school education, to the cancellation of all Sunday train services and to a disfranchisement of 'raw' Natives. Hofmeyr had to pay for these favours by voting with the Bond against motions disagreeable to Rhodes such as, for instance, an export tax on diamonds, suggested—as one of his many means of vengeance—by the 'Buccaneer'.

These political meanderings were, of course, only part of Rhodes' northern scheme, meant principally to cover his rear in the Cape by neutralizing the Bond. At the same time he wished to protect the northern territories from further German, Portuguese and Belgian penetration, to eliminate Krugerism, to finance his railway projects and to organize the pending occupation and the future policing of Mashonaland in the cheapest possible way. As Prime Minister of the Cape all these objects would certainly be attained smoothly and quickly.

If Britain preferred to colonize 'on the cheap' by means of private enterprise why should not Cecil Rhodes follow her example and let someone else pay for the expensive business of invading and occupying a large country? Rhodes had therefore conceived a plan whereby the Bechuanaland Police, which had been brought to a strength of about 800 men, should serve as a military protection to his pioneers by keeping Lobengula's *impis* in check. If good old Sir Hercules had still been ruling in Cape Town's Government House no difficulties would have been laid across his path. It was going to prove rather more difficult, if not impossible, to twist the old Governor's successor, Sir Henry Brougham Loch, around one's little finger. Downing Street had not looked with favour at the close financial interest of the former Governor in Rhodes' industrial enterprises. Sir Henry, they were certain, could not be 'squared' by anyone.

Carefully briefed and thoroughly warned, Loch came to South Africa with a slight bias against, and a strong distrust of, Rhodes. Still kept informed by his old friends about all happenings in Government House, Rhodes decided to overcome the new Governor's antipathy by taking him 'on the personal'. He had not, however, expected quite such a brusque refusal to his suggestion of using the Bechuanaland Police for his march into Mashonaland. Even his offer to pay for their work Loch brushed aside curtly. The Governor demanded categorically a proper military force organized and paid for by the Chartered Company.

Rhodes consulted military experts who told him that he would need at least 2,500 men for the invasion and occupation. Impossible! It would eat up at once the Chartered Company's entire capital of £1 million. Rhodes remembered that Selous had mentioned a plan of how to invade Mashonaland without passing through Matabeleland. Unfortunately he was at that moment not on very good terms with Selous as the hunter was one of the few in Bulawayo who had not received any compensation for his justified claims. One would need Selous now if only to keep him quiet! Selous knew Lobengula's realm better than anyone else, and, what was still more important, Selous, Rhodes was told, had enough proof to show that Mashonaland was a country independent of Lobengula. In Selous' opinion Mashonaland had never been conquered by the Matabele. There was no doubt, he maintained, that the Rudd concession, having no legal standing, was invalid and the Charter thus granted under false pretences.

In order to put some pressure on Rhodes, Selous secured a concession from one of the Mashona chiefs. But Rhodes was not unduly worried, knowing how easy it was to obtain the signature of a poor credulous chief. On the other hand, he did not want a man of Selous' reputation in the enemies' camp and therefore considered it wiser to appease him. In his talk with Selous,

Rhodes argued heatedly about the value of their concessions. Selous, as an experienced hunter, remained calm, and aimed at Rhodes' most vulnerable spot: his fear of adverse publicity in the English Press. Casually Selous remarked that he had prepared articles for some English papers advocating his views on the question. Rhodes saw at once, as he reported to the Duke of Abercorn in a letter dated March 1890, 'the danger of our position if a series of articles appeared in the papers from a man of Selous' position. . . .' It cost Rhodes £2,000 ('out of my own private fund') to settle with Selous and win him over to his side for the onslaught on Mashonaland. Selous now showed great enthusiasm. He had a private account to settle with Lobengula who had thrown him out of Bulawayo and forbidden him ever to set foot in Matabeleland again. Selous later explained his strange change of attitude by saying that he had then been in a very bad position financially and had therefore accepted a position in the Chartered Company as Adviser for the Mashonaland occupation. His acquisition was a windfall for Rhodes' company, even at the high salary of £3,000 a year, since there was no one whose knowledge of the Interior could compare with that of Selous'.

According to Selous' plan Matabeleland would be avoided altogether by building a road about 400 miles long from the border of British Bechuanaland leading directly to the eastern slopes of Mashonaland. Besides prospecting for gold, they could start bringing in settlers to cultivate this fertile land. Again Rhodes shuddered when he thought of the costs even with cheap Native labour. Another, cheaper way had to be found. The idea came to him of collecting a couple of hundred well-armed adventurous young men, paying them well and setting out on a sudden raid on Bulawayo, capturing fat 'Lob' and making him accept the *fait accompli*!

In his casual way Rhodes discussed this mad plan with several people, one of whom, after having wined well, boasted of how he would soon throw over the whole lot of bloody Kaffir chiefs and conquer all the Interior with a handful of chaps. This sodden talk came to the ears of Sir Henry Loch, who told Rhodes that silly rumours of an intended raid into Matabeleland were being passed round but that he had laughed them off as he could not imagine that Rhodes would run the risk of having his Charter recalled. . . . Rhodes took the hint. He had now to accept Selous' plan. But the more he pondered over it the more desperate did he become, all the more so because Dr Jameson from Bulawayo was urging him to hurry since he could not keep Lobengula sweet much longer.

Deeply worried, Rhodes was sitting at breakfast in the Kimberley Club when he saw the familiar, dark round face of little Frank Johnson. Though only twenty-three years old, this youngster had already shown his smartness, courage and business acumen in many a deal. He had been one of the many concession-hunters in Bulawayo, but had carried little favour with Lobengula. Rhodes, always keen to squeeze information out of others, invited him to his table. Rhodes began to talk, or rather think aloud, about Mashonaland, cursing those arrogant military experts who tried to make one believe that it would take 2,500 men, and at Colonial pay at that, for that little excursion to Mashonaland. Ridiculous!

Little Johnson agreed. He himself, he said, would venture on such an expedition with about 200 men, picked volunteers, at very small expense.

By lunch-time Johnson showed Rhodes sheets of paper covered with figures which gave an account of what he would need for 200 men in provisions, wagons, oxen, implements, arms, uniforms and horses. Rhodes, not interested in the details, became impatient and tried to pull out the last sheet with the final figure. But Johnson insisted on showing him each item until he concluded: '... And the whole amounts to exactly £94,100.' Five days later Rhodes signed a cheque for that amount.

When Rhodes submitted the new plan to the Governor, Sir Henry expressed his doubts about the safety of such an expedition without military cover and again demanded that Rhodes should provide protection by an adequate police force. Rhodes, still fighting shy of the expense, again suggested that the Bechuana-land Police should do the policing of Mashonaland and that he would pay for it. When Rhodes became insistent the Governor rang for his secretary and dictated a cable to the Colonial Office in which he reported Rhodes' suggestion and asked them to consider the repudiation of the Charter in the event of Rhodes' further insistence.

At last Rhodes was made to understand that Sir Henry Loch was not the man to accept instructions from him. He was forced to organize the British South Africa Chartered Company Police Force, consisting of about 500 men—and at Colonial pay!

On 10 March 1890 there stood on parade in Kimberley 184 hand-picked pioneers, well armed and in smart uniforms, each one as fine a specimen of South African manhood as one could wish for. In each one of them there burned the lust for adventure, the love of a free life on the veld and the hope of finding a secure future in a new and unknown land which would be conquered by their own hands. In Mashonaland each would be rewarded by a 3,000-acre farm and fifteen gold claims but until then they had to be satisfied with 7*s.* 6*d.* a day.

The pioneers first went to a spot on the northern frontier of Bechuanaland, where they were met by the Chartered Police and 200 Bechuanas hired from King Khama as road-makers and guides. Selous was there and Dr Jameson arrived from Bulawayo.

On Selous' advice two selected pure-bred white bulls were sent to Lobengula as a present which, according to Matabele custom, indicated the peaceful intentions of the giver. When after two days the messengers arrived to report Lobengula's acceptance Dr Jameson performed a dance of mad delight: 'That's all right! That will save us a lot of trouble!'

On 27 June 1890 Selous gave the signal for advance and the five hundred-odd men set out and made history. They endured the hazards of an almost tropical life with stoicism. These were not professional soldiers or down-and-out adventurers, but average young South Africans, most of them accustomed to a life of comfort and ease. Over them there always hovered the shadow of Lobengula. Twice he sent one of his *indunas* under *impi*-escort with the King's order to the columns to leave the country. Selous' fears grew: the wild bushy territory was simply inviting an ambush in the traditional Matabele style.

Lobengula, in his ignorance and keen belief in superstitions, must have thought, when he received the reports of his scouts, that the White Man had come to rob him of his country with the help of magic. What could poor lonely Lobengula do with all the might of his courageous *impis* against the witchcraft of the 'Man who made the Big Hole', who could make the sun—and if his *impis* did not lie even two or three suns—shine in the darkness of the night with a brilliance that hurt the eyes? What could poor lost Lobengula do against these white magicians who could produce storms with lightning sparks as high as mountains and make the ground roar and thunder so that the soil was thrown high into the air, leaving big holes into which a whole hut could fit?

With an eye on Native superstitions Selous had equipped the columns with powerful naval searchlights. The awe-inspiring thunderstorms were produced by dynamite charges laid outside the camp at night and periodically exploded by an electric wire.

On 15 August the columns reached the high veld and were now out of danger. A fort was erected named Fort Victoria, and another farther north, Fort Charter, to secure their line of communication. On 11 September 1890, well within ninety days as guaranteed by Johnson and Selous, they arrived at Mt. Hampden, their goal, destined to become the future centre of the Chartered country. A strong fort was built there and given the name of Salisbury in honour of the British Prime Minister.

It had been Rhodes' intention to accompany the pioneers on their march. Hofmeyr, however, had asked him to stay in Cape Town as a political crisis was calling for a change in government. The Governor sent for Rhodes to form a new government, and Rhodes accepted the mandate provided that Hofmeyr would come in with him. Hofmeyr declined but promised the full support of the Bond. On 17 July, a few days after his pioneers had crossed the border into Mashonaland, Cecil Rhodes, turned thirty-seven years old a few days earlier, became Prime Minister of the Cape Colony.

Rhodes did not find it as easy to form a Cabinet as to select the board of directors of a company, but finally he got together what he described as the 'Ministry of All the Talents' which included several prominent Cape Liberals such as his friends Merriman, Sauer and Rose-Innes.

His first parliamentary effort as Prime Minister turned out to be disappointing. Rhodes was unprepared in his subject—a Ballot Bill—and was very nervous, spoke badly and was almost inaudible to the House. The result of the first division resulted in a majority of one.

On 21 July came the expected attack in Parliament on his dual position as Prime Minister and Director of the Chartered Company to which Rhodes replied rather weakly that 'one position could be worked with the other, and each to the benefit of all'.

Many serious politicians and unbiased members of the public foresaw that Rhodes' not only dual but triple position would lead to unpleasant complications. It was pointed out that Rhodes, the Premier, would have to deal with contracts entered into with Rhodes, the Director of Chartered, and that Rhodes, the Premier, would have to decide important matters concerning Rhodes, the Diamond monopolist, Rhodes, the Goldfields Director, and Rhodes, the railway contractor. Olive Schreiner, the eminent South African authoress, expressed the feelings of many in the country when she wrote:

> The only big man we have here is Rhodes and the only big thing the Chartered Company. I feel a nervous, and almost painfully intense interest in the man and his career. I am so afraid of his making a mistake, as he would do, I think, if he accepted the Prime Ministership of this Colony, as there is some talk of his doing. I don't see how he can play the hand of the Chartered Company and the hand of the Colony at the same time.

Hofmeyr, when worried politicians asked him his opinion, replied that he preferred Rhodes to be exposed in his multiple private capacities to criticism by Parliament, which would be possible by censuring him as Premier, than to let him do what he liked without having to render account to the general public.

Others feared that Rhodes' expansive policy would involve the country in great expenses while the profits derived from such adventures would probably flow into the pockets of the shareholders of Rhodes' various companies. Voices were heard complaining about Rhodes' practice of 'squaring' the people whom he needed and that his activity in this respect, with the help of Chartered shares, was already noticeable in the changed attitude of several Bondsmen. A danger existed, they said, of a general corruption of public opinion by such nefarious methods and a further danger that he would now apply to the whole country his unpleasant spy-system which he had worked out to perfection in Kimberley. Men with so much money at their disposal, they feared, and with such great political and economic powers, might easily use their chances as a jumping-board into permanent dictatorial independence.

The English Tory Press hailed his nomination with great satisfaction. A writer in the August issue of *The Nineteenth Century*, after reminding the new Prime Minister that 'to implant English rule in all the outlying places of the Globe is the manifest destiny of our race', proceeded to teach him:

> . . . If the Dutch settlers set themselves in the way of development of South Africa after our British fashion, they will have to go to the wall. The principle of the survival of the fittest has decided that in the end it is the British, not the Dutch, element that must be supreme in the Cape as elsewhere.

This chauvinistic outburst did not tally with Rhodes' official policy, which had as its chief aim a reconciliation of Englishmen and Afrikaners with the prospect of a federation of all South African states, a union which he expected to be brought about by Free Trade, a Railway Convention, a Customs Union and 'closer and closer ties between the Cape and the neighbouring States'. However, with his finger raised in warning at the Transvaal about its own drive towards a federation under its *Vierkleur* flag, he said:

> It is customary to speak of a United South Africa as possible, within the near future. If we mean a complete Union with the same flag, I see very serious difficulties. I know myself that I am not prepared at any time to forfeit my flag. . . .

What would happen if 'the same flag' was the Union Jack, the speaker did not reveal; but it was interesting to learn that the Prime Minister—or was it the Director of the Chartered Company speaking?—expressed the certainty that 'within [his] lifetime the limits of the Cape Colony will stretch as far as the Zambezi', which would certainly be good business for the gentlemen of the Board and the shareholders of his Company, though the territory of this company was by Royal Charter meant to be part of the Empire under the direct control of Whitehall and not of the Cape. Rhodes once again, to please the Bond, wore the coat of the Colonial protagonist to scare away the 'Imperial Factor'.

As a result of Salisbury's policy of appeasement and his fear of expensive Colonial adventures, France, Portugal, Belgium and Germany had all been allowed to swallow large slices of Central Africa while Britain looked on. Salisbury's enthusiasm about the Cape to Cairo route had not lasted long.

Rhodes did not realize that changed conditions in European politics had forced England to re-direct her foreign policy in the last months. Therefore the latest moves in Downing Street concerning problems in Central Africa seemed to him enigmatic, contradictory and suicidal.

In March 1890 'the Pilot was dropped' in Berlin and Wilhelm II declared that he would from now on as 'his own Chancellor' steer the ship of State along 'the new course'. The Kaiser wanted to draw Britain into an Alliance which Salisbury tried to evade by all kinds of pretexts. Salisbury was willing to go so far as to 'keep in step with Germany' and even to make concessions in Africa. He therefore rejected the treaties which Stanley had made with various Native chiefs by which an all-British corridor from Lake Tanganyika to the Sudan would have been established and the Cape to Cairo route secured.

Germany immediately claimed these territories as falling within her sphere of influence. Britain protested only half-heartedly. This surrender, particularly of the Lake districts, could have been avoided since the Kaiser, not wishing to irritate England in view of other, more important, negotiations taking place at the time, had given instructions to the German Ambassador to drop the matter if Britain were insistent. Thus all Stanley's trouble and the propaganda campaign he had instigated 'to poke up the British Lion' had been in vain. On 1 July 1890 the Anglo-German Treaty was signed by which Britain gave Heligoland in exchange for Germany's consent to British influence over Nyasaland and the north-eastern corner of Mashonaland including the Stevenson Road, Uganda and the territories in the North beyond the Juba River to the confines of Egypt. In the south-west Britain conceded to Germany a strip of land, afterwards called 'Caprivi Zipfel'.

Rhodes and his friends raised a storm of indignation over this cession of the 'wasp-waist' to Germany by means of which the German south-west Colony was brought up to the Zambezi. They were still more angry when they heard that Salisbury had agreed to Germany's driving a wedge between Lake Nyasa and Tanganyika, thus cutting off for ever an all-British Cape to Cairo route.

Salisbury replied in Parliament that the only criticism 'had arisen from a very curious idea which has become prevalent in this country that there is some special advantage in handling a stretch of territory extending all the way from Cape Town to the sources of the Nile'.

To the Queen, Lord Salisbury reported his real intentions in signing the treaty:

> . . . any indefinite postponement of a settlement in Africa would render it very difficult to maintain terms of amity with Germany, and would force us to change our system of alliance in Europe. The alliance of France instead of the alliance of Germany must necessarily involve the early evacuation of Egypt under very unfavourable conditions.

Rhodes, who naturally knew nothing of Salisbury's true motives, rose in Parliament exactly eleven days after becoming Prime Minister, to give notice of the following motion:

> That this House regrets that the Government of this country was not directly represented in the recent arrangement entered into between the British Government and the German Empire in so far as those arrangements affected Territories south of the Zambezi and is of opinion that the Government of this colony should have a voice in any future proposed arrangement of boundaries south of that river.

Still worse was to come. Shortly before the pioneers had reached their goal in Mashonaland, Rhodes learnt that Lord Salisbury, on 20 August 1890, had signed a Convention with Portugal ceding the greater part of Barotseland and the whole of Manicaland to Portugal. Rhodes, who considered it a personal affront if Whitehall dared to make any move on the African continent without first consulting him, bombarded Downing Street with complaints, reproaches and fulminations. He wrote to the Foreign Office:

> I do not think I am claiming too much from your department in asking you to give some consideration to my views . . . and if you have any regard for the work I am doing, you will show it by now dropping the Anglo-Portuguese agreement.

Rhodes and his associates then showed—and unfortunately it was not the last occasion upon which they did so—how such complex colonial problems could be solved over the heads of governments, cabinets, ministers and diplomats. Shortly after his arrival in Fort Salisbury, Archibald Colquhoun, who had been nominated Administrator of the Chartered territories, together with Dr Jameson and Selous and a handful of Chartered police, had gone into Manicaland and made an agreement with the Chief by which, for the annual sum of £100, his country was ceded to the Chartered Company. This territory had been exploited for some time by a Portuguese syndicate. After learning of the agreement between the Chief and the Chartered Company the directors of the Portuguese syndicate charged a colourful adventurer, Manuel Antonio de Souza, also known as Captain Mor Goveia, a half-caste who specialized in gun- and rum-running, slave traffic and smuggling, to invade the Manica Chief's kraal and arrest him.

In an operetta-skirmish on 15 November 1890, Dr Jameson with a platoon of Chartered police overran the kraal, dispersed the Portuguese 'occupation army', arrested Goveia and a director of the Portuguese syndicate and sent them as 'prisoners of war' under escort to Cape Town. The Chartered Company was thus in full possession of Manicaland.

Since Dr Jameson's action, and the train of thought which moved him to infringe all existing civil, criminal and international laws, and also Rhodes' attitude towards this assumption of authority by officials of the Chartered Company constituted a remarkable precedent, it becomes necessary to make a closer investigation of the incident.

The Anglo-Portuguese Treaty was concluded on 20 August 1890. It can be assumed that the news of it had reached South Africa within at most a couple of days. Immediately after the pioneers had reached Fort Salisbury a postal service was established in Mashonaland and it was officially stated that a letter to Rhodes arrived at the first Bechuanaland postal station within five days. From Kimberley to Bechuanaland the weekly mail-coaches covered the 400 miles in three days. The treaty would have been known in the Company's headquarters at Fort Salisbury not later than 31 August. It can also be assumed that within the ten weeks till 15 November, Rhodes would have communicated with Dr Jameson, who was about 300 miles north of Fort Salisbury, and given him his instructions. It is also more than questionable whether Rhodes and Dr Jameson would have incurred the high costs of a military expedition into Manicaland, or risked the loss of the Charter, if the British authorities, perhaps not in

London or at the Cape, but certainly his friend Shippard in Bechuanaland, had not known about it. Perhaps this raid was the interpretation and practical demonstration of Lord Salisbury's answer to Rhodes' question of where to stop: 'Take all you can get and ask me afterwards.' No records exist which show that the Company was reprimanded for this action.

The tactics which Rhodes used to acquire Barotseland were hardly more commendable. A Kimberley merchant had obtained a concession for this territory of 200,000 square miles from its Paramount Chief Lewanika. It passed into the hands of a Kimberley syndicate and was finally acquired by Rhodes for £9,000 and 10,000 Chartered shares while the Chief received only an annual payment of £200 and 4 per cent royalty on mining. Lewanika had unsuccessfully asked the previous year for his country to be made a British protectorate. He now protested against the annexation by the Chartered Company. Rhodes tried to settle with the Chief on the basis of an increased annual payment of £2,000, but Lewanika beseeched Sir Henry Loch to be accepted as a 'Child of the Great White Queen'. With his letter he sent as a sign of his devotion two flawless large elephant tusks. The letter was intercepted by Sir Sidney Shippard upon whose recommendation the request was rejected and the tusks ended up as decorations in the board-room of the Chartered Company's London office, which strange fact the *Daily Chronicle* referred to as 'the meanest form of embezzlement, not from the Nation but from the Queen personally'.

Now that the Company had established headquarters in Fort Salisbury, the pioneers were disbanded and they set out to peg their gold claims. Hundreds of adventurous men were streaming into Mashonaland. Rhodes was burning with a desire to see with his own eyes the land of his dreams and only when Sir Henry Loch notified him officially of the Government's objection that the Prime Minister of the country should expose himself to the danger of being captured by Natives which might call for the use of the whole military force of the Colony at the Government's expense to rescue him, did he postpone his trip. Loch did, however, invite him to join his party which was to go to Bechuanaland as far as the Matabele border.

Together with two parliamentarians, members of the Bond, as his guests Rhodes joined the Governor's expedition, consisting of a Hussar escort, Bechuanaland Police and four big coaches laden only with provisions. Rhodes travelled alone in a Cape cart and kept aloof from the rest of the party. Just before sunset he would ride on ahead and choose the site for the camp. He chose the camp-sites not only for the beauty of their view but also for their cleanliness. A piece of paper, an old tin or a broken bottle would be sufficient reason for him to ride on, even if it meant having his dinner an hour later. In the morning he would insist that the camp was left as clean as it had been found. The same cleanliness he applied to himself in the veld: every day he appeared in a pair of immaculate white trousers, which did not remain clean for long, but of which Toni, his valet, an intelligent half-caste 'Cape boy', always had to keep a sufficient stock, his usual Norfolk jacket and a broad-brimmed slouch-hat. He shaved every morning, even when on trek: 'I believe I should shave if I were dying.' At about eleven o'clock a stop was always made to escape the midday heat and Rhodes, after fortifying himself with a bottle of champagne mixed with stout or Pilsener, would lie down in the shade of a tree. During the midday rest he would read pocket-editions of Marcus Aurelius, Plato's *Dialogues* and Gibbon or he would ponder over his crumpled old map of Africa, with compass, ruler, and pencil.

Every precaution had to be taken against lions because the country was, as Rhodes put it, 'lousy with lions'. Once two native servants leading a beautiful chestnut, who had strayed behind, were missed and later the bones of both men and of the horse were found with evidence that they had been devoured by lions. Another morning Rhodes himself had an unpleasant encounter with a lion not far from the camp. He was seen running for his life towards the camp, his pyjama trousers dangling down to his knees. When he arrived, breathless, he swore loudly at that 'King of Beasts' which did not respect even unavoidable human hygienic functions.

Finally they arrived at the farthest point of the Protectorate, Fort Macloutsie, from where Rhodes could look into the Land of Ophir. He wanted to go farther. Loch objected and was not particularly amiable after Rhodes' impolite seclusive behaviour on the way, which led him to speak of Rhodes as 'very gruff and abrupt, not to say surly'. Rhodes, annoyed at being restrained from going to Mashonaland, replied in a voice which cracked into its highest register:

'I have not come on this tiresome journey merely to see the British Protectorate but *my own protectorate.*'

The Governor did not like this arrogant description of the Chartered Company's concessioned territory in Mashonaland and dutifully reported his resentment to Whitehall. As a compromise Rhodes agreed that he would go as far as Tuli, the Company's first station.

On his way back from the North, Rhodes, in his new capacity as Prime Minister, wanted to look up President Kruger. This time a reception was arranged for him according to his position. A few miles outside Pretoria an officer saluted smartly when he met Rhodes' party and asked: 'Are these the wagons of President Rhodes?' Rhodes' red face indicated his embarrassment:

'Well, I am Rhodes—is there anything I can do for you?' He was welcomed as the guest of the Transvaal Government. Early the next morning he was fetched by a state-carriage and brought to the President's house under a military escort of honour. Together they drank coffee out of enormous cups and soon President Kruger was enveloped in clouds of smoke, which he puffed from his long-stemmed porcelain-headed pipe.

Conversation was slow. Kruger did not want to discuss Rhodes' railway projects. He had declined to have the Cape to Kimberley line, which had reached the Vaal River less than 100 miles from Pretoria, brought to his capital and had also objected to a railway connection with the Cape via Bloemfontein. Apparently he did not want any competition to his own railway, or, as he wanted to have it called, steam tramway, between Delagoa Bay and Pretoria, though it had not yet been completed owing to difficulties with the Portuguese Government, the shareholders and the constructors. Rhodes made great efforts to change the President's chilly attitude towards him:

'We must work together, your honour, I know that the Republic needs a seaport. You must have Delagoa Bay.'

An immense cloud of smoke was blown furiously out of the old man's mouth. Kruger, one could see, was having difficulty in controlling his temper. How dared this Englishman offer him a port which did not belong to him when he knew that the Transvaal had been striving for many years to obtain permission from Britain for an outlet to the sea in Swaziland? As soon as he was sure that he had regained his usual calm Kruger answered quietly:

'How can we work together that way? The port belongs to the Portuguese, and they will never give it up.'

'We must simply take it.'

'I can't take the property of other people. If the Portuguese will not sell it, I will not accept it, even if you were to offer it to me. A curse rests upon ill-gotten goods.'

The audience ended abruptly and was just as futile as had been a meeting six months previously between President Kruger and Sir Henry Loch and Rhodes at Blignauts Pont, where Loch had declined to cede Swaziland to the Transvaal and had declared Swaziland independent. A governing committee of three, representing Britain, the Transvaal and Swaziland was to have jurisdiction over the Whites. The outlet to the sea was mentioned in very vague terms. As a condition for this Convention the Governor asked for an official renunciation by the Transvaal of all territories in the North. Loch warned Kruger that Britain would consider any move of the Transvaal into Matabeleland or Mashonaland as a 'violation of the territory and an infringement of the right of H.M. Government'. Though he was not at all satisfied with this Swaziland Convention, Kruger signed it, but it was never ratified.

The vow of renunciation by the Transvaal was necessary to Rhodes because of the threat of an organized push of about 2,000 Boers into Mashonaland behind which stood General Joubert. Kruger was not really interested in this trek to the North and not only because his rival Joubert was connected with it.

When Rhodes at the end of November 1890 returned from his visit to Pretoria he found Cape Town in the midst of a severe financial crisis which had followed upon the closing of the doors of the Cape's leading bank, the Good Hope Bank, and of other colonial banks. Rhodes also experienced a great reverse in the price of Chartered shares which dropped from £3 to 12*s*. Only by an immediate personal appearance in London would he be able to save the situation, and thus at the end of November he sailed for England.

Soon after his arrival the Queen invited him, as the Prime Minister of the Cape, to dinner at Windsor. Her Majesty's interest in Rhodes was shown by the fact that he received the distinction of dining with her almost in private. Besides two ladies and two gentlemen of her personal suite Sir Henry Loch and Rhodes were the only guests.

The Queen had been well informed by Loch of Rhodes' political and financial activities. She had a remarkable memory, particularly where it concerned even the slightest anti-monarchist tendencies in someone's past and the name of Rhodes had reminded her immediately of his utterance about the 'elimination of the Imperial Factor'. Loch was able to dispel her scruples about Rhodes' loyalty. With satisfaction she noted in her journal that according to Loch, Rhodes—'a tremendous strong man'—was 'a very remarkable, honest, loyal man, and entirely anti-Republican'.

After dinner the Queen astonished Rhodes by her extensive knowledge of South African affairs. Her clear and determined views on Africa's future showed the business-like brain of a statesman. Rhodes took her observations as a cue for delivering his romantic virtuoso piece about painting those empty spaces in Africa red, British red, leading into the climax of his performance, the never-failing refrain of the 'Cape to Cairo' plan. The Queen was delighted. A very good judge of men, she decided that this 'tremendous strong man' could be relied on to fulfil his plans. Translating from Rhodes' enthusiastic language, she concluded the entry in her journal with the simple words:

> . . . He said Great Britain was the only country fit to colonize, no other nation succeeded. He hoped in time to see the English rule extend from the Cape to Egypt. He thought everything would be arranged and the difficulties got over.

CHAPTER XII

ON THE PERSONAL

FOR a place in which to make the laws of their land, people all over the world have built architectural absurdities in the form of medieval castles, Gothic cathedrals or Greek temples. A building was planned in 1874 for the Parliament of the Cape Colony which corresponded with these ideas in combining the features of a Renaissance palace, a classical theatre and the dome of a Baroque cathedral. The foundation-stone had already been laid when it was found that the design blatantly resembled a building in Illinois, that the foundation was faulty and that the costs would considerably exceed the stipulated amount. The plans were altered and the result was a red-brick monstrosity partly masked by sand-stone. Only clumsy Doric columns, completely out of style, remained of the architect's classical intentions, while the sun-heated glass roof reminded the perspiring law-makers during summer sessions of the intended colossal dome. After eleven years the building was completed at more than four times the original cost. Pressed into too narrow a space and without taking advantage of one of the world's most impressive views as background, Cape Town's House of Assembly presents an example of late Victorian architectural style at its worst. It looks like a public convenience with megalomaniac aspirations to become a Parthenon.

Sitting on the front bench on Mr Speaker's right, his long legs stretched out, his bulky body clothed in a crumpled, poorly tailored white linen suit, Cecil Rhodes, the Cape's Prime Minister, sprawled on the reddish-brown leather seat and apparently took no interest in, or even notice of, the debate. One might have suspected that he was fast asleep had he not from time to time suddenly jerked into another position or drawn his right hand, inch by inch, from the depth of his trouser-pocket and started to stroke his chin slowly with his forefinger. Strangers who saw him for the first time were disappointed that this should be the great Cecil Rhodes, master of the Cape's politics, of the world's diamonds, and of one of the world's greatest fortunes, the man who held the destiny of Africa in his grasp.

But those who knew Rhodes knew also that the dull, bored expression on his face was only a mask. It disappeared immediately, for example, when he was attacked for the delay in opening the railway which the Chartered Company had undertaken to build for the Cape Government a year before. A gleam appeared in his eyes. Though he did not change his recumbent position, his body was no longer relaxed. Every muscle seemed tensed for the spring. His right forefinger now stroked his chin furiously. He did away lightly with the attack, in a conversational tone such as he would have used when taking someone 'on the personal'. Yes, he said, his Company had defaulted the contract, but it was his birthday today, his fortieth birthday, and had he not done well for his country? What was a year? . . . And thus Rhodes, the defaulter, defended by Rhodes the Prime Minister simultaneously representing the defaulted party, the Cape Colony, got away with it, and no one would have dreamt of asking the Government to apply the high penalty stipulated by the contract in the event of default.

Though Rhodes was celebrating his fortieth birthday he gave the impression of being at least ten years older. His body had widened enormously at the waist, giving something elephantine to his appearance. Proudly he showed his friends the thick blue artery protruding on his wrist: 'Here you can see my heart beat. Nobody else has such a pulse!'

His health had been deteriorating after a bad fall from his horse the previous December. The shock had upset his mind and body to such an extent that his heart ailment, together with a subsequent anxiety-neurosis, came once more into evidence and was aggravated by the enormous amount of work and worries connected with his manifold official duties and private interests. He never recovered from this physical and mental breakdown. So as to keep himself in a condition in which he would be capable of attending to business, he doped himself liberally with champagne, heavy wines and strong beer. He began to worry so much about his health that his friends, not aware of the true nature of his illness, took him for a hypochondriac or even for a coward. He was a bad patient and when he suffered physical pain 'tears trickled down his cheeks'.

When the affected valves refused to perform their work as they should, Rhodes felt as if his whole heart was contracting in painful convulsive cramps. Fear of death would haunt him, the fear that sudden death would strike him, alone and lonely, and would take him away before his life's work was completed and his dreams fulfilled.

He became increasingly impatient and gave vent to frequent temperamental outbursts. His tense nerves were reflected in the intensity of his thoughts, the rapidity of his decisions and the suddenness of his actions. A strong belief in his own infallibility, strengthened by the flattery of his sycophants, made him inaccessible to advice on important questions. His rudeness, which at the beginning of his ascent had helped him overcome his feeling of social inferiority and which he later used, in the form of a large selection of the choicest expletives, as a safety-valve, could no longer be defined or excused in psychological terms. His choleric temperament had developed into calculated impudence. He often delighted in embarrassing people by his cutting remarks. One who knew him well spoke of his character as 'subject to the radical vice of phenomenal vindictiveness'.

Often when he knew he had gone too far with a friend he felt real remorse and tried to patch it up by being demonstratively amiable. At other times, while bristling with anger and swearing at his friends in the most abominable language, Rhodes would try hard to bridle his passion. He would throw himself into a chair, stare at his opponent and mutter to himself breathlessly: 'Now, let's talk this over quietly. Don't lose your temper. Keep calm—keep perfectly calm and cool.'

Rhodes, that 'bundle of inconsistencies' who could if he wished overflow with amiability, cultivated his rudeness as a personal characteristic to which he believed he was entitled as part of his unique personality. Once, at an official dinner in London, he sat next to a Cabinet Minister whom he bore an old grudge. When he was displeased with the Minister's answer in a harmless argument, Rhodes abruptly turned his back on him and ignored him the whole evening.

'It was very rude of me, I know,' he said, '*very* rude. People who live in London can't do these things—I can. I can do it on the basis of a barbarian!'

In Parliament, however, and also in his other political activities,

Rhodes aimed at offending no one and pleasing everyone in the country. Neither by temperament nor by inclination was Rhodes a politician. Constitutional rights, parliamentary procedure, political traditions had no meaning for him.

He had to learn the art of parliamentary horse-dealing—and very soon did he master it—so that he could say with genuine vexation of one of his opponents, a true Liberal: 'He has a conscience—but this is party politics!'

In order to please Hofmeyr and his Bond, Rhodes, often to the pained disappointment of his Liberal friends and admirers, passed laws dealing with Natives that stamped him in the eyes of the papers in England as 'an English-speaking Boer, thirsting for slavery'. This was the case particularly when he supported a Bill later known as the 'Strop Bill', by which an employer was given the right to apply corporal punishment to his Native labourers of both sexes for even the slightest offence. Also the otherwise sound law which gave the Natives in their Reservations individual land-titles with the right of passing them on from father to eldest son, and which gave them local government and encouraged education, lost its Liberal flavour by being coupled with a tax levy of ten shillings on non-workers, as a 'gentle stimulus to come forth and find the dignity of labour'; and as such 'labour' the work on their own land did not count.

The real idea behind this tax was revealed when Rhodes disclosed the difficulties of finding sufficient cheap labour for the mines. He complained that Natives in South Africa were overpaid at £3 or £4 a month and food, while in the North the pay was 4*s*. a month without food, and even in England, he emphasized, 'I find labour at 12*s*. a week, that is £2 10*s*. a month, producing export.'

Such methods of forcing the Natives into the mines provoked the eminent member of the Liberal Party in England, Sir William Harcourt, to ridicule Rhodes in the House with sarcastic acidity: 'Mr Rhodes is a very reasonable man. He only wants two things. Give him Protection and give him Slavery and he will be perfectly satisfied.'

His precarious position as Prime Minister soon became burdensome to Rhodes, who had never learnt the art of discretion. No one really trusted him—with the exception of Hofmeyr. And lately there was another Afrikaner, a brilliant young lawyer,

W. P. Schreiner, thirty-six years old, who had joined Rhodes' Cabinet as Attorney-General. Always an admirer of Rhodes', he became the second man to believe in Rhodes' political honesty without reservation.

The only group of people really satisfied were the Cape farmers, most of them good Bondsmen. Rhodes had repeatedly emphasized in his speeches in rural districts that he came of good old farming stock and that the love of the soil ran in his veins. Immediately after the occupation of Mashonaland, he had given orders to reserve for him a great tract of land in the most fertile district where he wanted to start a model farm. Soon after taking office Rhodes had created a Ministry of Agriculture, having recognized that the future of the Cape would depend a great deal on modernizing her backward farming industry. By importing the American ladybird, Rhodes saved the Cape's orange groves from destruction by insect pests; he protected the South African wool industry by introducing compulsory isolation of sheep affected by scab; from Turkey he brought some pure-bred Angora goats to be crossed with the poor Cape stock; and he procured Arab stallions to improve the indifferent local breed. By applying French viticultural methods to the Cape vines, and by having them grafted on to American varieties, he made them immune to the scourge of the *phylloxera* which had once brought ruin to the Cape's vineyards already. He tried to have the prohibitive English wine-tariff lowered by a preference to colonial wines and thus to revive the Cape's old wine trade with the mother country.

To the people of South Africa in general Rhodes remained a political enigma. They could not understand why their Prime Minister was still called 'a Colonial Imperialist' by the Afrikaners, and an 'English Boer Republican' by the English in the Cape; and a 'British Jingo' by the Transvaalers, while the English Press either still referred to him as 'the eliminator of the Imperial Factor' or praised him as the 'Colossus of Africa' and the 'Empire builder', if they were not attacking him as a 'humbug whose politics are a stalking-horse for his finance or his finance for his politics'.

In his predicament Rhodes lamented in a speech:

> It has been borne upon my mind of late that the best thing for a Prime Minister to do is to make as few public speeches as possible

> and especially is this the case in South Africa, for in South Africa we have to deal with the feelings of the English people who have lent us all the money we have borrowed; we have to deal with the sentiment of the neighbouring Republics; we have to deal with the development of the Northern territory. . . . I defy anyone to make a speech as Prime Minister of this Colony without hurting the feelings of someone . . . [*The Times*] thinks that I am too Afrikaner . . . *The Free State Express* slates me in the most fearful language because I am too much an Englishman. . . . But I do feel that I am steering the right course between Jingoism on the one side and sensitive feeling on the other. . . .

Yet Rhodes was not such a political tenderfoot as his friends as well as his foes imagined him, or perhaps rather wished him, to be. Intuition had led him to discover the basis of political success, which consists of the exploitation of the herd-instinct of the masses by means of appealing to 'sentiment'. Without realizing, probably, that these words revealed the secret of his success—and later of his downfall—he once told a friend:

> Sentiments rule half the world and as an explanation of this truth we can take the saying: 'We went far to the North, . . . we did it by the feeling of the people.' For after all, even if you have the wealth, it is impossible to carry out a conception unless you have the feeling of the people with you. . . . If you have an idea and it is a good idea, if you will only stick to it, you will come out all right.

'Sentiment' in the form of his old schoolboy-romanticism still kept the forty-year-old Rhodes as captivated as when it had first fired his imagination in his Oxford and early Kimberley days. In spite of his questionable stock-exchange manipulations, in spite of his many tricks when 'painting red, British red', the North, in spite of his various sharp practices and in spite of his methodical bribery, there still burnt in him, in that 'bundle of inconsistencies', the blazing fire of enthusiasm for his juvenile romantic idea of a secret society in preparation for the *Pax Britannica*. On his last visit to London he spent much time between his important business negotiations organizing the 'Society of the Elect'. The fact that he was able to infect with such fantastic madness a man like W. T. Stead can still be understood since the prominent publicist had found compensation for the dullness of journalistic routine work in the realms of mysticism, spiritualism and the collecting of all sorts of lost souls. It is far less comprehensible that a cold-blooded business-man of the worldliness of Lord Rothschild should, instead of rebuffing it with laughter, accept it by agreeing to act as executor of Rhodes' will as the representative of his ideas. Rhodes accordingly made a new, his fourth, will, by which he left his whole fortune to Lord Rothschild to be 'utilized in accordance with Stead's views for the Society of the Elect'. It was to be carried out by a 'Junta of Three' consisting of Stead as 'General', Lord Rothschild and Lord Milner, with Arthur Balfour and the Salvation Army General Booth as alternatives.

His present mood, at the time of his fortieth birthday, was hardly one of romanticism. He was waiting for the cue to enter upon the next act of his conquest of southern Africa. He had to exercise strict self-control in order not to show his hand and allow his opponents to call his bluff. Only a great bluff could save his plans. Watching Rhodes, it was easy to notice his poorly concealed anxiety. His nervousness spread throughout the country. People were expecting something to happen though they did not know what or where. His aim of attaining supreme power over the whole of South Africa in order to make the Cape the dominant factor of a future South African federation, naturally under his control, was no longer a secret. There were still two stumbling-blocks which would have to be removed before he could accomplish his final aim: the two men, Lobengula and 'Kroiger'—Rhodes never learnt to pronounce President Kruger's name correctly—would have to be eliminated from the scene before South Africa could come under Rhodes' complete control. The two men had shown themselves immune to all his methods of bribery, flattery and bluff. Only by force of arms could they be removed. South Africa's atmosphere was charged with the fear of war.

As the curve of war-fever climbed higher, so Rhodes appeared to become calmer. It was true that Mashonaland had been a great disappointment to him. But he could not very well blurt out that he considered that country only a stepping-stone, a small part of his scheme which took in the whole of the African continent.

He had to undergo the strenuous journey to Mashonaland via Beira to see for himself how the Chartered Company could be saved from threatened bankruptcy. Part of the way he had to travel in a dilapidated coastal steamer, where he was bunched together with his companions in a small stuffy cabin. Rhodes was lying in his bunk peacefully when the others started an uproar, having found beetles, cockroaches and all kinds of smaller insects crawling around them. How could Mr Rhodes remain so unconcerned?

'Well,' he answered, 'I cannot say I like them, but as I have had many a worse time than this in my life, I don't worry myself much about such minor discomforts. . . . Oh, my good friends, take the world as it is; how silly to be afraid of such harmless little things! Why, I treat them like flies. . . . One has to keep a sense of proportion.'

'To keep a sense of proportion' became Rhodes' motto during his stay in Mashonaland and was freely recommended by him to the many dissatisfied and almost riotous settlers who showered their bitter complaints upon him. Exceptionally long and heavy rains had caused a complete breakdown in the transport system, as the wagons which had to bring provisions over a stretch of 1,700 miles could not pass through the floods and mud. In consequence prices had soared enormously.

All along his way settlers told him of their dissatisfaction with their farms. Once Rhodes shrieked at them:

'Well, aren't you satisfied with me? Haven't I done enough for you? Do you blame me for opening this big new country?' Without giving them another glance, he swung himself into the saddle and galloped off.

Rhodes found 'a discontented population of about 1,500 people'. Those who had taken up the free farms of 3,000 acres allotted to each pioneer quickly sold them to land speculators for a song, often for not more than £100. In all of them there lived only the one thought—gold. True enough, there were auriferous rocks, but how could they ever hope to tackle this quartz reef with only pestle and mortar?

Those who did not go home stood by helplessly while their former farms were taken up by speculators and leased at *6d.* or *8d.* an acre, and all the land where they had discovered auriferous rocks passed into the hands of stock companies whose shares were torn out of the speculators' hands at high premiums on the London stock market.

As it was, gold was found in very small quantities. The directors of the Chartered Company in London bombarded

Rhodes with frantic cables asking him to let them know whether the gold-reef had yet been found. Neither Rhodes' optimism nor even the various Biblical references to the Queen of Sheba's gold-treasures often quoted by Rhodes offered a consolation to his London friends.

The London Board of the Chartered Company, wishing for an unbiased report on the real gold-prospects in Mashonaland, together with Rothschild, sent out two of the best-known geologists. The experts declared that they could find no signs of the presence of a real continuous gold-reef, and that the existing gold in Mashonaland occurred only to a relatively limited extent and principally in the form of a few rich pockets in the best mines, which would soon be exhausted. Only poor gold findings, they warned, could be expected, which did not warrant the investment of capital and still less the formation of stock companies.

To many it came as a bitter awakening from 'the dream of a lunatic'. Only Rhodes and, infected by his indefatigable optimism, Beit and Jameson, did not abandon faith in the gold and the future of Mashonaland. Before he had finished reading the report Rhodes crushed the copy in his hand, saying: 'Rubbish! They also told me I couldn't grow cotton in Natal! And who was right in the end, I ask you, about the blue ground in Kimberley? Me or the experts? Rubbish!'

Before Rhodes went to Mashonaland in 1891 he knew that the Chartered Company was bankrupt. The banks no longer accepted its cheques unless they were guaranteed by De Beers or by Rhodes personally. Lately the shareholders of De Beers had been remonstrating against Rhodes' high-handed manipulations with their company's funds for the benefit of the Chartered Company. The shareholders took exception to the fact that he and the other directors had formed a syndicate monopolizing the sale of the Company's diamonds. When they complained, too, that the Company spent money acquiring farms and breeding horses Rhodes replied:

'. . . We had a considerable quantity of diamonds on hand, and for amusement I put an advance of one shilling per carat on the price of diamonds . . . so that I may say the horses on our farms were really bought for the Company by the diamond buyers of Kimberley.'

They also objected to the Company's practice of making a

profit on their monopolized canteens and shops which supplied the Natives in the De Beers' compounds. A resolution was passed that this money, gained by the Company in the rather unsavoury way of overcharging their poor Natives for their miserable needs, should be 'devoted to useful public purposes as [Rhodes] in his discretion may determine'. Instead of using it for the benefit of these Natives, the fund, amounting to more than £25,000, was spent on such 'useful public purposes' as a deficit on an exhibition in Kimberley (£2,203), a local race-club (£1,200), a luxurious sanatorium for De Beers' white employees (£17,000), two volunteer regiments (£2,000) and a few hundred pounds on schools for white children.

In his Goldfields Company Rhodes' wings had also been clipped after Lord Rothschild had vehemently put a stop to the practice of his 'puzzling ally' of using the Company's funds for his northern dreams.

The full coffers of his two wealthy companies had thus passed out of Rhodes' grasp. No fresh money was coming in. The greater part of the capital of the Company in Mashonaland had been spent on equipping and feeding a police force of 600–800 men. Under the new administrator, Dr Jameson's rule, these expenses were reduced from £250,000 to £30,000 a year, by means of substituting a volunteer corps of settlers for the police force. Dr Jameson, like Rhodes, believed in Mashonaland, but knew that 'without a railway the Chartered Company might as well shut up shop'. Such a railway would have to connect Mashonaland with the port of Beira, only 400-odd miles from Salisbury. But how could they build a railway when money was not available? As the situation grew more precarious, so Rhodes grew up to it. If the Chartered Company needed money, one would have to get the money, he said, and all the amounts due to him from De Beers and Goldfields went straight into Chartered's account. He also borrowed on the security of his considerable shareholdings in his companies.

Rhodes now proceeded to round up his possessions. The gold of Gazaland was his next aim. The fact that this country belonged to the Portuguese did not deter him nor did he feel that the Anglo-Portuguese Agreement of the previous year for a *modus vivendi* on the *status quo* put him under the slightest obligation. Rhodes would not allow himself to be dictated to by an agreement which had been concluded behind his back. He would leave the matter in the hands of Dr Jameson. It was quite ridiculous to allow a degenerate people like the Portuguese to possess any colonies at all.

Dr Jameson acquired a concession to mineral rights in the usual form from the Paramount Chief of Gazaland against a paltry amount and the promise of guns. The only difficulty in having the Gaza concession ratified lay in finding a way to bring the guns to the Chief without being stopped by the watchful Portuguese. A gun-running expedition by steamer up the Limpopo River was arranged. The Portuguese stopped the expedition and fined the captain £2,000, but a Portuguese officer, his palms well greased, contented himself with a promissory note and even released the cargo of guns as being 'outdated and useless'. With the guns delivered, Dr Jameson received the confirmation of the concession. On his way back to Beira he was arrested and the steamer seized, but he was able to dispatch the precious document secretly by one of his companions. Dr Jameson was set free on his arrival at Beira, and thus ended his second successful raid on foreign territory.

A title without taking possession was not sufficient for Rhodes. He had to occupy Gazaland, and Gazaland was not all on which he had cast his eyes. Mashonaland had to have an outlet to the sea, as otherwise it would suffocate as a locked-in impotent inland island like the Transvaal. Beira was destined as the natural port of Mashonaland and the way to Beira lay through Manica and Gazaland, along, and during the floods on, the Pungwe River.

For many years, as often as he leant over his crumpled map of Africa, Rhodes' finger had come to rest on Beira, the coveted port on the Portuguese east coast.

In 1891 the Portuguese finances had sunk once more to a catastrophic level. Rhodes saw his chance to bargain for Beira. Together with the Rothschilds he offered to buy the port. The Portuguese Cabinet looked upon his offer favourably, but the promising negotiations had to cease when Downing Street intervened.

Later Rhodes again took up parleys and was very near success in obtaining Beira at the bargain price of £1,300,000, when J. B. Robinson, the 'Buccaneer', appeared on the scene and outbid Rhodes by a substantial amount. A new Cabinet came to power in Portugal and withdrew the offer.

If he could not pocket Beira by fair means, other ways would be sure to present themselves. The new Portuguese Government played into his hands by closing the Pungwe River and the port of Beira to men and goods connected with Rhodes' companies and by declaring martial law in all the districts of Manica. At the same time a volunteer corps arrived from Lisbon determined to restore the honour of their country by clearing Manica of Rhodes' police force.

If those dwarfs of Lisbon politicians wanted to fight him, Cecil Rhodes would teach them a lesson. An excuse for war could easily be found in this electrified atmosphere, and it would be war not against his Mashonaland Police but against the British Empire.

On his old map of Africa, Rhodes pointed out to his friends the immense vastnesses of space 'given over to savage life, with its waste of nature and contempt of human life'. Silently, he paced up and down the room until he came to a halt again in front of the map, and whispered excitedly:

'It is inevitable fate that all this should be changed; and I should like to be the agent of fate.'

Unafraid of the probable consequences, Rhodes, as the unauthorized 'agent of fate', hatched the dangerous plan of creating an 'incident' which would lead the British fleet to occupy Beira. Unfortunately Dr Jameson, already considered a specialist in such tasks, was not available. Rhodes' choice fell on Sir John Willoughby, one of the many titled hangers-on of the Chartered Company in Salisbury. This young ex-officer had all the qualities that were needed to have him turned overnight into a national hero by the English Press should something happen to him during the 'incident'. Willoughby sported the Eton tie, had gained his blue at Cambridge, had brought home a large collection of war decorations from the Egyptian Expedition and had once won the Derby. Possessing, moreover, the right amount of stupidity mixed with irritating arrogance which he dispensed freely among all outside his own coterie but showered especially upon everyone and everything 'foreign', he would not 'stand any nonsense' from any swarthy Portuguese.

Friends pointed out to Rhodes that the life of this blue-blooded flower of English nobility might be endangered—that he might easily be killed by a Portuguese bullet. Rhodes immediately replied:

'Not a bit—not a bit! They will only hit him in the leg—hit him in the leg—in the leg.' And, while vigorously rubbing his thighs, his screeching laughter echoed through the sudden deathly silence of the room.

They did not even hit Willoughby in the leg when he entered Beira harbour. All that the Portuguese did when he tried to enter the Pungwe River against their orders was to fire a blank shot over the bow of his 'flagship'. After protesting vehemently against this insult to the British flag, Sir John considered his mission fulfilled and quitted the scene, leaving to Rhodes the political exploitation of the 'incident'.

Misled by Rhodes' exaggerated reports, the English Press immediately turned the incident into the 'Beira Outrage'. Even Sir Henry Loch, who was not easily influenced by Rhodes, succumbed to the artificially aroused mass-hysteria and shared Rhodes' opinion that Portugal's affront constituted a *casus belli*. Lord Salisbury was surprised when he received from Loch, whom he considered a calm and reliable man, a cable strongly urging him 'to take action with the fleet'.

Through direct negotiations Lord Salisbury soon came to terms with the Portuguese Government, which immediately lifted the closure of Beira and the Pungwe River. To lay stress on the importance of the reopening of the port of Beira and of the free passage from there to Mashonaland, Salisbury dispatched a British cruiser and two gun-boats to Beira. The Portuguese Government had yielded on the question of Beira only on condition that Rhodes' police-troops were withdrawn from the territory of Manica which they had occupied without justification. The officer in command of the Chartered Company Police ordered his men to retreat, but only to occupy a strategically better position on the Manica hills.

Rhodes, fearing that a treaty would once more be signed without his being consulted and that again valuable concessions would be made by the British Government, cabled to Beit in London to safeguard the interests of the Chartered Company by presenting their claims to Lord Salisbury. He concluded his instructions:

> . . . I well know the predatory instincts of my countrymen. When they can't rob the foreigner, they rob one another; but I am damned if they're going to rob me!

Rhodes' interests were indeed well looked after when the Anglo-Portuguese Treaty was signed in June 1891: the Highlands, as well as the entire auriferous plateau of Manica and a narrow strip of Gazaland, were accorded to Rhodes. Concerning the question of Gazaland, however, neither Whitehall nor Lisbon was prepared to yield to Rhodes' demand of recognizing his concession for the whole territory. But Rhodes received full rights to use the port of Beira and the Pungwe River and was given a concession to build a railway from Beira to Mashonaland.

While Rhodes was busy brow-beating the Portuguese in the east, difficulties were arising on the southern border of Mashonaland, where an organized trek of Afrikaner burghers was threatening an invasion. They intended to found the 'Republic of the North' in the Banya district of Mashonaland to which they pretended to have acquired the rights from the local chiefs. The promoters of the scheme had previously offered this concession to Rhodes at an enormous figure, but he had pointed out to them that the territory fell under Lobengula's paramount power and thus under the Rudd concession.

The trek was favoured by General Joubert, the Commandant-General of the Transvaal and President Kruger's opponent in the approaching presidential elections of 1892. President Kruger, who opposed it because he knew it would affect his negotiations with London for Swaziland, issued a proclamation forbidding the trek, but Rhodes was still convinced that Kruger favoured and was secretly aiding it. The Colonial Office, too, feared a repetition of the Bechuanaland troubles. Consequently the British Government declared that Matabeleland and Mashonaland fell under the British sphere of influence and ordered the Bechuanaland Police to take up positions at the principal drifts on the Limpopo River. These Imperial troops, together with the Chartered Police, would, the High Commissioner warned the trekkers, prevent by force of arms any unauthorized crossing of the Limpopo.

These official precautions seemed to Rhodes insufficient to prevent Kruger from sponsoring the trek. He would send Dr Jameson and Sir John Willoughby to Pretoria and let the 'Old Dopper' know the exact meaning of Loch's shilly-shally proclamation.

During these last years Rhodes had learnt how to use to good advantage that loathsome political instrument—blackmail by the threat of war. If, contrary to expectations, it should not have the desired effect when applied to Kruger, one would have to create an 'incident' similar to the 'Beira Outrage', and would eventually have to go to war. Rhodes no longer doubted that war against the Transvaal would be the ultimate solution.

Bearing Rhodes' views in mind, the two raid specialists came to Pretoria. Willoughby first went alone to see the President and deliver Rhodes' message. Just as intended by his master, the arrogant haughtiness of the ex-guardsman had the most irritating effect on the President. Willoughby asked the President whether he realized that if the Boers attempted to cross the Limpopo into Mashonaland, he would have to reckon with the British Army.

Kruger, with his small inflamed eyes, looked at this young man whom the Prime Minister of the Cape Colony had chosen to send to threaten him, the aged President of a friendly neighbour-state, with war—war by the Queen of Great Britain, the suzerain power of his country! Kruger stood up. Looking the young officer straight in the eye, he said very slowly: 'I think we have reckoned with the British Army before!' With these words he left the room, his head held high. Willoughby remained in his seat for quite a while with open mouth. In his stupidity he could not explain this 'extraordinary behaviour'.

Yet Kruger felt that as a message from the Prime Minister of the Cape this threat would have to be taken seriously. He sent for the British Agent, Sir Jacobus de Wet, for an explanation, who immediately communicated with the High Commissioner. To everyone's relief there soon came a wire from Sir Henry Loch: 'Disown Willoughby and say Her Majesty's Government disown him altogether.'

The more intelligent Dr Jameson instantly realized that a blunder had been committed. He tried to repair it by visiting the President and applying all his charm to the old man. He scored a great success at least with another man, one of Rhodes' greatest antagonists and one of Britain's bitterest and most irreconcilable foes in South Africa: the Reverend S. J. Du Toit, who suddenly discovered his love for Britain and joined Rhodes' forces by declaring himself whole-heartedly against the trek. 'Squared?' 'On the personal?'

The trekkers who were sitting on the Transvaal bank of the Limpopo waiting for the signal from their leader to cross the river into Mashonaland were beginning to be bored. They had full confidence in their leader, a man well known throughout South Africa: whenever there was a rumour of gold or diamond findings, Colonel Ignatius Ferreira would appear among the first to dig; whenever there was a war against the Natives, Ferreira would be the first to volunteer, no matter whether it was under the flag of Britain, the Transvaal or Portugal, and fight in the front line with such foolhardiness that his name alone was sufficient to frighten many a Native chief.

Mashonaland must have been a dreamland for a man of his speculative optimism and he had thus taken over the leadership of the trek with enthusiasm. But to sit there for weeks doing nothing was more than his mercurial temperament could endure. Finally, to put an end to what was already becoming a comedy, Ferreira and a few others made a pretence of attempting to cross the river. They were promptly arrested by the Chartered Police. Dr Jameson, who had been waiting impatiently for this moment, tried to persuade the rest of the Boers to enter Mashonaland as registered settlers under the Company's rule. Only a very few accepted the offer.

Rhodes' next task, and the most difficult, so everyone in Rhodes' circle believed, still awaited him when he would have to face the shareholders of the Chartered Company at its second annual meeting scheduled in London for November 1892.

The capital of the Company had been spent. So far gold to no appreciable extent had been found. The shares of the Company, which soon after having been issued had climbed to £3 15*s.* and had been unloaded at that price on an unsuspecting public, were now unsaleable at a quotation of 10*s.* to 12*s.* Rhodes knew that it would be hard work not only to keep up the confidence of his shareholders but to instil in them fresh enthusiasm to such an extent that they would willingly grant him new and larger funds.

The *Spectator*, referring to Rhodes' light-hearted optimism in promising two years previously that 'Mashonaland consists not of one but of fifty Rands', hauled him over the coals:

> We are not inclined to take Mr Cecil Rhodes so entirely on trust as a great many people in this country show a disposition to do. . . . We should like to know much more exactly than any one seems to do, whether Rhodes is fighting for England or for his own hand. . . .

Rhodes had prepared his speech to the shareholders with painstaking care, employing all his well-worn and ever-successful bravura arias: the story of meeting General Gordon and how he would have 'squared the Mahdi', that he was proud to be called an adventurer and, to wind up, his old refrain of how he had always 'tried to combine the commercial with the imaginative, and up to the present never failed'. He appealed to the patriotism of his listeners when he asked them to oppose the 'scuttling out of colonial possessions: . . . I do not mean this on the basis of "Jingoism", or on the basis of the Empire on which the sun never sets, but on the basis of pure practical business.' He aimed at the proverbial sentimentality of the Englishwomen in his audience who could always be brought to the melting-point if called upon to fight the slave-trade:

> There are 14,000 shareholders in the various companies I represent, and if they like to send me, not a charitable contribution, but £10 each, there would be my line to Uganda. . . . There may be in various towns in England people who take an interest in Africa and in the suppression of the slave trade. If this telegraph is made, there will be an end to the slave trade and it will give us the keys to the continent. . . .

All now depended on regaining the confidence of his shareholders and re-establishing the trust of the stock exchange in his enterprises. What better recommendation could he furnish than the faith of such cautious bankers as Messrs Rothschild? Proudly he announced:

> Lord Rothschild, who I think, did not believe in the least degree in the Charter, but thought he was chucking his money into the sea, gave me £25,000.

The negative results of the two years' work in Mashonaland Rhodes went over lightly: 'My experience of the past is that, just as a Government, so as a Company we cannot expect to do more than balance revenue and expenditure. . . .' And he kept up their hopes for the great mineral wealth still to be discovered.

How could one possibly deny anything to so charming a man, so great a patriot and one so clever in financial matters? Rhodes received fresh confidence in, and new capital for, his company in full measure. And that was all he had wanted.

In his address Rhodes had made a deep bow to the new Liberal Cabinet, which had taken over the government in the summer of

1892. Rhodes recommended himself to the new masters in Whitehall by declaring:

'I am a Liberal myself!'

The extent of his Liberalism, so far, had been expressed merely by a contribution of £5,000 to the funds of that party.

Rhodes needed the goodwill of the ruling Liberals for his pending ventures. He had to have Uganda and he thanked heaven that only Gladstone and a few other Liberals now held to their anti-colonial policy.

In Lord Rothschild's son-in-law, Lord Rosebery, now Secretary of Foreign Affairs in Gladstone's Cabinet, Rhodes found an interested and enthusiastic backer of his scheme to save Uganda, which Rhodes described as 'the key to Central Africa'. The company which had a Charter for Uganda was asking for an annual subsidy of £40,000, whereas Rhodes offered to run it at £25,000 and to build a telegraphic line from Salisbury to Uganda without cost to the Government.

Sir William Harcourt, the Chancellor of the Exchequer in Gladstone's Cabinet, was, as a strong 'Little Englander', categorically opposed to colonial obligations. He would first have to be won over.

Harcourt was at first horrified by the Uganda scheme and even more shocked when Rhodes proposed that as a part of this plan the Cape should take over the administration of Bechuanaland and run it at £40,000, whereas now it was costing the British Government £100,000. Rhodes also mentioned, to Harcourt's consternation, that 'in a few years the Transvaal will be so flooded with English at the mines that there will be a majority there for annexation to the Cape Colony'. Yet, in spite of his distrust of Rhodes, Harcourt could not help being 'delighted with him', liking his 'hard sense and knowledge of affairs' and even agreeing with him that 'Jingoism is tolerable when it is done "on the cheap"'.

But on consideration Harcourt quickly changed his mind. He wrote a note to his Cabinet colleague Lord Ripon, the new Colonial Secretary, in which he opposed the amalgamation of Bechuanaland with the Cape:

> Of course, Henry Loch does not like to part with his own little despotism, and desires to keep his own niggers for himself, but this ought only to influence us. . . . In dealing with these Cape eels it is necessary to have sand on one's hands.

However, when Rosebery threatened to resign if Uganda were 'scuttled', Rhodes was given the sanction of the Cabinet to add it to his private empire which now stretched from the Limpopo across the Equator to the borders of the Sudan.

The new acquisition brought Rhodes' dreams still nearer to their complete realization. He would have rejoiced more about this latest victory had there not remained on the map of Africa the blot of the Transvaal. It was so near and yet so far and as time went on it seemed to recede still farther from his grasp.

Rhodes had nursed great hopes that the Presidential elections of 1892 would lead to civil war between Paul Kruger's followers and those of General Piet Joubert. 'Oom Paul' still held the confidence of the older generation, the conservative backvelders, but in the towns there had arisen a generation who were now clamouring for a change. It was a very close contest. The votes had to be counted three times, and each time they led to a different result until finally Kruger was declared elected with 7,854 votes against Joubert's 7,009.

Rhodes knew that the time to deal with Kruger had not yet arrived, and he felt his impotence painfully. One day, however, he would settle accounts with that old man 'Kroiger'!

Rhodes' mind was already occupied with plans for his next step: Lobengula would have to be eliminated so that the Chartered Company could take possession of Matabeleland and, of course, of the fat king's fabulous treasure chest of diamonds, his gold and ivory and his enormous stock of cattle. Rumours that his wealth, stored in old biscuit tins, now amounted to well over £10 million, had lately received confirmation from several sources. With Dr Jim, the experienced raider, sitting in Salisbury as administrator, it would not be difficult to arrange the necessary 'incident' to start the ball rolling. Moffat, now Her Majesty's Resident at Bulawayo, and still a willing instrument of Rhodes'—who officially paid his salary—was given the onerous duty of informing Lobengula of the transfer of the Lippert concession to the Chartered Company. The King understood the meaning of this message only too well, but he was determined to oppose the sale of this concession which had been a personal grant and could not, according to Native law, be passed on.

He also maintained that in spite of the Rudd concession he was still master over Mashonaland. All that he had ceded was the right to dig for gold. He therefore saw no hindrance to sending his *impi* into Mashonaland to 'bathe their spears in blood', to collect taxes or to go on punitive expeditions. There was, in fact, no boundary to show where Matabeleland ended and Mashonaland began.

An opportunity arose in June 1893 when Lobengula wanted to punish a petty Mashonaland chief living on the border, whose men had cut some 500 yards of telegraph wire and who had paid the fine imposed on him by the Company in cattle which belonged to Lobengula. In a letter addressed to the Company's officer-in-charge at Victoria, dated 29 June, Lobengula informed him of the coming punitive expedition against these cattle-thieves and pointed out that 'the *impi* in its progress will probably come across some white men, who are asked to understand that it has nothing to do with them'. Lobengula acted fully within his rights and even did more than was his duty by this warning.

To Dr Jameson this seemed a splendid opportunity for engineering the required 'incident'. He wired for Rhodes' consent. Rhodes, reading the telegram while sitting at his desk in Parliament, sent a messenger for a Bible. He smiled as he thumbed through the pages of the New Testament; and on a telegram form addressed to Dr Jameson, scribbled:

Read Luke XIV, 31.[1]

From Dr Jameson came the prompt reply: 'All right: have read Luke XIV, 31.' And he immediately went to work. He found the man for the job in one Captain Lendy, who by rights should no longer have been in the employ of the Chartered Company at all. Shortly before, he had been seriously reprimanded by the Colonial Office and was supposed to have been cashiered, for the barbarous torture under which he had put to death a Mashona headman for alleged theft.

When chasing the Mashona cattle-thieves, Lobengula's *impi*, which consisted of 300 men, reached the outskirts of Victoria, and, while looking for Mashona fugitives, they might possibly have entered the property of some settlers. The settlers thereupon, as Dr Jameson reported, had 'the jumps', sending away their

[1] 'Or what king, going to make war against another king, sitteth not down first, and consulteth whether he be able with ten thousand to meet him that cometh against him with twenty thousand?'

wives and children and barricading their houses. Not a single white person, however, was as much as touched by a Matabele.

Captain Lendy was told that if the *impi* did not leave Mashonaland within an hour, he should follow them with thirty-eight troopers. If he found that they were not moving off and if they resisted and attacked him, he should open fire. According to the testimony of Captain Newton, who as an old friend of Rhodes' must be considered, if not biased towards Rhodes, at least a neutral witness, there was 'nothing to show that any organized or individual resistance was offered'. This fact did not prevent a man of Captain Lendy's type from shooting about thirty Matabele.

In his report to the High Commissioner, Dr Jameson and Selous twisted the truth in maintaining that the Matabele *impi* had attacked Lendy's troops after having killed more than 400 Mashona, and emphasized that the lives of the white women and children had been jeopardized at Victoria. Not more than half a dozen Mashonas had in fact been the victims of the Matabele raid.

The High Commissioner censured Lendy, but only said 'that the punishment inflicted . . . appears disproportionate to the original offence' upon which the Colonial Secretary, Lord Ripon, observed that 'the full report by Captain Lendy . . . would have justified much stronger terms of remonstrance' and that he could not avoid the conclusion that 'Captain Lendy acted with recklessness and undue harshness'.

Dr Jameson did not care. He had succeeded in engineering an 'incident'. In order to remove any obstacles which Sir Henry Loch or the Colonial Office might put in his or Rhodes' way, *vox populi* would have to be raised to such a pitch that it would sound as though the settlers of Mashonaland were fearing for their very lives.

Nothing was easier than filling the people with the necessary war-spirit, and promptly at a mass-meeting in Salisbury a resolution demanding immediate strong action was passed and telegraphed to Government House in Cape Town.

In spite of this provocation Lobengula did not lose his head and exercised restraint in every respect. He defended his rights against the Company which seemed to have come 'not only to dig the gold but to rob me of my people and country as well'.

He appealed to the High Commissioner through Moffat, saying that he was 'not aware that a boundary exists between Dr Jameson and myself; who gave him the boundary lines? Let him come forward and show me the man that pointed out to him these boundaries.' The High Commissioner replied to Lobengula that it was also his desire that 'peace should be maintained'. In spite of these reassuring words Lobengula saw that the preparations for war in Salisbury were being intensified. As a last hope he wrote another pathetic letter to the Great White Queen, pleading for justice, with this touching outburst from a wounded heart: 'Your Majesty, what I want to know from you is: Why do your people kill me?'

The Queen replied through the High Commissioner: 'You can tell the King from me I have no intention of invading his country or of dragging him into war.'

When Rhodes' next monthly concession payment was tendered to Lobengula, the King refused acceptance because, as he told the messenger, it signified 'the price of his blood'. To show his peaceful intentions, and to rid himself of his obligations towards the Company, Lobengula returned the 1,500 rifles and the ammunition which he had received in part-payment of the Rudd concession.

In spite of these distinct signs of Lobengula's sincerity and the assurances of reliable traders and missionaries about his peaceful intentions, and in spite of repeated warnings from the High Commissioner not to provoke the King, Dr Jameson continued to prepare for the lethal stroke against 'that fat naked savage'.

Nothing could speak more against Rhodes' sincerity, nothing could better demonstrate his hypocrisy, than the cynical methods he employed in attracting volunteers for the intended campaign in Matabeleland. On 14 August 1893 Dr Jameson enlisted, by secret agreement, 672 men whom he promised by contract, in the name of the Company, each 6,000 acres of land of a minimum value of £9,000 to be chosen by them, and 20 gold claims in Matabeleland. Paragraph 7 of this shameless agreement referred bluntly to what is considered in every even half-civilized country as one of the greatest crimes in warfare:

> The loot shall be divided half to the British South Africa Company and the remainder to officers and men in equal shares.

It must here be stated clearly that the British authorities in Cape Town and in London knew nothing about this secret agreement and it remained unknown to them until 1913.

The expectation of loot from Lobengula's treasure cave of diamonds, gold and ivory and his herd of 500,000 head of cattle drove the men to such a frenzy of war-lust that they could scarcely be kept in check. Colonel H. Goold-Adams, the Commander of the Bechuanaland Police, reported to the High Commissioner on 18 September: 'Dr Jameson will not be able to keep the Salisbury and Victoria people much longer inactive.'

The High Commissioner, urged on by Whitehall, made every effort to frustrate Rhodes' attempt at invading Matabeleland and annihilating Lobengula. At the beginning of September he sent a message to Lobengula: 'Let there be peace between you and the white men! . . .' He encouraged the king to send his *indunas* to Cape Town, promising a safe conduct for them and that he would be 'glad to receive them if they come from you with words of friendship and of peace'.

At the end of September, Dr Jameson reported to the High Commissioner that a Matabele *impi* had fired on a police patrol. Though he had only Dr Jameson's word to rely on, Loch, who seemed not as yet to have been aware of the doctor's unbridled inventiveness, believed that a case of aggression by the Matabele had actually occurred. Perhaps he had begun to doubt Lobengula's sincerity, since his *indunas* who should have arrived weeks before had not even been reported to have crossed the border.

Poor honest Loch! How could he have known by what low means his highest assistants were working against him, against the Government and against their country, but to the advantage of their friend Cecil Rhodes? Three *indunas* had indeed arrived on the border. It was known that the aim of their mission to the High Commissioner was to prevent Rhodes' invasion of Matabeleland. Rhodes' interests therefore made it imperative that the *indunas* should proceed no farther. As soon as they crossed the border they were arrested 'by mistake' and two of them shot 'while attempting to escape', while the third was never seen or heard of again.

On 3 October Loch, under pressure from Dr Jameson, gave him 'discretionary powers to take the necessary measures to clear the border of Matabele *impis*'. On October 7 the troops of the

Chartered Company, well supplied with Maxim machine-guns and field artillery, left their camps in three columns consisting altogether of 897 white men and 555 Natives, and with Dr Jameson as Commander-in-Chief.

Two columns marched off in the direction of Bulawayo, while the third column went to join Goold-Adams' Bechuanaland Police to cover the left flank of the main body and thus create a diversion of Lobengula's forces.

When Dr Jameson and his expedition were already several days on the march, there suddenly appeared in Salisbury Cecil Rhodes escorted by twenty Cape Police. It was a very tired, a very sick-looking and a very subdued Rhodes who greeted the settlers. Dr Jameson had followed his orders well in improvising and keeping down the costs. Rhodes had had to scrape together every penny, to pledge everything he possessed and to borrow from all sides in order to provide money for this war.

During all this time Rhodes had prudently kept in the background. As Prime Minister of the Cape he had to avoid falling foul of Loch and the Colonial Office. He therefore left all the negotiations in Dr Jameson's hands, though he directed him secretly. If anything went wrong he could then always disown the doctor. When the critical moment arrived at the end of September, Rhodes went off to Mashonaland via Beira, but he stopped near Umtali, a little border-station, where he camped for many days without entering the town and avoiding contact with its inhabitants. Rhodes, in other words, had gone into hiding. One day a mounted Company policeman arrived at Rhodes' camp, and from his and his horse's exhausted condition it could be guessed how urgent was the letter which he handed to Rhodes. Rhodes' mood immediately changed, though only for the moment, from nervous anxiety to one of gaiety: Dr Jameson was reporting that he and his two columns had now passed Fort Charter. For this news Rhodes had been waiting all these long and dreary days in his hide-out. Now Dr Jameson could no longer be reached by telegraph and stopped in his march. To his friend Hans Sauer, Rhodes said, amid several outbursts of the usual piercing high laughter:

'I had to hide in the bush and to make it impossible to receive orders by cable from Whitehall prohibiting us from invading Matabeleland, but now that Dr Jim has disappeared into the blue nobody can deter us any longer from this adventure.'

However, although Whitehall had not succeeded in stopping Rhodes' march into Matabeleland, they did at least want to keep a control over the consequences, and therefore informed Rhodes that all future negotiations about peace terms with Lobengula would have to be conducted by, and under the complete control of, the High Commissioner.

Rhodes foamed with fury. Once again the 'Imperial Factor' was stepping in to try and rob him of the fruits of his work. In his rage, Rhodes appealed to his powerful colleagues on the Board of the Company, to exercise their influence on the Colonial Office. The Colonial Secretary was informed by them that 'the B.S.A.C. have asked the British Government nothing, and surely they have the right, in terms of the Charter, if victorious to settle the question with Lobengula, subject only to the approval of Lord Ripon'.

To his Afrikaner friends in Cape Town, Rhodes, in a telegram, was even more outspoken about the 'elimination of the Imperial Factor':

> I certainly intend to settle the question on South African lines. I had the idea and found the money and our people have had the courage to fight without help from home. Surely I should have a voice in the final settlement. I feel I can reckon on the people of the Cape Colony supporting me in this view.

Rhodes was successful in preventing, at least for the time being, any interference from the 'Imperial Factor', and the field seemed clear for his final settlement with Lobengula. The danger, however, that the 'Imperial Factor' might slip in at the last moment if Goold-Adams' Bechuanaland Police with Khama's Native troops were the first to enter Bulawayo, capture Lobengula and seize his treasure would have to be avoided at all costs.

The massing of Imperial troops on his borders worried Lobengula more than did the reports that three columns of Rhodes' troops had started to move towards Matabeleland. But he was not without hope. He believed firmly in the justness of his cause and was convinced that one Matabele with his assegai was the match of four Britishers in spite of their machine-guns.

With the same belief in their unconquerable strength, Lobengula's 5,000 men, singing their war-songs, marched along the Shangani River, straight into the murderous fire of the Maxim machine-guns, to be mowed down mercilessly in their hundreds by Rhodes' troops. As soon as one column was decimated the next moved in, and so it went on until only a few hundred men were left of the many thousand. A week later an even larger Matabele army was utterly wiped out at Imbembesi River.

Now they would come and seize him, Lobengula mused. But even though his best regiments had been lost he would continue to fight and go down fighting like a king, just as the great Zulu kings, Dingaan and Chaka, had done. Never would the white devils sit in his kraal, and when they came they would find nothing but ashes. He ordered his body-guard Bosungwana and ten selected young warriors of the royal regiment to load all his treasures on the big wagon.

When the costly load had been stored, Lobengula ordered the royal kraal to be burnt to the ground and with the help of a box of powder nothing remained but some burnt pieces of wood, a few broken bricks and mounds of ashes.

Smallpox was ravaging Matabeleland. German traders spread the rumour that Dr Jameson must have had a hand in this epidemic, or why had he had all his men and also his Natives vaccinated before the campaign began?

Lobengula went north towards the Shangani River. Two days after his flight, on 3 November, Bulawayo was occupied by Dr Jameson's two columns. The Bechuanaland Police, under Colonel Goold-Adams, obligingly left Jameson and his men alone for several days to gather all the glory, and, what was more, all the loot. There was great disappointment when it was found that the entire royal kraal had been burnt down and nothing was left of Lobengula's fabulous treasure.

Lobengula still wanted peace. When two captured troopers were brought to him he saw his chance of sending a message to Rhodes. He gave each a thousand golden sovereigns to bring to 'Ulodzi' and showed them the barrels full of gold which he told them their master Rhodes could have . . . 'and tell him they have beaten my regiments, killed my people, burnt my kraals, captured my cattle and that I want peace'.

The message was never delivered, the gold never handed over. The King felt that his end was near. Not far from the banks of the Zambezi he ordered a halt. He was too weak to continue, shaking with fever and his face red with smallpox. He had found a cave. The ten men who formed his escort were ordered to store all his possessions in the cave and to make the entrance inaccessible by rolling a tremendous rock in front of its small opening. When the work was done he had these men killed one after the other by his old and trusted body-guard, Bosungwana. A few days later, on 24 January 1894, Lobengula died and the old friend buried him sitting in his bath-chair. His friend made the grave unrecognizable by placing a large boulder over it. And the secret of the two places where Lobengula and his treasure were buried went with Bosungwana to his own grave when he died a few months later. Up to the present day many treasure hunters have searched in vain for the buried treasure of King Lobengula.

Before the year 1893 was out, Rhodes had arrived in Bulawayo and immediately went to work to establish the Company there firmly before any interference could come from Whitehall or Cape Town's Government House. Together with Dr Jameson he proceeded to mark out townships, distribute land, organize new companies, send out prospecting and surveying groups and start to share out Lobengula's country.

Rhodes, in his schoolboy-romanticism—or was it rather a case of simple vengeance?—insisted that the capital of his new province should be erected on the site of Lobengula's kraal Gu-Buluwayo, and for the location of the future Government House he chose the very spot of the King's goat-kraal and hut. His technical advisers, however, rejecting such romantic fancies, erected the town two miles north-west of the former royal kraal.

All the fears of the British Government in allowing a private person like Rhodes to conduct a private war for a joint-stock company against a country standing under the Queen's protectorate, had thus proved justified and Sir Henry Loch predicted that Rhodes' next step would lead to war by the Chartered Company against a foreign power instead of Natives. Rhodes, however, bombastically assured everyone of the 'peaceful policy' of his company.

The 'peaceful policy' of the Chartered Company was again demonstrated a few weeks later when Rhodes wanted to incorporate Pondoland in the Cape Colony against the will of its Chief and people. The Chief, Sigcau, was summoned to Rhodes and told in plain words that since his people were incapable of governing their country it would be annexed. The Chief was taken to a cornfield. Suddenly, at Rhodes' command, machine-guns began to spray their bullets into the high maize stacks which were mown down as if a ghost was running wildly over the field, cutting them down with a sharp sickle. Looking at the frightened Chief and pointing at the field and the machine-guns, Rhodes told him: 'And that will happen to you and your tribe if you give us further trouble!'

The ruthless methods employed by Rhodes in his conquests did not remain without critical repercussions in England. In the front row of the critics was Labouchere who, in *Truth*, continued his campaign against 'these filibustering and massacring expeditions . . . of Mr Rhodes and his pernicious company, a wretched, rotten, bankrupt set of marauders and murderers'.

Even Rhodes' friend, W. T. Stead, felt it his duty to censure him, and in Parliament, on three different occasions, the massacres in Matabeleland came under heavy attack.

An anonymous pamphlet, published in 1894 in Cambridge, expressed the popular abhorrence of liberal-minded British people as well as of all those whose conscience had been shocked by Rhodes. It bore the title:

THE MATABELELAND SCANDAL

by

One who remembers the punishment which fell upon Cain for killing his brother, and is jealous of the honour of Great Britain

It was a forceful *J'accuse* and stands as an echo of the actual sentiments moving thousands of Englishmen whom the poison of Jingoism and Rhodes' clever propaganda, as well as the temptations of the stock market, had left untouched.

All these attacks were much resented by Rhodes who feared increased difficulties with the Government for his future plans. Moreover, they had unduly influenced the share market, bringing down again the price of Chartered shares which had been improving so nicely of late.

At a banquet in Rhodes' honour, on his arrival in Cape Town, Dr Jameson feasted him as the great Empire-builder, announcing that the directors of the Company had decided to memorize his great deeds by naming the countries which he had opened up —Mashonaland and Matabeleland—Rhodesia.

In his reply Rhodes again emphasized that the volunteers had beaten the Matabele single-handed—without the help of anyone and without asking the British Government for a single sixpence.

This historical untruth was too much for the representative of the High Commissioner, the Government's Imperial Secretary, Sir Graham Bower. He stood up and pointed out the great part which the British Government had played, actively and passively, in opening up the North, by contributing both men and money to the campaign and to the subsequent policing of the territory. He later had to pay dearly for the annoyance thus caused to Rhodes, who never forgot it.

There were not many who took any interest in the welfare of the thousands of destitute Matabele. Rhodes had declared as the tenor of his policy, 'I prefer land to niggers', a cynical confession which contrasts grossly with the terms of the Charter granted by Her Majesty the Queen:

> . . . The Petitioners believe that the condition of the Natives inhabiting the said territories will be materially improved and their civilization advanced.

The Matabele had plenty of opportunity of learning what the white man meant by improved material conditions and an advance in civilization: syphilis, gin, forced labour, taxes, famine, prostitution, debauchery, physical deterioration, lust for money, and fraud.

CHAPTER XIII

GROOTE SCHUUR

THERE never was any rest for Rhodes. He had never learnt to relax. His brain worked endlessly, planning, scheming. The quiet beauty of Nature which soothes even the most turbulent of minds had a stimulating effect on him. He had loved the countryside since his earliest youth. When he first saw from the *stoep* of Hofmeyr's house in Camp Street the panorama of the Cape peninsula dominated by the severe majesty of Table Mountain he had fallen in love with the landscape. The noble simplicity of the old Dutch homesteads, the solidity, the clear shape and the superb craftsmanship of their furniture had captivated him. Here on the Cape peninsula, with Table Mountain always in view, he would settle down and build himself a house!

Until 1893, twenty-three years after his arrival in South Africa, Cecil Rhodes, the Prime Minister of the country and one of its richest inhabitants, had had no abode there which he could call his own. In 1891 he learnt by chance that an old Dutch house in Cape Town's suburb Rondebosch was for sale. This thatched building had served in the time of the Dutch East India Company as a barn for storage and later it passed through many hands until it became a large farm-house amid fields and woods and vineyards. Rhodes bought it in 1893 and restored its old Dutch name, Groote Schuur. Not wishing to be confined within the narrowness of a fairly populous area, he also bought all the adjoining land, including the slopes of the mountain, until he possessed altogether 1,500 acres, at a total cost of £60,000. By chance he met a young unknown architect, Herbert Baker, who aroused his interest by his fiery enthusiasm for the harmonious beauty of the old Dutch architecture. This was his man! He engaged him immediately and gave him full powers to restore Groote Schuur to its original state as shown in an old water-colour in Rhodes' possession. 'I want the big and simple, barbaric if you like', was his only directive to the young architect. On a half-sheet of paper, undated, he wrote an authorization for unlimited funds to be put at

Baker's disposal at his bank: 'Baker to be architect and clerk of works.'

As soon as work began, Rhodes gave it his full attention. In spite of his usual impatience with details, he now gave his architect explicit orders concerning even minor points. Rhodes had never before spent any money on himself except for the merest necessities, and he wanted now to give himself, without regard to costs, the very best that money could procure; something which would become a monument to his personality destined to live long after him and to bear testimony of him not as the 'Colossus', not as the politician, the land-grabber, the lucky speculator, the millionaire, the master of gold and diamonds, but of Rhodes the man, the lover of sylvan beauty, the connoisseur of antique art, the admirer of old Cape tradition and still more of Rhodes, the Squire, the Grandseigneur, the—Gentleman.

Everything in the house had to be large and spacious and, above all, absolutely solid and of the very best. Rhodes saw to it that for the material used on the house local products were given preference wherever possible. He would not allow foreign marble to be imported and was very proud of the fact that his bathroom, which caused a sensation by its splendour and luxury, had its roomy bath-tub hewn out of a single solid block of Paarl granite, while the huge massage-slab was of Cape marble and the whole room and floor were tiled with a local greenish marble.

The large back-*stoep*, supported by massive pillars and gaily floored with black-and-white checked marble, was designed to become the centre of life in Groote Schuur where up to fifty people could be entertained. Rhodes had seen at once that it would offer the best panorama with the grandiose background of a symphony in grey of the defiant buttresses and gorges and precipices of Table Mountain and Devil's Peak piercing the blueness of the sky.

All that was good in Rhodes, all his romantic longings which had not been throttled by his ambition for 'money—that is power', emerged in his urge to express his naked self derobed of the ugliness brought upon him by the 'struggle for life' and the 'survival of the fittest'. In his last years, when in a reflective mood, he repeatedly said that 'the greatest of all life's pleasures is the faculty of creation'. And it is remarkable that he did not mention as his creations the foundations of his private empire in Central

Africa, the Cape to Cairo line, the penetration of the African continent by telegraph and railway, the amassing of one of the greatest fortunes in the British Empire or the mastership over the diamond industry, but referred with pride to Groote Schuur and its park. He would point from the *stoep* in the back of his house towards the mountain view which grew, as it were, slowly out of the loveliness of eye-blinding blues and reds and purples and greens and yellows and mauves and whites of the flowers, out of the shrubs, the hedges and the trees, wild and tamed, to form, in harmonious set chords or in exciting strange dissonances, a sonorous chorus of colour to the glory of the sun. Then he would say:

'It is a thing of my own creation: creative genius, that's what I've got. It is a great thing to have.'

Even his 'foible of size' did not interfere with making the formal garden in the front and back of the house a full success. All the expert gardeners warned him that hydrangeas would not grow in the sandy soil of the hills around the house. 'They told me I couldn't grow cotton in Natal,' was Rhodes' reply, and he ordered whole acres on the hills and in the groves to be planted with hydrangeas. He wanted to have a 'blue lake of hydrangeas', and he succeeded. To this day at Christmas-time the hydrangeas fill the garden of Groote Schuur with a flower-lake in all the shades of blue, pink and purple.

His favourite flower, however, was the simple light blue blossom of the plumage shrub of which he had hedges built all around the terraces at the back of the house against masses of bougainvillaeas. Almost throughout the year a plumage blossom could be seen in Rhodes' buttonhole.

All his efforts were directed towards the enjoyment of an unobstructed view of the mountain. Although he hated to fell trees, a number of pines had to fall victim to the axe because he wanted to see the mountain from his bed as soon as he opened his eyes.

Rhodes' favourite seat was on the slopes of the mountain, where he had built himself a bench. To this spot he would often retreat on his rides, fastening his horse to an aloe plant. From there he would glance with satisfaction at the long rich grass which covered the paddocks like a thick green carpet. This grass was his pride, and no honour meant more to him than when later the grass (*Chloris Compressa*) was called 'Rhodes Grass'. He had found it growing on a farm near Queenstown, where French Moravian Brothers had cultivated it from seed which they had brought from India. After Rhodes' success with it, seed of the grass was exported to all parts of the world.

After his horticultural success Rhodes wanted to improve also the fauna on his estate. He imported from England several hundred nightingales, thrushes, rooks, starlings and chaffinches as well as squirrels. Of the birds only the starlings survived and multiplied to such an extent that today they have turned into a serious threat to the Cape's fruit crops, just as the squirrels have become a cursed pest beyond control. Such failure did not discourage Rhodes. He fenced off a large slice of land where wild animals, particularly South African species, could live in their natural surroundings, and he began a private zoological garden where he kept in cages lions, leopards, monkeys, baboons and a few birds of prey. The upkeep of the lions alone cost Rhodes more than £200 a year. Once, during a meat shortage, they had to be fed on imported cold-storage meat, the high cost of which Rhodes, with reference to the feeding of his lions, used as an argument in Parliament against the duty on meat.

One Sunday morning he saw a picture of the Temple of Theseus, and the idea occurred to him that the straight lines of the classical architecture in its marble whiteness would contrast splendidly with the greyness of the mountains and that such a structure was ideal for a lion-house. Baker was summoned immediately. He was horrified at the thought. He tried to dissuade Rhodes by telling him that the lions would immediately fight and kill each other. Rhodes replied excitedly:

'So much the better; it is their nature to, and they would enjoy themselves the more.'

But Rhodes soon forgot the project and began to occupy himself with the building of roads. With his own money he built one, eight miles long, leading from Rondebosch through his estate and the sun-drenched vineyards of Constantia, to the seaside at Hout Bay. On each side of 'Rhodes Drive' he planted trees: red-flowering gum trees, camphor trees and the only chestnut trees in the Cape.

It was not only for himself that he undertook all this work. His friends were to enjoy his house and park with him, and his whole estate was to be open to the public from morning to nightfall. Groote Schuur became Cape Town's most popular picnic spot, and people, white and black and brown, arrived there in every kind of vehicle to spend the day. Rhodes raised no objections to these mass invasions; on the contrary—'How delightful to see one's fellow-creatures about, enjoying themselves,' he said.

'Why do I love my garden? Because I love to dream there,' Rhodes confessed another time. And he wanted others 'to come and dream also'. Out of this idea grew a plan to create 'a cottage in the woods for poets and artists. If they live in beautiful surroundings', Rhodes explained, 'they will be better inspired to interpret through their art the beauty and grandeur of the country.' He built a roomy cottage amid the pine trees, and when it was almost completed he invited to live there the English poet who lay nearer than any other to his romantic heart: Rudyard Kipling was asked to come to 'The Woolsack' every year during the English winter and 'hang up his hat there'.

The imposing landscape held Rhodes spellbound. He once took Sir George Martin, the eminent organist of St Paul's Cathedral, to see 'my view'. After they had sat for many minutes Rhodes said to him, speaking hesitantly:

'Do you know why I brought you here? . . . Well, I have had many artists here and have wished them to paint this view but they can't do it. They can't grasp the enormous expanse. Now I want you, when you go back to think of this scene, and put it in your music at St Paul's.'

Rhodes' other contacts with art and literature were few. The pride of place in Rhodes' library was held by a sculpture of the bird Phoenix in soapstone, probably of Phoenician origin, found among the ruins of the Zimbabwe temples.

The Phoenix appealed to Rhodes' romantic vein particularly. He consulted many books on the subject and acquired a thorough knowledge of Africa's earliest times. The Phoenix bird Rhodes chose as his emblem and used it liberally for decorative purposes in his house. One copy was made for the Committee Room of the Cape Executive Council 'in order that members might in their deliberations realize their puniness when they contemplated that emblem of antiquity'.

In a cabinet, also in the library, Rhodes kept a collection of excavations in stone and bronze connected with the Phallic cult of the Phoenicians. His interest in the Phallus worship of some mysterious early settlers in Central Africa was misunderstood and maliciously misinterpreted by some visitors to Groote Schuur, giving rise to ugly rumours about Rhodes' abnormal sexuality. The scandalmongers linked their tales, the same as those which had already been whispered in Kimberley years before, with the fact that Rhodes had only bachelor friends, that he kept his private secretaries only as long as they were not married, and that there was not a single female servant employed at Groote Schuur.

Poor Rhodes, he never seemed able to escape scandalous rumours! At the beginning a great number of coloured and Native girls had been working in his house and kitchen, until he learnt that people in town had been spreading the maddest stories about wild orgies going on at Groote Schuur in which his chambermaids and scullery maids were supposed to be playing the leading parts. So disgusted was Rhodes that he immediately dismissed all female employees and did not allow even the wives of his men-servants and labourers to live on his estate.

Besides some very fine old French tapestry in the billiard-room and dining-room, there were few pictures on the walls. He was very proud of one picture, a portrait of a young woman by Sir Joshua Reynolds. Often he had the picture taken down and with his friends studied its details. Rhodes said that she represented his idea of female beauty, that he had known her from an illustration in a book and loved her since he was a lad of seven or eight. With a peculiar look in his eyes, he told his friends, as though in confidence: 'I call her my lady!'

Certain books, as we have seen, had played an influential part in Rhodes' spiritual development when the cultural impact received at Oxford had flung the intellectually sterile young digger from Kimberley too suddenly into the heights of classical civilization, the glaciers of philosophy and the crevasses of historical science. Those books which had first fertilized his brain in a belated and long-drawn-out puberty continued to feed Rhodes, the cynic, the unscrupulous hazarder, the arbitrary dictator, with the romantic ideas necessary to him as an antidote against the soul-destroying realism of his abject business methods. On his travels over the veld he always had handy in his ox-wagon pocket editions of his favourite books, especially a complete edition of Gibbon's *Decline and Fall of the Roman Empire*. Those same books, together with Bryce's *American Commonwealth*, Milner's *England in Egypt*, Mahan's *Influence of Sea Power* and some biographies of Napoleon, could always be found on the bookshelves in his bedroom.

Rhodes' great interest in Napoleon was shown by the many works of Napoleonic literature in his library. On several occasions Rhodes mentioned that there was not a single biography of the Corsican that he had not read, yet he could never be drawn into a discussion about Napoleon. Carlyle and Froude were also favourites of his. Novels only served him to kill time on his long journeys. Once, when he was about to leave for England, he asked his secretary how long they would be on board, and on being told twenty days, he gave orders to put forty of the latest novels into his cabin trunk: 'One for the morning, one for the afternoon, that means forty books,' Rhodes explained. A London bookseller had a standing order to send him weekly parcels of the most important new publications, but Rhodes rarely found the time to read them. If he thought a book might interest him, he gave it to one of his secretaries to make a summary for him, because, he said, he 'had not time to wade through books full of padding'.

He was still not interested, as he had already confessed at Oxford, 'in the class of people Dickens wrote about', and only a few of his books and several of Thackeray's novels, of which he liked *Vanity Fair* best, were to be found in his library. His acquaintance with even the well-known books of his time must have been very scanty. He once gave a friend's young daughter R. L. Stevenson's *Treasure Island* as a present saying:

'You ought to read it; it's a very good book—very instructive.'

'Have *you* read it, Mr Rhodes?' the child asked.

In annoyed tones and flushing red, Rhodes told her:

'Now you run away and play!'

It seems strange that the only work of fiction which aroused his admiration and which he considered a great novel, *The Choir Invisible*, should have been by an American author, James Lane Allen (1849–1925).

Another work of fiction, also by a foreigner, Emile Zola's *Germinal*, had a great effect on him too, though of a different kind: it pinched his social conscience. If Zola had known that his laboriously created *document humain* of the saga of the Rougon-Macquart family would help to improve the lot of miners in South Africa, he would certainly have rejoiced though he would hardly have understood why only workmen of a white skin should benefit.

It was in a London drawing-room that Rhodes stated:

'It was the reading of *Germinal* which caused me to realize the necessity of providing decent homes and harmless pleasures for the Kimberley miners.' But Rhodes' freshly awakened social conscience did not go so far as to make him think of the thousands of Natives, crammed together and locked up in De Beers' compounds.

No book fascinated Rhodes as much as did Gibbon's great work. It kept him under a spell until his end with never-abating strength. One would have thought that his real interest lay in Elizabethan times, in 'men of action' of the size of Raleigh or Drake, or in those of a later century—Clive or Hastings—whose qualities as 'Empire-builders' closely resembled his own. What was it then that caused him instead to devote himself to the period when the mighty Roman Empire was undergoing a process of decay? It was evident that Rhodes was not so much interested in the Roman Empire as in those deified despots who were the absolute masters of her fate. Yet the fascination which the degenerate Roman emperors, whose vices and perversities filled normal men with disgust, held for Rhodes, offers a psychological problem all the more difficult to solve because Rhodes, in his general, political, social and cultural conceptions, in his education and in his associations, was so thoroughly English.

Some other points in Rhodes' taste also form an apparently insoluble contradiction: only two men were represented by their likenesses in his house. In the drawing-room there stood a bronze bust of Robert Burns, though none of his works were to be found in his library nor did Rhodes ever allude to a liking for the poet or even to having read any of his works. For the privacy of his bedroom one would have thought that the 'great Empire-builder' would have chosen for inspiration a portrait of his Queen or at least that of one of England's national heroes. The Squire of Groote Schuur preferred, however, on opening his eyes in the morning, to look at a portrait of Prince Bismarck. Perhaps the portrait of the 'Iron Chancellor' was meant to serve Rhodes as a daily reminder of the dangers threatening South Africa from German *Machtpolitik*. Or was it expected to instil in him something of Bismarck's obduracy?

Rhodes' relationship to the Roman emperors was of quite a different nature, probably completely unpolitical and purely personal. He felt something 'foreign' in himself and thought that it might have originated in some Roman blood which his early ancestors, whose connection with an Aegean island was indicated by the family name, had brought with them to England. Whenever Rhodes was mistaken for a Jew he became very embarrassed. In his later years certain Semitic features became more conspicuous so that he never allowed photographs or paintings to be done in profile. His sister Edith once told a friend: 'There is no doubt of some Jewish blood in us and Cecil knows it as well as I do, but he prefers it to be Roman.' When Rhodes was given a gift of a medallion of Titus because he 'looked exactly like this Roman Emperor' his interest was immediately aroused and he obtained pictures of contemporary statues, busts and medals to make further comparisons. He liked to show these pictures of Titus to visitors and always pointed out: 'What a fine forehead he's got!' Once one of his servants had to hold a mirror so that Rhodes could see his profile in another mirror and compare it with that of Titus.

On his voyage to England after having acquired Groote Schuur, Rhodes spent all his time reading Gibbon. He found that the great historian dealt with the causes for Rome's political decadence rather than with personalities. He wanted to know all and everything about the Roman emperors with all the little details about their lives and characters. In London he consulted the old-established bookshop of Hatchards in Piccadilly, and asked them to procure for him a collection of all the authorities and sources used by Gibbon for his work, but in English translations. He was told that most of these works had never been translated into English. 'Then they will have to be translated,' was Rhodes' reply, and he gave the astonished bookseller what was certainly the strangest order ever given by a book-collector or received by a bookseller: Hatchards had to engage a staff of classical scholars, sometimes as many as twenty, who were kept busy for six years translating from the Latin and Greek and also procuring photographs of contemporary illustrations. Everyone working on the scheme was bound to absolute secrecy. Only one copy was made of each work, typed on special hand-made paper and bound together with the original text in red marocain-leather. Rhodes had forgotten that the later chapters of Gibbon's work dealt with early Christianity and was therefore surprised to receive volume after volume of works translated from Greek and Latin Church Fathers which dealt with intricate theological problems and casuistic ritual arguments. Urgent cables were sent to London to stop the supply of more theological sources and to arrange that further work should concentrate on the lives of the Roman emperors. The complete collection amounted to several hundred volumes at a cost of about £50,000.

The danger that his imagination might be fanned by the history of Rome and that the study of it might become an obsession and degenerate into grandiose delusions must have occurred to Rhodes. In his pocket edition of Marcus Aurelius' *Meditations* the following passage was underlined and often quoted by him:

> Take care always to remember that you are a Roman and let every action be done with perfect and unaffected gravity, humanity, freedom and justice. And be sure you entertain no fancies which may give check to these qualities. . . . Have a care you have not too much of a Caesar and that you are not dyed with that dye. This is easily learned, therefore guard against the infection. Be candid, virtuous, sincere and modestly grave.

It can hardly be maintained that Rhodes acted according to this wise advice of the Roman sage. But it has to be admitted in Rhodes' defence that his stupendous success would have turned the head of any man and filled him with an imperturbable sense of infallibility, a burning urge of self-importance and an unswerving sense of God-like elevation. The year 1895 had brought Rhodes to the pinnacle of his career: his Queen had honoured him ('such a remarkable man') by the nomination as Privy Councillor. He now became the Right Honourable Cecil Rhodes, P.C., ranking high on the social ladder. He was able to reply proudly to the Queen when she asked him what he had lately done:

'I have been adding new provinces of several hundred thousand square miles to Your Majesty's already wide dominions.'

But it was really his own empire which Rhodes had built up

in Africa between latitude 30 south and latitude 5 north. He had fulfilled the dream of his youth to paint the map of Africa red, British red. The Cape to Cairo railway scheme was progressing: Rhodesia was already linked by rail with the Cape and with the east coast. His telegraph line had reached Central Africa.

The financial difficulties of the last years had been overcome. The £1 shares of the British South Africa Chartered Company, though no dividends had ever been paid—and were not to be paid until 1923—had reached the fantastic price of more than £9.

At a shareholders' meeting of the Chartered Company Rhodes had strengthened popular optimism by saying: 'I think we may fairly say that we shall balance in the future. The new country is "mineralized" and all will be well.'

The appearance of the 'Colossus' at the shareholders' meeting had brought Rhodes a great personal success and enough publicity to raise Chartered shares still higher. A week later a lecture at the Imperial Institute, with the Prince of Wales as chairman, given by Dr Jameson who had just been decorated with the Order of the Bath, brought the valuable public royal sanction for Rhodes' enterprises. At a subsequent banquet Rhodes and Jameson were the guests of honour.

Although Rhodes had already said more than enough about Rhodesia's rosy future, Dr Jameson surpassed him in speaking about 'innumerable gold-fields'. It led people acquainted with Rhodesian conditions to ask 'whether his talk was the result of ignorance, windy hope, the dinner or a purely fraudulent intention, as every major statement was fantastically wrong'. Though no gold to any extent had as yet been found in Rhodesia, more than 200 mining companies had been floated and their shares had been taken up eagerly at a premium on the London Stock Exchange.

In the season of 1895 Cecil Rhodes was lionized by London Society. He was now generally accepted as belonging to the Prince of Wales' intimate set. No longer did he stay at the busy middle-class hotel, the Westminster Palace Hotel. Now he booked at the Burlington Hotel, where, at a daily price of £25, he occupied a suite consisting of a sitting-room, a dining-room and several bedrooms. There he held court like a sovereign, attended by his private secretaries, his servants and a whole bevy of minions.

Members of the Royal Family came to call on him; ambassadors of the great Powers left their cards; the scions of England's oldest noble families paid their respects to him. In his sitting-room there also assembled all those who had something to sell and his secretaries were hard put to it to prevent them from penetrating farther than the antechamber.

Not even the strongest barriers could keep out Rhodes' many friends. They flattered him; they made him drunk with their admiration; they encouraged him in his pride, his conceit and his belief in his own infallibility. The extent to which they went in their disgusting adoration can be judged by the words of W. T. Stead, who in the *Review of Reviews* spoke of Rhodes as 'the only man in the West with ideas that can be compared for the moment with those of the Pope for comprehensive scope and breadth of purpose'. Rhodes, always prone to self-assertion and presumptiveness, needed little encouragement. His great success killed all self-criticism in him.

At this time Rhodes commanded a yearly income, as he later stated on oath, of considerably more than £1 million. From De Beers alone he derived £300,000 to £400,000 and from Goldfields £200,000 to £300,000. His profits from his large share transactions were not included in this income. It was not the possession of his enormous wealth alone which led him to feel beyond good or evil and far above the accepted rules and laws governing the lives of ordinary citizens. He felt the power which his money had brought him. His aim of achieving power through wealth had now been realized, and he was determined to make use of this power in completing the ultimate goal of his ambitions—to become the absolute and supreme master over the whole of South Africa.

In his capacity as Prime Minister Rhodes checked any resistance by his old system of 'squaring'. No longer did he trouble to use his charm or joviality to take an opponent 'on the personal'. Brutal coercion had taken its place. To one of his critics, who had taken exception to Rhodes' triple business position as interfering with his Premiership, Rhodes gave a seat in his Cabinet. Once, when his Ministers were raising difficulties at a Cabinet meeting, he told them bluntly:

'You think I cannot fill your places in the Ministry. Well—I have another hungry dog to whom I can throw a bone—Mr X.'

Where his business was concerned, Rhodes did not shrink from anything which would further his interests. In the United States the Kinley Tariff imposed a duty on luxury goods so high that it made the export of diamonds to the United States almost impossible. A movement for the repeal of this high protective tariff was started in the United States in 1893. Rhodes, on the advice of American diamond merchants, charged an agent to do some extensive lobbying for him in Washington, and to suggest in his name 'in return for some support of the silver cause in the United States' the freeing of diamonds from any import duty.

In the United States, with presidential elections soon coming up, political feelings were running high in 1894 over the two issues of the Silver Purchase Act and the Tariff reform. At such a time of most serious political and economic upheaval Rhodes, the Prime Minister of a British Colony, decided to enter Washington's political arena. It did not occur to him that he had no official status that entitled him to interfere with a totally internal political matter of a foreign country. Neither could he claim the privilege of the freedom of action of a private individual. His many engagements did not allow him to visit the United States himself as he had planned. He thought that a letter would do just as well, and thus he sent to the President, with copies to all the Senators, a letter full of fulminant threats, promises and good advice.

Senator Henry Cabot Lodge, in the name of thirty-three other Senators, gave an appropriate answer to 'the recent astonishing communication to the President of the United States from the Premier of Cape Colony'. He wondered what right the sender had 'to suggest another proper exercise of this legitimate discrimination'.

Senator Lodge thought that such impertinence of foreign interference deserved a strong rebuke by coldly stating the actual facts in contrast to the distorted views of this arrogant man who was in control of a world diamond monopoly:

> . . . Since the discovery of the Kimberley diamond fields less than a quarter century ago, diamonds to the value $175,000,000 have been imported into the United States. . . . It is estimated that the country now absorbs from one third to a half of the annual product of these South African diamond mines, which are controlled by English investors, who have limited the output, created a trust and practically control the price of the diamonds of the world. . . .

A duty of 30 per cent on diamonds was suggested by these thirty-three Senators in order to

> check consumption and reduce the excessive artificial prices for these stones which now prevail and might induce people of Cape Colony to believe that the present attitude of Great Britain in relation to silver is not only unfair and unjust but is also injurious to the interests of that colony.

Such reverses did not discourage Rhodes for long. His position in England was now so firmly established that the few Liberal newspapers and financial journals which were still criticizing him sharply no longer worried him:

'Newspapers—do you think I care a continental fig what the newspapers may say? I am strong enough to do what I choose in spite of the whole pack of them!'

Nevertheless he never missed an opportunity to bring his influence to bear on newspapers. In South Africa he had brought several under his control. But it has to be said for the integrity of South African journalists that no editor ever wrote to his dictation or refrained from publishing something which Rhodes did not like. As long as the editors followed the big line of his policy he left them sufficient rope in as far as details were concerned and did not mind even an occasional criticism of some minor political problem. Rhodes never attempted to use any of his papers or any independent journalist for his financial manipulations.

Rhodes was, however, very sensitive about personal criticism in the Press, though in most cases he refrained from prosecution for libel. Only once, after the occupation of Matabeleland, did he sue several London publications for their personal attacks and brought successful actions for damages against them.

He was annoyed by an unfriendly comment in *The Saturday Review* just after his appointment as Privy Councillor and when he came to London its editor, Frank Harris, increased his attacks. With his knowledge of 'squaring', Rhodes found it easy to come to terms with Harris, though experience had lately taught him that people could be 'like many plants, or one should say, trees; once you start watering them you must continue to do so'.

Only rarely had Rhodes met people who refused to be either 'squared' or 'taken on the personal'. Not many had the strength of character of the devout missionary François Coillard, who, when offered the position of Commissioner of Barotseland as a bribe to help Rhodes persuade the tribal chiefs to sign their territories away, knelt down and prayed: 'Oh, my God, let not Thy servant be the martyr of a political transaction!'

Another exception was Samuel Cronwright. In 1894 he married the famous South African authoress Olive Schreiner, who at one time was an admiring friend of Rhodes', but later became one of his bitterest antagonists. The Cronwrights, for reasons of Olive's health, had moved to Kimberley, where they formed a new party with the aim of fighting Rhodes and the Bond, whom they accused of preparing war against the Transvaal in order to overthrow Kruger.

To utter such unfriendly political thoughts about the 'Colossus', particularly in his own citadel, was considered treason and blasphemy or perhaps only an attempt at blackmail. After Cronwright had delivered a lecture at the Kimberley Literary Society, the bitterness of which, in an attack on Rhodes, easily revealed the main author as his wife, the gentlemen in the De Beers boardroom thought that the time had come to put a stop to such dangerous activities.

If it was not possible to 'square' this obstinate fellow and his fanatical wife even though they needed the money badly, Rhodes would have to find some other means of counteracting their dangerous propaganda against himself and the Bond. He communicated with Hofmeyr, who recommended to him as a useful propagandist a young man, Jan Smuts, who had just returned from Cambridge. Hofmeyr reminded Rhodes that they had met Smuts seven years earlier as Head Student at the Stellenbosch Victoria College.

Rhodes engaged Smuts, who had just established himself as a barrister in Cape Town, to work for him by writing political articles and delivering speeches. One of his first tasks was to appear in Kimberley and, in answer to the Cronwright-Schreiners' fulminant challenge, to address the De Beers Mines Political and Debating Society on the subject of 'The Political Situation'.

When the president and secretary of the society went to the station to meet the speaker they were astonished to find a pale-faced, blue-eyed, ridiculously thin and tall young man 'without hair on his face', who looked no more than seventeen. They had expected Mr Jan Christiaan Smuts, the twenty-five-year-old Cape

Town advocate who, besides his Stellenbosch degrees in Literature and Science, had won the rare distinction of several prizes in Law at Cambridge and had been offered a fellowship there, to look rather different.

When the Mayor introduced the speaker to the 2,000-odd people who packed Kimberley's town hall that October evening in 1895, they were at first amused at the idea that this insignificant-looking bit of a lad should have anything to tell them about the political position that they did not already know. But they listened to him with growing interest. Though he did not tell them anything new, though they disagreed with him in almost everything he said, though they knew that most of his statements were far removed from fact, they soon fell under the spell of his oratorical power. When the people went home after having listened for two hours to his arguments they were convinced, at least for some time, that the Cronwright-Schreiners were false prophets and that Cecil Rhodes was indeed a wonderful, honest, altruistic, and benevolent man.

Rhodes could not have found a better propagandist. He was in urgent need of a strong defender not only of his ideas but still more of his own personality. By 1895 even old friends were complaining that success and his fabulous wealth had killed in Rhodes that old boyish 'magnetic' charm and the simple comradeship and warm cordiality which he had always shown towards them. It had lately been supplanted by a ridiculous pomposity, a repulsive arrogance bordering on megalomaniac disdain of everyone else. His cynicism, his tactlessness and his gruffness no longer knew any bounds and often, when applied on defenceless objects, took the form of mental sadism.

After the occupation of Matabeleland Rhodes had seen to it that the few sons of Lobengula who had not been killed were removed from the territory, in order to prevent any future trouble led by members of the Royal House. Three sons of the younger wives, all bright young lads, he took with him to Cape Town and had them educated there. Their holidays they spent at Groote Schuur.

One day he was telling some friends about Rhodesia and became confused about the dates. The three Matabele boys, aged fourteen, fifteen and eighteen, were working in the garden. Rhodes called to them, shouting from the *stoep*: 'Let me see, what year was it I killed your father?' His guests were still more shocked when the three boys—whether out of politeness or embarrassment—joined in the shrill staccato giggle with which Rhodes followed his words.

Another time, when Rhodes was showing visitors around his house, he pointed to his bed and said: 'This is where I lie and think in continents!'

Life at Groote Schuur was ruled by almost regal pomp which Rhodes' old friends found hard to reconcile with the unceremonious, unconventional, free and even coarse ways of the Cecil Rhodes of old. They did not feel at home in Groote Schuur, where evening dress was now *de rigueur*, though the master of the house often appeared in his usual day-time attire of white trousers, Norfolk sports jacket and *veldschoens*—coarse shoes made locally of untreated leather. To one of the first official dinners at Groote Schuur, Rhodes had invited all the high state dignitaries headed by the Chief Justice (later Lord) and Mrs De Villiers. All the guests had been asked to appear five minutes earlier than Mr Justice De Villiers. A ceremonial plan had been worked out, such as Rhodes had recently learnt at Sandringham and Windsor. The staff, who had been instructed accordingly, were under the direction of young J. Norris, a former Inniskilling Dragoon, who acted as major-domo, housekeeper, librarian, steward, bailiff and travelling secretary.

The guests were all assembled when both wings of the door were opened and Norris, solemnly marching ahead, announced in his sonorous dragoon-sergeant-major voice: 'His Honour the Right Honourable Chief Justice De Villiers. . . .' All eyes searched for Rhodes to welcome his guest of honour. There was no sign of Rhodes until they noticed the seat of his pants sticking out from beneath a sofa where he had gone in search of his shoe which he had slipped off because it pinched him.

Norris was probably the only one towards whom Rhodes only rarely employed his usual strong language. One of Norris' duties was always to carry a pocket dictionary with him as Rhodes was continually at war with the spelling of even the most common words. Norris used to say: '. . . And so I taught him the simple words and' (with a wink) 'he taught me the hard ones.' It was difficult for Norris to bring any kind of order into the household of Groote Schuur, the upkeep of which swallowed a monthly

£2,000 and even when closed £900. Without warning Rhodes would bring home for dinner up to twenty people when only eight guests had been prepared for. He hated to be alone at meals. Sometimes there were assembled at Rhodes' table the strangest and most varied collection of men: a stiff English nobleman and a clumsy sick trooper on leave from Rhodesia; an old spitting gold prospector and a titled 'remittance' man; a saintly missionary and a pompous *nouveau riche* Rand magnate; a scientist and a business man; a bishop and a wine-farmer; a mining engineer and an Afrikaner Karroo sheep-farmer could be found there sharing an uncomfortable meal.

Sometimes Rhodes invited guests on a Friday for the week-end without informing Norris, and they would number more than there were beds in the house. On one occasion Rhodes met a friend in Cape Town, and during the course of conversation he said: 'You must come out to Groote Schuur to stay with me for some days,' to which the friend replied indignantly: 'But, Mr Rhodes, I have been staying with you for the last week.'

Old friends were surprised by the type of men with whom Rhodes now surrounded himself. Though Rhodes had always proved himself to be a good judge of men after a short acquaintanceship, he now did not seem to mind the parasites, the spongers and the spittle-lickers who became predominant at his 'court' and were known as 'Rhodes' jackals'. It was particularly strange to see the great number of doctors whom Rhodes entrusted with the most important and delicate assignments which had nothing to do with their medical profession. After his lucky experience with Dr Jameson he must have thought that in every medico there slumbered a genius for colonial administration, a talent for diplomacy and a gift for political intrigue. Among the younger doctors, he had chosen as his special confidant Dr Rutherford Harris who had come out from England for health reasons a few years earlier. Since he spent most of his time hunting and since his medical abilities and his intelligence were none too great, he was not able to earn an income sufficient for a life of luxury to which he thought himself entitled. Dr Harris thought that he could do everything better than anyone else. He decided that he would speculate in mining shares and show those Kimberley Jew-boys of the Stock Exchange a thing or two. Within a few weeks all the savings for which his father had worked for a lifetime were lost. Rhodes engaged him and within a short time he had risen to the position of Secretary to the Chartered Company and also handled Rhodes' private, political and public affairs. When asked why he had given him such a position of trust, Rhodes, who like everyone else had a very low opinion of Dr Harris' intellectual and moral qualities, sighed and replied in a tone of resignation: 'There is something against everyone. I must take men as I find them.'

Even before later events had proved Harris' unreliability, his criminal corruptness, his pathological mendacity, his love for double-crossing intrigue, his disloyalty, his vain stupidity and stupid vanity and his arrogance, Rhodes described him as 'a rogue and at times a furious inebriate'. Dr Jameson, who knew him even better, spoke of him as 'a muddling ass—on the surface a genius but under the crust as thick as they are made'. A friend called him publicly 'an unmitigated liar' even before he was stamped in Parliament as 'the greatest and most unashamed liar, a perjurer of the meanest sort, a man without any moral sense'.

Such was the man whom Rhodes chose to represent him personally as well as the Chartered Company during the delicate negotiations with the British Government in 1895.

Why, Rhodes was asked, did he surround himself with so many doctors? 'I like doctors for my work, because their calling gives them such an insight into humanity,' was his reply to which he later added, followed by the usual squeaky laughter: 'and because when there is blood-letting to be done, they are less squeamish.'

In former times an answer such as this, dripping with savage cynicism, would not have shocked his friends—those few real and unselfish friends who did not buckle under the 'Colossus'. But they were beginning to detect behind this sardonic contempt for human values the ugliness of unmasked brutality, of unrestrained recklessness and of a morbid rancour. No longer did he try to control the eruptions of the boiling geysers of his temperament. No longer did he allow decisions to mature with the warmth of contemplation. No longer did he let his carefully laid plans ripen slowly into success. Everything had to be done quickly without regard to the means employed. He wanted to play God and use his powers to direct the fate of men, the destiny of nations, the future of a whole continent. What had once been 'imaginations' and 'dreams' had now become obsessions that did not allow natural obstacles or human obstructions to stop, delay or quieten his turbulent will.

The pain in his chest caused by the pressure of the heart, the wild pulsation of the 'water hammer' on his wrists and the frightful feeling as though the heart would burst, showed that his leaking heart-valves were working overtime. And every stroke of his heart, every pulsation on his wrist, seemed to be telling him: Hurry, hurry—your time is running out. Rhodes often said that he was sure he would not become older than forty-five years. He was now in his forty-first year. Only four more years were left in which to finish all his 'dreams' and his 'imaginations'. He sighed: 'The great fault of life is its shortness. Just as one is beginning to know the game, one has to stop!'

Rhodes began his race with Death. Faster! Hasten! No time must be lost! Each heart-stroke, each breath, each tick of the clock tortured him with the dreadful thought that Time was his master: 'It is a fearful thought to feel that you possess a patent, and to doubt whether your life will last you through the circumlocution of the forms of the Patent Office. . . . We do get older, and we do become a little hurried in our ideas because of that terrible time. Time you can never interfere with. . . .'

Those who had not seen him for some time did not recognize Rhodes. It was obvious that he was a very sick man. One friend observed that he looked 'thin, grey and haggard'. And another that he 'looks rather six years older than six months than when I saw him last. He has fallen away in flesh and there is a faraway appearance as though he had some special burden on his mind.'

People who met him in one of his inspired loquacious moods when he went on talking rapidly without pause and attracted everyone by the brilliance of his conversation noticed something strange in him which they would have attributed to the effects of inebriation had they not seen for themselves that he had drunk only moderately. Others maintained that he often gave the impression of being drugged. When they asked Dr Jameson, he discreetly shrugged his shoulders.

The thought of an early death was rarely far from Rhodes' mind. There were times when he wanted to forget his horror of death. Someone only needed to tell him how well and young he looked, that his mind was still young and that he would always be a boy, and Rhodes would immediately be in an exultant mood.

Pacing up and down the room he would repeat over and over again: 'I am a boy! I am a boy! Of course I shall never get old....' His eyes would suddenly regain their former lustre; his huge body would lose its slovenly curve and become erect and towering. He would stretch out his arms, his steps would sound full of energy and with a jubilant cry he would sink down on the sofa and repeat to himself: 'I never felt younger!—I never felt younger—never felt younger——'

In addition to the fear of an early death there now came to the surface his strong belief that he had been called upon by Fate to perform a special mission in life. He now considered himself more than the 'agent of fate': he thought he was Fate itself. What he had done up to now, his conquest of the North, had been described as 'the dream of a lunatic'. They knew now that 'the lunacy of the project . . . had passed from the era of imagination to practical completion'. And so Rhodes said, 'we have to complete with all the rapidity we can the project that is before us—that is the project of uniting the North and the South of Africa'. And there was no doubt in his mind that he had been ordained to shape the destiny of the African continent. From the musings in his library there remained firmly fixed in his mind the portraits, the lives, the deeds and the thoughts of the Roman emperors.

'. . . Was it not always the little things that changed the world and not the big things? All the great conquests of the world came from accident. . . . I was fortunate in forming an imaginative conception and succeeding within a period that was hardly equal to the term allotted to an Oxford student. . . They might discover the microbe of the rinderpest but would they ever find the microbe of the human imagination? . . . It came and thoughts came, and I was moved as a human atom to carry out those thoughts. . . .'

No power of imagination, no dreams, no musings over his old map, could help him now. Recently he had warned one of his associates: 'Don't deal with hypothetical cases—deal with facts.' Rhodes himself, however, could not free himself from his meditations over the completion of his great plans:

> When I find myself in uncongenial company, or when people are playing their games, or when I am alone in a railway carriage, I shut my eyes and think of my great idea. I turn it over in my mind and try to get a new light on it; it is the pleasantest companion that I have.

His conquest of the North was completed and needed only consolidation. But the peak of his work—the United States of Southern Africa—was still a long way from realization. Rhodes had at last learnt that the obstacle was no longer the obstinacy of a single old man, Paul Kruger, but the deeply rooted system of conservative Calvinism, reactionary xenophobia and corruption—which Rhodes described as Krugerism and which a contemporary critic called the 'political economy of Spain in the days of Phillip II applied by Kruger to the community of the most modern and progressive manufacturers ever assembled together in one spot'.

The Rand, where the gold output was ever increasing, gave the little Boer republic tremendous political and economic power. As the natural centre of South Africa the Transvaal had already in 1895 gained international importance. Johannesburg was an international town of 50,000 white inhabitants of which two-thirds were British. In a new community like Johannesburg where the chief interest of its population centred round the problem of getting rich quickly, it was not surprising that the percentage of low, even criminal elements was higher than in the older towns of other countries. A British general referred to Johannesburg, full of indignation, as 'Monte Carlo superimposed upon Sodom and Gomorrah!—probably the most corrupt, immoral and untruthful assemblage of beings at present in the world!'

A town such as this, grown suddenly out of the veld, with a highly developed industry and being linked, through *haute finance*, with the international share-market and banks, stood in gross contrast to the capital of the country, Pretoria, the little dreamy Boer town only forty miles away. The mentality of Pretoria's inhabitants had not changed in spite of the fact that the ox-wagon had been replaced by the railway. The influx of the foreigners had only strengthened their traditions by which they fortified themselves against any undesirable influence on the straitness of their ways, the primitiveness of the economy and the simplicity of their political system. The Uitlanders worshipped their idols in the temple of the Stock Exchange, whereas the Boers were still adhering to the laws of Moses. The new-comers were building up their future on bank-credit while the Boers saw security only in the possession of land and stock.

In the stagnated development of the Transvaal, Rhodes sensed a threat to the balance in South Africa, fearing that his plans would be frustrated and that Fate might direct the future of the continent without him.

At first Rhodes had tried to bring the Transvaal into his economic and political orbit, by the peaceful means of a customs union, a railway-tariff convention, treaties on post, on coinage and on the treatment of Natives and common laws which, he was sure, would sooner or later lead to closer relations and to the ultimate absorption of the small republic. Behind these proposals, the soundness of which many Boers did not deny, President Kruger saw only the bogy of British imperialism, represented by Rhodes, the ruthless land-grabber. He therefore declined all Rhodes' approaches. At their last interview, towards the end of 1894, Rhodes had come to the conclusion that he would never win over the 'old Dopper' by peaceful means. The only way left to him was the removal of Kruger and Krugerism by force. It was unlikely that any British Government would sanction war in Africa, since they had to be on the look-out for possible aggressive constellations by the big European Powers against Britain as a result of her 'splendid isolation'.

There were other means which could be employed; tactics, which in later years became known as 'cold war' and 'fifth-column', and were to lead in their combination to bloodless revolutions.

In Johannesburg the Uitlanders had been agitating for several years for the extension of the franchise to all aliens through the political machinery of the National Union. This perfectly legal and justified movement Rhodes decided to make his tool and to load it with revolutionary fervour and a spirit of conspiracy and fighting lust. He really believed that a 'revolution, like everything else, could be ordered for money', as Garrett later wrote in the *Cape Times*. He could count on the full understanding and support of the 'shrewd financiers, keen men of action, life-long worshippers of money and material success, to whom a belief in Cecil Rhodes became a substitute for religion'. He made the mistake of forgetting that Johannesburg was in the midst of a gold-share boom such as the world had never seen before. Rand shares, the aggregate value of which had amounted to £30 million sterling in 1894, rose to £150 million sterling in September 1895. Of the 183 gold-mines of the Rand, however, only 79 yielded any gold, and there were altogether only 25 companies which were able to declare dividends in 1896.

Rhodes now had no choice: he was forced into action. The Chartered Company was again in serious financial troubles. No gold of any intrinsic value had been found in Rhodesia and even the last prospects were fading. So far the long-threatened bankruptcy had been avoided only by the continual fresh issues of shares and debentures. Since its existence the deficit of the Company had reached the amount of £1,300,000—more than its original nominal capital—as the result of a cunning manipulation of its financial affairs by which all the profits were absorbed by Rhodes and his clique while the shareholders had to carry all the expenses. In spite of this, Rhodes and Beit by clever manœuvring were keeping the price of shares up to £8 to £9 though their real value was about three to five shillings. Rhodes and his friends made hay while the sun was still shining and unloaded large parcels of their own shares on the gullible public. They needed new funds to keep the Chartered Company afloat and to finance the planned Johannesburg 'revolution'. The main purpose in risking his position and fortune in a conspiracy against a friendly neighbour-state was to save that very position and fortune from ruin. If only he were able to 'Kimberlize' the Rand, monopolize its gold-fields by amalgamation and combine them with his empty Rhodesian gold-mines! Therein lay the Chartered Company's—and with it Cecil Rhodes'—only salvation. It was therefore imperative for him to bring the Transvaal under his thumb and eliminate Kruger.

Before Rhodes would risk his money on a revolution, he first tried to accomplish Kruger's removal by means of the blood of British soldiers and the money of the British and Cape tax-payers: he created a situation out of an unimportant issue which nearly led to war against the Transvaal.

There was a dispute between Kruger and Rhodes about the railway tariff on the fifty-two-mile stretch over Transvaal territory which formed the connection on the Cape line between the Vaal River and Johannesburg. Kruger had increased the freight-rate in October 1895 in order to attract the oversea traffic away from the Cape route to his Delagoa Bay–Johannesburg line. In answer to this challenge Rhodes reduced the rate from the Cape to the Transvaal border and organized an ox-wagon service to cover the fifty-two miles over Transvaal territory. The wagons had to cross the Vaal River on the Transvaal side through drifts. Kruger promptly closed the drifts.

Rhodes had found a new and an unexpected ally in the new master in the Colonial Office, Joseph Chamberlain. On studying closely the old London Convention of 1884, Rhodes found a suitable paragraph. He persuaded Chamberlain to turn the thumbscrews on the Transvaal Government. Chamberlain was willing to fall into line, provided that the Cape Government would bear half the costs of a military expedition and would supply some of the fighting force. Rhodes was in a quandary: he had to consider the Bond, Hofmeyr and his Afrikaner colleagues in the Cabinet. Using the Transvaal's high customs tariff on the Cape's wine and brandy as a weapon, he succeeded in bringing them all round nicely. An ultimatum was sent to Kruger from London. The old man was too wise to allow himself to be drawn into a war at an hour convenient to Rhodes and Chamberlain. On 5 November 1895 he reopened the drifts and the incident was closed.

When Chamberlain took over the Colonial Office, Rhodes had immediately begun to speed up his preparations for the final settlement with Kruger. Rhodes felt that pressure from within the Transvaal would have to be supplemented by pressure from without. A 'war of nerves' would have to put Kruger into such a state that the least provocation would act as dynamite and bring about the required situation where an intervention by—well, by whom?—probably, because it was cheaper, by the 'Imperial Factor', would make *tabula rasa* of Krugerism in the Transvaal for ever.

A field of operation was required from where Rhodes would be able to put pressure on the Transvaal in assistance to the planned Johannesburg rising. British Bechuanaland, which Rhodes had helped to secure for Britain, was about to be handed over to the Cape Colony as had been arranged in 1885. Rhodes had cast his eyes on the northern part of Bechuanaland, the British Bechuanaland Protectorate, which had been part of the Charter, but over which the Chartered Company had not as yet been given administrative powers. Rhodes now asked for the incorporation of this territory with Rhodesia.

At first, in the autumn of 1895, Whitehall seemed not disinclined to grant Rhodes' demand. Chamberlain, however, felt that behind Rhodes' haste lay some nefarious plan. He therefore purposely delayed his consent by going on holiday.

He had been right in his assumption that Rhodes was unduly anxious to obtain the consent. The three paramount chiefs of Bechuanaland, assisted by missionaries, were on their way to London to beg the Great White Queen not to allow them to suffer the same fate at Rhodes' hands as had been dealt out to Lobengula. Seeing that they were good Christians and had never allowed spirits to enter their lands, the London Missionary Society and all the forces of Exeter Hall, thoroughly assisted by the Liberal Press and by all the papers inimical to Rhodes, began such loud protests that the Government had to refuse Rhodes' demand. Boiling with rage, Rhodes let off steam in a cable to Dr Rutherford Harris:

> It is humiliating to be utterly beaten by these niggers. They think more of one Native at home than the whole of South Africa . . . I never objected to this part of the agreement, but I do object to being beaten by three canting Natives especially on the score of temperance when two of them . . . are known to be utter drunkards. The whole thing makes me ashamed of my own people.

Rhodes was not to be outwitted quite so easily. In November, behind the back of the British Government, he made a direct treaty with two minor chiefs by which he secured for himself, on the pretext of needing it for his railway line but really as a 'jumping-off ground', a strip of land north of Mafeking. The importance of the strip, though it was only six to ten miles wide, was the fact that it joined the western Transvaal border. Chamberlain, after some hesitation, confirmed the sale and also made no objections, though he was fully aware of the purpose, when Rhodes assembled there a strong and heavily armed military police force. Quite openly Rhodes recruited volunteers in Rhodesia, took over into his service the dissolved Bechuanaland Border Police and dispatched most of the Rhodesian Police to the railway strip. Headquarters were established at Pitsani, a little Native place near Mafeking on the Transvaal border. In command of this private army was Rhodes' raid specialist Sir John Willoughby.

The open arming of a private army was being carried out right under the nose of the highest official of the administration of the Bechuanaland Protectorate, Her Majesty's Commissioner, Sir Francis Newton, Rhodes' old Oxford friend. And in Government House in Cape Town Sir Graham Bower, the Imperial Secretary, also one of Rhodes' friends, was let into the secret of Pitsani by Rhodes, but prevented by his word of honour from speaking about it to anyone. Rhodes had told him: 'If trouble in Johannesburg comes, I am not going to sit still. You fellows are infernally slow. You can act if you like, but, if you do not act, I will.'

There was one man who had felt prophetically the storm-clouds gathering over his head and had feared that his good name would be sullied by the approaching mud-stream, finally to be buried in the 'South African graveyard of reputations': Sir Henry Loch preferred to return home dry and spotless and had thus retired from office in March 1895.

Since at that time Rhodes' good friend Rosebery was still occupying No. 10 Downing Street, Rhodes did not want Loch replaced by one of those Whitehall bureaucrats or by a pompous flag-waving, meddling, morning-coat-and-striped-trousers fellow. He wanted Sir Hercules Robinson back as High Commissioner. The Colonial Office was not very keen on recalling the old man from retirement, knowing full well his close personal and financial links with Rhodes. When Chamberlain referred to this point in the House of Commons Sir Hercules resigned from his various directorships. His nomination was thereupon welcomed since he was considered the most suitable person for the difficult position in the time of a crisis in South Africa. Chamberlain eventually dropped his objections.

After Robinson's nomination Rhodes wrote to him:

'. . . If we should ever come to difference, I promise you that I'll see in it a sign that I'm wrong.'

Robinson folded the letter carefully and put it in his pocket-book, saying: 'This letter I'll keep.'

With the ailing senile man installed in Government House and his friend Sir Graham Bower muted, Rhodes felt himself completely unhindered and uncontrolled. The last remnants of his conscience went overboard. The Prime Minister of the Cape Colony, one of Her Majesty's Privy Councillors bound by several holy oaths, instigated and took an active part in the smuggling of arms from the Cape into the Transvaal, arms which were destined to help conspirators against the lawful government of a friendly foreign state!

It was the end of Cecil Rhodes as a responsible politician. He had turned a political adventurer. And for what? For geological reasons! Nature had had the silly idea of embedding gold in the rocks of the Witwatersrand.

PART III

CHAPTER XIV

THE UPSET APPLECART

THE year was drawing to a close. Between Christmas Eve and the first days of January business life in Cape Town, following an old custom, stops almost completely. The sky is far too blue, the sun too hot, the sea too inviting, the shady slopes of the mountains too attractive and the consequences of celebrating over the Christmas holidays too exhausting to work before another string of days of merry-making, the New Year holidays, begins. Thus, whoever could afford it closed his store, his office or his workshop and enjoyed the cool breeze of the Atlantic at Sea Point. Those who were more enterprising suffered willingly the jolts and bumps of the cape-carts in an uncomfortable sixteen-mile journey to one of the rising fishing villages like Muizenberg on the False Bay coast, to have a dip in the warmer waters of the Indian Ocean. The Malays of the town, though strict Mohammedans, took the opportunity of the Christian festival to make gay, the womenfolk by dressing in the brightest colours and the men, only their fezes and their brown faces indicating their eastern origin, by competing in choir-singing, street against street, district against district. Cape Town's numerous half-castes, the Cape Coloured, forgot all the misery of their lives during this time of the year by abandoning themselves completely to the celebration of their carnival season. For weeks they had saved pennies to make themselves fancy-dress costumes from the cheapest material, in which they paraded through the town dancing and singing to the accompaniment of accordions, guitars or mouth-organs.

Everyone, whether rich or poor, indulged in some form of pleasure and rejoiced in a happy festival mood. There was nothing to worry the sedate inhabitants of Cape Town. Business men could look back on a prosperous year. The Kimberley mines had been busy; on the Rand everyone had prospered. Money—there had been plenty of it in the country, much of it due to the long and tremendous boom on the share market. There had lately been a little set-back, but that was probably only a passing phase.

Wool prices had been satisfactory and, though the farmers had as usual been complaining, they had actually not experienced such good times for many years. One had to admit that Mr Rhodes with his 'Cabinet of All Talents' had done well. The 'Colossus' himself, as cautious merchants in the City Club often remarked, had his fingers in too many pies and often took rather hazardous risks. But why grumble, when he always got away with it? Rumours had it that something was brewing on the Rand. People just arrived from Johannesburg were actually speaking about a revolution of the Uitlanders there against the Boer Government. It was amazing, really, how long they tolerated the shame of dancing to Oom Paul's tune. These rumours and the drop in prices on the 'Kaffir Circus' on the London Stock Exchange were indeed a little disturbing. Perhaps one should worry about it? But after all Mr Rhodes and his new boss in London, Mr Joseph Chamberlain, had lately been showing the 'Old Dopper' in Pretoria that he could no longer make sport of the British Lion. In Government House, since the unapproachable Sir Henry Loch had been replaced by dear old Sir Hercules Robinson, there now prevailed a more energetic tone dictated by the 'Colossus', who made sure that the old boy would jolly well let him do as he liked.

At home, in the old country, the wind was blowing another way too: Lord Rosebery was swept out of office with his party, the Liberals, by a Tory tidal wave. With a majority of 152 Lord Salisbury took over the reins for the third time. The effect of a militant imperialism was immediately noticeable in Britain's foreign politics: in spite of her 'splendid isolation' in confronting the Triple Alliance under German leadership as well as a Franco-Russian Entente, Lord Salisbury allowed the British Lion to roar so vehemently that only a few weeks ago war had seemed imminent between Britain and the United States for such a trifling cause as a disputed boundary between Venezuela and British Guiana. In the Far East trouble was brewing as a result of Russian penetration and in the Near East the Armenian Massacres by the Turks were used by the Russians with French help as a threat to force the Dardanelles and seize from the 'Sick Man of Europe' his much-coveted capital, Istanbul. The new masters in Whitehall did not content themselves with the vocal efforts of the British Lion, but were resolved to regain Britain's former prestige as the deciding factor in the balance of power in Europe by means of the plain international language of naval guns. A British squadron was lying ready outside the Dardanelles.

Much as Salisbury desired to come to terms with Germany, he was determined not to allow his country to become involved in the Kaiser's mad *Machtpolitik*. Salisbury gave the Kaiser a lecture on Britain's unwillingness to have her foreign policy dictated in the future by the Wilhelmstrasse. He spoke with such forthrightness and vehemence that from that August day in 1895 dated the beginnings of tense relations between the two countries.

The people at the Cape were not very interested in high politics conducted 6,000 miles away; still less were they interested in the Kaiser's little intrigues with which they thought, though erroneously as they were to learn only a short while afterwards, South Africa had nothing whatsoever to do.

Among the people who could not join in Cape Town's general merry-making and enjoy a carefree holiday during the Christmas season of 1895 was the Cape's Prime Minister, Cecil Rhodes.

As usual, Rhodes was already up when his boy Toni came to waken him at day-break. They all knew that the *baas* had to be handled carefully in the morning, the time of day when he was the most irritable. Almost every morning his servant found him leaning out of the large bay-window looking at the mountain view. He often wondered whether his master ever slept at all since he rarely found him in bed. Before dressing, Rhodes would walk through the house to see that all the windows were wide open. On his way downstairs he would check the time of each of the numerous antique grandfather clocks. Still in his pyjamas he would call for one of his secretaries, all young South African men known as 'Rhodes' Lambs'. Rhodes hated letters, both writing and receiving them. Important letters were sometimes not answered for days. Telegrams he answered immediately and often dictated his reply sitting in his bath. He took a childish pleasure in having his correspondence conducted by telegram or cable, and the longer they were the more he enjoyed it. Very often, when a thought struck him, he would call in his secretary, using his favourite expression: 'Come now, let us make a telegram.'

Though Rhodes as the head of the many and large companies

handled millions, he was extremely careless where his own financial affairs were concerned. Rarely did he know how much ready money was at his disposal, and often he would transfer large amounts before they were due to him. When worried bankers informed him that there were no funds in his private account he would think nothing of taking the required sums from De Beers or Goldfields. Let his co-directors just dare to make difficulties. . . . Were not De Beers, Goldfields, the Chartered Company and the many large and small dependencies his very own property?

What shares and how many he actually owned no one, least of all himself, could tell. Some of the shares were entered in the names of friends, secretaries or employees. His staff found valuable share certificates crumbled up in the trouser-pockets of discarded suits, as bookmarks in his library, among private letters in his desk. His banks were often puzzled when they were presented with large cheques, bearing Rhodes' signature, written in pencil on odd pieces of paper.

Sometimes it was still dark when Rhodes set out on his morning rides. He mostly rode alone, accompanied only by Toni or one of his secretaries. Often they covered twenty-five miles; Rhodes always had a certain destination in mind and his favourite ride was along the mountain slopes towards the sea. He was mostly silent during the rides. 'I think horse exercise increases the activity of the brain,' he used to say. He liked small, quiet horses which were easy to mount. 'One doesn't want to spend one's energy and time in mounting,' he said. The horse had to be a good 'walker' and he was never seen to trot. His seat was still as bad as in his earlier days, perhaps even worse, riding as he did with long stirrups and holding the reins loosely in his hands. He would sit on the horse as though half asleep. Because of the droll figure which he cut on horseback the miners in Kimberley had nicknamed him 'Jack Ashore'.

At breakfast, especially at week-ends, there was always open table at Groote Schuur. Business friends and politicians were told: 'Come out on Sunday and have breakfast with me and we'll go and see the lions.' On weekdays Rhodes went the six miles to town by cape-cart and was back for lunch. In the afternoons he slept till tea-time which he took at five o'clock on the back *stoep*. He hated to dine alone, and thus there were always numerous guests for dinner.

On Saturday, 28 December 1895, his house was full of guests. Beit was there and Rutherford Harris, both having recently returned from London. From Johannesburg there had arrived Charles Leonard, the President of the National Union, and Frederic Hamilton, the editor of the *Star*. 'Matabele' Thompson and Edmund Garrett, the young editor of the *Cape Times*, and a number of others were there for the day.

Everyone remarked on Rhodes' nervousness. Still more obvious was the excitement of Beit, who was pacing up and down, endlessly lighting cigarettes and tossing them away after a few puffs.

The guests noticed that Rhodes did not touch his tea. He ordered drinks contrary to his habit of not touching liquor until shortly before dinner. Those who knew him well also knew that a storm was brewing, since only recently Rhodes had declared: 'Under the stress of worries I have sometimes taken liquor between meals, but I mean to do so no more.'

He called to Leonard and Hamilton: 'Come with me and look at the hydrangeas!' The three men were seen sitting together on a bench, and Rhodes' purple face and squeaky voice, which sometimes penetrated through the clear summer air, showed that he was in a great rage. Charles Leonard, the leader of the Reform Movement, had left his Johannesburg £10,000 law practice, and had come down to Cape Town together with Hamilton to discuss with Rhodes the most recent developments in the pending revolt which had originally been planned for 28 December. During the last few days a controversy had arisen among the Reformers about the flag. It had been understood from the beginning that the rising would take place under the Transvaal *Vierkleur* flag. Dr Jameson had considered this as 'merely talk' in order to bring over many of the non-British followers. He was convinced that the Union Jack would be hoisted as a matter of course. Now many Reformers belonging to other nationalities wanted an assurance from the Committee that nothing would be changed and that they would march under the Transvaal flag, since their common aim was reform and not annexation of the Transvaal by Britain. They considered the sudden change to the Union Jack a betrayal. The enthusiasm of most of the conspirators, in as far as they had been able to become enthusiastic at all about a revolutionary movement treated as a business proposition, had faded. Dr Jameson, particularly, had aroused everyone's suspicions. He had been in

Johannesburg shortly before Christmas, and in his usual cynical way had shown so much impatience that many thought of giving up the plan for the time being and starting afresh later. The big mine-owners, the financiers and some of the leading executives who sat on the Reform Committee did not like the predominant rôle which Rhodes and his friends had usurped. True enough, he and Beit had contributed lavish sums. But so had they and others. It was easy for Rhodes to talk sitting snugly at Groote Schuur, whereas they would have to risk their necks. President Kruger had warned, in one of his latest speeches: '. . . Before one can kill a tortoise, it must put its head out.' The hint had not fallen on deaf ears. Should they risk their lives to pull the chestnuts out of the fire for Rhodes so that he might become master of the Transvaal?

Rhodes' mistake lay in leaving the execution of the planned revolution to those of his subordinates who were the least suited for the job—men like the three doctors, Jameson, Harris and a recent addition to his collection of medical handymen, a Dr Wolff from Kimberley, and especially his elder brother, Colonel Frank Rhodes. This gallant and amiable cavalry officer had no experience whatsoever in handling civilians, still less in dealing with millionaires playing at conspirators. Cecil Rhodes had installed the colonel nominally as his representative at Goldfields, but actually to manage the Reform Movement for him. Frank had unreserved faith in his brother, but others had little trust in Cecil Rhodes. Rhodes' unpopularity was fanned by his old enemy Sir J. B. Robinson, 'the Buccaneer'. Though Robinson had accepted a baronetcy from his Queen, he had become a staunch propagandist of Krugerism. It paid good dividends for his own extensive interests on the Rand and it gave him a better opportunity to lash out at Rhodes.

On one point Robinson's opinion was shared by all clear-headed men on the Rand. Lately they had been asking whether the whole Reform Movement had not been instigated principally for the benefit of a few mine magnates and a handful of speculators, or perhaps only for the advantage of British imperialism represented by Cecil Rhodes. Actually, the great mass of miners had hardly anything to complain about. It made little difference to them whether they were being exploited under the *Vierkleur* flag or the Union Jack. Working conditions were not ideal, but they were paid good wages.

Paul Kruger and his wife. A photograph taken during the South African War

Olive Schreiner

Princess Radziwill

Lionel Phillips, Beit's junior partner, had hit the nail on the head when he told Rhodes and Beit: '. . . as to the franchise I do not think many people care a fig about it'. The recently amended Transvaal Naturalization Law compared well with the laws of other countries and was, in fact, more liberal than the British one.

Rhodes, before 1894, had never expressed a word of sympathy for the Uitlanders. He was too much of a realist to imagine that he could supply the Rand miners with enthusiasm for the coming revolution with the same ease as he had supplied them with rifles and ammunition. Enthusiasm, there was no doubt about it, was sadly lacking even among the staunchest British patriots. Among the workmen a revolution managed by 'bloody capitalists' naturally aroused their suspicions. All that they could expect was that President Kruger would be replaced by President Rhodes. However, they tried to make the best of it. Various 'Rifle Clubs' had been formed where men were drilled in the evenings. Attendance was paid—out of Rhodes' funds—at the rate of £1 per drill.

So little did the leading conspirators understand the men and conditions with which they would have to deal that they fixed the date for the revolution for the December week when the greatest races of the year took place in Johannesburg. Yet even without the races they would not have succeeded in moving many Uitlanders to fight. When rumours went through the town that zero-hour was near there was a complete rout. A rush for the trains to the Cape and Natal began. Ugly scenes took place when thousands rushed the trains, climbing through windows and hanging on to footboards. Many well-known figures left in disguise. It was a general *sauve qui peut* in the hour of danger.

Though a number of men looked forward to the 'fun' provided by a 'little revolution' and there were others in whom still blossomed a spirit of revenge ('Remember Majuba'), there was no doubt in the minds of the impartial that the only people really interested in an uprising of the Uitlanders were Rhodes, Beit and a handful of other mine magnates. Even men near the Rhodes group were aware of the true position and objected to the rising.

Rhodes did not care. He dragged them into it, one and all. Even the question of the franchise of the Uitlanders was only a pretext for him: 'I do not like the idea of British subjects becoming burghers, and that is why I prefer that burghers should become British subjects. . . .' Politics had always served Rhodes as an instrument for his financial interests. This time, too, his grievances against the Transvaal were of a purely economic nature and all political differences were artificially exaggerated in order to camouflage the real issue. The Chamber of Mines, under Rhodes' direction, had complained about the gold-mining laws of the Transvaal though they were lenient in comparison with those of most other states. Taxation of the mines in the Transvaal, another complaint, amounted to only 5 per cent on the profits and was actually only rarely enforced. Rhodes himself, in Rhodesia, had fixed the tax at 50 per cent. One of the main grievances was Kruger's refusal to allow the mines to cage the Natives in compounds on the Kimberley system. The mine-lords complained that 10 per cent of the gold was stolen by the Natives, which was in fact more than improbable.

For years the mine-owners had been trying to induce the Transvaal to give them title-deeds to their mines. According to Transvaal law private landed property had never been recognized by the State, and this constitutional principle referred not only to mines but also to all land in town and country. Only leases for ninety-nine years were given. All minerals were considered national property, and the Government granted only mining rights.

The main attacks against the Pretoria Government by the Rand lords were directed at a dynamite monopoly held by Beit's cousins, the brothers Lippert, who made an enormous profit out of it. The total cost to the mining industry of this dynamite monopoly amounted to £600,000 a year, which worked out at not even a minimal fraction of 1 per cent of their working costs and almost nothing of their profits. In later years under British rule, the dynamite monopoly was acquired by De Beers, which still possesses it to this day, protected by heavy duty and rail tariffs.

These demands were made issues of great importance by an industry which in the case of bona fide companies paid yearly dividends of 30 to 60 per cent and could afford to provide each of their directors with a bonus of £200,000 to £400,000 a year. They could not seriously maintain that their existence depended on these questions.

All this could and would have been settled by negotiations with the Transvaal Government, and during the last few months there had been very promising signs of a friendly understanding. The conspirators, however, were afraid of any amicable settlement of the differences between the Uitlanders and Kruger that would deprive them of the chance to take action. In order not to be forestalled by Kruger, as in the affair of the closing of the drifts, the revolution would have to take place soon.

Many sober-minded people in Johannesburg refused to allow Rhodes to lead them by the nose. Among them were several of the big mine-owners, men like Abe Bailey and especially Barney Barnato. It seemed strange that Barnato, 'that cunning little Jew', had to preach to those dyed-in-the-wool Jingoes, who had always looked down on him as 'more or less a foreigner', what allegiance to the Queen and to the country of his birth, and what pride in one's British nationality really signified. He, like every decent Britisher, would never barter his British nationality for financial advantages. He vehemently declined to join the Reform Committee and was seriously upset when he learnt that his junior partner, his nephew S. B. Joel, had become a member.

As the date originally fixed for the revolution drew nearer many of the conspirators in Johannesburg began to get cold feet. With Dr Jameson's permanent coaxing and Dr Rutherford Harris' drunken jabbering, they began to shudder at the thought of having placed the fate of a town, the lives of thousands of human beings, the future of a valuable industry and the destiny of a country, perhaps of a continent, in the hands of these two men whose unreliability needed no further proof.

It had been arranged that Dr Jameson should set out from Pitsani on 28 December, when the rising in Johannesburg was to take place, and march his column to their aid. Now, with arms as yet insufficient, with thousands of men running away and with the flag question not yet settled, the leaders in Johannesburg decided to postpone the date for at least ten days, if not longer. The chief leader, Charles Leonard, after having signed a fulminating manifesto calling a mass-meeting for 6 January, left Johannesburg for Cape Town on Christmas Day, in order, as he said, to confer with Rhodes. In Johannesburg, however, people said openly that he had chosen the better part of valour by running away.

There now began a frantic exchange of telegrams between the Reform Committee and Dr Jameson, who was pulling madly at the leash on the border. All their telegraphic correspondence was conducted in code, not a private code but in one of the popular commercial codes available in every book store. Only the names and special references were expressed in special secret words. It was symptomatic of the mentality of these merchant-adventurers that they chose as code-words for their revolution terms borrowed from company promoting such as 'flotation', 'shareholders' meeting' and 'diamonds'. Dr Jameson's troops became 'foreign subscribers'.

Still, on 23 December, Harris sent a wire to Dr Jameson, reading (decoded):

> Company will be floated next Saturday [28 December] 12 o'clock at night: they are anxious you must not start before 8 o'clock and secure telegraph office silence. We suspect Transvaal is getting aware slightly.

At the same time Dr Harris, who had been given the appropriate code-name of 'Cactus', tried to goad on the Johannesburg cold-footed revolutionaries:

> Dr Jameson says he cannot give extension of refusal for flotation beyond December, as Transvaal Boers opposition shareholders hold meeting on Limpopo. . .

Colonel Frank Rhodes, however, was too experienced a soldier to imagine that action could be taken when the leaders had become lukewarm; the chief leader had preferred to seek security in Cape Town, and what was left of the rank and file was at the races. He wired to Cape Town, with the consent of the Committee, on 26 December:

> It is absolutely necessary to postpone flotation. Charles Leonard left last night for Cape Town.

Dr Jameson's brother, who held an executive position in Goldfields and was one of the leading conspirators, telegraphed his brother simultaneously via Cape Town:

> It is absolutely necessary to postpone flotation through unforeseen circumstances here altogether unexpected, and until we have C. J. Rhodes' absolute pledge that authority of Imperial Government will not be insisted on [refers to the Union Jack]. . .

To this message, when forwarding it to Pitsani, Rutherford Harris added:

> Charles Leonard will therefore arrive Cape Town Saturday morning; so you must not move until you hear from us again. Too awful. Very sorry.

The conspirators, knowing Dr Jameson's impatience and obstinacy, did not want to leave the matter of stopping him to a few telegrams which he could deny having received. They therefore dispatched two messengers to Pitsani, Captain Holden and Major Heany; and so as to be doubly sure, the one was sent by rail and the other by road.

In spite of all wires from Rhodes, Frank Rhodes, Harris, the whole Reform Committee and individual members, Dr Jameson clearly did not want to wait.

On Friday, 27 December at three o'clock, he wired to Harris that his troops had gone forward, but that he would try to stop them and that he expected telegraphic authorization the next morning to proceed. Two hours later he threatened that if the Johannesburgers 'do not we will make our own flotation'. After receiving the Johannesburg wires he discovered that the real cause for the delay lay in the fact that his co-conspirators in Johannesburg had succumbed to an attack of mortal funk. In his rage he sent Colonel Rhodes the scornful message:

> Grave suspicion has been aroused. Surely, in your estimation, do you consider that races is of the utmost importance compared to immense risks of discovery, daily expected by which under these circumstances it will be necessary to act prematurely? Let J. H. Hammond inform weak partners [the] more delay [the] more danger. Dr Wolff will explain fully reasons to anticipate rather than postpone action. Do all you can to hasten the completion of works.

There followed a telegraphic bombardment of Dr Jameson from Cape Town and from Johannesburg to stop him and make him wait for Major Heany, who was due to arrive on a special train. Even Rutherford Harris sobered up sufficiently to see the disaster which a rash action by Jameson would bring about. He tried to pacify him by a wire sent on the morning of Saturday, the 28th:

> You are quite right with regard to the cause of delay of flotation, but Ch. Leonard and Hamilton of *Star*, inform us movement not popular in Johannesburg; when you have seen Major Heany, let us know by wire what he says; we cannot have fiasco.

'No, we must not risk a f*y*asco——, we mustn't risk a f*y*-asco——, no f*y*-asco,' Rhodes said over and over again as he walked up and down the path between the hydrangeas.

Rhodes had always preached: 'If you cannot manage a thing one way, try another!' And thus he now told the two Reform envoys with a shrug of the shoulders: 'Another time!' and he recommended them half-heartedly to 'go on quietly'. The envoys, obviously greatly relieved, echoed: 'Another time', and were starting to speak about a 'new programme' when Rhodes left them abruptly. By his flushed face one could see his contempt for those 'mugwumps', as he called them, who at every opportunity waved the Union Jack and shouted themselves hoarse with Jingo phrases, until it came to action.

Rhodes went into the house, took 'Little Beit' aside and told him about the 'biggest game of bluff that was ever played'. In the meantime the Imperial Secretary, Sir Graham Bower, for whom he had sent, had arrived and Rhodes told him:

'You will be glad to hear that the revolution at Johannesburg has fizzled out like a damp squib.' Rhodes took him into the garden and unburdened his heart, telling him, much to Bower's surprise, that he had financed and organized the revolution. He ended with a sigh:

'Well, I am still a rich man, and can spend the balance of my money in developing the North.'

Dr Rutherford Harris was having a late breakfast at Three Anchor Bay, a suburb of Cape Town, when he heard the Sunday morning quietness disturbed by the noise of rapidly trotting horses. While the cab was still moving, out jumped Stevens, the clerk of the local office of the Chartered Company. When he had arrived for duty he had found two urgent telegrams from Pitsani which he had quickly decoded and because of their importance he had brought them out to Harris immediately. Harris hurried to Groote Schuur.

Lunch had just been served. When they saw his pale face and were told that two telegrams had arrived from Dr Jameson, Rhodes, Beit, Leonard and Thompson got up immediately and left together with Dr Harris for the privacy of Rhodes' bedroom. The one telegram was dated Saturday 28 at 5 p.m. and said that '. . . unless I hear definitely to the contrary, shall leave tomorrow evening . . .' Without waiting for a reply Jameson had sent another telegram to Cape Town on Sunday morning at nine o'clock announcing: 'Shall leave tonight for the Transvaal.'

Rhodes sat on the edge of his bed. His face turned ashen and seemed suddenly haggard. After a long pause he jumped up and began to pace up and down the small room, repeating over and over again: 'Now just be cool. Let's think this thing out. Now just be cool. Let's think this——' After a while he stopped his pacing. Turning to Thompson, he said: 'Look, Thompson, look what that damn fool Jameson has done! Why did he do it? Tell me, Thompson, why did he do it?' His voice cracked and again and again he shrieked: 'Why did he do it?—Why? . . .'

Beit sat shrunken into himself and appeared smaller than ever. He tore vehemently at his moustache, his other hand holding tightly a bottle of headache tablets from which he took one from time to time.

It took several hours until Rhodes had made up his mind. In the afternoon he wired to Pitsani:

> Heartily reciprocate your wishes with regard to Protectorate, but the Colonial Office machinery moves slowly, as you know. We are, however, doing our utmost to get immediate transference of what we are justly entitled to. Things in Johannesburg I yet hope to see amicably settled, and a little patience and common sense is only necessary. On no account whatever must you move. I strongly object to such a course.

Unfortunately the line to Pitsani was dead. The telegram never left the Cape Town post office. To the meaning of the first two sentences no clue has ever been found. Rhodes, though he could have used this message to prove that he had made every effort up to the last minute to stop Dr Jameson and thus exonerate himself from the blame of having been largely instrumental in the

Jameson Raid, never did so because he did not want his friend to bear the whole brunt of accusation. This noble and unselfish attitude of Rhodes' showed throughout the whole affair, the only pleasant and agreeable feature in a cobweb of intrigues, lies, perjuries and blackmail.

Towards evening Schreiner, the Attorney-General in Rhodes' Cabinet, came to see Rhodes. Like his other colleagues Schreiner, a staunch friend, an almost loving admirer and a devoted follower, knew nothing of Rhodes' association with the Johannesburg conspiracy. But having heard rumours, he thought it best to tax Rhodes with it directly. He saw him only for a few minutes. Schreiner asked: 'Have you seen Charlie Leonard?'

'Yes,' replied Rhodes, trying to sound nonchalant, 'I have seen him.'

'For goodness' sake,' Schreiner said, and put great emphasis on his words to express his serious concern, 'keep yourself clear from that entanglement at Johannesburg. If there is any disturbance, they are sure to try and mix you up with it.'

Rhodes shrugged his shoulders and stood up, saying: 'Oh! That's all right! That's all right—all right. Good night!'

At eleven o'clock on Sunday night the Imperial Secretary, Sir Graham Bower, was disturbed in his slumbers by Rhodes' servant with a message that his master was anxious to speak to him at once. Bower was amazed to find Rhodes a crushed man, who told him: 'Jameson has gone into the Transvaal. Here is a telegram I've sent to stop him, and it may yet come all right—I'll resign tomorrow, but I know what this means. It means war. I'm a ruined man, but there must be no recriminations. I will take the blame.'

No one found much sleep that night.

While the people in Cape Town were enjoying themselves on the beaches to escape the heat of the day the churches in Johannesburg were overcrowded. And while from a pulpit a clergyman was advocating the Uitlander cause by fulminating against bluster and funk, 180 miles away an abhorrent act against international law, against human rights and common sense was being committed.

The Honourable Leander Starr Jameson, M.D., Companion of the Most Honourable Order of the Bath and Administrator of Rhodesia, was very bored in the camp at Pitsani. One could not play poker all day long. The company around him got on his nerves: these young officers could talk of nothing but women, racing and society gossip.

In his boredom he began to read. When he had returned from his skirmish with the Portuguese in Manicaland many people flattered him by comparing him with Clive. He took Macaulay's *Life of Clive* out of his kit and began to fly through the pages. Since his 'filibustering expedition', as his invasion of Manicaland had been called in Parliament, and his extermination of the Matabele *impis* by machine-guns, Rhodes had considered him, and he had been inclined to agree, as a military genius of the rank of a Marlborough, Wellington, Napoleon or Moltke. Macaulay now confirmed to him that the comparison between him and Clive had been well chosen. Suddenly he banged his fists on the table and to the astonishment of his companions he almost shouted:

'Well, you may say what you like, but Clive would have done it.'

He also remembered what Rhodes had once told a young officer in Uganda whom he reproached for having followed instructions too closely:

'You cannot expect a Prime Minister to write down that you are to seize ports, etc. But, when he gives you orders to the contrary, disobey them.'

He thought that he now understood Rhodes' orders not to move. He assembled his men on parade at 3 p.m. and told them that although he could not force them to go with him to the aid of Johannesburg he expected them to come as volunteers. He took from his pocket a letter dated 20 December and signed by members of the Reform Committee which told of the critical situation in Johannesburg:

> . . . Not to go into detail, we may say that the Government has called into existence all the elements necessary for armed conflict. . . .
>
> What we have to consider is, what will be the condition of things here in the event of conflict?
>
> Thousands of unarmed men, women and children of our race will be at the mercy of well-armed Boers. . . . We cannot contemplate the future without the gravest apprehension. . . .
>
> It is under these circumstances that we feel constrained to call upon you to come to our aid . . . and we cannot but believe that you, and the men under you, will not fail to come to the rescue of people who would be so situated. . . .

At first Dr Jameson's appeal had only a lukewarm reception, but when he read the passage about the plight of thousands of women and children there was a stir among the soldiers. None of these simple mercenaries could have guessed that the use of the 'Letter of Invitation' was a bluff. This letter had been written several weeks before as a draft by Charles Leonard to be sent to Dr Jameson as soon as the revolution began. When the conspiracy was postponed or rather had 'fizzled out like a damp squib', Leonard had asked Dr Jameson to return the letter. Casually Jameson had replied: 'Oh, that letter. Why? Awfully sorry, old man, but it has gone down to Cape Town by the last train.'

Now, on this Saturday afternoon, Jameson had forged the date to read 20 December.

Similarly he deceived his officers. He had told them in private conversations that the expedition was 'in the service of the Queen', that the whole scheme was known to and approved of by the authorities and that especially 'Chamberlain was in it up to the neck'. Those officers who were still in doubt about the legality of the expedition were soothed by Jameson and the rest with the words: 'Never mind, you won't be left!' with a wink which was meant as a reference to Rhodes.

At five o'clock Dr Jameson sent the previously mentioned telegram that he was leaving 'unless he heard definitely to the contrary'.

The canteens were opened for free drinks and towards evening everyone was in a more or less alcoholic state. When Dr Jameson gave orders for the telegraph wires to be cut ('secure Telegraph Office silence') some of his men were so drunk that they cut instead about 100 yards of barbed-wire fencing, as a result of which the line to Pretoria was not interrupted. Thus it happened that the Transvaal Government knew about the events at Pitsani earlier than did the High Commissioner in Cape Town.

On Monday morning, 30 December at 5.30, Dr Jameson crossed the Transvaal border with only 512 mounted men—instead of the 1,500 promised to the Reformers—30 pack-horses, 8 machine-guns, 1 twelve-and-a-half-pounder and 2 seven-pounders, all under the military command of the old filibuster, Sir John Willoughby. One invalided officer accompanied the column in a dog-cart as he 'wanted not to miss the fun'. Among the troopers, apart from the well-trained former Bechuanaland Police volunteers, were many most unmilitary characters picked up by Dr Harris in Cape Town, men who had never so much as sat on a horse or handled a gun. Unaccustomed to drinks like champagne, whisky and liqueur, many fell from their horses and quite a number deserted. On the road from Pitsani to the Transvaal there were found the next day rifles, ammunition, haversacks, bandoliers and even saddles.

The next day Major Heany, bringing Rhodes' message to stop Jameson, caught up with the raiders. Jameson walked up and down for about twenty minutes. When he returned the following dialogue took place:

'I am going!'

'Thought you would.'

'And what are you going to do?'

'Going with you.'

'Thought you would.'

Jameson was the only one in 'civvies', wearing a 'terai' hat with a dented crown and a light-fawn dust-coat. He must have felt more like Napoleon than Clive, perhaps even like Caesar crossing the Rubicon and sighing: 'The die is cast.' But it seems more probable that Jameson did not think at all. Habitual gamblers for high stakes never think of consequences.

Jameson's self-aggrandisement had deteriorated into an amoral, anarchistic, superman consciousness. 'The ten Commandments are out of date!' he once told Stead. And another time:

'Why morals or religion should have anything to say in political questions I fail to see. . . . What difference can it make in a man as a legislator what his morals are if he has genius and intellect and can use them?'

Unfortunately Dr Jameson believed himself to be a man of genius and was determined to use it 'in the public interest of his country' for the 'Caesarian Operation' he was about to perform.

On Monday, 30 December, Rhodes was up early and left the house on horseback, accompanied by Toni. Messengers were sent out and many callers came, but he was nowhere to be found. Bower, Schreiner, Hofmeyr and especially Sir Hercules Robinson were anxious to see him. Rhodes avoided them purposely. He was waiting for further developments: perhaps that Jameson had been stopped in the meanwhile; perhaps that the fire of revolution had been relit in Johannesburg; or perhaps that the 'Imperial Factor' would step in and come to the aid of the Uitlanders? He wanted to gain time.

A formal letter from Bower was left in his house:

> I have called several times at your office this morning for the purpose of conveying to you His Excellency's instructions for the immediate recall of Dr Jameson. . . .

to which Rhodes scribbled a very informal reply:

> My dear Bower,
>
> Jameson has gone in without my authority. I hope one message may have stopped him. I am sorry to have missed you.

Something had to be done. By now Jameson's invasion of the Transvaal would have become public knowledge, even if he had been stopped. Too much was at stake: the Charter, the Goldfields, his Premiership, his P.C., his fortune, his future and the future of his 'dreams'. Something had to be done.

Schreiner, the most faithful of his followers, had called several times while Rhodes was hiding in the mountains. He had at first been unwilling to believe the reports from the local police. He had wired back asking for confirmation of the 'agitated telegram'. To his consternation he had to accept the fact that Dr Jameson had indeed committed this outrage and that probably Rhodes. . . . So strong was still his belief in Rhodes that he could not imagine that Rhodes, his friend Rhodes, could have committed such perfidy.

Late at night Rhodes asked Schreiner to come and see him. When Schreiner entered the library Rhodes, his hair dishevelled, his eyes bloodshot, his face greyish-green and haggard, was staring into space. Schreiner knew that here was 'a man he had never seen before: utterly dejected and different in appearance . . . absolutely broken down in spirit, ruined'.

Without any introduction Rhodes cried out:

'Yes, yes, it is true—yes, yes, it's true—it's true: old Jameson has upset my applecart. It is all true—— Poor old Jameson. Twenty years we have been friends, and now he goes in and ruins me. I cannot hinder him. I cannot go and destroy him—— Go and write out your resignation—— Go, I know you will.'

Schreiner replied: 'It is not a question of my writing out my resignation.'

For many hours the two men talked. As Schreiner walked over the lawns and saw in the moonlight the majestic buttresses of Table Mountain he remembered a scene on the *stoep* of Groote Schuur when Rhodes had said, pointing to the mountain:

'In a few years you and I will be gone, and other little ants will be running about the foot of the mountain. If you think of that you can't worry.'

Now the great man, the 'Colossus', was broken down—— Schreiner stopped. A thought, a sudden ugly and terrible suspicion struck him. He wanted to suppress it. What if Rhodes was only acting a part?—— No, he was really broken down, and he was not the man to play that part—— If he did, he was the best actor——

And Schreiner in that hour felt 'what hundreds of people are feeling in South Africa today; they have lost their leader. Yes, they have lost him absolutely, a leader who cemented around him such loyalty and devotion. . . .'

Will Schreiner, a lovable character—highly intelligent, a great scholar, a splendid lawyer, an honest and captivating parliamentarian—was of German parentage. He possessed a romantic sense which even the dryness of Roman Law, the sobering atmosphere of Cambridge's stuffy lecture-rooms or the freezing traditionalism of London's Inns of Court had been unable to kill, and he needed a man like Rhodes—'a man of action'—to develop his paradoxical endowments. He loved Rhodes; he admired him; he acknowledged his superiority.

And Rhodes, unsentimental in spite of his occasional romanticism, recognized the value of, and also felt flattered by, the younger man's devotional admiration. Schreiner could not be bought: 'the obstinate fellow', Rhodes had called him when he insisted on paying his own election expenses.

Rhodes had played on Schreiner's sentiments with great virtuosity, knowing that the only way he could 'square' 'the obstinate fellow' was by affection. Just a year before, after Rhodes' nomination as P.C., he had written to Schreiner:

> I am just going up the Acropolis. I wished to say to you, how pleased I am we have come together and are at last getting to know one another. We may do much if we do not weary of each other and the work. Do not think this claptrap; it comes from my innermost thought. Read and tear up.

With a man of Rhodes' unsentimental make-up this letter, a unique product of his pen, should be taken as almost a declaration of love. Rhodes' affection for Schreiner was sincere. That very Sunday, in the afternoon when he still denied his implication in the Johannesburg conspiracy, Rhodes had written to Schreiner's mother in Grahamstown:

> My dear Madam, — Your son says you would like to have my photograph. It is pleasant to think you have a thought for me. I send it you and ask you to remember that I have tried always to do my best for the country of my adoption. The future has trouble in store but time will right everything, for it is only time that tells the truth. You wonder why I write you so openly. The reason is that I am very fond of your son. He is to me the most straightforward and honourable man that I have ever met and I know he must owe a great deal to his Mother. Put my letter away and do not let him know how I have written, but the words will be pleasant to you as his Mother and they are from my heart. . .

Schreiner's heart was sore when he found in the soul of his friend instead of the expected gold nothing but sham. He had lost more than a friend. As a result of the perfidy of this man he saw smashed to pieces the cherished dream of racial peace, the hope of a united South Africa, the vision of Africa's golden future.

Another old friend, Merriman, also turned his back on Rhodes in disgust, though he had himself been in sympathy with the Reform Movement. 'The Raid', Merriman said later, 'was not only wrong in its inception, but it is the deceit and treachery which accompanied it that I object to; and the Raid has put Mr Kruger into his old position and rehabilitated him in the civilized world: that is the pity of it, and for that we have to thank Mr Rhodes . . . I do say, Mr Rhodes is unworthy of the trust of the country!'

Even Rhodes' faithful mouthpiece, young Garrett of the *Cape Times*, was shocked. The 'Colossus', with a forced smile, tried to joke:

'Well, there is a little history being made; that is all.'

The last day of the year, Tuesday, 31 December, also saw Rhodes' separation from another friend. As on the previous day, Rhodes had hidden from the world in order to avoid being forced into action. To win time was all he wanted so as to give Dr Jameson a chance to 'finish his job'. For that reason, too, he did not resign. As long as he was still Prime Minister he might be able to help lift his upset 'applecart'. Until the very last minute Rhodes hoped for Jameson's success.

In the morning a Cabinet meeting was held. After about forty-five minutes of discussing current affairs, Rhodes left so that 'the others may talk freely'. The Ministers agreed that they would have to hand in their resignation to Rhodes. Schreiner declared that he would leave the Ministry the minute blood was shed.

Bower came into Schreiner's room to obtain the Cabinet's consent for a proclamation to the inhabitants of Johannesburg by which the High Commissioner, on behalf of the British Government, repudiated Dr Jameson's action. It had been suggested and drafted by Hofmeyr.

This proclamation, as was later proved, at least averted civil war in the Transvaal and a consequent war between Britain and the Boers. Unfortunately its effect was weakened by Garrett, who had helped in editing the final text. Before the proclamation was published in Johannesburg he wired to his colleague on the Johannesburg *Star* not to misunderstand this official pronouncement 'putting Jameson formally in the wrong', as the Imperial authorities had no other way out. He ended with the wish and the hope: 'Don't let this weaken or divide you.' As a result, the Reformers in Johannesburg assumed that the British Government really approved of Dr Jameson's march into the Transvaal and pretended only officially to be against it.

All these events came as a bolt out of the blue to Hofmeyr. He expected Rhodes not only to resign but to repudiate openly and clearly Dr Jameson's action. Rhodes' immediate resignation or dismissal had also been expected in Pretoria. The mood of men in high positions was expressed in a telegram to Hofmeyr from a judge:

> Has the moment not arrived for High Commissioner to dismiss Rhodes and keep him in custody, so as to prevent more mischief in Chartered Company?

Hofmeyr, when he learnt of the Raid, had telegraphed to Kruger: 'I hope your burghers will acquit themselves like heroes against Jameson's filibusters.'

This telegram proclaimed to Kruger as well as to the British authorities the definite identification of Hofmeyr and the Bond with Kruger's defence of his rights, his condemnation of Jameson and the severance of political co-operation between the Afrikaners of the Cape and Rhodes. Hofmeyr felt that Rhodes' and Jameson's folly 'threw back the cause of civilization in South Africa for 25 years'. His first words on hearing the news were: 'If Rhodes is behind it, then he is no more a friend of mine.'

Now, on Tuesday afternoon, he had to settle the final account with his former friend. They met in Bower's room in Government House. Hofmeyr began the interview:

'You will not pretend to me that you have mixed yourself up with this outrage from an overwhelming sympathy with the poor, down-trodden working men who are now drawing big wages on the Rand?'

Rhodes, not accustomed to such sarcasm, least of all from Hofmeyr, replied, downcast:

'No, I shall not pretend.'

Rhodes declared that he would resign, to which Hofmeyr replied:

'Rhodes, mere resignation will not clear you. . . . Issue a proclamation or manifesto as fast as it can be printed, repudiating Jameson's move, instantly dismissing or suspending him as Administrator of Rhodesia, and providing that the criminal law will be enforced to the utmost against him.'

'It's making an outlaw of the doctor—making an outlaw of the doctor—— Well, you see, Jameson has been such an old friend—such an old friend—— Of course, I cannot do it—cannot do it—cannot do it.'

Hofmeyr replied very softly:

'Quite, quite—I understand—— That's quite enough—— You need say no more.'

Hofmeyr was a sick man, suffering from a weak heart. His nerves were frayed by the excitement. And he really loved Rhodes. He turned away and busied himself with cleaning his eye-glasses. Turning again towards Rhodes, he said:

'I could explain better if you had ever been married. I have not yet forgotten the relation of perfect trust and intimacy which a man has with his wife. We have often disagreed, you and I, but I would not have thought of our distrusting each other in any joint undertaking. So it was till now; and now you have let me go on being apparently intimate while you knew that this was preparing and said nothing.'

And so they parted. Returning home in his carriage, Rhodes told Dr Harris about the conversation. So as to conceal how deeply he had been touched, he joked in his usual way: 'And you'll see how old Hofmeyr will slobber at my funeral—slobber at my funeral—slobber——' Even stupid Dr Harris looked at his chief in consternation when the usual shrill staccato chuckling started and would not stop. Almost suffocating, Rhodes tried to repeat between shouts of laughter: 'Slobber at my funeral——' When he had recovered from this hysterical attack he said: 'I am no longer pulled two ways; Jameson has decided me.'

Hofmeyr, sitting on his *stoep* that evening, was still quieter than usual. When he told some friends about the interview he ended by saying:

'I had the feeling as if my wife had deceived me with my best friend. . . . Rhodes imagines himself a young king, the equal of the Almighty—perhaps a Clive and Warren Hastings rolled into one!'

CHAPTER XV

A LITTLE HISTORY BEING MADE

MR. JOSEPH CHAMBERLAIN, Her Majesty's Secretary of State for the Colonies, stood in front of a large mirror in the dressing-room of his house, Highbury. He always spent considerable time over his toilet. In public he appeared mostly in formal morning-coat and striped trousers, and invariably with an exquisite specimen of an orchid in his buttonhole. Europe's largest and most expensive collection of orchids was reared in his hot-houses at Highbury, the upkeep of which and the purchase of ever new additions from all parts of the tropical world swallowed, it was said, an amount exceeding his ministerial salary.

Chamberlain never forgot a slight, least of all when it touched his craze for orchids. Gossip-mongers had taken delight in reporting to him Rhodes' frequent squib:

'Some people spend their time in growing orchids, others spend their time in making empires.'

It was also reported to Chamberlain that Kruger, when shown a picture of him with his monocle in his eye and a large orchid in his buttonhole, had shaken his head and said:

'What foolishness for a man to give so much money for so small a thing! And then he can only see half of that for he has only one eye!'

These remarks contributed towards Chamberlain's dislike of the two men, yet both of them were to become instrumental in the fulfilment of his dreams of a lifetime: to make the world feel the power of Joseph Chamberlain from Birmingham.

Chamberlain had never shown scruples in choosing the means towards his goal. He was as unscrupulous in his political life as he had been in his business methods, changing sides whenever it seemed opportune and sacrificing his greatest friends. Labouchere, who had once been his friend, said of him: 'Judas compared with Chamberlain was a most respectable character.' The nickname 'Judas' remained with him.

By June 1895, when Lord Salisbury had offered him a seat in his Cabinet, the 'Birmingham Ironmonger' had become a considerable factor in Tory politics. Forgotten was his revolutionary, his Radical, his Liberal, his Free Trade and his 'Little Englander' past. 'Judas' had become *plus royal que le roi*.

The time was ripe for a man of Chamberlain's uncompromising chauvinism and imperialism. A tidal wave of Jingoism at the last elections had drowned the old Liberal thought and had almost swept the Liberal Party out of existence. The mind of the English public was no longer open to reason. They now had new prophets who would bring them salvation: Cecil Rhodes, Barney Barnato and Whitaker Wright; J. B. Robinson, Abey Bailey and Alfred Beit. Devoutly they looked towards the Stock Exchange.

Politicians were astonished at Chamberlain's appointment as Colonial Secretary. He had been offered the War Office, but insisted on taking over the Colonial portfolio because he foresaw that it would have to become the centre of gravity in Britain's foreign policy. Chamberlain became the driving force of English politics. From the Colonial Office he set out to open up a new era of British *Weltpolitik*. In his electioneering speeches he had made it clear that his imperialism was not restricted to empty phrases, and that in Africa particularly Britain would brook no attempts to dispute her superior position.

The Liberals feared the worst: a renegade from their own ranks, he was; a man who only eleven years ago had fought tooth and nail against the annexation of the Transvaal. And an apostate, history had taught them, will go to any length to make people forget his past.

Rhodes received the news of Chamberlain's appointment 'with horror'. For Rhodes, Chamberlain signified the incarnation of the 'Imperial Factor'. And Chamberlain would not be as easy to handle as had been his noble predecessors.

Rhodes opened the relations with a formal letter:

> I am glad you have taken the Colonial Office even if you differ with me as to my part of the world. I know full well you will always come to a decision and before your assumption of office the difficulty was to get anything decided whether yes or no. . . .

Chamberlain answered in cool tones with a few generalities:

> . . . As far as I understand your main lines of policy I believe that I am in general agreement with you, and if we ever differ on points of detail I hope as sensible men of business we shall be able to give and take, and so come to an understanding. . . .

In actual fact each man was afraid of the other. Chamberlain realized that if he wanted to succeed in his policy in Africa he would have to co-operate with Rhodes, the 'uncrowned Emperor of South Africa'. Rhodes was not only a very considerable political factor in African politics, but, as a result of his financial and social infiltration into all parties and even into the highest circles at home, he would be able to make his weight felt in the British Parliament.

It took a man of Chamberlain's political instinct only a few weeks to be transformed from a bombastic demagogue into a creative statesman. He transferred his turbulent ambitions to external political issues as soon as he had been initiated into the secrets and aims of Britain's traditional Colonial policy, as handled by the Permanent Secretaries who always kept themselves independent of changing party politics. He learnt that, since the Suez Canal could easily be blocked in the event of war, the security of the sea-route to India depended upon keeping a firm grip on the Cape and securing its hinterland as well. The Dutch element in the Cape had therefore to be humoured. In order to defend this 'Gibraltar of the two Oceans' against German, French and Belgian surprises from the rear, it was essential to keep the back doors to South Africa well guarded by means of a ring of colonial possessions which would at the same time protect the rear of the Sudan and the entry into Egypt against intruders.

England's position, as the undisputed financier of the world, was dependent on the gold-mines of the Rand which were producing already a quarter of the world's entire output, with ever-increasing yields. As long as Britain controlled the gold of the world she would play a decisive rôle in all world affairs. Thus in order to fortify her position in the world, the pending issues in Africa would first have to be cleared up. For that reason the gold-fields of the Rand which were for the greater part owned by British companies, financed by British investors, and worked by British experts and workmen would have to be brought under the

Union Jack. And the Boer Government at Pretoria would have to be removed, by fair means or foul, before the Germans could forestall Britain by a sudden blow from their impulsive Kaiser.

Chamberlain's eyes had been opened by a speech delivered to the German Club in Pretoria by President Kruger on the occasion of the Kaiser's birthday banquet held in January of that year, 1895:

> . . . I always thought before [1884] that our Republic was regarded as a child amongst other countries, but the Kaiser received me as the representative of a grown-up Republic . . . I know I may count on the Germans in future . . . I feel certain when the time comes for the Republic to wear still larger clothes, you will have done much to bring it about. . . . The time is coming for our friendship to be more firmly established than ever.

It became clear to Chamberlain that fast action in the Transvaal was imperative. He had already shown his willingness to go to war against the Transvaal when Kruger had closed the drifts. But Kruger in his wisdom had not done him the favour of giving cause for war.

Chamberlain had also learnt that according to tradition the Colonial Office welcomed and encouraged men like Rhodes and did not mind their making huge profits as long as they proved themselves useful by doing all the dirty work which the Government itself could not handle for reasons of foreign policy or because of the 'negrophil cranks'.

From the files Chamberlain learnt further that already as far back as 1893 his predecessor, on the recommendation of Sir Henry Loch, had sanctioned a revolution by the Uitlanders against the Kruger régime with the ultimate aim of bringing the Transvaal under the Union Jack. In 1894, when a disturbance occurred in Johannesburg during a visit of the High Commissioner to Pretoria to confer with Kruger about the commandeering of Uitlanders for commandos against the Natives, Loch had kept the Bechuanaland Police in readiness on the Transvaal border to move into Johannesburg at a moment's notice.

His predecessor, Lord Ripon, Chamberlain found, had received confidential information from the High Commissioner in June 1894 about a conversation in Pretoria between Loch and Lionel Phillips. The contents of this astonishing interview became general knowledge in Rhodes' camp through a letter to 'dear Beit' from Phillips, his junior partner:

> Sir Henry Loch . . . asked me some very pointed questions, such as what arms were already in Johannesburg, whether the population could hold the place for six days until help could arrive etc. and stated further, that, if there had been 3,000 rifles and ammunition here, he would certainly have come over. He further informed me in a significant way that they had prolonged the Swazi Agreement [with the Transvaal] for 6 months and said he supposed in that time Johannesburg would be better prepared—as much as to say, if things are safer, then we shall actively intervene.

Lord Ripon had reported to the Prime Minister, Lord Rosebery, in September 1894:

> We might make war on the Boers . . . or we might play off the British element . . . against the Boer element and give the Boer Government thereby a lot of trouble. To go to war with the Boers . . . I hold to be out of the question. It would be very costly, it would require a large force. . . .
>
> To press our complaints against the Transvaal on account of their treatment of British subjects and support the latter in their claims would be a course having in it more elements of ultimate success than may at first appear, but would be, no doubt, uncertain in its effects and would be represented as mean and cowardly . . . for which last I for one should not care.

As a result of his discoveries, Chamberlain was satisfied that his Liberal predecessors had acted or would have acted exactly as he was going to act and thus, no matter what he chose to do in the Transvaal, the Liberals would have to give their consent.

Shortly after Chamberlain had been established in the Colonial Office Rhodes had charged Dr Rutherford Harris with the task of sounding the new man. Chamberlain, suspicious of everything coming from Rhodes, asked his collaborators, Lord Selborne, the Parliamentary Under-Secretary of State, and the two Permanent Under-Secretaries, Sir Robert Meade and Mr E. Fairfield, to be present at the interview. Dr Harris was introduced by Earl Grey, one of the directors of the Chartered Company and a personal friend of both Chamberlain and Rhodes.

It is not known whether Dr Harris had, as was his habit, taken rather more liquor with his lunch than was good for him. At any rate, he was very loquacious and in the course of his tirades he referred—in confidence—to the unrest at Johannesburg by making what he later called 'guarded allusions to the desirability of there being a police force near the border'. He said something like: 'We shall be here [on the border] and if a rising takes place in Johannesburg, of course we could not stand by and see them tightly pressed. . . .'

Chamberlain's coolness sank to an arctic temperature when he interrupted the doctor's jabbering:

'I am here in an official capacity. I can only hear information of which I can make official use.'

He put the doctor off by adding that he had full confidence in the High Commissioner to do the right thing at the right time.

The cool reception which he had received at the Colonial Office did not prevent Dr Harris from cabling to Rhodes fantastic reports, from which Rhodes must have gained the impression that Chamberlain had sanctioned all his plans. Yet the snub must have been strong enough even for Dr Harris to notice that Chamberlain was not willing to become an accessory to Rhodes' conspiracy. He therefore confided all further news of happenings in Johannesburg to Fairfield, a personal friend, knowing that it would finally reach Chamberlain's ears. Probably on Rhodes' instructions he also won over Flora Shaw, the editor of the Colonial Section of *The Times*.

She was a valuable ally. At the Colonial Office, Flora Shaw was *persona grata* and held in high esteem for her thorough knowledge, her discretion and her reliability. Believing in Rhodes' 'mission', she became his staunch admirer, ally and co-conspirator. When Dr Harris returned to South Africa she took over his duties of keeping Rhodes informed about happenings in the Colonial Office and of acting as Rhodes' go-between with Chamberlain. She gave her help for no reason other than her conviction that the Uitlanders' cause was right and that Kruger and his Boer Government formed a disturbing element for the peace and further development of South Africa. Even in the planned Raid she could see nothing wrong. She gave the foreign correspondents of *The Times* a memorandum with the necessary advance 'dope', so that they would fall into line when the event came off.

She had recently interviewed Dr Leyds, Kruger's State Secretary, who, on the pretext of 'seeing a throat specialist', had spent several weeks in Berlin. She had learnt that all the non-official Germans whom the Transvaal Secretary had met had assured him that 'he might rely on German help if England interfered on behalf of the Uitlanders. . . .' She also drew the attention of the Colonial Office to an article published in the *Gaulois* which warned that 'whatever happens in the Transvaal nothing can be allowed to take place to the benefit of England'. How serious was the view taken by the military authorities was shown by the fact that the War Office was planning to direct a second troopship to Cape Town.

The situation was rapidly mounting to a climax. Fate could still be guided, however, if Chamberlain had a wish to do so. In his hands he held Britain's immediate future. Experts in the Colonial Office saw the implications of what threatened the country: already early in the year Germany had intimated to Rosebery that she claimed the right to support President Kruger. Krupp had received large orders from Pretoria for artillery guns, machine-guns and ammunition. German instructors were busy training the Transvaal artillery.

The situation was so precarious that the Colonial Office considered it necessary to prompt its chief by a letter, on 18 December, that he 'may wish the Uitlander movement to be postponed for a year or so'. Besides the political reasons, another consideration was mentioned. '. . . if it takes place there will probably be a "slump" in the South African mining market which . . . may produce a serious crisis in the City'. Britain's Colonial Office acting as the guardian angel of the Stock Exchange, its jobbers and punters! Chamberlain replied that the present time seemed to him more convenient for action since foreign intervention in South Africa was the more probable the longer the delay.

A day later the Colonial Office informed its holidaying chief that Maguire, Rhodes' partner, had been informed accordingly and had replied that Johannesburg would begin to 'move' in about ten days (29 December) and that postponement for a year was impossible as 'Johannesburg is so full of bad characters, for whom there is no legitimate employment, that nothing can be done to keep them quiet, except to set them fighting.' A solution of the unemployment problem by revolution!

Maguire cabled to Rhodes the information which he had just received at the Colonial Office. The same statement and probably with more details and reasons were given to Flora Shaw by Fairfield, who did not know that she was now also acting as Rhodes' confidential agent in London.

A week previously Flora Shaw had cabled to Rhodes:

> Delay dangerous; sympathy now complete, but will depend very much upon action before European powers give time to enter a protest which as European situation considered serious might paralyse Government: general feeling in the Stock Market very suspicious.

After receiving Fairfield's latest confidential comments she cabled to Rhodes on 20 December:

> Chamberlain is sound in case of interference of foreign powers, but have special reason to believe wishes you to do it immediately.

When Rhodes received Harris' mendacious report about his interview with Chamberlain, and when he heard that Lord Grey had later given Chamberlain further details about Rhodes' plan, including the information about troops being assembled at the 'jumping-off strip' at Pitsani, he could not but believe that the Colonial Secretary was 'in it up to the neck'.

What Chamberlain—without experience in this kind of conspiracy and also not yet used to intercourse with men reared on the moral morass of South Africa—really believed was that *a* raid, not The Raid, was to take place and that Rhodes' police-troops would march on Johannesburg only after the rising, so as to keep order on the Rand, and only after receiving orders from the High Commissioner, who would hurry to Johannesburg to act as arbitrator. Such was the information which Sir Hercules Robinson had given Chamberlain with a warning that 'a fiasco would be most disastrous', the same thought about a 'fyasco' which Rhodes had expressed at almost the same hour.

When Chamberlain was dressing on that evening of Monday, 30 December, he was not thinking of South African affairs. Robinson, in his latest dispatch, had cabled that the movement had collapsed. And Chamberlain was not sorry. After dinner, however, there arrived a messenger from the Colonial Office, and it would have to be bad news with which they would worry him so late at night. . . .

His face white and pearls of sweat on his forehead, Chamberlain sat in his study as though paralysed. On his desk lay the message that Jameson had invaded the Transvaal, but that the High Commissioner was still trying to stop him. 'If this succeeds, it will ruin me. I am going up to London to crush it,' he told his wife.

After a few hours' sleep he was at his desk and immediately he sent a cable to Sir Hercules Robinson instructing him to declare the Raid 'an act of war, or rather of filibustering', to make it clear to Rhodes that if the Chartered Company were involved in this 'marauding action' he would withdraw the Charter and liquidate the Company, and for the rest approving of Robinson's measures in trying to stop Jameson.

When Rhodes learnt of this cable he was at first speechless. Then he sent for his secretary: 'Let us make a telegram to Flora Shaw':

> Inform Chamberlain that I shall get through all right if he supports me but must not send cable like he sent to High Commissioner. Today the crux is, I will win and South Africa will belong to England.

On Tuesday, 31 December, the entire English Press condemned Dr Jameson's Raid unanimously and hurled heavy accusations at Rhodes.

The next day, the first day of the year 1896, *The Times* published the 'Letter of Invitation' with its sobby reference to 'women and children' which Harris, on Rhodes' instructions, had cabled to Flora Shaw. This time the date of the letter was falsified to read 28 December, the third time the date had been altered. Rhodes had counted on the Englishman's sentimental sympathy with women and children in distress. And he was right. Overnight Dr Jameson, the 'raiding filibuster', the 'mad law-breaker', the 'foolish marauder', was turned into the gallant knight-errant, the *chevalier sans reproche* by the English Press.

The attitude of the English public towards the whole issue of Jameson's Raid had changed. The Raid had come as a shock to the English people, but not a wholly unwelcome shock. For years the Jingoes had been drumming into their heads: 'Remember Majuba.' They had also seen to it that the Boers were depicted as hoary savages on the lowest level of civilization. It was therefore not surprising that Dr Jameson was considered a hero by the masses.

To his consternation Chamberlain found that with the rise in the Doctor's popularity his own prestige decreased. The Jingo papers turned against him, accusing him of lack of backbone in bending to old Kruger's will and 'leaving unarmed Englishmen at the mercy of the Boers'.

Full of bitterness, Chamberlain complained in a letter to his wife that 'they have been waiting to jump on me', but at the same time he congratulated himself for having stood firm and separated himself from 'what was a disgraceful exhibition of filibustering'. He added that his messenger had met Jameson who had refused to obey the order to return. Sadly he concluded: '. . . so this is the end.'

In the room next to that of the Secretary of State for Foreign Affairs on the first floor of an ugly grey building in the Wilhelmstrasse sat Friedrich August Baron von Holstein. It was no secret that since he had managed to eject the Bismarcks, father and son, from the grace of the young Kaiser and out of office, he was the supreme ruler over Germany's foreign politics, no matter who was the official head of the *Auswaertige Amt*. Ambassadors, foreign ministers and his own superiors not only regarded him as a Machiavellian genius, but in personal dealings they were as afraid as first offenders before a judge. He looked more like a third-rate pensioned civil servant than a diplomat. He had no social ambitions or any interests other than to play his clever game on the chessboard of world politics. He never went to court; he never accepted invitations from anyone; he even declined the commands of the Kaiser for personal reports. During the last five years he had seen his imperial master only twice when the Emperor had come to his office.

Bismarck had hated him, the 'man with the hyaena-eyes', and Holstein had fought against the Bismarckian system of upholding the European balance of power through the Triple Alliance, while having at the same time a reassurance pact with Russia. In Holstein's opinion this traditional German policy was outdated. He wanted to draw Britain into the orbit of German alliances.

Germany's courtship of Britain found little response in

Whitehall. The Kaiser had thought in 1895 that with Salisbury at the head of a new Tory Government and simultaneously its Foreign Secretary, a German-British alliance was assured. When Salisbury gave the Kaiser the cold shoulder, Holstein maintained that the only way was to squeeze Britain into a tight corner somewhere and force her into an alliance.

When the first news of the Raid reached Berlin on Tuesday, 30 December, Baron von Holstein rejoiced. Here he had Albion in just the tight corner for which he had always hoped. He drafted a Note to be handed to Salisbury by the German Ambassador to St James, Count Hatzfeldt, asking the British Prime Minister to repudiate Jameson's violation of Transvaal territory immediately. In the event of the British Government's declining to do so, Hatzfeldt was instructed to demand his passport.

Thanks be to Providence for having established the good and healthy custom for Englishmen to take, whenever they can, a prolonged week-end holiday in the country. On New Year's Eve no responsible official was present at No. 10 Downing Street. Since the previous Saturday they had been indulging in their New Year celebrations. Hatzfeldt did not consider it etiquette to let such an important document lie there for several days and therefore took it home again, asking the Wilhelmstrasse for further instructions. In the meantime Holstein, the Kaiser and his Ministers had calmed down considerably. In the hang-over mood of New Year's Day, Hatzfeldt was instructed to destroy the ultimatum Note and replace it by another, a more conciliatory verbal *démarche*, stating that the German Government, because of the large German financial investments and industrial interests in the Transvaal, was anxious to have the *status quo* of the Republic maintained. This change of attitude was largely due to the refusal of the Portuguese Government to allow a contingent of fifty men of the German Marine Corps to pass through Delagoa Bay and to Kruger's refusal to let German troops enter his territory even to 'safeguard the German Consulate at Johannesburg'. Prince Hohenlohe, the seventy-seven-year-old German Chancellor who had had an interview with Dr Leyds only a few days before, warned the Kaiser: 'Dr Leyds is a suspicious man; he detests the idea of a German protectorate as much as a British one!' Holstein therefore suggested that they wait for further developments in the Transvaal.

They did not have to wait long. On 2 January, at Krugersdorp, twenty miles west of Johannesburg, Dr Jameson surrendered to a superior Boer commando under General Cronje after heavy fighting during which Jameson lost twenty-seven men killed and thirty wounded. The Boers lost two men. In Johannesburg, according to the latest reports, everything was quiet.

The next morning, 3 January, the Kaiser held a conference at the Chancellery. His shrill excited voice and quick manner of speaking indicated that the Almighty War Lord was in one of those dangerous moods that usually ended in some rash order being given with none having a chance to discuss or contradict.

Almost shouting at them, the Kaiser announced that at last the hour had struck to bring Britain down on her knees by uniting the European Powers against her. He would take over the Protectorate of the Transvaal, for which purpose he intended to dispatch marines and troops to Africa. He had already ordered the cruiser *Seeadler* to proceed to Delagoa Bay.

Old Prince Hohenlohe—or 'Uncle Chlodwig' as the Emperor called him—usually fell asleep during such long tirades. This amazing proposition kept him wide awake. He was the only one who dared to interrupt the Kaiser. In the slow and quiet tones of an old man he asked:

'Does Your Majesty realize that such a step would mean without any doubt war with England?'

'Yes, but only on land!'

Carefully Baron Marschall von Bieberstein tried to explain to the Kaiser the folly of military action, but he was not even allowed to finish his sentence. The Emperor had become even more agitated and was shouting, swearing and banging his fist on the table as he had not been seen to do since the day of Bismarck's dismissal. When he saw that even his naval advisors were not going to support him, he shouted angrily: 'Go and call Holstein!'

Holstein declined to come. He would rather resign than undergo the ordeal of wasting his time with 'that megalomaniac neurotic'. Besides, the matter did not concern his department at all, but should be handled by the Colonial Office. In charge of the Colonial Office was an old *Geheimrat*, the prototype of the unimaginative German bureaucrat. Helplessly he ran over to Holstein and asked him for advice. Holstein had merely not wanted to be drawn out of his anonymity and shoulder responsibilities; behind the scenes he was as usual quite willing to make the puppets dance according to his own tune. He refused to do anything before the other Great Powers were sounded.

The old *Geheimrat* suggested to Bieberstein that a telegram of congratulations should be sent to President Kruger. Bieberstein found the idea '*colossal*'.

The draft was brought to the Kaiser, who, upon hearing Prince Hohenlohe's and Bieberstein's opinions, agreed to sign it, after having deleted several offensive phrases:

> I tender you my sincere congratulations that, without appealing to the help of friendly Powers, you and your people have been successful in opposing with your own forces the armed bands which have broken into your country to disturb the peace, and in restoring order and maintaining the independence of your country against attacks from without.
>
> Signed: Wilhelm, I.R.

In the last minute Bieberstein had corrected the draft, taking out the original phrase 'the dignity of your Government' and replacing it by 'the independence of your country', in order to 'make it more pungent'. He should have known that the independence of the Transvaal was abolished by the Pretoria Convention of 1881.

Admiral Knorr, somewhat hard of hearing, had not understood the telegram properly. When he read it he almost imploringly asked the Kaiser not to send it. The Kaiser, already at the door, asked Prince Hohenlohe to hold up the telegram until the matter could be discussed again. 'Sorry, Your Majesty, it is already gone,' was the reply.

When the Queen read the Kaiser's telegram to Kruger she remarked to Salisbury: 'Outrageous and very unfriendly towards us!'

The next day she wrote a letter to the Kaiser which in its calm dignity and wise restraint presents an excellent example of her great statesmanship:

> My dear William, — As your Grandmother to whom you have always shown so much affection and of whose example you have always spoken with so much respect, I feel I cannot refrain from expressing my deep regret at the telegram you sent President Kruger.

It is considered very unfriendly towards this country, which I feel sure it is not intended to be, and has, I grieve to say, made a very painful impression here. The action of Dr Jameson was of course very wrong and totally unwarranted; but considering the very peculiar position in which the Transvaal stands towards Great Britain, I think it would have been far better to have said nothing. Our great wish has always been to keep on the best of terms with Germany, trying to act together, but I fear your Agents in the Colonies do the very reverse, which deeply grieves us. Let me hope that you will try and check this. . . .

I hope you will take my remarks in good part, as they are entirely dictated by my desire for your good.[1]

Upon receiving this letter the Kaiser immediately replied to his 'Most beloved Grandmama', giving the reasons for his action in pompous words and empty phrases. He had acted, he said, 'in the name of peace' which, 'following your glorious example', he wanted 'to maintain everywhere'. 'The men were acting in open disobedience to your orders,' he continued, referring to the declaration of the British Government and her Ambassador. 'They were rebels. . . . Now to me, rebels against the will of her most gracious Majesty the Queen are the most execrable beings in the world, and I was so incensed at the idea of your orders having been disobeyed . . . that I thought it necessary to show that publicly. I challenge anybody who is a Gentleman to point out where there is anything hostile to England in this.'

The damage had been done. There was more than one 'Gentleman' whom the Kaiser could have challenged. All the newspapers, the whole English Nation one might say, stood up as one man against this German interference. The English Press fulminated against Germany and the Kaiser to such a degree that, on the advice of the Queen, Salisbury had to calm down public opinion. The German Ambassador saw the imminent danger of war and warned Berlin that 'British ministers must be guided in some measure by the voice of the people.'

So as to show the Germans that he meant business, Salisbury mobilized a naval flying squadron to be sent to South Africa. The Wilhelmstrasse began to back out.

From then onward Britain relinquished her 'splendid isolation' and entered the cauldron of European politics. She soon sought

[1] By permission from *The Letters of Queen Victoria*, published by John Murray.

to come to an understanding with France and Russia in order to repair the 'balance of power' on the Continent.

On 2 January, Rhodes learnt of Jameson's ignominious surrender. The dreaded 'fyasco' had finally occurred. He would have to try to save what he could from the disaster. Both the Charter and his position as Privy Councillor were essential for his future, if there was to be a future at all. In the afternoon he wrote out his resignation as Prime Minister. The document was scarcely completed when he felt that he had perhaps acted too rashly. Why should he resign and thus accept responsibility for the Raid? At any rate, the High Commissioner was ill and had asked him to continue until a new Government could be formed.

On leaving Government House, Rhodes almost collapsed, but he still tried to give his friends the impression that nothing could touch him. When Rhodes found a new phrase he would use it *ad nauseam* at every opportunity. This time he repeated over and over again: 'Well, there is a little history being made; that's all—a little history being made. . . .'

When he arrived home and saw the grey faces of his friends and collaborators, Rhodes shouted in a hoarse falsetto: 'Jameson, at any rate, tried to *do* something. All of you down here do nothing at all—except jabber, jabber, jabber!'

With these words he rushed up the stairs and locked himself in his bedroom. In his hand he held a letter which contained Schreiner's resignation. 'Blood has been shed and the position I fill I can no longer hold under you,' he wrote, and ended with the words: 'I have had no more bitter sorrow in my life, than my loss of you.'

Rhodes crushed the letter and put it into his trouser-pocket, muttering: 'Yes, I ought to have told Schreiner . . . I should have told him. . . . I was very fond of Schreiner. It was wrong. I ought to have told him. . . .' Toni was waiting for orders on the landing when he heard alarming noises coming from his master's room. Were they deep sighs, cries of pain, or could it be that the *baas* was sobbing? It went on for a long time. The faithful servant was relieved when he heard his master's footsteps in the room. Rhodes called for whisky. When Toni was summoned again after some time, he saw that the bottle had been almost emptied. Rhodes

Rondebosch. Groote Schuur, Rhodes' home near Cape Town
From an old photograph

Parliament House, Cape Town, with Table Mountain in the background

Muizenberg. The cott
in which Rhodes died

The grave of Rhodes
the Matopo Hills

ordered his horse to be saddled and with his servant went up into the mountains. For three days he tried to escape from himself, from his friends and from being forced to a decision. Late at night he would slip into the house by a back door and lock himself immediately into his bedroom, where the servants would hear him roaming up and down without a break. In the morning before day-break he would ride away again into the mountains. He ate nothing except an occasional sandwich, but drank, according to Toni, bottle after bottle of whisky, though he showed no signs of being affected by the alcohol in any way. They rode from one place to another. Somewhere they would stop and Rhodes would sit on a rock for hours, his elbows resting on his knees, his head between his hands, brooding. It was thought afterwards that Rhodes was trying to gather enough 'Dutch courage' to commit suicide. Many of his intimates feared such a step. It seems more likely that he needed the alcohol to calm his nerves and to stimulate his heart, which must have suffered under the strain of the past weeks.

Rhodes tried to persuade himself that his actions had been dictated by fear of German infiltration into the Transvaal, just as he had saved Bechuanaland and the North from falling into German hands. But no one would swallow such a tale today, he told himself:

'Nobody and nothing can defend me, for I am indefensible. I did not send Jameson over the border—— I would not have done anything so suicidal to the policy I had laboured all these years for—— But one is morally culpable—morally culpable. Why did I not make it my duty to know more, and take care to prevent Jameson going over the border? I am indefensible—indefensible—— Now, I shall have to face the music!——

'We are in the trough of the wave; you have to think of tomorrow—— If you only knew what was in front of you, you would never attempt a thing——

'But Jameson was very nearly a success. Of course, the proper course would have been for Jameson to have put his bag on the train and gone to the Johannesburg races—— Instead of arming that mob in Johannesburg a couple of hundred men could have gone to Pretoria with knobkerries and seized the President, members of the Raad and the Arsenal, and the whole thing would have been over——'

He tried to sleep in the shade of a tree where Toni had laid out a rug for him on the grass. After a few minutes he jumped up again. Rhodes had always been able to fall asleep immediately whenever he wished and had once boasted that if he was told on going to bed that all Cape Town was in flames he would fall asleep at once all the same and sleep right through the night. And now sleep would not come. The portraits of the Roman emperors in his library came to his mind:

'They staked all their fortunes in one great battle and often lost. How they must have felt sitting in the midst of the stricken field when all their hopes had perished and everything had gone to rack and ruin. And yet the world has jogged along fairly well after all. . . . And in spite of whatever happens to us, the race moves on. . .'

It was Saturday night, the third day of Rhodes' flight into the mountains, and just a week since Jameson had 'taken the bit between his teeth and bolted off', just a week since he, the 'Colossus', 'the uncrowned King of South Africa', 'the modern Midas', 'the Elizabethan Prodigy', had been hurled from the summit of his career into the depths of ignominy, the icy floods of contempt, the dirty morass of calumny. He hurried home. His loneliness pressed heavily upon him.

He thirsted for the friendship of his old collaborators, the independent, straightforward companions of his political life, men like Hofmeyr, Schreiner and Merriman, who, as opposed to his intimate business associates, had never attempted to gain a personal advantage out of the friendship. As soon as he arrived at Groote Schuur he called for his secretary. A bundle of telegrams was brought to him. Mechanically he opened a few, but dropped them on the floor without reading them. He took up again his nervous pacing of the room. The secretary wanted to retire discreetly. Rhodes stopped him, almost imploringly: 'Don't go away; stay here for a little while.'

Interrupting the silence only by an occasional deep sigh, Rhodes walked from the window to the bathroom door, from one wall to another. He was bathed in sweat. Exhausted, he sank into the arm-chair at the window and kicked angrily at the heap of telegrams on the floor. Finally he said over and over again: 'Now that I am down, I shall find out who are my real friends—— Now that . . .'

In his naïvety Rhodes had seriously believed that Hofmeyr, Schreiner and perhaps also Merriman would believe in his complete innocence and stick to him. He read a note sent to him by Hofmeyr, who had also feared during Rhodes' three days of flight and heavy drinking that the 'Colossus' might lose his head and do away with himself. In a few lines Hofmeyr tried to tell him that though their political association must needs be at an end, his personal feelings of friendship and sympathy for his friend's plight remained untouched by the recent events.

Rhodes almost upset the arm-chair as he leapt out of it and flung the letter on the floor. Stamping on it, he shouted at his astonished secretary:

'Go back and tell him that I want friends while I'm alive. I don't want any of his post-mortem snivelling.'

The next morning, before the sun was up, he wrote a note to Schreiner:

> It is Sunday. A merciful Providence will now guide us to a decision. I really mean it and no chaff. . . .

Schreiner was away at his fishing cottage at False Bay and could therefore not accede to Rhodes' demand to come and see him. Also worried by many rumours of Rhodes' wanderings, he wrote him a note in which can be felt the sincerity of a great friendship —words inspired by a sore heart and dictated by a character of sterling quality:

> Whatever you suffer or whatever you seem to have lost or to be losing, do not let them induce you to do anything small. You must go on living your life on big lines. Rest and wait and your grip will return. I am so anxious about you, and my anxiety about your health is less than my apprehension, foolish perhaps, that you may be persuaded not to take and acknowledge your full responsibility for what has occurred. . . . You will understand how my heart yearns towards you. As for me, I am all right in a way—and I dream still.

On Sunday evening there arrived unexpectedly at Groote Schuur the Archbishop of Cape Town. He refused to accept the response that Rhodes was unable to see him. Friends had asked him to go out to Groote Schuur as they themselves had not been admitted and feared that the worst might happen. The Archbishop finally saw Rhodes in his bedroom and spoke to him at some length, telling him that his Christian duty bade him not give up. Rhodes appeared much relieved by the soothing words of the Archbishop.

The next few days brought one crushing blow after the other. From Pretoria came the news that the 'Boers show a tendency to get out of hand and demand the execution of Jameson'. On 6 January a new Government was formed at the Cape, and Rhodes was not even consulted by his successor. Secretly he had hoped —so little did he as yet realize the seriousness of his position— that his influence was still strong enough to prevent the formation of a government in which he was not present at least in spirit.

On 7 January after an ultimatum from the Transvaal Government, Johannesburg surrendered unconditionally. The comic-opera revolution had ended in Gilbert-and-Sullivan style just as it had begun.

The leaders of the Reform Committee, among them Frank Rhodes, Lionel Phillips, Rhodes' American mining expert J. H. Hammond, and Barnato's nephew Solly Joel, were arrested and taken to prison in Pretoria. The only pleasant tidings which Rhodes heard that day was the news that President Kruger, upon the personal intervention of the Queen, had magnanimously consented to hand over Dr Jameson and the other officers under arrest to the British authorities for punishment.

No one to whom Rhodes could unburden his heart came near him. And in him there burnt a desire for activity, anger at being pushed aside, and fear that his voice would no longer be heard. Only Hofmeyr and the Bond had the power to pave the way for Rhodes to return to the politics of the Cape.

Rhodes swallowed his pride and asked a cousin of Hofmeyr's to arrange a meeting between them. Only after his cousin's appeal to 'display the Christian spirit of forgiveness' did Hofmeyr give his consent. He met Rhodes and in his face he saw written the mental and physical agony which Rhodes had endured during the last few days. 'What am I to do?' Rhodes asked Hofmeyr. 'Live it down!'—'How can I do it? Am I to get rid of myself?'

Hofmeyr could only advise his former ally to resign from Parliament and to keep away from politics for a while. Rhodes, he insisted, must declare publicly by a manifesto that he condemned Jameson's deplorable action whole-heartedly. A declaration of this kind, for which every decent man in the Cape had now been waiting for more than a week, was necessary in the interests of reconciliation and peace.

Hofmeyr had the impression that Rhodes' thoughts were straying during the conversation. Repeatedly he interrupted Hofmeyr to lament his fate: his whole life's work would be destroyed and his life would no longer be worth living if the Charter were revoked. He seemed to worry only about the Charter. Was Hofmeyr going to attack him and agitate for the cancellation of the Charter? If such an attack had to be expected he could not go away from Cape Town; otherwise he might leave for Rhodesia very soon.

Rhodes remained very vague. Immediately after receiving Hofmeyr's promise that he had no intention of attacking him concerning the Charter—which he asked him to repeat the next day in front of a mutual friend—he seemed to be filled with new life. He shook Hofmeyr's hand and said casually that he would consider Hofmeyr's advice and that they could talk matters over again 'when times are more settled'.

On his way home Hofmeyr realized that Rhodes was helplessly lost, still 'imagining himself a young king, the equal of the Almighty'. He felt that 'the white ants had begun again to eat away all that was noble in this unhappy man, poisoning his weak character with the honey of flattery'.

The staff of Groote Schuur was surprised when told that Rhodes was leaving for Kimberley immediately. Forgotten—if ever he had contemplated it seriously—was the thought of suicide. The old fighting spirit had returned.

His friends in Kimberley certainly came up to the occasion. They had stirred up the whole town to give Rhodes a rousing welcome. When Rhodes saw the masses of people pushing towards him, when he heard the cheers, he became intoxicated again with the greatness of his personality and believed that all these people had come to show him that they stood behind him. These good people of Kimberley, he thought, were certainly not alone. The whole of South Africa, he was convinced, was behind him. And he would not fail them.

He waved to them happily, feeling like a victorious Roman emperor welcomed home in triumphal procession. 'Speech! Speech!' they shouted. He was careful at first, but encouraged by their cheering he let himself go, uttering dark threats, making obscure allegations and indulging in generalizing accusations. He ended the short speech with the words:

> There is an idea abroad that my public career had come to an end. On the contrary, I think it is just beginning, and I have a firm belief that I shall live to do useful work for this country.

His former friends in Cape Town were disagreeably surprised by Rhodes' quick political resurrection. Their astonishment increased when they learnt about a telegraphic interview with Rhodes published in the *New York World* (14 January 1896):

> CAPE TOWN, 12 JANUARY 1896.
>
> The position is that within the Transvaal there are 70,000 newcomers and an old population of 14,000.
>
> With the development of the gold industry to a fuller extent the newcomers will probably amount to 500,000 in five years.
>
> From time to time the position will be upset by the attempts of the new population to claim common civil rights, which eventually they certainly must get.
>
> Statesmanship should give them some rights now, as the present state is impossible for the newcomers, who own more than half the soil of the Transvaal, and nine-tenths of the wealth of the country.
>
> The new males outnumber the old in population five to one, and are composed largely of Americans, including the principal mine managers.
>
> England is the only great power in South Africa.
>
> She is now threatened with German interference, which she is bound to resent and resist.
>
> In this she should have America's sympathy. Blood is thicker than water.
>
> Americans above all nations insist on civil rights in one's industries here at the Cape.
>
> In the Transvaal all my managers are Americans.
>
> And yet we have the spectacle of the two great English-speaking nations of the world almost on the verge of war about some barren land in South America, whereas by working in perfect harmony the peace of the world would be assured.
>
> C. J. RHODES.

This statement of Rhodes' had just the opposite effect of what he had expected. He had blatantly demonstrated his political ignorance outside his own narrow sphere, particularly where it concerned American public opinion. From the editorial comment on his interview, published in the same issue of the *New York World*, it was clear that all decent people condemned his (and Chamberlain's) policy of aggression in South Africa:

THE TROUBLE IN AFRICA

> The cable message of ex-Premier Cecil Rhodes of Cape Colony to the World . . . is a declaration that the doom of the Boer Republic has been declared, that the English influence, the mining influence, the greed of gain and the spirit of the age, all working against this picturesque relic of individual freedom, cannot fail to destroy it. . .
>
> It may be wrong for the Boers to refuse political rights to the Uitlanders. But if it is, the way to right the wrong is not to send a swift and secret expedition armed with Winchesters and Maxims to surprise a peaceful, orderly, legal and presumably unarmed civil government. . . .
>
> The Jameson raid will have to be settled for in full before any demand is made on the people of the United States for sympathy with the raiders.

When Rhodes' attempt at influencing American public opinion became known in South Africa, Hofmeyr condemned the cabled interview as a 'bundle of lies, distortions and humbug'. Not one of Rhodes' facts or figures corresponded with the truth.

The New York interview was followed by a similar declaration of Rhodes' given to *The Times* which Hofmeyr described as 'filled with mischievous fictions'. No, Rhodes had learnt nothing. His former collaborators would still have to teach him a lesson in spite of all their former friendship. Hofmeyr no longer felt himself bound to spare Rhodes and wired to him that he had the full intention, in case Rhodes continued to spread such ghastly lies, of cabling 'an exposure signed by himself and other prominent men'. The telegram bore the signatures of all Rhodes' former political friends, among them his successor Sir Gordon Sprigg, Hofmeyr, Schreiner, Merriman and Sauer.

Rhodes stayed in Kimberley for only a few days. Then, without telling anyone, he left for England.

It could no longer be denied that Chamberlain was in a quandary. Everything had gone wrong since those eventful last days of the Old and first days of the New Year. The fiasco of the Raid, the ridiculous Johannesburg 'revolution', the capture of Jameson and all his officers and the arrest of the leading 'Reformers' was bad enough. Still worse—that silly ass of a guards officer, Major the Honourable 'Bobby' White, acting as Jameson's aide-de-camp, had carefully kept in his kit not only all telegrams, messages, orders and correspondence but also the secret code and had allowed it to fall into the hands of the Boers. Chamberlain's name appeared in these documents in various connections. They were now probably busy in Pretoria, using them to compromise him and the Government as having been in the know all along. What they thought and did in Pretoria, Chamberlain did not care. The only trouble was that he had firmly assured Salisbury that the Colonial Office had been taken completely by surprise and had had no previous knowledge of Rhodes' and Jameson's machinations. As a result of this declaration Salisbury had made solemn statements to the foreign Powers and the Queen had written to various monarchs that the British Government had been in no way involved.

A scapegoat would have to be found. Rumours were already going round that Chamberlain had been 'in it up to the neck'. Chamberlain's ambitions went beyond the Colonial Office, and South Africa was not going to be the graveyard of his reputation. Rhodes, life and soul of it all, would have to be the scapegoat.

Rhodes had been warned. The news that he was already on his way to England was anything but welcome to Chamberlain. With what kind of adversary he had to deal Chamberlain was to learn the very day, 4 February, on which Rhodes arrived.

Rhodes had sent Mr Bourchier Hawkesley, the solicitor of the Chartered Company, to the Colonial Office to warn Chamberlain through Hawkesley's 'very great personal friend' Fairfield that Rhodes would make use of certain telegrams in his possession, proving beyond doubt Chamberlain's knowledge and approval of the Raid, should Chamberlain make any attempt to cancel the Charter, proceed against Rhodes or deprive him of his title of Privy Councillor.

Chamberlain, in the clutches of a guilty conscience, asked Fairfield to write a private letter to Hawkesley with a request to come to him with the compromising telegrams. Instead of going to the Colonial Office, Hawkesley sent his 'very great personal friend' an arrogant note: 'Mr Chamberlain knows what I know, and can shape his course with this knowledge. . . . As I hope I made clear to you there is not the slightest intention to make use whatever of confidential communications. . . .'

Through Lord Grey's intervention Chamberlain was allowed to see copies of the telegrams. Unfortunately for him there were not only the twisted reports of Rutherford Harris but altogether seven different reports by absolutely reliable witnesses such as Lord Grey, Hawkesley, Maguire and Flora Shaw, who had all cabled to Rhodes independently about interviews which they had had with Chamberlain and his chief advisers in the Colonial Office. From these telegrams there remained no doubt that Chamberlain had known everything not only about the activities of the Reformers in preparing an armed uprising but also about the preparations of Dr Jameson for his Raid. Though 'Chamberlain will do anything to assist', one of the telegrams stated, 'you are aware' [according to another text] 'Chamberlain states Dr Jameson's plan must not be mentioned to him'.

When Chamberlain read these telegrams he was consumed with rage. It now became clear to him 'that there was a deliberate plot to commit the Colonial Office . . . to a general approval of Rhodes' plans and then to use this afterwards as a screen for the whole conspiracy'. No, Chamberlain could do nothing to fight this 'blackmailing scheme' instigated by people whom he called 'a dishonourable lot from top to bottom'. Chamberlain was ready to appease Cecil Rhodes.

On 6 February, Rhodes entered Chamberlain's office. Rhodes was not sure whether Chamberlain would fall into the trap. He still counted with the possibility of being sent to prison. On his arrival he had learnt that a Parliamentary Inquiry would probably be opened against him. As usual when he was in a tight corner, Rhodes tried to conceal his true feelings behind cynicism: 'I don't mind doing a stretch. Well, I suppose I should go along all right. There are a lot of books I have been wanting to read for many years now without having an opportunity of doing so. I should go in for a course of reading.'

For so peaceful and friendly a reception as he was given by Chamberlain, Rhodes was certainly not prepared. For one hour and forty minutes the two men were closeted together.

Chamberlain told Rhodes that he did not intend to revoke the Charter, though for the only reason that the Government did not want to be burdened with the heavy annual deficit in Rhodesia. He did not, however, yield to Rhodes' demand to drop the idea of a Parliamentary Inquiry in spite of all Rhodes' efforts. About the compromising telegrams not a word was mentioned.

When Rhodes came out of the room no trace of despair remained on his face. It shone with the glow of his old self-satisfaction. But this time no court was held in the Burlington Hotel. He strongly felt the animosity of London towards him. He considered himself 'hunted, hounded and harassed', especially by the general opinion that the Raid had been organized as a stock-exchange manœuvre in his and his friends' financial interests.

Labouchere in *Truth*, as well as the *Morning Leader*, the *Daily News* and several financial papers pointed to the enormous profits which Rhodes, Beit and their partners had derived from off-loading the majority of their holdings in the Chartered Company on the public at a time when shares which had cost them £1 stood at £8–£10 each. Between July 1895 and the beginning of 1896 Rhodes had made more than £1 million, Beit even more, and they had not forgotten their old friends who also had been allowed to make their 'pile', altogether a profit of £3,250,000 for the group.

Gold-share fever, the wildest speculations, the greatest share swindles flourished as never before. It was therefore not surprising that some papers sounded a sharp warning against the financing methods of the Chartered Company. 'Labby' in *Truth* spoke of 'this wretched, rotten, bankrupt set of marauders and murderers'.—'A group of exceedingly shady financiers has carried on a gambling establishment with the Union Jack flying over it.'

No wonder that Rhodes became nervous once again. He had learnt that when Parliament was to meet on 11 February, the Raid would be one of the first topics of debate. His political and legal advisers cautioned him to leave the country as soon as possible, and thus avoid being called to the Bar of the House and perhaps have criminal proceedings instituted against him. 'Hunted, hounded and harassed', he left London on 10 February, only five days after his arrival, and proceeded in the greatest secrecy on a German steamer via the Suez Canal to Rhodesia. Only there did he feel safe and free. That for which he had come to England he had achieved: Chamberlain would not dare to deprive him of the Charter. By means of a clever whispering campaign that Chamberlain had been 'in it up to the neck' Rhodes was no longer held entirely responsible for the happenings in South Africa. Joseph Chamberlain had been forced by Rhodes to defend Rhodes in order to save himself, his reputation and his future.

Rhodes sneaked away from London. It had been expected that he would at least wait for the arrival of his friend Dr Jameson, who together with his officers was being brought to London as a prisoner on a warship. It would have been chivalrous, people said, to testify on behalf of his old friend or at least to give him some moral support. There were also the other men, the unfortunate conspirators of the Reform Committee including his brother Frank, who were awaiting trial in the Pretoria jail. All that Rhodes did for his brother was to ask his sister Edith to go there and 'look after Frank'.

Rhodes, seeking to save his own skin, was already on the high seas when Parliament was washing all his dirty linen in public.

The 13th February 1896 was a great day in the House. Everyone knew that Joseph Chamberlain would have to fight a battle royal for his very life. Not a muscle moved in his face when Harcourt, very carefully, since he still believed in Chamberlain's innocence, fired off his accusations and exposed 'the squalid and sordid picture of stock-jobbing imperialism'. He ended his condemnation of Rhodes with the warning that 'we do not desire to extend the Empire or gain wealth *per fas et nefas*—by fraud, falsehood and crime!'

Chamberlain rose from his seat. He assured the House 'to the best of my knowledge and belief that everybody, that Mr Rhodes, that the Chartered Company, that the Reform Committee of Johannesburg, and the High Commissioner were all equally ignorant of the intention or action of Dr Jameson'.

If this was not the truth, it was at least clever politics. It must have been the sharp edge of the poised dagger of blackmail which made him launch out on a smug eulogy of the man whom the whole world, including the majority of English people, considered justly to have been the curse of South Africa:

> . . . A few weeks ago Mr Rhodes was I think the most powerful man in South Africa. . . . He goes back almost as a private individual, having not the control of a single policeman . . . and for the moment at all events, having seen his work jeopardized, possibly destroyed—the work he set himself of consolidating and bringing together the Dutch and English races.
>
> I am not to pronounce upon Mr Rhodes, but I say it would be an act of ingratitude if we were, even now, when suspicion hangs over him, to forget the great services he has rendered. I believe he is capable of great service still . . . even if he has done wrong in the past, he may do a great deal to repair that wrong, and recover the confidence and gratitude of his fellow-citizens. . . .

CHAPTER XVI

'. . . ALL BUT THE BOILS'

It was not only the heat of the Rhodesian summer which robbed Rhodes of sleep during the months which followed his hurried London visit to interview Chamberlain at the beginning of 1896. The disasters which befell him from the time of his return to Africa till the end of 1897 would have broken a stronger man.

On 30 May 1896, in Pretoria, Frank Rhodes, Lionel Phillips, Farrar and Hammond were condemned to death and the others to two years' imprisonment and a fine of £2,000 each. President Kruger realized, however, that the Johannesburg conspirators had merely been instruments in the hands of Rhodes. When a deputation of his burghers had come to him after the capture of Dr Jameson he had thundered at them:

'Bah! You are always tap, tap, tapping at the *tail* of the snake; why don't you cut his *head* off?'

He decided to pardon the prisoners and commuted the capital sentences to fines of £25,000 each with banishment for fifteen years.

The news came as a great relief to Rhodes, who willingly paid the fines. His share of the expenses for the miscarried revolt and Raid—the other half being carried by Beit—amounted to more than £250,000. Further and even greater amounts, Rhodes feared, would be demanded of him by the British Government in payment of damages caused by the Raid, for which the Transvaal was asking £677,938 3*s.* 3*d.* 'for actual outlay' and £1 million for 'moral and intellectual damage'.

Another danger threatened Rhodes: Kruger demanded his trial before an English criminal court. Rhodes was certain that Salisbury and his Cabinet would throw him to the wolves if they could derive even the smallest advantage from it. That much was clear after the treatment which had been meted out to poor Jameson who after a seven-day trial had been sentenced to fifteen months' imprisonment and his officers to terms of between five and ten months. Only after a general uproar in the Press were they given the privileges of First Division prisoners. After the sentence Rhodes, through his lawyer Hawkesley, declared in the London papers that he was willing to return from Rhodesia immediately and stand his trial, in case Her Majesty's Government 'might think fit to call upon him to do so'.

The news from England upset Rhodes badly, especially when he heard that even his friend Stead had censured him publicly, in the *Review of Reviews*, and was 'very anxious to have him sent to prison . . . believing that it would have been much better for him, for the cause of the Empire, and for the future of South Africa'.

The next blow came in the form of a short note from the Colonial Office that Rhodes and Beit must resign from the Board of Directors of the Chartered Company, which hurt his pride even though he had expected it. Something which also pained him a great deal was the news that he had been black-balled in London by the Travellers' Club, an incident which Labouchere had broadcast with great glee.

In the Cape Parliament, where Rhodes had ruled for five years as the supreme and unchallenged master, the 'mugwumps', as he had called them, sat in judgment upon him. After long and acrimonious debates, Parliament resolved to nominate a Select Committee to investigate the Raid and Rhodes' activities. Three former members of Rhodes' Cabinet, Schreiner, Innes and Merriman, were among the seven members of this committee. Rhodes was notified accordingly 'in order to afford him an opportunity to lay before the Committee such evidence or statements as he might wish to adduce'. Rhodes did not even consider this notification worthy of a reply. The findings of the Committee in a majority report which filled 700-odd pages were summarized in the concluding sentence:

> They are reluctantly forced to the conclusion . . . that the part taken by him [Rhodes] in the organization which led to the inroad headed by Dr Jameson, was not consistent with his duty as Prime Minister of the Colony.

About the verdict Rhodes did not care. His one fear was that the Cape Parliament would try to deprive him of the Charter. Merriman introduced a motion that the Chartered Company was 'not consistent with the peace and prosperity of South Africa', and that the Queen should be asked for 'the revocation or alteration of the Charter'. The motion was defeated by a large majority —60 votes to 11—and principally through the intervention of Schreiner, who concluded a masterpiece of oratory with the words:

> ... I would just say that nothing ... has caused me in any way to waver in the estimate I hold as to the motives of Mr Rhodes. Misguided though they were, they were the highest of motives. The supreme powers that Mr Rhodes has are fit to adorn a position of the highest eminence and I am sorry to think that these great powers have not been coupled in this matter with more respect for what is right and what is wrong. ... The aim of Mr Rhodes was a high one. I wish it had been a right one.

No friendship did Rhodes miss more nor did any condemnation cause him greater grief than that of Schreiner. All that he felt for his former friend he put down in a letter which he wrote to him from the veld in Rhodesia:

> ... I want to tell you that you need not fear as to the North, the people are fond of me and I will fulfil every pledge I gave in the House as to closer union and similar laws and eventual union.
>
> You said once 'supposing you died'. I am dead in a way but everything will be carried out as I foretold by my presence here. I am not going to die physically. I am not going to run away from Africa. I will remain here unofficially and carry out the big idea. ...
>
> You will say why did you not speak to me? I reply I was not going to mix you up. ... Why did you not counsel waiting for the future? My reply is that Kruger is temporary. ...
>
> I write this to you because you can give me nothing ... and it gives me an opportunity of expressing my thoughts and clearing some doubts in my mind. ... I have only one regret. I am afraid my conduct has caused division in your family. Your mother must be a lovable woman. I am afraid she has too high an opinion of myself ... I go by the golden rule which you gave me. Possess your soul in patience. Yrs. C. J. Rhodes.

The series of disasters had not yet come to an end. The year 1896 was drawing to a close. One morning Lord Grey, the new Administrator of Rhodesia, received a telegraphic message from Cape Town for Rhodes. He knew that a sudden shock might kill

Rhodes, whose health had suffered under the excitement of the past few months. He therefore held back the telegram for several hours. They were riding together over the veld near Bulawayo. Rhodes was speaking, as he often did of late, about the many misfortunes which the year had brought him. It seemed more difficult than before to tell him the sad news. Lord Grey stammered: 'Well, Mr Rhodes, I am sorry, there is more bad news....' Rhodes stopped the horse. His face turned yellow. Grey told him news had come from Cape Town that Groote Schuur had burnt down to the ground. Rhodes sighed with relief and muttered in a hoarse voice:

'Oh, thank God, thank God! I was afraid that something had happened to Dr Jim. Oh, thank God, thank God!'

Back from his ride, Rhodes sent a telegram to his architect asking him to begin immediately with the rebuilding and furnishing of Groote Schuur exactly as it had been before except for the thatched roof which was to be replaced by shingles.

Unpleasant comments about Rhodes appeared in the English Press when it became known that several troopers had had to go to court to obtain compensation from the Chartered Company for injuries sustained in the Raid. Rhodes, who knew nothing about the case, was accused of 'meanness towards men who do his dirty work'. Still harder words were used when the Company lodged an appeal against the judgment. As soon as Rhodes read about the accusations he cabled orders to settle the matter immediately and withdraw the appeal.

Meanness was one fault of which Rhodes was never guilty. In Rhodesia the demands on his purse were particularly heavy. Lord Grey once asked him why he spoilt the people, most of them obviously undeserving cases, by giving away cheques of £20 or even £50 whenever a fellow told him a sob-story. Rhodes explained:

'Well, a man once came to me in Cape Town and said he was on his beam ends, could I lend him something? I didn't like the fellow's face and refused, and that same night he committed suicide. That was a lesson to me; and since then I have never dared to refuse money to folks who are hard up!'

The public accusations of meanness in England, unjustified as they were, therefore hurt Rhodes to the quick. Not only old foes like Labouchere but also responsible men like Harcourt accused

Rhodes in Parliament of sordid financial motives in connection with the Raid. During a debate on Chamberlain's motion to nominate a Select Committee of the House of Commons to inquire into the Raid, Harcourt had called Rhodes 'a rogue and a liar'. Rhodes had moved heaven and earth, particularly through Hawkesley's 'rather foxy pressure' on Chamberlain, to prevent such an inquiry. Chamberlain, in his despair, had taken Harcourt into his confidence and Harcourt had replied: 'To me the blackmailing part of the transaction is the basest and blackest of the whole.' Hawkesley also failed in his impudent demand to have the Committee packed with Rhodes' friends. The only man on the Committee favourably disposed towards Rhodes was George Wyndham, 'the delight and ornament of the House, and the charm of every private society he honoured with his presence'.

Another member nominated to the Committee was Labouchere. Lord Grey, who as Administrator of Rhodesia was a Government official, had the audacity to write a letter to Chamberlain—who, though a personal friend, was also the Colonial Secretary and therefore his chief—in which he called the nomination of Labouchere 'an intolerable insult to Rhodes'. The letter also contained another threatening reference to the compromising cables. This time Chamberlain would not allow himself to be brow-beaten since he knew that he had Harcourt on his side and with him the Liberals.

Still thinking that he had Chamberlain 'in his pocket', Rhodes was anxious to take Harcourt 'on the personal'. He knew that he would not be able to silence him, but perhaps he would be able to put him in a more lenient frame of mind.

Rhodes was never a great letter-writer. He preferred to conduct his correspondence by telegrams which excluded any emotional outbursts. When he did write a letter, and personally at that, it was a matter of the greatest importance. Much to the surprise of his secretary, he asked for pen, ink and paper to be brought to him and began to write a letter to the Right Honourable Sir William Harcourt, M.P., Leader of Her Majesty's Opposition:

> . . . I should be sorry to think that you thought I was 'capable but not honest'. I have tried to unite South Africa and no sordid motive has influenced me.
>
> You might say why do I write, certainly not to mitigate your censure, but in case we come to grief I wish you to know that I feel

that, whatever you have said, you have said it from a sense of public duty, and that I hope you will understand in the future that I understand the reasons of your censure, though bitter, and I am still pleased to think that you had an affection for me. But remove from your mind the idea of sordid motive. . . .

I am minded to tear this up, but the outlook is gloomy, and I would not like you to misunderstand me. If I get through, well, tear this up; if I do not, I think when you are sitting in that smoking room at Rothschild's you will be pleased to think that I understood your reasons, but I could not go out from here to an uncertainty without saying, blame me as you like but do not do the cruel thing of attributing my conduct to sordid motives. Good-bye.

You make one mistake—the Dutch in Africa are not all with Kruger, and my action was not English v. Dutch. But we would not have the German element, and the Pretorian Government must go.

Rhodes was right in saying that the outlook was gloomy. The Chartered Company, which Rhodes had still prevented from being declared insolvent, now faced final catastrophe. The Matabele were in open revolt; rinderpest was devastating the country; famine was taking its toll throughout the North; no gold had been found; the settlers were dissatisfied and on the point of quitting; the Company lacked the most urgent means, all fresh financial sources had been cut off and Chartered shares were almost worthless. Rhodes therefore had every reason to lament: 'I feel like Job, all but the boils.'

When Rhodes had travelled to Salisbury from Beira in April 1896, he had seen the veld covered with the skeletons of thousands of cattle, all victims of the rinderpest. And by the precautions which most settlers had taken to fortify their homesteads he knew that Rhodesia was in flames, set alight by a Matabele rising. It was bitter news to him. Though Rhodes had now been in close contact with Natives for more than a quarter-century, he still did not have any knowledge of their mentality. For him they were 'children, just emerging from barbarism'. Yet he realized that something positive would have to be done to solve the Native problem:

. . . They are increasing enormously: their locations are too small for them. The old diminution by pestilence and wars has ceased. We have put nothing in the place of their old tribal war and intrigue which were excellent things in their way to keep their minds employed. We have instead placed canteens in their midst and never taught them the dignity of labour. . . .

One of the main reasons for discontent in the country, which certainly did not contribute towards teaching the Natives 'the dignity of labour', was the existence of slavery which had been introduced by the Company and about which the British Resident, Sir Richard Martin, later reported to the High Commissioner: 'Compulsory labour does undoubtedly exist in Matabeleland if not in Mashonaland. . . . Labour procured by the various Native Commissioners for the various requirements of the Government [Company], mining companies and private persons . . . a labour system synonymous with slavery. . . .'

Indunas began to rouse their people from their lethargy by telling them that they had not really been beaten and that Lobengula was still alive. The Matabele listened joyfully to anyone willing to give them a lead. After Lobengula's death they had been left, as Selous had stated at the time, 'like a swarm of bees bereft of their queen'. They had lost their king, their leader, the father of their nation. They had been robbed of their cattle; their huts had been burnt down to make room for the settlers and for mining camps or had just been left empty. Homeless, starving and sick, destitute and hopeless, they had nowhere to go. The Company had expropriated their land and deprived them of all ownership rights. Only two Matabele in the whole country, who had bought garden plots from the Company, still possessed any soil. The Matabele masses had finally been crammed into a 'location' situated in the worst part of the country which was devoid of fertile soil, water and game and where fever made life impossible. A British official described this territory as 'graveyards but not homesteads'. Moreover, after Lobengula's death, the Company had appropriated all the cattle of the country without investigating property rights. And, worst of all, the white police had been replaced by Mashonas who searched for cattle bearing the Company's brand-mark with systematic cruelty.

Reports told of the massing of large *impis* and from all parts of Matabeleland came the sound of war-cries: *Tshayai Bulala*—beat them, kill them. At first single settlers were shot. Then whole white families were massacred.

The settlers blamed the 'Four R's' for the dreadful events in Rhodesia: Rhodes, Rinderpest, Raid and Rebellion.

Rhodes was less interested in investigating the causes of the uprising than in suppressing it as quickly and cheaply as possible. With the help of Lord Grey he organized in Salisbury and Bulawayo volunteer detachments of settlers, including many of his pioneers. Bulawayo with its 4,000 inhabitants was besieged by an army of 15,000 Matabele warriors, among them some of Lobengula's *élite* troops which he had kept in reserve at the time of the invasion of Matabeleland. A relief column of volunteers under Colonel Plumer was sent to Bulawayo, defeated this Matabele army and thus relieved the beleaguered town. The British Government had sent out a detachment of regular British troops from Mafeking and insisted that the Rhodesian volunteer corps should be put under the command of regular British officers.

Rhodes, though still suffering from frequent attacks of malaria, left Salisbury with one of the volunteer columns towards the middle of April. He was in one of his worst moods. According to his calculations every day of this unforeseen war was costing the Company £4,000. In view of the insolvent state of the Company he would not be able to finance the campaign for long.

During the march into Matabeleland, Rhodes kept to himself. He always pitched his tent two or three miles away from the camp. He wanted to be alone because he hated the usual officers' mess conversations.

In his detachment were four colonels and soon they began to argue about seniority. Rhodes ended the argument by saying: 'Gentlemen, I am a colonel too, honorary colonel of the Kimberley Light Horse, and you'll think me a funny fellow—I am a funny fellow—but you must remember I am one of Her Majesty's Privy Councillors and therefore I am naturally the senior of all of you. And so that's settled!' His impulsive behaviour did not increase his popularity with the warrior caste. From Whitehall came a cable: 'Hear you have appointed yourself Colonel. Wire explanation.' Rhodes did not reply.

Throughout the march he rode in front of the troops, which was not without danger since several attacks from Matabele snipers had taken place. He was asked rather to keep with the main body or in the rear. Rhodes replied: 'If I am in front, they will all aim at me and all miss; while if I ride behind, I may be hit by accident.'

His detachment soon came under fire. The Matabele had by now learnt the proper use of fire-arms and the dum-dum bullets of their elephant guns were particularly feared. During the first attack by the Matabele, in the old Zulu tradition of massed frontal rushes, Rhodes walked calmly along the lines of his troops as though unaware of the danger around him.

Clad as usual in white flannel trousers, of which Toni even in this campaign had to see that there was a fresh pair ready every morning, Norfolk jacket and large grey slouch-hat, Rhodes offered a good target for the bullets which whistled about him. Rhodes was unarmed; a hunting-crop was all he carried. A desperate 'Colossus'—a colossus with clay feet, ruined, facing bankruptcy, 'hunted, hounded and harassed', derobed of his power, abandoned by most of his friends and mocked by his enemies—was he trying to find a bullet for a melodramatic exit?

When the rain of bullets became denser, Rhodes no longer pretended to enjoy the battle. Later he confessed to Garrett: 'I was in a funk all the time and more afraid to be thought afraid.'

He soon learnt from experienced troopers how to take cover. He still thought that it was unbecoming for him to throw himself to the ground. Once, when a bullet almost hit him, he turned to his secretary almost apologetically:

'D'you know, it was a very near thing. I might have been hit in the stomach—very unpleasant—— I should have been very angry—— I was never in such a funk in my life—hit in the stomach—— Absurd, isn't it, how you can't help ducking—— Not a bit of good——'

The Matabele were, of course, mowed down like ripe corn by the machine-guns. Rhodes led an attack himself against the kraal of a Native chief, marching in front of the troops and wildly swinging his riding-crop. In trying to escape, the encircled Natives ran straight into the machine-guns, which within a few minutes slaughtered more than seventy of them, 'like rats' as Rhodes proudly announced.

After the 'battle' there was an argument in the camp about the number of Natives killed. 'Very well,' said Rhodes, 'we'll count them again!' Alone, ignoring the darkness of the night and the possibility of an ambush, Rhodes climbed up the steep hill to the 'battle scene' and counted the bodies by walking from corpse to corpse.

Even hardened old troopers were shocked when they heard Rhodes, after the first big encounter, speak of his own troops' casualties in this cynical way: 'You'll admit that for 300 men who went out to fight the Natives numbering about 6,000, the record of a butcher's bill of about 75 is a very fair one.' His first question after every encounter was: 'How many Natives were killed?' Once one of the subalterns answered: 'Very few, sir, the Natives threw down their arms, went on their knees and begged for mercy.' Rhodes looked at the young officer as though he had not understood him: 'Well, you should not spare them. You should kill all you can, as it serves as a lesson to them when they talk things over by their fires at night. They count up the killed and say so and so is dead and so and so is no longer here and they begin to fear you.'

An old Native chief had told Rhodes: 'You may wipe out the Matabele but you cannot make dogs of them.' He remembered these words when he arrived in Bulawayo, where the three columns met and General Sir Frederick Carrington took over the command. The military position had become impossible. In spite of their many defeats strong Matabele forces had retreated in full order into the Matopo Hills. Nature had given them a fortress, stronger and better built than could have been designed by military genius. There they were well protected from the murderous mower-guns of the white man. They had brought with them into the caves their women and children and sufficient food to last them until the next harvest. There was no longer a single Matabele to be seen. From their inaccessible natural fortress they had brought the offensive of the British troops to a complete standstill.

The rainy season was about to begin and no military action would be possible for months. Carrington decided that all he could do was to break up the campaign and start again later with a stronger force of regular troops consisting of at least 5,000 men.

If the General had his way the consequences, Rhodes realized, would be a still longer campaign costing between £4 million and

£5 million and leading to the irreparable ruin of the Company as well as his own bankruptcy. After long arguments Carrington agreed to give Rhodes a chance by leaving the troops there for a few more weeks but declined to take any responsibility.

Rhodes still lived in his own tent, two miles away from the main body and not only fully visible to the enemy from the hills but within easy range of their bullets.

In those days of solitude a resurrection took place within Rhodes. He found the way back to himself. He had overcome his despondency and felt his old strength of mind return to him. The wildly beating heart reminded him in sleepless nights of the short span of life left to him. Not more than fifty years at the most, he was certain, were allotted to him. Only six years remained. Faster and faster he would have to go. This expensive war would have to be brought to an end so that he could continue and finish the great work of which he had dreamt for the last twenty years, 'to paint this map red, British red'. 'Cape to Cairo—Cape to Cairo . . . British red—British red. . . .' What a wonderful feeling to be a Britisher! Once, in juvenile enthusiasm, he had believed that one could 'eliminate the "British Factor" from South Africa'. How stupid he had been! No part of Africa was left in perpetuity to be ruled by pygmy races. Only the English race was now striving, and would be likely to continue doing so in the future by her most practical and effective work, to spread justice, liberty and peace over all parts of the world——Was not the English race God's chosen instrument for bringing Justice, Liberty and Peace?

Thus Rhodes had turned into a true Jingo, a natural development foreseen by Britain's Jingoes who had seen in him the incarnation of their creed.

One night, when Lord Grey had come over from Bulawayo to spend a few days with him in his outpost, Rhodes, clad only in his flannel nightshirt, woke him up. Rubbing his eyes, Grey inquired: 'What's the matter, Rhodes? Is the tent on fire?'

'No, no,' replied Rhodes, and his eyes sparkled, 'but I just wanted to ask you, have you ever thought how lucky you are to have been born an Englishman?'

Day and night Rhodes sought for a solution to end this war and to bring peace to the country so that he could turn again to his real work. He remembered how during the campaign against the Basutos in 1882 General Gordon had wanted to ask the Basuto *indunas* to meet him at a *pitso*—conference—which he would attend alone and unarmed, and so pacify his opponents.

He would have to do it—to do it alone. He would have to set everything, including his own life, on this gamble. His life's work was at stake. It was worth staking one's own life on it. He would take the *indunas* and if necessary all the Matabele *impis* 'on the personal'. As interpreter, he had at his disposal Johann Colenbrander, a man who had been popular with the Matabele since he had accompanied Lobengula's envoys to London. Colenbrander's handyman was a young Swazi, John Grootboom.

For six weeks Rhodes waited in his camp to find a Native capable of persuading the Matabele to take up negotiations. Through Grootboom he was finally brought into contact with an ancient witch-like Native woman, one of the wives of Umziligazi, Lobengula's father, though not the mother of the last king. In her old brain there still lived the memory of the great king's advice always to live in peace with the White Man. Rhodes put all his charm to work on this shrivelled old woman, and it was not long before she fell under his spell. He himself was greatly impressed by her natural wisdom and gained great respect for her. He had her photograph taken and this picture, until his death, hung in his bedroom next to that of Prince Bismarck and of the Duchess of Sutherland. Through the old woman and with the help of Grootboom, Babyaan came to Rhodes' camp and stayed there. Babyaan told Rhodes that the older *indunas* were willing to surrender but, though near starvation, they were afraid of the young warriors. Rhodes wanted Babyaan to return to the other side and use his influence as a leading *induna*. Babyaan, however, explained: 'No, it's better this way: when they see me sitting here and getting fatter and fatter every day they'll say: "Look at Babyaan—he fought as long as he thought there was a hope, and then he surrendered and now he gets fatter every day. Let us go and do the same."'

Though Rhodes thought, and told him so, that the old boy's concern was for his stomach rather than for peace, he admitted that according to history the stomach rules the destiny of nations.

Rhodes' patience was taxed to the utmost and his nerves

strained to breaking-point. He was faced by thousands of well-armed Natives. During the day he could see them distinctly within shooting distance when they crawled out of their crevices and caves and from behind the big boulders to look at him curiously. Without paying any attention to them, Rhodes followed his daily routine. By going out on his long rides completely unarmed and accompanied only by Colenbrander and Toni, he showed them that he was not afraid of them.

In the seventh week his patience was rewarded. In the hills there appeared a white flag. Rhodes showed no signs of excitement. He took with him Colenbrander, Dr Sauer, Grootboom and a Johannesburg journalist, V. Stent. Higher and higher they went, over *kopjes*, through dark forests, over stony canyons. Behind them, as soon as they passed an open space, they would notice hundreds of heavily armed Matabele crawling out of their shelters. Rhodes' retreat was cut off. Even now Rhodes showed no signs of fear. He knew that he was being watched by thousands of enemy eyes and that everything depended on his personal conduct to convince them of his peaceful intentions.

They arrived at the appointed meeting-place, a large ant-heap. Should they dismount? Rhodes decided: 'Dismount, dismount, of course. It will give them confidence. They are nervous, too. How can they know that we haven't prepared an ambush for them behind the hill?'

No signs of the *indunas*. Grootboom was the first to detect the white flag high up in the hills, which drew nearer and was followed by a long procession of Matabele. A flush of excitement mounted on Rhodes' face. His voice sounded hoarse and strange when he exclaimed: 'Yes, yes, there they are! There they are— This is one of those moments in life that make it worth living —worth living. . . . There they come!'

They sat down to the *indaba* in a semicircle; the chiefs in the middle surrounded by about forty *indunas*, and with hundreds of Natives jostling each other in the background. Rhodes sat alone on a large stone opposite, with Colenbrander behind him and his other two companions a few yards farther along.

Gradually the din of voices, the clatter of arms, the shuffle of feet died down. The few seconds of absolute silence increased the tension on both sides. Rhodes gave them—after he had practised it well with Colenbrander—the traditional salute of peace:

'*Mehle 'mhlopi*—My eyes are white!'

The *indunas* rose from the ground and shouted:

'*Mehla 'mhlopi, 'nkoos*—Our eyes are white, Chief!'

Natives are great debaters. They delight in oratory. Chief Somabulane, a member of the royal house, voiced the complaints of the Matabele in a long speech, which Rhodes did not once interrupt. When his turn came, Rhodes, through his interpreter, told them that the Native police would be abolished. It was like a cry of relief when the *indunas* echoed their thanks:

'*Ea bongo—ea bongo.*'

Rhodes asked Colenbrander to say in his name that all he wanted to know was: 'Is it peace? Are the eyes white?'

Somabulane declared that they would lay down their arms. Rhodes tried to control himself but in his excitement he could not help repeating over and over again 'That's good—that's good—— He'll send in his arms—send in his arms—that's good——'

It became evident during the ensuing negotiations that Rhodes' influence over the Natives was almost hypnotic. The *indunas* expressed their fear that all Rhodes' promises would be forgotten when Rhodes himself was gone. So he promised to stay with them until everything was settled. They now called him *Baba*—father—and *Umlamula M'Kunzi*—the 'man who separated the Fighting Bulls'.

Rhodes thought that they had now completely delivered themselves into his hands. He wanted to give them a lecture and reprimanded them for having killed women and children: '. . . that wasn't right; that wasn't the deeds of brave men; that was the work of dogs!'

Pandemonium broke out in the ranks of the young warriors. They pushed forward. Assegais were brandished threateningly. Somabulane tried to silence them by a few sharp words of command. He began a new formal speech with accusations that it had been the White Man who had started slaying women and children.

Colenbrander became worried. He whispered to Rhodes that he should rather change the subject. Rhodes finally gave way: 'Well, all that is over. And now you have come to make peace.' And all the *indunas* in unison once more gave assurances of peace.

Triumphantly Rhodes returned to his camp. He had achieved what those military gentlemen, the experts, had believed to be possible only with an armed force of at least 5,000 men which would have cost him millions and millions.

The next morning he sent Dr Sauer and Stent to Bulawayo, to announce the conclusion of peace. They had to promise, however, to keep back the good news for several hours to enable Rhodes to cable his orders to the Stock Exchange before it became general knowledge. Even in the hour of triumph Rhodes did not neglect business!

Rhodes invited several ladies from Bulawayo to his camp to attend the negotiations which still followed. On one occasion Lady Grey told Rhodes how much everyone admired the courage, patience and self-control which he had shown in those past trying weeks. Rhodes gazed up at the stars with a dreamy look, when he replied:

'Well, well. I should like to be like Cincinnatus, who gave up a throne and went and grew cabbages. Such a peaceful life—such a peaceful life—— And, believe me, I'd grow very good cabbages, too.'

In the same philosophic vein he told his secretary while riding through the Matopos:

'There is one thing I hope for you, and that is, that while still a young man, you may never have everything you want. Take myself, for instance: I am not an old man, and I don't think there is anything I want. I've been P.M. of the Cape, there is De Beers and the railways, and there is a big country called after me, and I have more money than I can spend. You might ask: "But wouldn't you like to be P.M. again?" Well, I answer you very fairly—I should take it if it were offered to me, but certainly don't crave for it.'

While waiting for the conclusion of negotiations Rhodes explored the Matopos. He was overwhelmed, when coming to the top of one of the highest hills, by the majestic beauty of the view. He liked to sit there and look at what he named 'the World's View!'

'. . . When I die, I mean to be buried here, and I shall have the bones of those brave men who helped me take the country brought from Zimbabwe.'

When he saw the wealth of water rushing down the mountain in rivers and rivulets he immediately conceived the idea of harnessing it and using it to irrigate parts of the 120,000 acres which made up the farm he owned in the district. He gave orders to build a dam with a reservoir holding 50 million gallons of water to be completed in not longer than a year. He also investigated the chances of continuing his railway schemes. His technical adviser was told: 'We propose now to go on and cross the centre just below the Victoria Falls. I should like to have the spray of the water over the carriages. . . . Imagine, sitting in one's compartment and the spray of the Falls splashing against the windows —the train travelling through a curtain of spray of the Victoria Falls—a curtain of spray of the Falls——'

Neither Rhodes nor Lord Grey had the right to conclude an official peace, as Chamberlain, fearing unpleasant surprises, had made the negotiations subject to the approval of the High Commissioner. The Resident Commissioner, Sir Richard Martin, considered Rhodes' peace-terms too lenient and refused to give his consent. In a rough scene Rhodes declared to Martin that in the case of an official veto to his peace-terms 'I'll go back to the Matabele and throw in my lot with them to carry through my policy of forgiveness.'

Martin gave up resistance and sealed the peace pact in a solemn *indaba*.

Before Rhodes left Rhodesia towards the end of 1896 he had to settle the claims of various settlers for damages suffered as a result of the war. On this mission he came to the Gwelo district. Enormous claims had been submitted there for what he knew to have been primitive huts. Rhodes wrote out cheques without asking any questions, though he had to pay everything from his private pocket. Among the settlers he observed an old Scotsman, a blacksmith, who was standing quietly in a corner. Rhodes asked him: 'And what do I owe you?' 'Nothing; I've lost nothing.' 'Write that man out a cheque for twenty-five pounds. He's the only man who told me the truth today.'

There was still Grootboom to be rewarded. 'You have done a great thing for me. What can I do for you?'

'I would like a horse with a saddle and bridle, sir.'

'You'll have much more than that.'

'I don't want it. I want to go North to help the missionaries.'

Rhodes was touched. He told one of the Company's secretaries: 'Give Grootboom whenever he asks for it 100 acres of land, a wagon, a span of oxen, twelve cows, a horse and £100.'

Grootboom still refused to accept the gift. Shortly afterwards he left Rhodesia and was never heard of again. When Rhodes heard of Grootboom's departure he scribbled a few lines on an old envelope. After his death when his Last Will dealing with millions was opened, his friends were astonished to read of a legacy to one John Grootboom of '100 acres of land, a wagon, a span. . . .'

At the end of 1896, before leaving for England to attend the Committee of Inquiry, Rhodes went to the Cape in spite of the warnings of his friends that there might be demonstrations against him. Stepping on to the gangway at Port Elizabeth he noticed a black mass of people on the quay. Immediately he regretted not having listened to his friends' advice.

Walking down the gangway, however, he was deafened by the cheers of thousands. They removed the horses from his carriage and forty men drew it to the Town Hall.

The old Duke of Cambridge had told Rhodes shortly after the Raid: 'Never mind, my boy, you'll live it all down in five years' time.' Not even a year had passed and the people of the Cape were acclaiming him wildly. These demonstrations, and also those which followed in Kimberley and even in the citadel of Afrikanerdom, Paarl, were spontaneous and sincere. They were not, however, as Rhodes wished to believe, an expression of political sympathy. South Africans, no matter to which section of the populace they belong, have always the greatest respect and admiration for deeds of courage and determination, and the applause for Rhodes was meant as a sign of recognition for the outstanding bravery he had shown in facing unarmed the hordes of Matabele in the Matopos.

In his first public speeches after his return Rhodes followed the recommendations of his friends by showing discretion and restraint. They feared demonstrations of protest in Cape Town, but his reception there was overwhelming. Rhodes, deeply moved, muttered: 'It's beautiful to see one's fellow-beings feel so kindly to one—— Such appreciation as this generally comes after a man is dead.'

Friends had arranged a private luncheon-party for him in which also a few of his former political followers participated. With great anxiety they awaited Rhodes' speech, his first political utterance since the Raid, from which they expected a clarification of his attitude towards the Raid. Their expectations were surpassed. Rhodes acknowledged his fault:

> . . . I do not so much regret joining in an attempt to force President Kruger into a juster and more reasonable policy . . . but what has been a burden to me is that I was Prime Minister at the time, and that I had given a promise that I would not do anything incompatible with the joint position I held as Director of the Chartered Company and Premier of the Cape Colony. On every ground I was bound to resign if I took such a course as assisting in a revolution against an officially friendly State; and I did not.

Here Rhodes made a long and dramatic pause. The tension among his listeners became evident. Some leaned forward so that not a single word should be lost. Rhodes continued in a softer voice and speaking extremely slowly:

> I can only say that I will do my best to make atonement for my error by untiring devotion to the best interests of South Africa.

Thunderous applause followed. Rhodes promised, since the speech had been 'off the record', to repeat his 'confession of error and promise of atonement' at a public meeting in the City Hall the same night.

The wild enthusiasm and flattering words of welcome had intoxicated Rhodes. Not once did he look at the notes which he had put on the table when he started to speak at the City Hall. After the applause which greeted his words, repeated from his first speech after the Raid in Kimberley, that 'his public life was not, as some people had believed, at an end but was just beginning', he seemed to forget everything around him.

It was the old Rhodes, unrepenting, aggressive and obstinate. Defiantly he accused Kruger of suppressing the Uitlanders and threatened him with vengeance. This part of his speech did not arouse as much angry comment as did, especially in England, his phrase: 'I am going home to face the unctuous rectitude of my countrymen. . . .'

Did he not say once that he never prepared a speech and could not the expression 'unctuous rectitude' be excused as having merely slipped from his tongue? 'No, no,' replied Rhodes with a wink, 'that I had ready three days before I spoke.'

CHAPTER XVII

UNCTUOUS RECTITUDE

MOST of the first-class cabins on the mailship *Dunvegan Castle* bound for England from South Africa at the beginning of January 1897 were unoccupied. The passengers missed the usual gaiety on board and by the time the ship approached the Equator everyone had become too lazy to do anything but gossip. With a number of eminent people on board such as 'the two multi-millionaires' Rhodes and Beit, a Cabinet Minister Mr 'Will' Schreiner, his sister the world-famous South African authoress Olive Schreiner, and the redoubtable Dr Rutherford Harris, sufficient variety of gossip was assured.

The trip also provided something strongly reminiscent of those exciting adventures of Sherlock Holmes running in the *Strand Magazine* at the time. Olive Schreiner had spent most of the journey lying alone in a deck-chair on the upper deck. Everyone on board was therefore astonished when one morning the stout little woman came tripping along breathlessly and stormed the bridge. Flourishing her sunshade she made straight for the captain. From her frantic tale he gathered that someone had burgled her cabin, had forced open one of her trunks and stolen from it the manuscript of her latest work, *Trooper Peter Halket of Mashonaland*. And she knew, she said, she knew for certain that no one could have committed the crime except one of Mr Rhodes' henchmen, since only he was interested in suppressing this book with its sensational disclosures of the murder, the rape, the robbery and the injustice committed by Mr Rhodes' gang of marauders in Mashonaland. Soothingly the captain suggested that before any steps were taken a thorough search should be made of all her luggage. Stewards unpacked her large trunk, on the bottom of which, she said, she had put the manuscript before she left home. Nothing was found. There was some more luggage but she ridiculed the idea of finding the book there. Finally some other trunks were opened. At the bottom of one of her smaller bags the manuscript was found and handed to her. 'He must have put it there as soon as he learnt that I had found him out,' she said. Nothing would convince her that no one could have tampered with the lock. 'Young man, you don't know with what sort of people we've to deal.'

After this incident Olive Schreiner explained to a few sympathetic listeners that she felt it her Christian duty to expose Cecil Rhodes, of whom her Peter Halket said: 'He's death on niggers, is Rhodes! . . .' And she quoted to them from her book: 'Why, if God Almighty came [to Mashonaland] and hadn't half a million in shares, they wouldn't think much of him.'

Between their whiskies the passengers whispered what an extraordinary woman this Olive Schreiner was. There was a time when she had adored Rhodes as the saviour of South Africa. The fact that Olive Schreiner was not on speaking terms with her brother Will also aroused much comment. She took no notice of him though he was observed to be trying hard to approach her. It had not escaped observation either, that the relationship between Rhodes and his former colleague Schreiner was of a peculiar nature. It was amusing to watch how Schreiner, whenever he saw Rhodes coming in his direction, quickly walked away to another part of the ship.

Schreiner, always upright and true, was still struggling with his conscience whether to abandon his love for Rhodes. Politically he had completely divorced himself from Rhodes, but he still believed that he might remain friends with him. Lately strong doubts about Rhodes' personal honesty had gnawed at him: Rhodes, 'gaming with men's lives and the fate of a country', would, as he had been told recently, have made gigantic profits if the Raid had gone according to plan. If these suspicions about Rhodes' financial interest in the Raid proved to be true, then Rhodes would cease to exist for him also as a person. He purposely avoided Rhodes because to his lawyer's mind it appeared unseemly as a witness at the coming inquiry that he should expose himself to being perhaps unconsciously influenced by Rhodes.

Rhodes, however, was in high spirits. In his ears there still lingered the ovations he had received at a civic reception in Cape Town. It was music to his love-thirsty soul to hear the Mayor end his speech with the words: 'We, as friends, say to our guest, "You have done great things for Africa and we want you back again!"'

No, Rhodes was not worried. Every day he rehearsed with Dr Harris, Garrett and his two secretaries answers to possible questions at the Inquiry.

As soon as he arrived in London, however, Rhodes seemed to show signs of nervousness. During the first few days he calmed down, at least outwardly, and even became a little boisterous when he proudly announced: 'All the bus drivers touched their hats to me. So I know I am all right.' But his friends knew better. Rhodes was far from popular in England and they therefore asked him again to declare that the phrase 'unctuous rectitude' had been a misunderstanding and that what he had said was in fact 'anxious rectitude'. 'No,' Rhodes replied, 'I am going to stick to the "unctuous rectitude".'

He became angry when Garrett suggested that before the Inquiry began he should express his regrets about the Raid: 'I've already said so much; but I'm not going on saying it, and crawling in the dust to please you or anybody. So I told some Dutch constituents of mine who made advance, after abusing one like a pickpocket at the time. "Oh," they said, "do say you repent! Only *tell* us you repent!"—"That's my business," I answered. I know what my idea was—no race feeling at all—and what my motive was; and it all went wrong, and I and others made mistakes, and that's all about it.'

All Rhodes' friends, such as Rosebery, Wyndham and Rothschild, tried privately to use their influence on Chamberlain to drop the Inquiry at the last minute. Immediately after his arrival Rhodes went to see Chamberlain. For two hours and twenty minutes they hurled threats, reproaches and accusations at each other. Chamberlain, possibly fearing that misinterpretations of his words might follow or that Rhodes would once again resort to blackmail, insisted on having the Colonial Under-Secretary, Lord Selborne, a son-in-law of Lord Salisbury's, present at the interview.

Rhodes, full of his old self-assurance, told Chamberlain with his usual haughtiness that it would be best for all concerned if the whole Committee were scrapped. It was no longer necessary, he said, since the Cape inquiry had completely exhausted the issue.

Trying as a last resort to take Chamberlain 'on the personal', he came forward with one of his virtuoso pieces:

'. . . What is my reputation or your reputation compared with the interests of the country? In twenty years you'll be gone, snuffed out, but the country will remain. . . .'

Chamberlain, himself far too accomplished in the art of playing on other people's emotions, coldly told Rhodes that it was impossible to scrap the Inquiry, since its abandonment would cause greater harm to the country than if it took place.

His real reasons, which Chamberlain did not reveal to him, had nothing to do with Rhodes. Chamberlain needed the Inquiry in order to clear himself of the charges, which had turned from whispered rumours into loud accusations, that he had not only sanctioned the Raid but had been its real instigator. The Liberal papers said so very plainly. Some verses by Sir Wilfred Lawson threw Chamberlain into a rage:

> If Jameson makes a wicked raid,
> And strikes a treacherous blow,
> On searching records, I'm afraid
> You'll find it worked by 'Joe'.
>
> If bullying Kruger is the scheme,
> At which we're never slow,
> The wretched business, it would seem,
> Is all arranged by 'Joe'.

Lord Salisbury was an old, sickly man. Chamberlain saw his great chance and was determined that it should not escape him. Premier of England? As such, an unblemished political reputation was necessary. He would see to it that he came out of the Inquiry immaculate, no matter what happened to that 'blackmailing blackguard'.

When Rhodes left the Colonial Office, his face purple and his hair dishevelled, his secretary knew that a storm was brewing. On the way home Rhodes threw his top-hat on the floor of the carriage and with a deep sigh said to himself: 'The man who wrote "It is possible for a new country to be connected by cable *too soon* with Downing Street" knew well what he was talking about.'

When he got back to his hotel he found Dr Jameson's old servant awaiting him. He had come unknown to his master, who had been released from prison before his time was up because of sickness. The doctor was fretting as Mr Rhodes had neither visited him nor sent a message. 'And', added the servant, 'I thought I should let you know, but please, Dr Jameson must not hear that I came to you.'

Rhodes jumped into his carriage. His eyes glistened suspiciously when, standing at the doctor's bedside, he clasped his thin hand and said: 'Both of us have had a rough time, but you had a rougher time than I!'

The Grand Committee Room in the Palace of Westminster, where the Inquiry took place beginning on Friday, 5 February 1897, and continuing for the next five months, was cold and bare. The only spot of colour was contributed by a huge map of Africa on one of the yawning white walls. On one side of the room was a long, horseshoe-shaped table with numerous chairs around it, a single small table—the 'dock'—in the middle and behind it the table of the counsel for the 'defence'.

In the back of the hall, a large space had been allotted to the Press. A few seats were reserved for the Peers, in the front row of which the Prince of Wales, spruce and elegant as always and appearing rather tired from the strain of the night before, could be seen passing his time in chatting to the right and left as he waited for the Committee to arrive. Just like the Lords Rosebery and Rothschild next to him, he seemed to consider the whole business of the Inquiry a huge joke.

When the sixteen members of the Committee had finally taken their seats the air immediately became charged with electrifying tension. Stead, sitting in the front row, whispered to his former apprentice Garrett: 'Over the door of this room they should have inscribed the words of the American statesman W. J. Bryan: "You shall not crucify mankind on a Cross of Gold!"'

When the Chairman called upon the Right Honourable Cecil John Rhodes to take his seat as witness at the small table, those who had known him in the days of his glory only eighteen months before were shocked. Others who had never seen him before were bitterly disappointed. Why, was this indeed Mr Rhodes, the multi-millionaire, the 'uncrowned King of Africa', the 'Colossus', the man whom the African Natives had dubbed 'the man who swallows countries for his breakfast', who 'thought in continents', the ruler over South Africa's diamonds and gold, the 'Elizabethan prodigy', the man who had boasted that he could 'square' anybody, the conqueror of half a continent, the great Empire-builder!

The unfavourable impression was increased when Rhodes read a declaration in his squeaky voice, jumping from one leg to the other and reading so quickly that he stumbled over words and sometimes became almost inaudible. The statement was not very elucidating and consisted mostly of generalities. Only at the end did he gain any attention.

> . . . I must admit that in all my actions I was greatly influenced by my belief that the policy of the present Government of the South African Republic was to introduce the influence of another foreign Power into the already complicated system of South Africa, and thereby render more difficult in the future the closer union of the different states.

Harcourt smiled. Labouchere sneered. Chamberlain, monocle in his eye, seemed engrossed in a file. 'The German bogy once again', a foreign journalist commented to his neighbour under his breath. Rhodes, in spite of his daily practice during his voyage to England, cut a deplorable figure under cross-examination. His 'usual grandeur or grandiosity of self-assurance' was gone. His answers were evasive, verbose and not to the point. When driven into a tight corner he often replied sharply: 'You want an answer. Well, I think you had better get it from the High Commissioner.'

The lunch hour arrived. So as not to lose time the Committee did not adjourn but had light refreshments served on trays from the buffet of the House. In front of Rhodes was placed a meagre ham sandwich decoratively sprinkled with a a few leaves of cress, and a large tankard of foaming stout. Everyone's eyes were focused on Rhodes who munched his sandwich unconcernedly and took long draughts of beer with obvious enjoyment. His pleasure in so simple a repast immediately won him the sympathy of people who had probably fancied that a multi-millionaire fed exclusively on caviare and champagne. Even the ever-hostile 'Labby' remarked: 'I hate the sight of this Jerry Empire builder, but I can't help liking his ham sandwich and tankard of stout.'

After the luncheon interval Rhodes seemed to undergo a complete change in his behaviour and attitude and even in his physical appearance. It was as if he had taken off his coat, pulled up his sleeves and said: come, now, let us fight this thing out. During lunch he had studied the faces of the men who were sitting in judgment over him. The shadow of a smile had flitted over his face. In the evening he explained to friends: 'Looking at those faces I could not help thinking that there was not a single man among them who in Africa wouldn't be my subordinate.'

Rhodes quickly gained the upper hand. He seemed to be trying to take the whole Committee 'on the personal' by ingratiating remarks of repentance such as: 'I dare say it's morally wrong.' He emphasized that he wished to take full responsibility for all that had happened but that he could not have known all the details, busy as he had been in his triple position:

> . . . so that if some of my answers appear to be evasive, I may say they are not evasive through my shirking of responsibility; they are only evasive because I do not remember the particular telegrams; probably they were not submitted to me; but yet I do not wish to say I repudiate responsibility for them at all.

Whenever an awkward question was asked, Rhodes would reply: 'That's a fair question—a very fair question,' but his answer would nevertheless be non-committal. When Harcourt referred to the 'manufactured revolution' Rhodes appeared indignant. 'Well,' Harcourt retorted calmly, 'we'll call it a subsidized revolution.' When a question became too embarrassing for him Rhodes would ask for time to refresh his memory and the Committee would, of course, never receive the answer. A certain telegram? 'Oh, it may seem absurd to you, but I haven't read the Blue Book containing the correspondence quoted.'

He was as smooth as an eel and at times it was amusing to watch how he played with the Committee. Harcourt, referring to the 'order given to Dr Jameson a day before the Raid to "secure telegraphic office silence"', wanted to know what it meant. Rhodes replied: 'I do not know what it means. It seems absurd, doesn't it?' This was too much for Harcourt, who shouted angrily: 'It is not at all absurd, Mr Rhodes, because it was the thing that was done.'

What about certain telegrams allegedly implicating the Colonial Office? 'Oh, these telegrams. . . . They are in the hands of my legal advisers. . . .' Rhodes would not allow them to be produced; he stated that he would refuse to answer questions which might prejudice a third party and, besides, he added with a smile, he really did not remember their contents.

Here would have been a chance for Rhodes to exonerate himself. By tabling the telegrams incriminating Chamberlain he could prove that he had acted not only in conjunction with the Colonial Office but as an agent of the Government. Why then did Rhodes make every effort not to involve Chamberlain in the Raid and the Johannesburg revolt? What made Rhodes play guardian angel to the Colonial Secretary instead of using him as a scapegoat? These were questions that were on everyone's lips.

The Committee swallowed Rhodes' evasions and all his circumlocutions, evident untruths, and direct lies without the slightest attempt from any side to throw light on the matter.

On the third day Harcourt gave up in disgust. Labouchere now stepped in. Labouchere's hatred for Rhodes was well known. In his journal he had never minced words, as could be seen from the damages and fines he had to pay regularly for libel suits. Now at the Inquiry, under the protection of his parliamentary immunity, an even greater unloading of dirt was expected.

Labouchere's cross-examination resembled 'the act of an infuriated bull-terrier who barked at a cat sitting behind a gate and was so occupied with his vocal efforts that he failed to see the open gate by which he might have caught his feline enemy'.

He asked Rhodes dozens of questions about the financial aspects of the Raid which might have brought some elucidating replies. Often Labouchere was on the right track, but he was no match for Rhodes, who was able to answer such questions and yet say nothing. Thus he replied to Labouchere: 'Yes, I had sold Chartered shares before the Raid, because I needed money for my railway and telegraph lines. Surely there was nothing wrong in selling shares?' It did not occur to Labouchere to demand that Rhodes should produce his private bank accounts or to summon through the Stock Exchange all those brokers who had sold and bought shares on behalf of Rhodes and his friends.

Rhodes did not waver in refusing to answer questions concerning the suppressed telegrams. Labouchere lost his temper.

'Mr Rhodes, at the commencement of your examination you took an oath to tell not only the truth but the whole truth.'

Rhodes, with an expression of great astonishment: 'Did I?'

'Yes, you did, Mr Rhodes.'

'Well, it would depend upon the powers of the Committee. As to this point of making statements which would bring in the names and affect the positions of third parties, I've thought about it very carefully, and I do not think I am justified in answering that. . . .'

Labouchere gave up. Later when the ordeal was over Rhodes no longer felt any malice towards 'Labby'. He told Stead: 'Labby fills for me the rôle of a court jester in olden times. . . . He is my court jester, and he does his fooling with a will; and what is more, so far as I am concerned, free, gratis and for nothing.'

When they saw that neither Harcourt, the great lawyer, nor Labouchere, the great hater, could get anything out of Rhodes, the Committee dismissed Rhodes. Everyone was apparently relieved.

For six days Rhodes had sat in the witness chair, having answered about 2,000 questions. His last triumph had come at the end when he addressed the Committee in words of heavy sarcasm dressed in a coating of urbane politeness:

'Would you like to have me up again? I'll be happy to come, but you must remember that my work in Rhodesia keeps me very busy.'

He was not asked to appear again. They had had quite enough of him. When he came home to his hotel on the last day Dr Sauer asked him why everyone, even members of the Opposition, were treating him so leniently, hardly ever putting questions to him which might compromise certain persons. Rhodes smiled when he told Sauer:

'They dare not do it; we also have a cat in the bag which, if we let it out, would show that one of their big men knew all about it.'

The 'big man' was not Chamberlain but Lord Rosebery, with whom Rhodes, at a time when the Liberals were still in power and Rosebery was Prime Minister, had discussed the planned Raid. Rosebery had probably warned Harcourt about the possibility that the former Liberal Government might be dragged in by Rhodes if Rhodes were pressed too hard.

Beit was the next witness. He cut a most pathetic figure, with his nerves on edge and always on the point of either crying or fainting. For one who had always shunned publicity, this public exposure was a great ordeal and turned into real torture once Labouchere began to turn on the thumb-screws of his cross-examination. Yet Labby failed once more, since he either indulged in generalities to which he could expect no concrete answer from the witness, or went into details without knowing how to extract the truth.

General amusement followed when Dr Rutherford Harris appeared in the witness chair and told such tall stories that the Committee, although already accustomed to perjured testimony, was amazed. And whenever it suited his purpose he hid behind his 'defective memory'.

Harcourt had to summon all his powers of self-control to express in parliamentary language the Committee's disgust with this permanent perjurer: 'I suppose, Dr Harris, that you would rather not state the *exact* fractions of what you call truth and of what is not truth in this evidence of yours?'

Even Flora Shaw allowed her *esprit de corps* and her loyalty to Rhodes and to Chamberlain to cause her a sudden loss of memory. In spite of her telegrams to Rhodes in which she had given him Chamberlain's messages, she now declared on oath that 'she never at any time gave the Colonial Office information about the plan and never at any time received information from the Colonial Office about the plan'.

Her evidence as well as that of the other witnesses had been well prepared beforehand. Flora Shaw had discussed her evidence at some length with Chamberlain and had also been briefed by Dr Harris. At the end of that day's sitting Harcourt whispered to Chamberlain: 'Rhodes is not really a clever man, or he would not have trusted his fate to Dr Rutherford Harris and Flora Shaw!'

Rhodes and his friends hoped to tire out the Committee, so that it would one day adjourn *sine die* without ever issuing a report on its findings. The longer the Inquiry lasted the more it moved away from the real subject of investigation—to wit, the Raid and its instigator—and centred instead on Chamberlain and his part in it.

How far would Chamberlain stick out his neck?—that was the burning question on everyone's lips when he was called to the witness chair. He categorically denied all knowledge of the Raid: he had known only that a spontaneous and justified rising of the malcontent Uitlanders was expected to take place. No collaboration from his side with Rhodes or any of Rhodes' men!

Chamberlain had no alternative but to perjure himself. According to a secret agreement with Rhodes he could not attack Rhodes without bringing on a revengeful disclosure of his implication in the Raid. The sword of Damocles was hanging over his head ready to drop at Rhodes' command and end the political life of Joseph Chamberlain. So as to save his career Chamberlain had willingly bought Rhodes' discretion for a promise not to deprive him of the Charter and his Privy Councillorship.

Not only did Chamberlain have to whitewash himself but he also had to clear the Colonial Office of the charge of active conspiracy. Nothing was easier for 'Judas'. He had found his scapegoats. So as to save face for the Colonial Office he sacrificed three innocent men: Sir Robert Meade, the chief Permanent Under-Secretary of State for the Colonies, and Chamberlain's right-hand man; Sir Graham Bower, the Imperial Secretary to the High Commissioner, both old and merited Civil Service men; and Rhodes' old friend Captain Newton, the Commissioner of Bechuanaland.

Sir Robert Meade, as well as old Sir Hercules Robinson, were excused from appearing as witnesses because of illness. Since Meade had conducted most of the talks with Flora Shaw and Dr Harris on Chamberlain's behalf, Chamberlain was happy to have someone to blame for all the indiscretions committed by the Colonial Office. Meade through his absence was unable to contradict Chamberlain when he said that he knew nothing about the negotiations between Meade and Rhodes' party.

Bower became a victim of his loyalty to Rhodes. He had given him his word of honour before the Raid to keep all his knowledge of the preliminary conversations and reports absolutely secret. Bower was a man of honour who would never break his word. For the same reason of loyal decency he also refused to compromise his chief, the High Commissioner, and also refrained from testifying as a Crown witness against his highest superior, the Colonial Secretary.

Before the Inquiry Bower had pleaded with Rhodes to have out all the truth so as to save his, Bower's, reputation, but Rhodes had refused to 'give away the man [Chamberlain] who tried to do more to help him than any other Colonial Secretary', adding 'I'll tell no lies. Mr Chamberlain can do his own lying if he pleases. That's not my affair!'

They certainly all lied amply in the end to protect each other according to their agreement. No one on the Committee had the bright idea of asking for the files of the Colonial Office to be laid on the table of the Committee, a procedure which would have cleared up many doubtful points. Everyone did his best to suppress the truth.

The dramatic climax to the proceedings came when Rhodes' lawyer Hawkesley appeared before the Committee and was told by the Chairman: 'We therefore call on you, Mr Hawkesley, to produce the telegrams.'

Not a sound could be heard until Hawkesley pronounced in a determined voice:

'I can only say, with very great respect. . . . I still feel that my duty compels me to act upon the instructions I have received from Mr Rhodes . . . to make these telegrams not available. . . .'

The Committee had full powers to compel Rhodes to return to London and to send him and Hawkesley to the Clock Tower for an indefinite period until they gave up the telegrams. It would have been still easier to have summoned the cable company to supply copies.

The Committee had two good reasons for not insisting on bringing the telegrams to light. If they had used force Rhodes would have become the great martyr—a most undesirable result. Only recently, it was reported, he had quoted with a salvo of his ear-splitting staccato laughter, the words of Oliver Wendell Holmes, that it was not perhaps so difficult to knock a man down, but that the trouble was the man might get up and give his assailant a thrashing. Moreover, foreign politics made it imperative that under no circumstances should any facts connecting the British Government with the Raid become known in view of Salisbury's and the Queen's denials. Britain's position in foreign politics was far from satisfactory and complications were expected in several quarters.

The English Press could not be expected to grasp what was going on behind the scenes of the Committee Room. Especially in the Liberal papers, but also in Conservative circles, people expressed their astonishment at the 'infamy of the prolonged masquerade of an inquiry, tempered by mendacity'. Everyone had the impression—and they were not far wrong—that 'efforts were being made to prevent the truth being brought to light'.

It was no easy task for Harcourt, who referred to the Inquiry as 'the most demoralizing transaction in the 60 years' reign', to draft the Report of the Committee after it had been sitting for five months. He endeavoured, as he wrote to Chamberlain, to 'put the matter as regards yourself and the telegrams in a shape which I hope you will find satisfactory'. About Rhodes, 'that arch-liar', he had not changed his opinion: '. . . the mendacity of the man is sickening. . . .'

All members of the Committee had agreed that it would be best to terminate the whole matter as quickly as possible before it developed into something like a British Dreyfus Case. Harcourt and Chamberlain thus concocted a verdict for the Committee Report which would satisfy political demands and calm down the public while at the same time it would give Rhodes no cause to continue his vendetta by blackmail. It contained a strong censure of Rhodes for his activities in the Johannesburg revolt, affirmed his moral responsibility for the Raid and condemned his deception of the High Commissioner.

The Report also contained a full exoneration of Sir Hercules Robinson, who for having kept his mouth shut so diplomatically was raised to the peerage with the title of Lord Rosmead. It gave Chamberlain and the Colonial Office a clean bill of health, condemning instead poor Sir Graham Bower. Only Labouchere dissented and presented a Minority Report in which he was able to give vent to his feelings. Though many of his colleagues on the Committee agreed with him, they found his condemnation of Rhodes expressed somewhat harshly: '. . . he abused the high positions which he held by engaging in a conspiracy in the success of which his own pecuniary interests were largely involved'.

The report of the Commission was not the end of the *cause célèbre*. On 26 July a debate on the Colonial Estimates provided an opportunity for a discussion on the findings of the Inquiry. There had been rumours that exciting surprises might be expected: that the Radical members would refuse to accept the Report and would move for the withdrawal of the Charter from Rhodes' Company, for the cancellation of Rhodes' P.C. and for orders to call Hawkesley to the Bar of the House to produce the missing cables.

The debate showed that the attack by the Radicals was really aimed at the renegade from their ranks, Chamberlain, the 'Judas'. Harcourt, on the other hand, defended Chamberlain but refused to spare Rhodes: '. . . You cannot say as the Roman Emperor said, *non olet*; there is a noisome odour of the Stock Exchange about it. . . . It is a squalid and sordid picture of stock-jobbing imperialism . . . privateers . . . these unscrupulous men who have deceived everybody, who have ruined the character of the British nation for honesty and fair dealing. . . .'

All eyes were fixed on Chamberlain. He sat, as usual, in sartorial elegance, with his eyes closed. He was certainly not asleep, and several people in the House knew only too well what thoughts were probably keeping the Right Honourable Gentleman wide awake. In the morning he had been warned that a certain Member (Maguire) would take the ominous telegrams to the House. He would keep them in his pocket, to be laid on the Table of the House at a given signal from a friend of Rhodes' in the gallery—probably Hawkesley—in case Chamberlain and his Party did not repel any attempts by the Opposition against Rhodes' Charter, his P.C. and his honour.

By now, however, a great number of members of the Opposition had been persuaded by Harcourt's criminologistic reasoning that the mysterious telegrams were nothing but one of Rhodes' dirty tricks, as was explained in a clause in the Committee's Report on the insertion of which Harcourt had insisted:

> Your Committee fully accept the statements of the Secretary of State for the Colonies and of the Under Secretary, and entirely exonerate the officials of the Colonial Office of having been, in any sense, cognisant of the plans which led up to the incursion of Dr Jameson's force into the South African Republic. It is clear from the evidence of Mr Hawkesley, and his letter of 5 February 1896, that the telegrams in question conveyed the impression that the action of Mr Rhodes was known and approved at the Colonial Office. The fact that Mr Rhodes (after having authorized that they should be shown to Mr Chamberlain) has refused to allow them to be produced before the Committee leads to the conclusion that he is aware that any statements purporting to implicate the Colonial Office contained in them were unfounded, and the use made of them in support of his action in South Africa was not justified. It cannot reasonably be doubted, having regard to the use already made of these telegrams, that they would have been produced to your Committee if their contents could in any way have relieved Mr Rhodes or his subordinates from the responsibility now attaching to them.

Chamberlain did not very often use notes. This time when he rose to speak he took out of his pocket a whole sheaf of closely written pages. In the dim light of the House the colour of his complexion resembled that of old parchment.

It was certainly one of the greatest speeches ever rendered in a place which had been the scene of some of the finest oratory. Chamberlain was fighting for his political life. His future was at stake. The prize was Britain's premiership. He did not struggle wildly like a drowning man. His strokes at the beginning were composed, skilful, and moderate. And when he at last saw land, he lashed out at those who were responsible for his cold immersion. His speech was constructed like a Shakespearian monologue with the main theme of his innocence pronounced in different keys and various modulations, finally reaching the dramatic climax with the fanfare-call:

> . . . It is impossible to suppose if you think me such a fool, that any English minister could be such a knave as to do what is attributed to me . . . that I was myself a party to the Raid, and approved the policy of which the Raid was a part. . . .

The House remained surprisingly calm and only a few cheers were heard. They were waiting for Chamberlain's attitude towards the demand of punishment for Rhodes. It had of course been expected that he would refuse to support the motion of the Radicals, but even his intimate followers were surprised that he should motivate his refusal by whitewashing—nay, by paying tribute to—Rhodes, the man who in the Report of the Committee, signed by Chamberlain, had been declared indirectly 'a liar, a coward and a blackmailer'. Now Chamberlain maintained that 'there has been nothing proved—and in my opinion there exists nothing—which affects Mr Rhodes' personal position as a man of honour. . .'

Harcourt was in a rage over this betrayal. Other Liberals considered this triumph of Rhodes over Chamberlain the saddest hour in Britain's parliamentary history. It did not help. The 'Chartered Libertines' had carried a victory over political morality. The motion of the Radicals was defeated by a majority of 304 to 77.

In the evening after his oratorical performance, Chamberlain tried to explain to some of his intimates, or rather to excuse, his incomprehensible canonization of Rhodes, after having only recently called him openly a 'blackmailer, blackguard and traitor':

'Have you and others thought what would be the consequences of driving Rhodes to the wall? If in his desperation he joined forces with the extreme Dutch element and took advantage of the prejudice so easily aroused against the "unctuous rectitude" of a British Government, we could hardly keep the Cape Colony without a war. Is it worth while to risk this for the satisfaction of depriving Rhodes of the barren honour of his P.C.?'

England's prestige abroad, as a result of the parliamentary comedy of the Inquiry, had suffered a set-back more serious than that of losing a war. *Le Temps* wrote:

> The Committee sacrifices everything including the honour of England, to its desire to preserve the reputation of that meddlesome and imperious statesman [Chamberlain]. The evil is wrought and irreparable. It is now proved that the Queen's Government has plotted in time of peace the invasion of a friendly country, and that there is no majority in Great Britain to condemn the crime. It is the apotheosis of the Birmingham statesman; it is also the abdication of the conscience of Great Britain. . . .

In Germany Parliament and Press jubilated over 'Perfidious Albion' which was 'now facing bankruptcy of the Parliamentary System'. The *Berliner National Zeitung* summarized the general opinion in the country:

> . . . If in England they are content with this procedure [of the Inquiry], the fact will not be without importance in the world's eyes as indicating the measure of morality which obtains in English politics as soon as the extension of English territory comes into question.

Also in Russia voices were raised in indignation. The Moscow *Gazette* spoke of 'this scandalous and disgraceful sham of investigation', which 'is instructive illustration of the fact that in England's Parliament the end justifies the means'.

Hofmeyr indicated his contempt with delicate restraint:

> The whole finish of the Enquiry is deplorable and disappointing especially in view of the loyal attitude of the Bond and of the Dutch generally in the time of the Jubilee. All we asked, all we wanted, was fair play, not vindictive punishment. The Dutch belief in English fair play, in Imperial thoroughness and impartiality, has received a serious shock. . . . The Commons have decided for continued suspicion instead of a clear and honest understanding.

The English Press, in as far as it was not bound by party loyalty, condemned the way in which the Inquiry had been conducted. The *Westminster Budget* published an amusing epitaph on the Inquiry:

> It respected confidences, it discovered the obvious, it avoided the obscure, it compromised no man . . . fortified by unctuous rectitude and unsuspicious disposition, it was unsparing of whitewash . . . dyed in the odour of inanity. . . . Let resignations wait. . . .

The *Investor's Review* surpassed even Labouchere in its vituperations:

> Mr Cecil Rhodes as 'unctuous rebel' . . . the unscrupulous master of the Jameson bullybumpkins. . . . The brutal insolence of their hero's conduct, his obvious determination to browbeat home opinion . . . disgusted all honourable men. This was not at all the kind of behaviour they looked for in the man their overheated imagination had endowed with all manly virtues. Englishmen do not object to a little dignity even in their freebooters and Rhodes exhibited himself far too much in the unsavoury part of a sort of bar-tender braggart masquerading as rebel for all but the strongest stomached or best paid of his supports to be other than shocked. . . .

On the Stock Exchange many jokes were cracked about the 'Committee of No-Inquiry' which, during its long session, had destroyed only one reputation, its own.

These opinions, censures and judgments of Rhodes were for the most part prompted by party political considerations, influenced by national motives or blackened by purely personal vindictiveness. It is therefore interesting to hear the opinion of a famous man, trained as a journalist and experienced as a writer. Mark Twain, the great American author, came to South Africa at a time when Rhodes' star was already waning and it was left to him to write the best sketch of this strange comet which passed over South Africa for about three decades, changing the political, economic and social face of a whole continent. In *More Tramps Abroad* Mark Twain wrote:

> I know quite well that whether Rhodes is the lofty and worshipful patriot and statesman that multitudes believe him to be, or Satan come again, as the rest of the world account him, he is still the most imposing figure in the British Empire outside England. When he stands on the Cape his shadow falls to the Zambezi. . . .

That he is an extraordinary man and not an accident of fortune, not even his dearest South African enemies were willing to deny. The whole South African world seemed to stand in a kind of shuddering awe; friend and enemy alike: it was as if he were deputy God on the one side, deputy Satan on the other, proprietor of the people, able to make them or ruin them by his breath, worshipped by many, hated by many, but blasphemed by none among the judicious, and even by the indiscreet in guarded whispers only.

What is the secret of his formidable supremacy? One says it is his prodigious wealth . . . ; another says it is his personal magnetism . . . ; another says it is his majestic ideas, his vast scheme for the territorial aggrandisement of England, his patriotic and unselfish ambition to spread her beneficent protection and her just rule over the pagan wastes of Africa . . . ; and another says he wants the earth and wants it for his own and that the belief that he will get it and let his friends in on the ground floor is *the* secret. . . .

One fact is sure: he keeps his prominence and a vast following, no matter what he does. He 'deceives' the Duke of Fife—it is the Duke's word—but that does not destroy the Duke's loyalty to him. He tricks the Reformers into immense trouble, with his Raid, but most of them believe he meant well. He weeps over the harshly-taxed Johannesburgers and makes them his friends; at the same time he taxes his Charter settlers 50 per cent and so wins their affection and their confidence. . . . He raids and robs and slays and enslaves the Matabele and gets worlds of Charter-Christian applause for it. He has beguiled England into buying Charter waste-paper for Bank of England notes, ton for ton, and the ravished still burn incense to him as the Eventual God of Plenty. He has done everything he could think of to pull himself down to the ground . . . ; yet there he stands, to this day, upon his dizzy summit under the dome of the sky, an apparent permanency, the marvel of the time, the mystery of the age, an Archangel with wings, to half the world, Satan with tail to the other half.

I admire him, I frankly confess it; and when his time comes, I shall buy a piece of the rope for a keepsake.[1]

[1] Reprinted by permission of Messrs Chatto & Windus Ltd.

CHAPTER XVIII

WAR

THE Rhodesia Express syncopated its metallic march of speed and power through the night. For once the 'up' train to Bulawayo had left dead on time. The officials of the Rhodesia Railway Company had received a warning that the 'Old Man' was travelling on it in his private coach. It was June 1897.

Wherever Rhodes showed himself a general expression of sympathy could be heard, especially among the simple people: 'Poor old Rhodes . . . these London "swells" treated him like a criminal and all his friends left him in the lurch. . . .'

He had brought home with him from London nothing but a Pyrrhic victory. Though he had boasted, before he left for England to 'face the music', that his political career was just beginning, he had already sensed that it would not be easy to pick up the reins that had slipped from his hands. One of those Cape Town 'mugwumps' had actually had the impudence to tell him straight to his face that his best retreat would be 'a hermit's cell somewhere on the Zambezi'. At the Colonial Office they had called him 'the hustler'. And old Goschen had asked: 'Were you not acting in rather a hurry, Mr Rhodes?' Of course he had been, and still was, in a hurry!—— They ought to come and see the knot on his wrist and watch how the heart laboured to keep him going! And for how long still?—— Not older than fifty—— And next week he would be celebrating his forty-fourth birthday.

The state of Rhodes' health had become known also outside the circle of his friends. Newspapers had already discussed the question of a successor. From all parts of the Empire there arrived anxious inquiries. Rhodes answered them all himself, in carefully worded statements so as not to upset the alarmed stock market.

Only the other day in London an old friend, a digger from Kimberley, had asked whether he had enjoyed his success in life and whether it had been worth all the trouble. Was it? Was it? Yes, he had enjoyed it, certainly he had enjoyed it! It was worth the candle. At the time when he thought that Kruger was going to hang Frank and he had not been sure they mightn't hang him too, he didn't like it——'No, the great fault of life is its shortness. Just when one is beginning to know the game, one has to stop—has to stop—to stop——' One thing he had learnt: 'I honestly believe that my years of trouble have made me a better man. I had a life of uninterrupted success, and then I had two years of considerable trouble, and I found . . . that I had an individuality that could stand trouble. . .'

The train rattled on. Rhodes, in his bed, tossed about from side to side. But no matter how he turned, the wildly palpitating heart morsed its maddening rhythm into his ears, broadcasting, as it were, his death-sentence. After such nights of torture Rhodes would need many hours to recover. Everyone would keep away. But that morning his secretary could not avoid entering his sleeping compartment at the first sign of his chief's being awake. He found a grumbling ill-humoured Rhodes. 'What do you want?' The secretary reported that the night before, after Rhodes had already retired, a telegram had arrived with the news that Barney Barnato, on his way to England, had committed suicide by jumping overboard.

All the colour left Rhodes' face. Just as suddenly he turned crimson with fury. Why had the telegram not been brought to him immediately upon its arrival? He barked at the secretary:

'I suppose you thought this would affect me and I should not sleep. Why, do you imagine I should be in the least affected if you were to fall under the wheels of this train now?'

Barnato's suicide upset Rhodes deeply and not only because of the probability of a new crisis on the stock market. Rhodes had always retained a soft spot for Barnato. Perhaps Rhodes also felt in some way responsible for Barnato's mental collapse. Barnato had been excluded from the secret of the Raid. Unlike Rhodes, Beit and their friends, he had therefore not been able to make financial arrangements beforehand. Not only had he made no profits but he had lost more than £3 millions. In the autumn of 1895 speculation on the 'Kaffir Circus' had reached such dimensions that a crash could be predicted even by the uninitiated outsider. The value of the South African shares on the market amounted to more than £300 millions which, however, yielded only £2 millions in dividends.

When in September 1895 large parcels of South African gold

shares were offered, the provenance of which was unknown, prices began to crumble. These mysterious sales were repeated in ever-increasing quantities. The crash on the London Stock Exchange began on the Jewish Day of Atonement. Barnato bought up whatever came on the market and thus prevented a general breakdown in prices and saved London's money market from a consequent crisis of catastrophic proportions. Everyone wondered what could have moved Barnato, who had always operated timidly and only within his own restricted field, to act as the saviour of the stock market. Strange as it may seem Barnato had acted completely altruistically. The Lord Mayor of London gave a banquet at the Mansion House in honour of Barnato 'in recognition of his exertions to keep up prices and prevent a panic'.

The New Year brought Barnato a sad awakening: he had spent his '*kosher* money' to fill the pockets of Rhodes, Beit & Co., who had used the Raid for a gigantic bear-speculation. His friend Rhodes had made a dupe of him.

Even if he had been asked, Barnato would not have participated in the Johannesburg conspiracy, because in his opinion 'men do not come to the Transvaal to vote, they come to earn money'. Without his knowledge his nephew Solly Joel had participated in the Reform movement. Now he was sitting in jail in Pretoria with the others, awaiting trial. Barnato took the next ship to South Africa: 'How can I face the boy's poor mother if I don't get him out of *tronk*?'

And he did not mince his words when at the trial he told the presiding judge in the most precise terms what he thought of Transvaal justice. The judge finally interrupted him: 'Mr Barnato, you are no gentleman.' As fast as a revolver shot came Barney's reply: 'And you are no judge!'

A few days later Barnato gave notice to all his employees. Advertisements announced the auction of his multiple property in Johannesburg. Several of his mines closed down. Barnato, clad all in black, went to Pretoria to see Kruger.

In Pretoria Barnato's intended sell-out was not considered an empty threat. They knew his stubbornness. The loss in revenue and the crisis which would inevitably follow would be ruinous to the Transvaal. The President promised Barnato the greatest leniency towards the condemned Reformers.

From the excitement of those days Barnato never recovered.

And yet he had no reason to worry: he had surmounted the crisis almost unscathed, as the loss of £3 millions had soon been partially recovered. But he imagined that he had lost most of his fortune. Everywhere he saw enemies waiting to destroy him. When threatening letters arrived, he lost all hold over himself. His cries of 'they're after me' echoed through the house. 'They're after me! . . .' 'Yes, oh yes, poor old Dad, bless his memory, used to say to the boys: If a man is going to hit you, hit him first and say: 'If you try that, I'll hit you again.'" . . . No, no—too weak for that now. . . . They're after me. . . . No one ever knew or ever can know how hard I worked for it all. If I have made millions, I have worked for them as few men ever can have worked. . . . I go to bed with my work, sleep with it, dream of it, and wake up with it. . . . And. . . . They're after me! They're after me!——'

He sailed for England on a holiday accompanied by his family. During the trip he was calm and drank only moderately. One day when he had been lying in a deck-chair he suddenly stood up and with a piercing cry of 'they're after me' jumped over the rails.

The tragic end of Barnato weighed heavily on Rhodes' mind. It reminded him of the probability of his own sudden death. He revised his last will and sent it to his financial manager, Sir Lewis Michell: '. . . It will amuse you. I am almost superstitious. I knew Barnato would not outlive me, so I made no arrangement with him. If Beit had not made the arrangement with me, he would have also died first. Now the thought has come that I might go first and my ideas be lost. . . .'

In England, in spite of his victory over his compatriots' 'unctuous rectitude', Rhodes had to swallow many humiliations. Lord Salisbury made no secret of his contempt for him. He cut him ostentatiously wherever they met, even at the table of the Prince of Wales.

When he had been dismissed by the Committee, Rhodes had booked his return passage from England on the *Tantallon Castle* only after he had made sure that Schreiner was travelling on the same ship. He kept his departure secret so that Schreiner should not escape him at the last minute. He had to talk to Schreiner, and now that all was over the hatchet would have to be buried between them and everything be forgotten and forgiven. Rhodes needed Schreiner, without whom he would never win back the confidence of the moderate Afrikaners.

Rhodes found it impossible to believe that anyone should have principles which he would not give up after having received a good treatment 'on the personal' from him. All his wooing of Schreiner was wasted. Schreiner had had his suspicions about Rhodes' financial interest in the Raid confirmed by the Inquiry. It had broken his last link of friendship with Rhodes. He would fight him now, tooth and nail. Schreiner, together with Merriman, Sauer and Solomon, all former Ministers under Rhodes, attached themselves to the Bond. Rhodes, with what was left of his former Afrikaner followers and with the majority of the English-speaking elements, formed the Progressive Party, financed principally by himself. The country was now clearly divided into two racial political factions: Afrikaner and English. Rhodes' twenty years of working for a reconciliation policy between the two races had been utterly wrecked.

For some time Rhodes was able to keep his party—though without him—in the saddle, thanks to the peculiar election methods prevailing in South Africa at the time. However, one could not permanently *corriger la fortune* at elections, and soon the Progressive Party was in the minority. Schreiner, backed by the Bond, became Prime Minister.

Schreiner had succeeded in ousting Rhodes and his 'capitalistic Caesarism and bastard imperialism'. He regarded Rhodes 'as the greatest enemy of the Imperial policy', if, as he assumed, 'the British Government was set on a peaceful course'.

His loss of political power affected Rhodes so deeply that he sometimes lost complete control over himself.

Several of his friends did not believe that Rhodes' strange behaviour in the years from 1897 until his death was due only to his weak heart. Molteno, who had observed him closely, now regarded Rhodes as 'more a candidate for mental treatment than serious political canvassing'. Others had noticed also the great physical deterioration in him since the days of the Raid. His complexion had taken on a still darker hue; his swollen face appeared distorted and his eyes recalled the expression of an old retriever dog.

No one asked for Rhodes' advice. He was left out in the cold. In his own new party the English voters had not yet completely forgotten his liaison with the Bond and his repeated proclamation of the 'elimination of the Imperial Factor'. Jingoism in England was flourishing as never before and Rhodes saw the necessity of transplanting the new type of vociferous chauvinism to the Cape. Parties were all right during election time: between elections the people should be given an opportunity to wave their flags and voice their patriotic feelings. He therefore founded a movement, the South African League, which on the outside was a harmless patriotic society, but in fact did its best, as the Cape Government soon complained to the High Commissioner, 'to foment and excite ill-will between the two principal European races'.

Responsible people in South Africa were seriously worried about the hooliganism, hitherto unknown in South African politics, which Rhodes' South African League had provoked but of which, through repercussions on his opponents, the victim was mostly Rhodes himself. Since the time when Groote Schuur had been rebuilt nineteen fires had broken out, all of which were proved to be the work of incendiaries. On his estate valuable birds' eggs were smashed, the kangaroos and ostriches in the paddocks were poisoned or clubbed to death, almost 2,000 young trees were uprooted and broken and an attempt to liberate the lions from their cages was frustrated only at the last minute.

Rhodes was so disgusted by this savage warfare against him that he wanted to leave South Africa. Should he go to Rhodesia? It seemed senseless. By the grace of Chamberlain he had again been admitted as Managing Director of the Chartered Company, having been elected by his shareholders with great acclaim. At the same time, however, the dictatorial powers which he had wielded in Rhodesia were narrowed down by Chamberlain through the introduction of a legislative council superseding him. Though not much gold had as yet been found and, according to expert opinion, would never be found to any extent, Rhodes still fed his shareholders with hopes of great gold-reefs and managed once more to obtain fresh capital. The Chartered Company now had the respectable amount of £5 millions of their shareholders' money invested in Rhodesia without having as yet paid a penny in dividends. The optimism of the small shareholders and of the thousands of foreign speculators was by no means shared by English bankers and financial experts. The shares, shortly after the shareholders' meeting, had reached their lowest level.

Rhodesia would be able to get on very well without him, with Lord Grey in charge and the Legislative Council acting as Chamberlain's watchdogs. There was nothing for him to do any more in South Africa. Thrown on the rubbish heap! Even his interest in Goldfields and De Beers had begun to weaken: 'The only trouble with regard to the industry is that it is becoming a matter of course and uninteresting. It goes like clockwork. There is an element of certainty there was not in the past; but I will admit that to my mind it has not the interest it had in the past when one had to use one's mind and brain.'

The thought of being condemned to political impotence deprived him of the ability to enjoy his existence. All his money, the millions he had gathered and the half-million pounds which constituted his regular income, had become valueless to him. 'Money is power', he had often said in his earlier days. At the zenith of his life he had to find out how wrong this notion had been.

He confided in Garrett. It was shortly before the elections that sealed Rhodes' fate of political eclipse in the Cape. He did not speak 'off the record' and knew that his words would be printed the next day, in the *Cape Times*.

A leading place again in Cape politics? Garrett wanted to know. This master of journalistic art had struck the right keynote. Rhodes replied:

> . . . Don't talk as if it was *I* who want your Cape politics. You want *me*. You can't do without me. You discuss 'Ought Rhodes to do this?' and 'Will Rhodes keep in the background?' and so on—I am quite willing to keep out, but you have to take the feeling of the people, and the feeling of the people . . . is that somebody is wanted to fight a certain thing for them, and there is nobody else able and willing to fight it. You say, 'Oh, but that's your ambition, you want to get back into power'—I reply quite fairly, no, humanly speaking, as for ambition at the Cape, I have had everything. There is no more to offer, only work and worry. As for the North—well there we are really creating a country. . . . Really there are many other things to think of besides Cape Town parish pump. . . . The Cape [is] a sort of Bond-ridden place—Bond, varied by unctuous rectitude and all sorts of wobbling. . . . I really believe they say 'Oh, this is Rhodes' amiable lunacy—we must humour him because after all he does work for the country.' You see, it's very amusing.

Localism here and in Johannesburg, and in Natal and in the Cape Colony; and that's where I think, to be frank, that I might perhaps be able to be of a certain use, because I have a certain influence, with a good many people in all these places, and you know my idea—Colonial Federation. . . .

Poor Rhodes, he still cherished illusions and wish-dreams far removed from reality. Politicians fought shy of having their names linked with his or even of being seen in his company. One of his former followers once came to him at Groote Schuur, bringing him some presents, but asking that his visit be kept secret. Rhodes concealed his annoyance but he took his revenge: the visitor had left behind his umbrella which had his name engraved on the handle. Rhodes had it placed on the table in the entrance hall for everyone to see.

It now began to dawn upon Rhodes that his political power had vanished. All that remained of his former glory was a certain sentimental value attached to his name as founder of the diamond industry and conqueror of the North. He was no longer needed. Chamberlain had indicated to Molteno, that 'when things have been settled in the Sudan, the whole weight of the British Government will be thrown against the Transvaal and in clearing up affairs in South Africa'. The 'Imperial Factor' had taken over the task of shaping the fate of South Africa and Joseph Chamberlain, *à la Jupiter tonans*, would direct the powers from Whitehall. Since gods no longer appeared on earth personally, Chamberlain would have to send a demigod hero to South Africa as his handyman. He made the best possible choice: acclaimed by all and sundry as the perfect representative of England's militant Imperialism, the new creed of the country which had been brought to full bloom through the patriotic exaltations on the occasion of a beloved Queen's Diamond Jubilee, Sir Alfred Milner was appointed, in February 1897, as High Commissioner in South Africa. The 'South African graveyard of reputations' was yawning for a new victim.

Chamberlain had picked on Milner not only for his administrative abilities and brilliant intellect but rather for his well-known strength of character bordering almost on recalcitrant stubbornness which he thought would firmly resist any possible attempts by Rhodes to bully him, to 'square' him, or to 'take him on the personal'. Chamberlain had warned Milner against Rhodes. He had also given him strict orders to suppress any anti-British movement in the Cape. He asked him to settle the Uitlander question with or without Kruger, with the ultimate aim of a South African Federation under the Union Jack.

Rhodes had expected to be consulted by Milner immediately upon the High Commissioner's arrival. No word came from Government House. Swallowing his pride, Rhodes went to see Milner unasked. He tried hard to apply all his magnetic charm on the new man for a treatment 'on the personal', but he soon realized that the stern and inanimate features of the new High Commissioner would not thaw. He never went there again. Neither did he invite the High Commissioner to Groote Schuur after Milner's remark had been reported to him: 'The less Rhodes and I are seen together the better.'

Though Rhodes, at the time of the Matabele *indaba*, had expressed a wish to be able to grow cabbages like the Roman Emperor Cincinnatus, he was not fully satisfied now that he had nothing else to do but devote all his time to his various agricultural enterprises. He had become the biggest farmer in the world. In Rhodesia his two farms, one of 100,000 and the other of 70,000 acres, occupied him only as long as he was able to design plans for dams, organize the cultivation and direct the management. As soon as details had to be dealt with he lost patience and left them to his managers. Before the elections of 1897 he had acquired a great number of large farms in the Paarl and Stellenbosch districts where most of the farmers were followers of Hofmeyr. It was said that he had acquired these farms for the sole purpose of settling his old English retainers from Kimberley, Johannesburg and Rhodesia there so as to win a majority for his party in these districts. These rumours were contradicted by the fact that Rhodes immediately began to combine these farms into a single giant fruit farm. The 'Rhodes Fruit Farm' became the first, biggest and most progressive agricultural enterprise in South Africa, the pioneer of today's Cape fruit industry.

Most of his time Rhodes spent in Rhodesia. He loved to ride up the Matopo Hills for recuperation. He had been seriously ill, following severe attacks of malaria. Dr Jameson hurried to

Rhodes' farm near Bulawayo to nurse him. The two friends often sat together on the 'View of the World'. Once Rhodes pointed at the weather-beaten heavy boulders and lay down flat on the biggest of them saying almost ceremoniously: 'Here I want to be buried—— As somebody said: They'll get the country and all I'll get is six foot by four—six foot by four. . . .' Jameson looked at his friend in consternation. No shrieking laughter followed. Jameson then knew that Rhodes' health was even worse than the symptoms had indicated.

Feeling that the span of life left to him was no more than a score of months, at the most a couple of years, Rhodes, as though in a frenzy, urged everyone around him to hurry with the completion of his various schemes. His main project, the Cape to Cairo railway, was already more than 1,300 miles nearer realization. For the ceremonial opening of the railway line over the Zambezi he had, upon Lord Grey's advice, invited Milner. They had not met since that first futile encounter at Government House the year before.

At first, remembering Milner's offensive chilliness towards him, Rhodes wanted to pay him back in his own coin and remained coldly aloof. Now that there was no longer any danger of Rhodes crossing his path and eclipsing him, Milner softened considerably. They had two long talks together unburdening their hearts to each other, and found out that, after all, their opinions, aims and intentions were identical. Each, however, distrusted the other, fearing that at the critical moment the one might steal the other's thunder. They both agreed that 'Krugerism' would have to be destroyed. Rhodes blamed the old Boer President, recently re-elected for the fourth time by an overwhelming majority, for every failure in his latest enterprises: the Raid, the Johannesburg revolution—they had only broken down because of 'old Kroiger'. The financial crisis, the slump on the stock market, the labour difficulties, the lost Cape elections—it was all the fault of 'that damn' old Dopper'.

To Milner the Transvaal appeared as 'two wholly antagonistic systems—a medieval race oligarchy, and a modern industrial state [which] simply could not exist permanently side by side'. Only about the method to be employed did the two men differ; Rhodes was opposed to war, but only because of the cost. He preferred the quicker, cheaper and easier way of a 'jump on the Transvaal'.

In Milner's righteous civil-servant bureaucratic mind there arose the fear that Rhodes might once again spring on them some ugly surprise. He immediately changed the subject. He found Rhodes, as he reported home, 'undaunted and unbroken . . . but also untaught and quite capable, unless he be guided, of making shipwreck of his own ambition and our permanent shipwreck'.

In Whitehall they had expected Rhodes to lie low for some years and to be satisfied with building up what he had acquired. Rhodes, with his insatiable appetite, demanded more: the British Protectorate of Bechuanaland had been promised to him; he now wanted this promise fulfilled. Milner, thinking of the uproar which would be caused among the Exeter Hall people and the 'Little Englanders' if the demand were granted, was horrified. 'Men are ruled by their foibles and your foible, Mr Rhodes, is size', he told him. The only way, Milner suggested to Chamberlain, by which Rhodes should be allowed to incorporate Bechuanaland with Rhodesia, was to make him 'earn it by his good behaviour'. For the time being he found Rhodesia still 'in a pretty handsome mess' which was due to the fact that Rhodes 'is a great developer but a bad administrator'. And he considered Rhodes personally 'too self-willed, too violent, too sanguine and too much in a hurry'.

Outwardly they got along well together, though between them there always remained a feeling of suspicion and jealousy. And both suffered from the same kind of stubbornness, so that Rhodes once remarked:

'I find him, his mind once made up, unmovable—so much so that we tacitly agree to drop at once any subject that we do not agree on. I allow he makes his decisions slowly, but once made they are irrevocable.'

Such tolerance and patience Rhodes showed only rarely, even towards people with whom he wanted to ingratiate himself. He tried to avoid differences with Milner because he did not wish to interfere with Milner's 'mission' even indirectly: 'A burnt child dreads the fire. I keep aloof from the whole Transvaal crisis so that no one may be able to say if things go wrong that Rhodes is in it again.'

Besides, he needed Milner's good will for his railway scheme, which was nearest to his heart now that there was no longer anything else for him to do in Africa. Next on his programme was the continuation of the railway line up to Tanganyika. He needed it not only for his Cape to Cairo scheme but also in order to establish new mineral 'milestones' there. On the Rhodesian-Congo border his men had discovered the rich copper belt and the coal-mines of Katanga. Without a rail connection it would be useless. Funds would have to be found to finance both these projects. With this object in view Rhodes left for England at the end of 1898. If the copper and coal in his new mines were to pay, he would have to find cheap money for the railway extension which he would be able to obtain only from the British Government. It was most unlikely that they would grant his request. Rhodes, however, conceived the ingenious idea that the British Treasury should merely guarantee his railway company's issue of £3 million debentures which would enable him to obtain the money from the public at Government rates of 2½ per cent, whereas otherwise he would have to offer at least 3½ per cent.

Chamberlain was not disinclined to listen to Rhodes' proposition but he was afraid to have the Colonial Office mixed up in any of Rhodes' financial schemes. So as to get rid of him politely he gave Rhodes a recommendation to his Cabinet colleague 'Black Michael' Hicks-Beach, the Chancellor of the Exchequer. Chamberlain could well imagine the meeting between these two men—Rhodes who 'is very unreasonable in the way he expects all his demands to be taken on trust' and 'Black Michael' who had inherited from Lord Randolph Churchill the title of being England's rudest man: there would probably be a hell of a row.

The reception which Rhodes was given by Hicks-Beach surpassed even Chamberlain's expectations. The Chancellor who had no faith in the Cape to Cairo route suspected that all Rhodes was out for was to boom Chartered shares by 'creating the impression that the Chartered Company was to be reinforced by Imperial credit'.

It did not take long before the two men were at loggerheads. 'Black Michael' told Rhodes—or rather shouted at him: 'It's all right, Mr Rhodes—you can't bluff me.' Rhodes jumped up from his chair, his face purple. He had to fight for breath before he squeaked in highest falsetto: 'You should be ashamed of yourself—ashamed of yourself!' Excitedly he marched up and down the room, his hands deeply buried in his trouser-pockets. Someone—an assistant or a clerk—came into the room. Rhodes checked his pacing and, stepping in front of the intruder, he shouted: 'What d'you think? The damned fellow said I was trying to bluff him! I'm going home tomorrow. . . .'

Hicks-Beach was not the only one who refused to believe in the possibility and soundness of the Cape to Cairo route. Railway experts, pointing to the enormous costs, estimated at fifteen to twenty millions, doubted whether interest could ever be paid on such large capital. They also questioned the necessity of an overland route which would not shorten the distance from London to the Cape. Colonel Prout, in a technical railway journal, described the idea as enticing and admitted that 'nothing quite so spectacular has been done in history since the time of Alexander the Great'. But he also rejected the project as uneconomic. A quarter of the route would go parallel to navigable waters; half of the distance would run through uncivilized country and three-fifths of it through areas in which no white man could live.

They all misunderstood Rhodes' idea and still believed that he was motivated only by the romantic ideas and imperialistic 'dreams' of his schoolboy 'imagination'. In the meantime, however, Rhodes, in spite of, or perhaps because of, his fierce Jingoism was beginning to think in terms of absolute *Realpolitik* as far as his enterprises in the North were concerned. Sentimental considerations would not have moved him to change the railroad a single mile. The plans were laid with 'some immediate and material objects in view', namely, to keep up with the geological, industrial and commercial exploitation of the newly opened countries. He pleaded with Harcourt:

> Look at the matter. You get the railway to Lake Tanganyika, you have Her Majesty's sanction for the railway to Uganda . . . and then you have Kitchner coming down from Khartoum. . . . It is not imaginative; it is practical. That gives you Africa—the whole of it . . . the conquest of Africa by the English nation is a practical question now.

Harcourt refused to be convinced. He sneered at the scheme: '. . . What a noble and generous offer! Only it is not the Chartered Company who is to pay for this—it is the British taxpayer. . . . This prospectus is not only for English publication and English consumption, but it is a notice to other countries who must wickedly imagine that they have some claim to some share in portions of Africa. . . .'

The coffers of the British Exchequer were closed to Rhodes. He had to find—and he did find—the necessary funds among private investors, relying to a great extent on investment by German and French speculators. He had repeatedly been censured by the English Press for using foreign money markets in his unorthodox financing methods.

The question of the route farther north had now become acute. The Tanganyika line to Uganda would have to go through German and Belgian Congo territory. He had to hurry: Kitchener, from 'a post to the south of Fashoda', asked him jokingly in a telegram: 'When are you coming up?' Rhodes replied in the same vein. . . . 'If you don't look sharp, in spite of your victory, I shall reach Uganda before you.'

He had no faith in British diplomacy. He would go to Brussels and Berlin himself and discuss the matter personally with King Leopold and the Kaiser. Was he not himself a kind of sovereign, the Ruler of Rhodesia?

He ran down the thickly carpeted marble staircase of the Palace of Laeken towards the Palace gate so fast that the elderly court flunkey who wished to show him out could scarcely follow him. He ignored the polite question: 'Does *Monsieur* not wish to see His Majesty's hot-houses with the famous orchids?' Orchids? He suppressed a round English curse. Reminded him of another damn' fellow who also grew those useless blossoms and who could have behaved just as atrociously.

When Rhodes reached his carriage he wiped the sweat from his brow and spat out his words to his secretary breathlessly: 'Satan, I tell you that man is Satan!'

Later, when he had recuperated a little, he added: 'I thought I was clever—but I was no match for King Leopold.'

In his opinion of Leopold II, King of the Belgians and master over the Congo, Rhodes did not stand alone. He merited his name of Leopold the Unloved. Just as he himself was hated, so he hated everyone who threatened to disturb him in his business or his private pleasures. His greatest aversion, next to his own family, was the English Queen, who detested him as much as she had loved his father, Uncle Leopold.

Instead of discussing Rhodes' projects of telegraphs and railways during the audience, the Belgian king gave him a lecture on British perfidy. When at the end Rhodes timidly asked permission for his railway line to go through Congo territory, Leopold became abusive. How dared he even ask? Had not Rhodes been responsible for having robbed the Congo of the Katanga basin, where copper, coal and iron had been found in such abundance? And then there was still the strip in the territory formerly held by the French and now taken over by the British, that Rosebery had promised him!

The King stood up and when Rhodes was already at the door he shouted at him: 'Give it back to me and you may traverse the Congo as you please. But until I get it back, I'll be damned if ever a yard of your telegraph wire or a single rail of your Cape to Cairo railway will cross my country.' Bismarck had been right, Rhodes told himself, when he had said: 'Apparently no one ever leaves Leopold with a whole shirt.'

In Berlin, where Rhodes arrived on 11 March 1899, the reception was totally different. Baron von Holstein had received a report from German East Africa that Rhodes might visit Berlin on his next European trip. Immediately numerous telegrams were dispatched from the Wilhelmstrasse to the German Ambassador in London to inquire whether 'Sir Rhodes'—a German could not imagine a prominent person without a title—'is a man with whom compensation politics on the larger scale can be discussed—that is to say . . . is his influence strong enough in England to drive them through even against Lord Salisbury's *vis inertiae*? . . .'

Holstein wished to exchange railway concessions in German East Africa for the cessation of England's resistance to Germany's acquisition of Samoa and her interests in Morocco. He also hoped to gain an improvement in Anglo-German relations from Rhodes' visit. Salisbury had been inaccessible to the German Ambassador for weeks. At the moment the two countries seemed not far from breaking off diplomatic relations.

The German Foreign Secretary, suave Baron Bernhard von Bülow, immediately took Rhodes in hand. He wished to sound the man and his ways so as to be able to prepare the Kaiser for their first meeting. The next morning Rhodes was invited to an 'informal' audience with the Kaiser for the late afternoon.

Wilhelm received his guest in his study where, behind a large desk, he sat on a peculiar seat built in the form of a horse's back topped by a leather saddle complete with stirrups.

Two men sat facing each other who were the very personification of *Machtpolitik* and of a *fin de siècle* sham-romanticism. Both believed that they had been selected as instruments of destiny to spread and materialize the gospel of nationalism. They thirsted for power as a compensation for the hidden weaknesses of their own personalities. Only in a state of climactic crisis could the German Emperor find a confirmation of his own importance and thus overcome his gnawing inferiority complex. Cecil Rhodes also needed the stimulus of ever new and complicated situations to feel the weight of his personality and thus escape from the painful dissatisfaction with his existence. These two men admired each other. Unconsciously each saw himself mirrored in the other.

They soon warmed up. Rhodes, employing his charm with all the stops pulled out to their furthest limit, fascinated the Kaiser and gave him the feeling that now at last he had found a congenial character who had full understanding for his complex genius. The Kaiser led the conversation to colonial questions, complaining bitterly that there was nothing left for Germany on which to build up a colonial empire. Rhodes had been waiting for this topic. He had learnt about the Kaiser's latest foible of planning a Berlin–Baghdad railway line. Rhodes now fired the Kaiser's imagination by pointing out the possibility of conquering the Middle East not by the might of the sword but by railways, dams and water pipe-lines.

Rhodes felt at once that the magic name of Mesopotamia had won his case for him. 'The Baghdad Railway', the Kaiser said, 'is Germany's task, just as the Cape to Cairo line is yours.' Together they bent over maps and spent their time building bridges here and dams there—real miracles of engineering—and canals through deserts and railways across mountains. Two schoolboys playing a geographical game!

The ground had now been well prepared, Rhodes decided, for him to come out with his own business: 'Oh, that stupid Jameson Raid', he said. It had all been the fault of Kruger, who did not allow the Cape to Cairo line to run through the Transvaal, a demand which, after all 'was not unjust and would certainly have met with German support'.—And without Kruger there would have been no Raid and (with a twinkle in his eye) no unfortunate telegram.—'Oh, for that telegram', Rhodes continued after having made sure that the Kaiser was smiling, 'I have to be extremely grateful to Your Majesty. You see, Sir, I got myself into a bad scrape, and I was coming home to be whipped by Grandmamma, when you kindly stepped in and sent that telegram, and you got the whipping instead of me—I was the naughty boy and I never got whipped at all.'

All he wanted, Rhodes explained, was the right for his telegraph and railway line to pass through German territory in East Africa. The Kaiser agreed provided that his Ministers had no objections. He made the condition, however, that German material should be used and that Rhodes should exert his influence in London for a favourable settlement of the Samoa question.

The Kaiser was about to touch on another subject when to his great amusement Rhodes, who did not care for such nonsense of court etiquette as waiting to be graciously dismissed, pulled out his watch and, proffering his hand to his imperial host—another crime against court rule—said to him with a smile: 'Well, Your Majesty, good-bye. I've got to go now, as I have some people coming to dinner.'

The Kaiser pressed his hand warmly: 'I wish I had a minister like you.' Rhodes replied: 'If I had met you before 1896, there never would have been any Jameson Raid.'

When the Kaiser told von Bülow about his meeting with Rhodes he said: 'When Napoleon met Goethe at Erfurt he exclaimed: "Voilà un homme!" I can say the same of Rhodes: I've met a man!'

Several other meetings between the Kaiser and Rhodes followed. Rhodes received the confirmation of their agreement with the proviso of England's approval of the Samoa cession. He left Berlin not quite satisfied with his success, which he called 'a most just bargain but all ifs and ans'. However, his opinion of the Germans, who for the last twenty years had conveniently served him as a bogey, had changed. He had turned into a champion of an Anglo-German *entente* and of Germany's colonial expansion anywhere in the world—except, of course, in Africa.

One other triumph Rhodes carried away from Berlin. So as to please Whitehall the Germans had now begun to end their flirtation with the Boers. Dr Leyds, who had arrived in Berlin before Rhodes, again 'to see a throat-specialist', was no longer received by von Bülow. He was told by a junior clerk in the Wilhelmstrasse: 'On behalf of his Majesty I have to express to you the Emperor's urgent wish that you and your Government should at least cease agitating in German papers against an Anglo-German *rapprochement*.'

To the Prince of Wales went Rhodes' full report about his visit. The letter was later forwarded to the Queen:

> . . . I feel sure he is most anxious to work with England, and I think he is fond of the English; he must be so, for after all he is half an Englishman. I think he is very sensitive, for he spoke about the way the English papers have abused him. I heard in Berlin, on good authority, and I am sure, Sir, you will not mind my repeating it, that he thinks you do not like him, and that he is very anxious to gain your good opinion. . . . I am sure of this, that, if you showed him good feeling when he came to England, it would immensely influence his mind.

During a short stay in England Rhodes was fêted as though there had never been a Raid or an Inquiry. He felt highly flattered when his old University bestowed on him, together with Lord Kitchener, the honorary degree of Doctor of Law. After the ceremony Rhodes proudly remarked to his friends: 'They gave me a greater reception than Lord Kitchener, and you must remember that they were not mere undergraduates of eighteen, but Masters of Arts, gentlemen with grey beards. . . .'

Rhodes believed in his infallibility more than ever before. It was said that his intercourse with crowned heads, who had treated him as an equal, had altogether turned his head. He became completely arbitrary in his actions and refused to discuss his dispositions or explain his orders even to his colleagues. When Rhodes heard that Sammy Marks, one of Johannesburg's multi-millionaires and a personal friend of Kruger's, had presented the President with a pair of sculptured lions for the entrance portal of his residence, Rhodes decided that it would be a good idea to send the President a pair of real lions as a gift for Pretoria's new Zoological Gardens. Friends warned him that the gift might be misinterpreted and taken as a political allegory—the British Lion. Rhodes, however, argued, shouted and raved, and off went the lions to Pretoria. They were sent back by return as unwanted.

Rhodes returned to South Africa in August 1899 just in time: the war against the Transvaal began in October. Milner had fulfilled his mission; the Uitlander franchise served as a convenient pretext. The real reason for going to war remained obscure to many. A prominent writer stated: 'Surely we never before went to war when there was so much uncertainty about the *casus belli*.' The masses were fed with sufficiently intoxicating patriotic slogans and a novelty was added to the old numbers of the usual musical Jingo programme by a new song to the tune of 'John Brown's Body': 'We'll hang old Kruger on a sour apple tree. . . .'

Those who knew the country, however, realized that the war, just like the Raid and previous wars in South Africa, had been started primarily for geological reasons. Nevertheless Her Majesty's Secretary for War felt that the occasion called for a note of 'felicitations' to his colleague Chamberlain, to which he added: 'My soldiers are in ecstasies.'

Ecstatic would hardly have been the word to express Rhodes' state of mind. Until the last moment he had not believed in the possibility of war. In London he had declared that 'Kruger is only bluffing' and shortly before the outbreak of hostilities he had cabled to Beit: 'Kruger will yield everything the Home Government demand. . . . Nothing will make Kruger fire a shot.'

Clear-headed Englishmen who remained sober in the turmoil of wild chauvinism were dubbed 'Little Englanders' or simply 'traitors' and beaten up. Even a British general, Sir William Butler, who had substituted for Milner as High Commissioner for a while shortly before the war, objected to the way a *casus belli* had been manufactured. He as well as many others realized that the war would be nothing but a 'financial crusade'. He thought he saw through Rhodes' schemes. 'When Rhodesia proved a failure, the Transvaal became the next necessary acquisition to save the market.' There was no reason for war.

Rhodes had carefully kept in the background so that no one could blame him for having instigated this war. Although for economic reasons he would have liked to attain his goal of destroying Krugerism without a war, he had advocated political pressure within and without the Transvaal. He had done more than anyone else in South Africa to poison the atmosphere from behind the scenes, by the noisy Jingoism of his South African

League, by the aggressive policy of his Progressive Party in the Cape Parliament and by the war propaganda in his newspapers. Milner could be and was highly satisfied with Rhodes' underhand war-mongering!

Young J. C. Smuts had been promoted from Attorney-General of the Transvaal to become Kruger's Assistant Secretary of State. In his new capacity he had immediately offered Britain a franchise of the Uitlanders after five years' residence, as well as ten seats in the First Raad. It was not sufficient: Milner, in a published dispatch, spoke of 'the spectacle of thousands of British subjects kept permanently in the position of helots. . . .' Remembering the effect of Dr Jameson's infamous 'Women and Children Letter' of 1895, headlines in the Press screamed: 'Brutal Ill-Treatment of Women and Children' (*News of the World*); 'Brutality to Women' (*Daily Mail*).

It was the ugly cancerous growth of commercial imperialism spreading over the auriferous soil of South Africa that must be held responsible for this war. The main driving force was not Rhodes alone. Chamberlain, too, was blamed:

> Mr Chamberlain has raised a separate variety of Rhodes' financial or speculative imperialism dependent upon a supposed connection between Trade and the Flag, and a confusion between emporium and imperium. Perhaps it may be called provisionally 'Emporialism'. (Hirst.)

Some even went so far, according to Stead in his *Review of Reviews*, as to accuse Chamberlain of having private interests in the war, since the Chamberlain family was closely connected with various armament concerns whose main business was contracts with the Admiralty and the War Office. Also the fact that his son Austen Chamberlain held the position of director in the Bank of Africa was considered, to say the least of it, as strange. Lloyd George, who was one of the most aggressive 'Little Englanders', was once heckled at a meeting: 'You oppose any expansion of the Empire', to which the pugnacious little Welshman retorted: 'I only note that the more the Empire expands, the more the Chamberlains contract.'

The connection between *haute finance* and politics created, as a leading Liberal politician expressed it, a 'dirty moral squalor'.

Neutral foreign onlookers, like the respectable *Nouvelle Revue*, were repelled by Britain's frivolous policy of going to war against a peaceful nation for no other than financial reasons:

> These people [the financiers] have let loose the war not with a light heart, but with a single eye to the operations on the Stock Exchange. To that end they have endangered their country, and exposed the Empire to infinite damage in the estimation of mankind.

Rhodes did indeed look upon the war as a speculative business transaction with economic rather than political aims, and as the logical continuation of his Raid politics. He sneered at Chamberlain's 'pride in the war' and at his boast that if he, Chamberlain, was credited by his opponents with having been the 'author of the war, such an exploit would be a feather in [his] cap'. To friends Rhodes remarked:

'Three years ago I made a raid and everybody said I was wrong. Now the Queen's Government are preparing another raid, and everybody says they are right.'

The events leading to the state of war had exonerated Rhodes completely. Triumphantly he was able to show that he had always been right:

'. . . When I began this business of annexation, both sides [of Parliament] were most timid. They would ask one to stop at Kimberley, then they asked one to stop at Khama's country. I remember Lord Salisbury's chief agent [Sir Hercules Robinson] imploring me to stop at the Zambezi. Now they won't stop anywhere. They have found out that the world is not quite big enough for British trade and the British flag.'

When he had waged war against the Natives in the North Rhodes had never been disturbed by the sacrifice of human lives. War for him meant the continuation of business by other means. He made his point of view quite clear when he said:

'The British flag is the greatest commercial asset. . . . We are not going to war for the amusement of royal families, as in the past, but we mean practical business.'

The same cynical tendency was expressed in a telegram from Rhodes' friends to Kruger just before hostilities began: 'For what you are about to receive may the Lord make you truly thankful.' President Kruger was wiser. He had once warned his State

Secretary Dr Leyds: 'Young man, you don't know the English. I do. You should argue with them—dispute with them—negotiate with them—but don't fight with them.' However, in a cable to the *New York World* he expressed his iron determination to defend the freedom of the Boers:

> ... The Republics are determined, if they must belong to England that a price will have to be paid which will stagger humanity.

The results were anything but what the foolish cynics in Whitehall had expected: the English were beaten thoroughly in the first months of the war and warfare was carried into their own territories, the Cape and Natal. Once again English generals had to learn that war, and especially war in Africa, differed somewhat from manœuvres at Sandhurst or Aldershot.

When Rhodes told his friends that he was going to Kimberley, which the Boers were threatening to cut off and besiege, they tried to dissuade him. He refused to listen. That's where his place was in the hour of danger! If it was to be destroyed, if his life's work was to be wiped out by the Boers, he would go down with it.

Having Rhodes within the precincts of the besieged town signified an increased risk for Kimberley: the Boers would muster their greater forces to take the town and capture Rhodes. They had already made it known that they were holding ready an iron cage in which to bring him to Pretoria for judgment. The Mayor and several of Rhodes' friends in Kimberley therefore begged of him to stay away from Kimberley as long as it was besieged, but their entreaties fell on deaf ears.

A beleaguered town was not a place for someone as restless as Rhodes, unaccustomed as he was to having his activities curtailed in space and sphere. After having victoriously fought wars on his own in spite of all warnings of the military experts, after he had ruled a large country with almost dictatorial powers, how could he submit, under martial law, to the orders of a military commander of only the rank of a colonel? According to him Rhodes and Kimberley were one. He had 'made the town'. The greater part of the town—De Beers—was his property. Most of its inhabitants were in his employ or were indirectly dependent on him. And the town contained the greatest asset of the Cape

Colony, his diamond mines. It was therefore to be expected that he would feel himself not only responsible for the security of his men and property but also entitled to conduct all the necessary arrangements for the defence of the town.

Rhodes showed clearly that he did not think much of the military qualities of the Commander, Colonel R. G. Kekewich. He had seriously expected at least a general. Already in the early stages of the siege, in preposterous telegrams to Milner and to the Commander-in-Chief, General Sir Redvers Buller, Rhodes had demanded that a strong force for the relief of Kimberley should be put on the march without delay.

As soon as he was settled in Kimberley, Rhodes began to organize the defences. Before any of the military experts he had recognized that the great initial successes of the Boers were the result of strategy based on the great mobility of their troops. Rhodes, at his own expense, bought 1,000 horses and smuggled them through the Boer lines into Kimberley. So as to strengthen the weak garrison he organized mounted volunteer troops which were able to meet the Boers on equal terms, all his men being good riders and splendid shots.

Rhodes, of course, believed that these troops, the Diamond Fields Light Horse and the Kimberley Light Horse, were his own personal guards—regiments which only he, their Honorary Colonel, had the right to dispose. Colonel Kekewich was naturally of a different opinion. The first clash occurred. Others followed. Rhodes had established his own military cabinet, intelligence service, provision-commissariat, hygienic departments, labour corps, armament depots and medical branch, all under his authority without regard to Kekewich's orders. There was a moment when even the calm and gentle Kekewich came very near to having Rhodes court-martialled. No other officer would have stood for an answer such as Rhodes gave him during an argument: 'You military are working only for medals, orders, titles and promotion, but I am working for the people.'

When the military heliograph station was no longer at his disposal, Rhodes made the De Beers engineers build one for his own private use. Previously his messages had been censored; now he could say what he liked. Officers maliciously spread the rumour that Rhodes' telegraph only served his Stock Exchange speculations. These rumours were partly justified: Rhodes, or De Beers, owned all the mines in Kimberley except one. Now, with the guns roaring all around him, he negotiated with the directors by heliograph via Cape Town and succeeded in bringing this last independent diamond mine under his control.

Rhodes did not seem to mind the grenades exploding and the bullets flying around him. Conspicuous in his well-known apparel of light sports jacket and white trousers, and his notorious somewhat soiled large slouch-hat, he served the enemy as an easy target. Nevertheless he took his usual ride outside the fortifications every morning. Later, accompanied only by his secretary, he was often seen to go out on private reconnaissance very near the Boer line, the aim of many Boer snipers whose bullets never went far from their mark. Was he looking out as he had done in the Matabele campaign for the bullet to end his life and thus put a stop to this horrible and frustrating wait for relief to arrive? They were already eating horse-meat in Kimberley. Rhodes organized soup-kitchens, but many people grumbled that he was living far too well himself in the Sanatorium where, it was said, chickens were being kept in bedrooms. His friends advised him to eat publicly at one of his soup-kitchens so as to dispel these rumours. He could not swallow any horse-meat soup, he said, little knowing that it had been his chief nourishment for the last weeks. Once the Kimberley Club's £3,000-a-year chef served the meat of a two-year-old colt to Rhodes as 'grilled prime veal fillet *garni a la siège*'.

A great problem was the Natives in the compounds. Work in the mines had come to a standstill after the first few weeks. If the Natives were dismissed from the compounds a crime wave would sweep the town. Rhodes organized the Natives into road-making gangs. They built the famous Siege Avenue, more than a mile long, which is still the pride of the city.

Kekewich's few light guns were no match for the Boers' heavy Krupp artillery. Rhodes conceived the idea of making heavy guns in the De Beers workshop. Within a short time 'Long Cecil' and 'St Cecilia' began to send their 30-lb shells into the Boer lines. Each bore the inscription 'With C. J. R.'s compliments.' The Boers promptly retaliated with a Krupp 100-pounder. The Krupp guns of the Boers caused great losses in human lives as well as considerable damage to the town. It was Rhodes who had the women and children brought into safety in one of the mines before the military authorities of Kimberley even gave them a thought.

The heavy bombardment, the lack of food and even more the fact that after three months of siege hope of relief was no nearer, although an English force under Lord Methuen was only twenty miles away, frayed everyone's nerves. Rhodes especially suffered under what he called 'Methuen's masterful inactivity'. Kekewich, too, was almost at the end of his tether. But never, even when all seemed hopeless and under Rhodes' constant provocations, did he lose his imperturbability. Rhodes hated this war, or rather the way in which it was being conducted. Interviewed by a young journalist, he burst out:

'People imagine that I am a warlike sort of person. I am not. I do not believe in war. I think so many things should be tried before going to the arbitrament of war. Some of these colonels think that all you have to do is to cry out "Attention!", hold up your sword, and the world will quail before you. Nonsense. I like soldiers like "Chinese" Gordon who went through the Taiping rebellion armed with a walking-stick.'

He would have liked to end the war. It was his firm conviction that 'Kruger was not such an ass as to resist to the end'. Lord Methuen was so near to Kimberley. Why, for heaven's sake, did he not push through? Rhodes sent telegram after telegram to Headquarters, giving military advice, threatening, cajoling, ridiculing. He delivered public speeches, published articles and gave interviews over his heliograph to English papers in which he accused the highest authorities of blundering inefficiency and asked for replacement of the leading generals. At Headquarters Lords Roberts and Kitchener, who knew him, merely smiled. Lord Methuen, however, did not possess as much sense of humour and instructed Colonel Kekewich to 'tell Mr Rhodes that on my entry into Kimberley he and his friends must take their immediate departure'. Kekewich had this dispatch shown to Rhodes, with the result that relations between them were broken off almost altogether.

Kimberley was not far from surrender and Rhodes seriously contemplated personal negotiations with the Boers when it was relieved on 15 February. No one was happier than Kekewich who for five months had had to wage war on two fronts. In his final report to Lord Roberts he complained about Rhodes: 'I have put up with this man as long as possible.' But the General replied dryly: 'I wish you had understood, Colonel, "that man" was a power in Africa and should have been honoured.' Rhodes decided to bury the past and at his instigation the directors of De Beers presented Kekewich with some selected diamonds as a souvenir of the siege.

Work—work—some work to do was what Rhodes wanted. If they would only listen to him the war would be over in a few weeks. They had now followed his example and made the British infantry more mobile. Nevertheless they could not compete in mobility with the Boers. The stumbling-block lay in the cumbersome British provisions system. Advance troops always had to wait until the service corps caught up with them. The Boers carried their provisions, some sticks of *biltong*—sun-dried game meat—in their saddle-bags. Rhodes planned a system whereby the British troops would become more independent of their bases of supply. He telegraphed to Lords Roberts and Kitchener that he was willing to take over the organization of the supply of provisions for the troops provided that 'I have full power and no one to interfere with me. . . . Reply sharp as otherwise I am going to Cape Town.'

They preferred to let him go to Cape Town. There, however, the atmosphere was anything but pleasant. The Afrikaners resented the way Milner was treating them—as if they all were traitors. Civil and military authorities advised Rhodes in the interests of internal peace and of his own safety to leave the Cape as soon as possible. Rhodes went to Rhodesia, where he was far too occupied to take an interest any longer in a war in which they ignored his advice and went from one blunder to the next.

A few months later the picture on the war front had changed. Lord Roberts had seized Pretoria from the retreating Boers. Somewhat prematurely he declared the war over and left to Kitchener what he thought were mopping-up operations. Rhodes was surprised at such ignorance.

An opportunity for venting his opinion on the situation arose when he was called upon as President of the South African League to preside over a meeting in Cape Town to celebrate the victory. His face, stern and grim, showed that he was in no mood to join in the exultant flag-waving and triumphant hurrah-shouting of the assembly which filled only half the hall. Ignoring the ovation, he hurried to the platform and growled at them:

> You think you have beaten the Dutch! But it is not so. The Dutch are not beaten; what is beaten is Krugerism, a corrupt and evil government, no more Dutch in essence than English. No! The Dutch are as vigorous and unconquered today as they have ever been; the country is still as much theirs as it is yours, and you will have to live and work with them hereafter as in the past. . . .

His speech had great repercussions. Milner realized that the war had turned Rhodes the politician into Rhodes the statesman. He and a few others now saw what Rhodes had always preached, that the only possible future for South Africa lay in a reconciliation of the two races by a federal system. Should Rhodes be asked to lead the South African states into a union of a nation? The Raid was not yet forgotten and the memory of Rhodes' betrayal of his Afrikaner friends was still too fresh and painful in their memory. Rhodes went back to Rhodesia. There, he felt, was his place. His mission in South Africa was completed. He had painted the map of South Africa red, British red. On the credit side of the balance sheet he could proudly show that the 250,000 square miles of British territory in Africa had been extended in scarcely twenty years to two million square miles. On the debit side, however, there stood in blood-red letters the expense account which for the Boer War alone amounted to:

British casualties:	7,582 killed	
	13,139 died of disease	
	21,157 wounded	
	1,853 missing	
Boer casualties:	6,000 killed	
	16,000 children	Died in British concentration camps
	4,000 women	
British war costs:	£222,000,000	

CHAPTER XIX

SO MANY WORLDS

W. T. STEAD once remarked: 'The history of South Africa would have been different if Rhodes, Dr Jameson, Beit and Milner had been married men.' The fact that Rhodes remained a bachelor and took no interest in women led to many comments, rumours and insinuations which followed him throughout his life. It was generally accepted that he 'hated women'. Once, when the subject was under discussion, Rhodes remarked casually: 'Women! Of course I don't hate women. I like them, but I don't want them always fussing about.'

Having acquired, as a result of his irregular life, all the habits of a spoilt bachelor, with complete freedom of movement and independence of set household rules, he would have considered a wife only as a disturbance. As a trial his sister Edith once acted as hostess at Groote Schuur. It did not last long and ended in a 'capital row'. Brother and sister were temperamentally too much alike. Rhodes, referring to this brief episode, said: 'Groote Schuur is not big enough for two Rhodes to live there together.' But it had nothing to do, he added, with a dislike of the other sex. The Queen, on his second visit to Windsor, referred to these rumours when she said: 'I've been told, Mr Rhodes, that you are a woman-hater.' Rhodes later claimed to have replied: 'How could I possibly hate a sex to which Your Majesty belongs.'

The gossip-mongers were never busier than at the time when Rhodes, at the height of his career, came to London regularly and the hostesses of Mayfair competed in lionizing him. Some of the society women would not accept a simple 'No' for an answer. One of them used to wait for hours, sitting in her carriage in front of his hotel, to catch him and take him for a triumphal ride to the 'Row'. Rhodes mostly gave her the slip by using a back-door.

Rhodes' mail regularly brought him what is known today as 'fan mail', from more or less hysterical female admirers. The wife of a British officer in China wrote to him with every overseas mail for many years until his death. She told him of her deep love for him, her 'Prince', her 'Emperor', her 'Hero'. Her husband with whom, as she wrote, she lived in happy union did not object to her letters. She signed them by her full name. Anxiously she gave him advice about his health and seemed very worried that he might be overworking. At first Rhodes was flattered, but he never answered her. Later he did not even read her letters. The same fate was dealt out to the ardent love-letters of a London woman, 'Sarah', who, however, was not satisfied with the expression of her platonic affection *par distance*: she beseeched him constantly in the most pleading terms to meet her in Hyde Park.

It was certainly more than his name, his millions and his position that attracted women. One of the few in whose company he felt comfortable, the Duchess of Sutherland, confessed: 'He could conquer hearts as effectually as any beauty that sets herself to subjugate mankind.' And another of his female admirers said: '. . . he had great grey eyes and a smile of singular and persuasive charm . . . like the sun on a granite hill.'

There was only one occasion on which Rhodes showed and expressed an interest in female beauty. During the first Matabele War he and his secretary were riding over the hills when they met Lobengula's youngest daughter, 'the Princess', as Rhodes liked to call her, a girl of sixteen or seventeen with a bronze-coloured, slim, and graceful body and a face of serene nobility. Her name, *N'Tupusela*, could not have been better chosen; it meant 'Rosy Hue in the East before Daybreak'. Rhodes stopped his horse and pointed at the girl whose lithe movements seemed to express a silent music: 'Now, I want you to see my idea of a really beautiful Native girl. . . .' Without pausing, he continued a conversation about a financial transaction.

To the same secretary he once explained, without any introduction, his flushed face indicating how the subject embarrassed him:

'You may ask why I never married, and do you know? I answer you very fairly that I have not yet seen the woman whom I could get on in the same house with.'

The question—or was it the rumours about his misogyny that worried him?—seemed to occupy him a great deal. To another of his secretaries he gave a different explanation:

'I know everybody asks why I do not marry. I cannot get married. I have too much work on my hands. I should always be away from home and should not be able to do my duty as a husband towards my wife. A married man should be at home and give the attention and advice which a wife expects from a husband.'

For the same reason, that of a dual loyalty, Rhodes wanted only young unmarried men as secretaries. As soon as they married he transferred them to one of his companies. He considered their marriage as an act of disloyalty. At the wedding of one of his secretaries he congratulated the bride by saying: 'I am very jealous of you!' When another secretary became engaged he barked at the bridegroom: 'I hate people getting married; they simply become machines, and have no ideas beyond their respective spouses and offspring.'

Experienced medical men among his friends, such as Dr Jameson and Dr Smartt, must have realized that the origin of Rhodes' heart-disease excluded the possibility of his ever getting married. All of them were therefore not a little astonished when they noticed shortly before the Matabele War that Rhodes was taking a deep interest in a pretty eighteen-year-old girl who had just left school, Maria Elizabeth Schickerling. It seemed obvious that Rhodes was in fact courting the girl. She was often asked to Groote Schuur with her parents; he frequently sent her presents of flowers and chocolates and once a beautiful ebony-topped glove-box. Rhodes took her to the theatre several times, but the shy girl would not go alone with him, always bringing along a sister or a cousin as chaperon. It seemed clear that Rhodes wanted to marry her and her parents appeared to favour the match. Maria Elizabeth, however, had more sense than her parents and did not believe in the possibility of marital happiness between a man of forty and a girl less than half his age. It is questionable whether Rhodes really had matrimonial intentions. Probably he was only temporarily fascinated by the youth, the beauty and the naïvety of a well-brought-up young lady.

True friendship based on mutual esteem linked him for almost a quarter of a century to an old lady, Mrs Maria Margaretha Koopmans-De Wet, who was generally acknowledged as the 'Uncrowned Queen of South Africa'. She came of an old Dutch family which had been established in the town as merchants for more than two centuries. After the death of her husband she had taken over her family's old residence in Strand Street overlooking the bay. There she ruled as the centre of a new Afrikaner culture which had been reared on the old Dutch civilization of the Cape. Her position as a living link between the old and the new culture attracted to her *salon* everyone of significance in the Colony's cultural, political or social life. For sixty years Mrs Koopmans-De Wet acted as unofficial political adviser to Ministers, Governors and diplomats, as *mater confessor*, oracle and judge. President Kruger was a personal friend, as were Hofmeyr, Schreiner and Sauer. Young Smuts sat at her feet and listened with wide eyes to the old woman's wise and prophetic words, many of which were later to come true.

Hofmeyr introduced Rhodes to the Koopmans *salon* just after he had been elected to Parliament. At first the old lady was a little baffled by this young man from the Kimberley diggings who seemed to have a patent solution for every South African problem. She did not keep back her own opinions. Often she told him that as yet he knew nothing of South Africa: 'It takes five years to become acclimatized to South Africa; another five years to like it; and another five years to know it.' Rhodes kept surprisingly quiet when Mrs Koopmans-De Wet lectured to him or scolded him. She liked him, however, because she was convinced of the sincerity of his intention to reconcile the two races. She had great respect for his intellect, except for the disturbing predominance of his materialism against which she persistently put up a battle.

Rhodes grew so accustomed to her 'telling him home-truths' that when he became Prime Minister he often consulted her before making important decisions. It was often difficult for her to follow him in his political meanderings or to approve of his strange company of satellites. Gradually she found it almost impossible to understand his motives. Nevertheless she never ceased to defend him against the increasing number of his critics.

Then came the Raid. When Mrs Koopmans heard about Rhodes' loneliness and the danger that he might harm himself, she let him know that she expected him to come and see her. For three hours they were closeted together in Mrs Koopmans' private sitting-room. Neither of them ever disclosed what was said during the interview. Eye-witnesses, however, reported that when he left Mrs Koopmans' house, there appeared for the first time in many days the old gleam in Rhodes' eyes though they looked as if tears had reddened them.

Though the intimacy of their friendship had come to an end, she retained her respect for Rhodes as a man until the end, while he still held her in high esteem.

Rhodes' strange friendship with Olive Schreiner lasted for only a few years. It ended in hatred. Olive Schreiner's hatred, however, was only love in a different key. Everything that Nature had bestowed on this genius of a woman—'the only person of genius that any of the Colonies has produced'—every episode of her life, her very existence, was contradictory.

The contradiction in her intellect was partly due to hereditary influences. Jewish blood pulsated in her veins, which was derived from her mother's side though dating back several generations. There was indeed something of the fighting spirit of the Old Testament prophets in this little woman. And fight was what she did all her life.

It was her misfortune to have been brought up in Darkest Africa where no humanitarian feelings were squandered on Natives and where the battle for survival between men and the beasts of the veld was still in progress. A mission station did not give an anaemic young girl the necessary sense of realism with which to accommodate herself to such a life. The realism of frontier life was met in the house of her parents by pious hymns and Wesleyan prayers, supplemented by German fairy-tales and German Romantic poetry. In young Olive's impressionable mind there arose the first contradiction: the Bible mixed with the sensual German romanticism fomented dissension in her brain.

When to this strange intoxicating concoction was added the sobering medicine of Spencer's 'relativity of knowledge' as served in his *First Principles*, and when into a famished intellect was poured Darwin, Gibbon and Buckle, it is not surprising that out of the little mission house there stepped a revolutionist. She thirsted for freedom. She wanted to live her own life. For the young governess who for a pittance of £30 a year had to teach children on lonely farms there was little hope of realizing such wish-dreams. She needed an antidote to the sedate routine of her life. She procured it for herself. In the first man she met she already saw her redeemer, according to the pattern of Grimm's fairy-tales. All the sentimentality of the German Romantics she poured into her love. It did not take much disillusionment to sober her up and bring her to a state of psychological conflict, after which she had in fact been hankering.

Olive wanted to break out of the prison of her ego. The newly awakened spirit within her was to conjure out of her intellect a new, a fantastic existence by the magic of pen and paper.

Here she could say everything she did not dare to mention in South Africa's narrow-minded atmosphere: she gave account to herself of the realities which she had not previously had the courage to face; she expressed her longing for liberty, for love and for the warmth of companionship with such realism that she wondered at it herself; she lived her life over again with full consciousness of her sins, her faults and her failings; and she lived her future life as she would like to live it, pouring into it all her lusts, her desires, her hopes and her expectations; she accused herself and at the same time defended her actions; she wanted to be free, not only free from the manacles of conventional lies, but free from herself;—she filled page after page.

When she went to England to stay with one of her brothers she took the neatly wrapped manuscript along with her. George Meredith as reader of a London publishing house recognized her great literary talent: twenty-four-year-old Olive Schreiner became world-famous in 1883 as the author of the sensational book *The Story of an African Farm*, the topic of conversation in the literary *salons*, the drawing-rooms and the cafés of three continents. Olive Schreiner was celebrated by English, American, French, German and Russian critics as the champion of women's rights, as the courageous propagandist of 'free love' and the brave bearer of the testimony of Agnosticism.

Her unexpected fame carried in itself the contradiction in her literary value. The plot of her story is feeble; its construction shows the inexperienced beginner; most of her figures are drawn from cliché patterns; and her philosophy, courageous as are her thoughts, does not fit into the frame. The greatness of her work lies in the beauty of the language with which she paints the extraordinary atmosphere of the South African landscape. In her lyricism can be felt the influence of the German Romantics. Her language sometimes had the simple forcefulness of the Old

Testament. And some passages recall the poetry of the Evangelists. Above all, the perfectly worded ending has never been surpassed.

Her fame brought her in contact with many literary celebrities. W. T. Stead called her 'the categorical imperative in petticoats'. He introduced her to the circle of his friends, where she was approached by a young *littérateur* of her own age. Havelock Ellis, the scion of a seafaring family, had recently taken up the study of medicine, not so much with the aim of curing disease as to investigate the mystery of sex. He recognized the contradictions in Olive Schreiner's nature which, in spite of her strength and 'for all her keen vision of the external world', could rarely adjust itself to the surroundings. He experienced a tantalizing crazy love for her. Only after he had at last been cured of his passion did he realize that behind the iron façade of her intellectualism there lay 'a child, a trustful, idealizing, imaginative, helpless child'.

Olive Schreiner feared nothing and no one more than herself. She would rather fight against Nature than succumb to her passionate temperament. She was afraid of losing herself in passion. In the naïvety of her maidenish romanticism she believed that she could sublimate sex by platonic sentimentality. Olive Schreiner, the apostle of 'free love', tortured poor Ellis for years by refusing him her body. She even expected the poor young healthy man to 'control the animal in him' when sharing the same room with her on holiday travels. Once she wrote to him: 'When passion enters into a relationship it does spoil the holy sweetness.' The thirty-year-old woman ran away from sex. And she openly confessed her fear to Ellis: 'In that you are myself, I love you, and am near to you, but in that you are a man I am afraid of you, I shrink from you.'

Such madness could not last, but it went on for five years. The only profit that Ellis gained from this nerve-racking love-affair was interesting studies for his *Psychology of Sex*. Olive's health was failing under the English climate, and frequent attacks of asthma made a permanent stay in the dry atmosphere of the Karroo imperative. She returned to South Africa. She lived in a small cottage in the lonely village of Matjesfontein, where besides her work there was no distraction other than to watch the Cape Town trains to Kimberley and to the Rand at the little station.

Olive Schreiner, who had been active in England's Liberal

movement, took a great interest in the politics of the Cape. In her admiration for Rhodes, who was about to take over the Colony's Premiership, she found herself for a time in full accord with her family. Her mother had elevated the 'Colossus' to a household-saint to whom and for whom she prayed. Poor little 'Mamsie', tired and resigned, had found peace in Catholicism and rest for her body and soul in a little convent cell. Will Schreiner, now a Minister in Rhodes' Cabinet, led the family in the hymns of praise to his new friend.

Here was a figure after Olive's own romantic heart: adventurer, pioneer, discoverer of hidden fortunes, a Croesus, one who 'thinks in continents', a man of action, a friend to the poor—— Was he not like a knight in shining armour from one of Papa's German fairy books? To a friend she confessed: 'I feel a curious and almost painfully intense interest in the man and his career.'

She went to the House to hear him speak in 1890. Her heart was in flames. To her brother Will she opened wide the sluices of her heart: 'It's not love, it's not admiration . . . it's not that I think him noble or good . . . it's the deliberate feeling "that man belongs to me". . . .'

In November 1890 they met for the first time. Rhodes' train stopped at the little Karroo station for an hour to allow the passengers to dine. He recognized her as she stood on the platform by her resemblance to her brother Will: a tiny, rather stoutish woman—'a big person in a small compass', as the man who later became her husband gallantly expressed it, or, as she described herself, 'a tall person cut short'.

Rhodes and Olive Schreiner resembled each other in many respects, besides that of being often taken for Jews. Just like Rhodes she had received her first enlightenment on the evolutionary facts of life with the shock of a child whose belief in Father Christmas is suddenly destroyed. Darwin gave both of them intellectual indigestion. The idea of Evolution widened their horizons with such vehemence that they lost their way in the labyrinth of Materialism. Into their adult life they dragged the heavy load of shattered ideals. They never surmounted the storms and upheavals of their puberty completely. They could not rid themselves of their juvenile romanticism which upset the harmony of their minds. Just like Rhodes, Olive's mentality and actions were influenced by her ill-health. The irregular working of his heart and the disorder of her respiratory organs created a permanent tension in them which they tried to overcome by accelerated activity.

The thoughts of these two people rotated round South Africa. They both loved the country. Yet Rhodes never changed and never wanted to change from being thoroughly English. England remained his 'home'. He felt happy in South Africa because he liked the landscape, the people with their easy manners and the open-air life. And he loved South Africa because the country had dealt kindly with him. But his love for South Africa came nowhere near the Roman cosmopolitan maxim of *Ubi bene, ibi patria*. Olive Schreiner loved South Africa as a child loves its mother, seeing everything in it as the most beautiful on earth. South Africa was a part, the most essential part, of her emotional and intellectual make-up. And she felt that she was a component of this country: Boer, English or Native were for her not members of a different race or language group but all South Africans. That which Rhodes aspired to achieve by the political means of a Federation was in her mind already a fact, in spite of state boundaries. 'I learnt to love the Boer; but more, I learnt to admire him', she said; and she meant it because she also saw his faults.

Though they differed widely in many spheres of their mentality there remained sufficient points of contact for a friendship based on mutual admiration. Olive Schreiner, with her higher intelligence, recognized the chasm between them but believed that it was only because 'our friends are so different that we could never become close friends'. When she asked Rhodes why he surrounded himself with friends of that kind he lost his temper and almost shouted at her: 'Those men my friends! They are not my friends! They are my tools, and when I have done with them, I throw them away!' Nevertheless she found him 'even higher and nobler than [she] had expected'.

They walked together over the purple veld and Rhodes became infected with the 'sense of wild exhilaration and freedom' which Olive always found in the breezy Karroo. Olive rejoiced at finding Rhodes not the 'huge hard-headed man of the world' she had expected but 'so curiously like a little child, that one feels so tender to him'. He spoke to her about her *African Farm* with an intelligence and enthusiasm such as no one, in her opinion, had ever shown before in talking about her work. It was no empty compliment which he paid her: the book was always on his bedside-table and among the few which he took on his travels. Before he had met Olive Schreiner, Rhodes had told friends that the book had 'enraptured him again and again and again', that it was 'a work of profound genius'.

Later when Rhodes described this first conversation with Olive Schreiner, he said: 'She has me on her brain', but he was not sure whether the reason was political or personal. He told her bluntly that 'after this book that was her own life anything else she wrote would be mere twaddle'. Olive replied angrily that she had plenty more books planned but was reluctant to 'reveal her innermost thoughts to the public'. Rhodes interrupted her: 'That's nonsense, you've done it already.'

They parted as good friends. When in Cape Town she was a frequent and welcome guest at Groote Schuur and every time disregarding all rules of precedence, Rhodes would ask the male guest of honour to take her in to dinner, or he himself would act as her table partner. People often remarked on the fact that Olive Schreiner was the only person who could make Rhodes listen quietly for any length of time.

Her romantic ideas about the 'man of genius' could not fail to suffer disillusionment upon closer acquaintance. While she retained her 'strong personal admiration for Rhodes' genius' she soon began to express her 'strong detestation of his methods', especially his attitude towards Natives. It came as a shock to her when he told her one day at the dinner-table: 'I prefer land to niggers.' Though she often censured him harshly and, as W. T. Stead called it, 'expended no small portion of her vast resources of vituperative eloquence upon Rhodes', she never allowed anyone to belittle Rhodes or even to question his greatness. To such a critic she once exclaimed: 'Great man? Of course he is! Who ever denied that?'

She published her revised opinion of Rhodes in a series of parables in which she pretended that 'it came to pass that Cecil Rhodes died'. The Devil claimed him. However, the gates, doors and windows of Hell proved all too small to take Rhodes in. The *Bon Dieu*, hearing the commotion, asked for the reason. The Devil explained that he had tried every way but could not get Cecil Rhodes into Hell: 'He is too big!' 'Ah,' said the *Bon Dieu*, 'then, I suppose Cecil must come here after all.'

In view of Olive Schreiner's temperament, it seems not unlikely that personal factors were, if not the main, at least contributory reasons for her final rupture with Rhodes. Towards 1893 rumours were heard that Rhodes was engaged to marry Olive Schreiner.

Full of indignation, Olive denied that there was any truth in it. All she wanted, she told a friend, was to have a 'mother's friendship', where men 'come and tell me their troubles and feelings'. She declined to discuss her relations with Rhodes even with her best friends, because, if 'such a beautiful thing has happened to a human being that they absolutely love another soul it must seem a terrible desecration to have other human beings finding it out and discussing it'.

No, Olive Schreiner refused to say anything more on the subject. It seems probable, however, that Cecil Rhodes, though he had no objections to receiving the adoration of a famous authoress, and though he liked her company and found her useful as an intellectual ornament to Groote Schuur, would not allow himself to be 'mothered' by her or permit her to interfere with his private life, his business or his politics. Neither does it seem likely that he would accept the role of romantic lover in a platonic love intrigue. Perhaps he took the longing for 'mother's friendship' of this almost forty-year-old eternal flapper as an attempt to catch him in the meshes of matrimony. Whenever Rhodes suspected even the slightest attempts in that direction he broke off all connections immediately. The rumours about an engagement could not have failed to reach his ears. Thereafter he saw very little of Olive Schreiner.

Olive Schreiner grew ever more censorious of Rhodes. The Matabele War and Lobengula's tragic end, Rhodes' intensified propaganda campaign against Kruger, the conditions in Rhodesia and his almost dictatorial rule in the Cape offered sufficient fuel for her attacks. She found a helpful and enthusiastic ally in a young farmer, Samuel Cronwright, who expressed his liberal ideas in a provincial newspaper in forceful 'leaders'. After two years of wooing, the forty-year-old spinster married the young man eight years her junior, who adopted the name of Cronwright-Schreiner.

Their common antagonism towards Rhodes formed the firmest link in this strange union. Both saw in him the greatest enemy to peace in South Africa. Rhodes' attempts to 'square' Cronwright-Schreiner when he brought his political propaganda campaign into Kimberley, the very heart of Rhodes' domain, was, as we have seen, doomed to failure.

After the shock of the sudden death of her only child, which was suffocated in its mother's bed a few weeks after its birth, Olive Schreiner's health deteriorated rapidly. She became harder, harsher and more vehement. The 'child in her' disappeared and instead there came to the surface the doctrinal, hard-hitting, intolerant intellectual Valkyrie. The Schreiner family was split into camps. The mother continued to see Rhodes as a superman. Will Schreiner was proud of his friendship with Rhodes. Those who were for Cecil Rhodes were, she decreed, against Olive Schreiner. Thus she sacrificed her family to her hatred for Rhodes.

When the Jameson Raid confirmed her damnatory opinion of Rhodes she felt no sense of triumph. Tempting offers for critical articles on Rhodes and the Raid reached her from large newspapers and magazines all over the world. Though she needed the money badly she declined without hesitation to profit by Rhodes' downfall: 'I attacked Rhodes frankly and fearlessly and endlessly when he was in power, and therefore I can afford to be quiet now. . . . My feelings are a strange mixture of intense personal sympathy with Rhodes in his downfall, and an almost awful sense of relief that the terrible power which was threatening to crush all South Africa is broken. . . . It is too terrible to think of what the results would have been if Jameson had not been defeated.'

The Raid had wrecked once and for all the idealized picture of the fairy-tale prince which Olive Schreiner had painted for herself before she had met Rhodes. The end had come. She did not thirst for revenge. As a conclusion to this disappointing chapter she had to justify herself to her own conscience. Years ago he had told her that anything she might write after *The Story of an African Farm* would be 'mere twaddle'. Now she would show him that Olive Schreiner still had something to say to the world. She sat down and wrote a book to show the monster Rhodes to the world —and to herself. *Trooper Peter Halket* appeared in London in 1897 just when the Parliamentary Inquiry was in session. Even Rhodes' opponents disapproved of the moment chosen for its publication. The book caused a sensation not only because it accused Rhodes of the murder, rape, theft and torture committed by Chartered Company troops in Matabeleland but because of its frontispiece, a repulsive picture omitted in later editions, of three hanged Natives dangling from trees. It was an unmitigated condemnation of Rhodes as a man, a politician and a colonizer.

The last woman to cross Rhodes' path was so extraordinary that he failed to understand her until it was too late. Princess Catherine Maria Radziwill, *née* Countess Rzewuski, came of an old Polish family. At the age of fifteen she was married to Prince Radziwill whose family ranked among the leading aristocrats of three countries. The prince belonged to the junior branch whose members had no money of their own but were kept by the head of the house. Catherine Radziwill, through her name, her ravishing youthful beauty and her intelligence, soon became a greatly admired member of the court in Berlin where the young couple occupied the family palace in the Wilhelmstrasse. She became a friend of the old Kaiser and the Empress and later attached herself to Queen Victoria's eldest daughter, the consort of Crown Prince Frederick. She associated not only with the crowned heads of Europe and with famous statesmen, but also with socialist agitators, artists, circus riders, authors and journalists. Her linguistic talent which enabled her to converse in five languages—Russian, Polish, German, French and English—made her *salon* a cosmopolitan rendezvous.

Princess Catherine's curiosity thirsted for a wider knowledge of the world. Her temperament demanded an outlet for her manifold though superficial interests. She loved to talk and especially to gossip and found a rich field of activity for her garrulity at the Berlin court. In this hotbed of intrigue, the Russian Princess had sufficient opportunity to acquaint herself with international politics. She herself took an active part in it by reporting interesting details to the Tzar. Bismarck, who was still in full power at the time, soon found out that this Russian princess was working against him and an indiscreet novel which she wrote about Berlin court life offered him a welcome pretext to have her banished from the Berlin court.

Princess Radziwill began to travel. It was said that she toured Europe in the company of a circus rider. The allowance which she received from the Radziwill family could not cover her extravagances. Pawnbrokers and money-lenders became regular visitors to her rooms. She flitted from one town to the other, from one country to the next. Everywhere she succeeded in forcing her way into political circles after the aristocratic *salons* had been closed to her. Politics from being a hobby became an obsession with her. She believed that she was destined to play a leading rôle in international affairs.

The Princess had no inhibitions. Those whom she wanted to meet she managed to meet somehow. Her greatest efforts were directed at becoming acquainted with the millionaire rulers of the financial world. Such friendships, she had discovered, brought many advantages: one dined and wined well in their homes; the hospitality of their country seats provided a cheap holiday in luxury; they all loved to show their importance by dropping useful tips for the share market. Their share tips one could hawk to other people and thus establish one's position as a prophetess.

There was one person whom she had not been able to ensnare in spite of prolonged efforts. Only once did she succeed in obtaining an invitation to a dinner party in Rhodes' honour, but she failed to gain his attention.

During the second Matabele campaign when Rhodes was camping on the veld, his secretary one day handed him a thick blue envelope which bore a large embossed crown and was marked 'private'. When he opened the letter, a small Russian gold coin dropped out. Rhodes had to read through the communication twice before he could understand it. The coat of arms and the large crown startled him. Princess Radziwill? Who on earth was Princess Radziwill? His secretary reminded him that she had often called at the Burlington Hotel but he had not wished to receive her.

A strange letter: she wrote that she was 'blessed or cursed with the gift of second sight' and had had a foreboding that his life, a life so precious to the British Empire, to the future of South Africa and also to his many admirers—to whom she was proud to belong—was in danger as an attempt on it would be made within the next six months. She asked him to accept the enclosed gold coin as a talisman. With Matabele warriors lying in ambush for him behind every tree it was not difficult, Rhodes decided, to predict danger to his life even if one was not blessed with the supernatural faculties of a Cassandra. He told his secretary to thank the lady in the usual form and, occupied as he was with more important matters, he immediately forgot about her.

He was reminded of her existence again a few months later

when he received another letter. This time she asked him for advice as to how she should invest a recent inheritance of £150,000. It was more likely that the Princess at the time did not own even 150,000 farthings, as she was considerably in debt. Rhodes, though he rarely used a pen, answered the letter personally. A real princess, and one who apparently owned some money, could not be given an answer through a secretary. He declined to give advice, carefully explaining that experience had taught him how people when they had luck forgot to thank him and when his tips proved wrong blamed him for their losses.

When Rhodes left London for South Africa in 1900 he was exhausted. His business had detained him longer than he had planned, so that he had had to postpone his departure five times. The Union Line always made great efforts to provide this eminent passenger with all possible amenities and the greatest comfort in absolute privacy. At his departure, an official representative of the ship's company found it necessary to inform him that a Princess Radziwill had inquired several times at their London office by which ship Mr Rhodes was travelling, but that of course they had refused to give any information. She must have learnt about it from other sources, however, because every time Mr Rhodes cancelled his booking so did the Princess, until finally she booked her passage on this ship. Of course her request to have a cabin next to that of Mr Rhodes' suite had been refused, since as usual the whole wing of the deck had been reserved for Mr Rhodes and his party. Also as usual, it had been arranged for Mr Rhodes to use the captain's deck, and in the dining-saloon the usual corner partition had been reserved for him and his party.

They had just finished the fish course when the door was thrown open and in swept Princess Radziwill. Dramatically she paused at the door. Her entrance, as well as her whole appearance, was obviously designed to cause a sensation, though her elegance was a little outmoded and just on the verge of being shop-worn. Her approach was heralded by a dense cloud of perfume and the sound of rustling silk, brocade and taffeta, as though to warn men to be on their guard. According to her own calculations she was just over forty, but, in spite of her cosmetic and sartorial efforts, there remained sufficient evidence of her real age which was nearer fifty.

With a studied expression of bored unconcern she glanced over the dining-saloon. When she saw Rhodes in a corner she put on an exaggerated act of sheer surprise and restrained joy. Before Rhodes had a chance to prepare himself against her menacing intrusion she stood beside him. He could not help offering her a chair. Though—on his instructions—it was pointed out to her that another table had been reserved for her, she took all her meals at Rhodes' table.

At first Rhodes was interested in her conversation. She had come well prepared. The weeks of waiting for her departure she had spent in reading up everything available on South Africa and Rhodes, so that he should consider her well informed and sharing his opinions. During the first few days he was amused by her stories. She took his interest for encouragement and began to discuss delicate subjects with such frankness that Rhodes was often made to blush. She told him about a cruel husband who was ruining her life so that she had decided to save herself by a separation. It would take a long time to procure a divorce and she therefore wanted to spend a year in South Africa.

These confidences made Rhodes feel uneasy. His embarrassment reached its climax when one day the Princess fainted into his arms. Helplessly Rhodes had to hold the 200-odd pounds of aristocratic flesh until his secretary came to his rescue. For the rest of the journey Rhodes took his meals in his private saloon.

She came to Groote Schuur so often that Rhodes frequently had to hide, and when at the end of 1900 he returned from Rhodesia he was pestered again by her ambuscades. In the meanwhile she had started a political journal, *Greater Britain*, which Rhodes had helped to finance. When her paper quoted remarks which he had uttered casually at table, he declined to discuss politics any longer with her or in her presence. The Princess, however, still tried to draw him into political discussions until finally he had to raise his voice and tell her that she would have to stay away from his house if she did not comply with his wishes.

In Rhodesia, shortly before Rhodes left for England in July 1901, his doctor and friend Dr Scholtz told him that the Princess was in financial difficulties, owing about £3,000. Rhodes told him to pay her debts as well as her fare to England and asked him to see that she left South Africa as soon as possible. The Princess, however, stayed on in Cape Town. She still pretended to be on the best of terms with Rhodes. Knowing that the surest and quickest way of making a rumour public property was to confide in another woman under the seal of secrecy, she whispered to her best friend that Rhodes, when in Cape Town, came to see her every night in her hotel room, entering the hotel in disguise by a secret passage. A few days later she confessed to the same friend, again in greatest confidence, that she was engaged to marry Rhodes but that they both wished to postpone the official announcement until a later date. Not long afterwards she consulted her friend as to which rooms she should occupy at Groote Schuur.

Rhodes, who knew nothing about the calumnies spread by the Princess, arrived in London in July 1901. His friends were shocked when they saw him: death was plainly written on his face. His doctors were anxious to get him out of the heat of London into a cooler climate. He himself felt ill. The pain in his chest never stopped and made breathing difficult. He often sat up whole nights. During the day Rhodes forgot his ailment. He worked as hard as ever.

Once, when Dr Jameson examined him, Rhodes asked him: 'At any rate, Jameson, death from the heart is clean and quick, there is nothing repulsive or lingering about it; it is a clean death, isn't it?'

Dr Jameson was by no means a soft man, but he had to turn away quickly so as not to show his embarrassment. 'Yes, of course—of course,' he replied and allowed his words to sound as casual as possible.

Finally his doctors succeeded in persuading him to take a long rest. He hired a shooting-lodge in Perthshire, to which he invited his friends, Jameson, Beit, Maguire and others. Among the guests one week-end was a young red-haired former Hussar lieutenant who had made a name for himself as a war correspondent and through a courageous escape from a Boer war-prisoners' camp. His name was Winston Spencer Churchill. Though only in his middle twenties this young man entertained the whole party by his witty stories, quick repartee and inexhaustible humour. Rhodes, though he had disliked the father, became very fond of the son, admiring his sparkling intellect, his energy and his zeal, 'powers which,' Rhodes said, 'in conjunction with his dash and "go", must inevitably bring him to the front'.

In October 1901 Rhodes together with Beit, Jameson, Metcalfe and his secretaries travelled to the Continent. It was Rhodes' first pleasure trip. Besides Brussels and Berlin he knew no other towns. They first went to Paris, where he felt well enough to spend many hours visiting museums which he enjoyed immensely. Next he and his party motored to the South of Italy, after short stops at Lucerne and Venice. In Florence they stayed for several days. It was Rhodes' first experience of travelling in a motor-car and the speed gave him a boyish pleasure.

On his way to and from Beira Rhodes had often passed through the Suez Canal and every time he had said that the next time he would spend a few weeks in Egypt. He now travelled from Cairo up the Nile. During the journey he talked for hours about Egyptian history. The Pharaohs he admired because many of them, like true 'men of action', had taken up the fight against Nature to save their nation from destruction by famine. He was impressed by the ancient irrigation works, especially by the Nile dam at Assuan, which he compared with his plans to provide water for the sun-drenched thirsty soil of Rhodesia.

His mind wandered down to his own South African domain. By now he had probably admitted to himself that the discovery of the Land of Ophir, of a new Rand reef, would always remain no more than a 'dream'. One would possibly find other, less valuable minerals, such as copper and coal there which were already being mined in paying quantities. He consoled himself with the thought that the future of the country would depend largely on its agricultural products. A rich soil was there and a suitable climate, sufficient and cheap labour and a good transport system. Rhodesia might easily become the granary and cattle-kraal of the Empire. And Rhodes, who regarded agriculture as an industry like any other productive enterprise, had realized that in order to grow crops or rear cattle, one had to employ scientific methods and invest a lot of money before profits could be reaped. He wrote regularly to his farm managers in Rhodesia, always giving them exact orders on how to proceed with the next crop. He sent them several bags of Egyptian maize after he had noticed that it grew there with a minimum of water and under conditions very similar to those in Rhodesia. These samples of maize grew exceptionally well on Rhodesian soil and have since become the standard crop there.

When Rhodes saw a team of donkeys plodding along the tow-path of the Nile, he compared them with the far weaker though larger Rhodesian breed. He selected thirty stallions to be crossed with the Rhodesian donkey and the result, still noticeable today, shows Rhodes' great foresight.

In spite of the warm weather Rhodes did not tire of sight-seeing, especially among the excavated ruins. He loved Egypt. One evening, sitting on the terrace of his hotel in Cairo, he told his friends that he could find true happiness in the peace and pure atmosphere of the desert where, in the shadow of the Pyramids, he would forget the dirt and accusations flung at him. He closed his eyes and, speaking softer and slower than he had ever done before, he painted an almost poetic picture of the quiet loveliness of the Nile.

Every day, as they travelled south, the Egyptian December sun became stronger until the heat and the flies, mosquitoes and other loathsome insects made the journey most unpleasant. Rhodes' improved health began to deteriorate again so rapidly that Dr Jameson insisted on an immediate return to England. Rhodes' repeated heart-attacks were not improved by cabled reports from Cape Town informing him that promissory bills bearing his endorsement and the signature of the Princess Radziwill had been negotiated there.

Rhodes immediately cabled instructions to his Cape Town manager to insert advertisements in all the papers warning people that he had never signed any bills and would not be responsible for them.

In January 1902 he arrived in London. All signs that he had benefited by his holiday had vanished. A great deal of work as well as excitement and annoyance awaited him. His health broke down completely. It was the first time that his energy proved insufficient to overcome the weakness of his heart. He became even more impatient than usual when his doctors confined him to bed. For the pettiest reasons he jumped out of bed, ran across the room and swore and shouted until he fell into a chair exhausted and doubled up from the tantalizing pains in his chest. Whoever dared to argue with him would immediately have a cascade of curses poured over him. Those who differed with him on any point were 'up to mischief'. He could not bear to be kept waiting. If he ordered refreshments and they were not brought to him within a minute or two his face became distorted and black with rage.

If his friends arrived only a few minutes after the appointed time he felt neglected and almost ready to cry. To Dr Jameson he complained: 'A third of your life is lost in waiting for people who fail to keep their appointments and trying to find out if your friends are telling the truth.'

With the object of removing Rhodes as quickly as possible from London, where he only insisted on exerting himself in spite of his serious condition, Dr Jameson advised him to buy a country estate. Thus Rhodes became the squire of the old Dalham Hall estate near Newmarket which he bought unseen from photographs. He made his final decision as soon as he saw in the game book that 1,700 partridges had been shot there in the first four days of the season. To Jameson he said jokingly that he had 'dotted the earth with resting houses, having a shooting-box in Scotland, his country place near Newmarket, his two farms in Rhodesia, his fruit-farm in the Cape Western Province, his little house in Kimberley, his suite in the Burlington Hotel and, of course, Groote Schuur. And all I'll soon need,' he continued, 'as that damned rude fellow said, will be a place six foot by four—six foot by four—six . . .'

Preparations were already being made for Rhodes to take up residence at Dalham Hall when news came from Cape Town that again promissory notes bearing Rhodes' endorsement, to a total value of about £25,000, had been negotiated by Princess Radziwill. She had succeeded in having most of them discounted. Those who had advanced money to the Princess against these bills now sued Rhodes when they found that his endorsement was not honoured.

Rhodes fumed with rage. He immediately decided to leave for Cape Town so as to be present at court. Dr Jameson and other friends tried to dissuade him from exposing himself to the heat of a Cape summer, but Rhodes would not hear of asking permission to give evidence on commission in London, fearing that an admission of his state of health would seriously affect the share market.

'Damn that woman! Why can't she leave me alone?' he groaned and, clutching his chest, he sighed: 'I know it will upset me. The heat of Egypt bowled me over, and to go back to the Cape now that the hot weather has set in is more than I can stand. Look at my pulse! . . .' A last attempt was made to have the case postponed until cooler weather set in, but reports from Cape Town indicated that a postponement would be regarded as an admission that Rhodes was afraid to face the music. Rhodes shouted: 'Me afraid of facing the music? Me afraid! Of course I'll face the music; damn that woman!' Friends tried to tell him that after all £25,000 was a comparatively paltry amount which he should rather forgo than endanger his health. He replied: 'It's not the money, but no risk will prevent me clearing my character of any stain in connection with that woman.'

On 16 January 1902 Rhodes together with Dr Jameson and some members of his staff left for Cape Town. The day after his arrival the civil case against Rhodes for payment of the bills came up in court. Rhodes was able to prove that he had never signed any bill and demonstrated that his signature had been forged with the help of tracing paper. The Princess, who was called as witness, did not appear. Rhodes won the case.

Rhodes' legal friends immediately advised him to institute criminal proceedings for forgery and fraud against the Princess, but he declared firmly that he was not interested in having her prosecuted. The Public Prosecutor, however, had already taken up the case *ex officio* and the next day the Princess was arrested, but admitted to bail.

When the preliminary examination began in the Magistrate's Court the next day the Princess sent in a medical certificate excusing her absence. The magistrate decided to hold court in the cottage which she had rented in Muizenberg.

Rhodes, called as a witness, repeated that he had not signed any bills and that the letters used by the Princess to convince people of the incredible fact that he should have given her a number of blank promissory notes to be filled in by her for any amount required, were forgeries.

The Princess seemed to be blissfully unaware of her precarious situation. Haughtily she looked through her lorgnette at the lawyers and witnesses, giggled into her lace handkerchief or talked happily to her solicitor. The forgeries she had committed were of such infantile clumsiness that one wondered how anyone could have believed in the genuineness of the bills and letters. One of her silly artifices had been to send herself telegrams in the name of Rhodes' London lawyers, for which purpose she had bribed a telegraph boy to alter the name of the Cape Town sending-office to read London E.C.2. Probably the men who discounted the bills, at the enormous rate of 40 per cent, thought that Rhodes would pay them in the end so as not to be involved in a scandal.

Taking her cue from the case of the mysterious telegrams at the Committee of Inquiry, Princess Radziwill claimed that she had in her possession discreet letters and confidential documents which referred to Rhodes and Milner. In the interest of the British Empire, she could not reveal them though they would prove her innocence beyond a doubt. She had acted, she said, not only with the consent of Mr Rhodes, but in his interests in order to save his reputation. Mr Rhodes, she maintained, was only being misled by his friends who wanted to destroy her because she knew too much.

Poor Princess Radziwill! Up to her neck in debt and with all her credit exhausted, she had taken these desperate steps in the hope that Rhodes would not let her down. What was £25,000 to a man who possessed millions? And now he was allowing his jealous minions to influence him to be 'so nasty' to her. The prosecutor and magistrate, too, were being 'awfully rude' to a lady of her rank, making such a fuss about some little stories she told them as though a woman in trouble wasn't allowed to tell a few little white lies. If they would only communicate with the Tsar or her friend the Kaiser; if only her brother were at home—if only they would give her some time. It would be so easy to get this ridiculous amount of £25,000—not quite 250,000 roubles, a sum which a Rzewuski would think nothing of betting on a card in the Nobility Club of St Petersburg. She would throw the money in their faces. A shame how they treated Princess Radziwill, *née* Countess Rzewuski, the friend of Royalty! . . . She had to suffer because she had believed and still believed in Rhodes. She would keep quiet and could not reveal her secrets because Cecil Rhodes was still her friend. He would undoubtedly settle this trifling matter the next day.

The Princess was cruelly awakened from her day-dreams when the magistrate announced that the accused was indicted on twenty-four counts of fraud and forgery. The case was sent for trial at the Criminal Session of the Supreme Court. A few weeks later she was sentenced to two years' imprisonment.

Rhodes left court immediately after giving evidence. When he arrived at Groote Schuur the pain in his chest was stronger than ever before. The intensity of the pain increased and spread to his neck, down his arms and to his shaking hands. He felt as though somebody was drawing together the inside of his chest with barbed-wire, pulling it tighter and tighter until his heart could no longer beat freely and breathing became almost impossible. Large drops of sweat covered his face. Yet he felt cold and shivered. Everything in the room whirled around him. He could not move.

At first he did not know where he was. It was his own bed. But how had he got there? There was Dr Jim with his friendly face, trying hard to smile, leaning over him, holding his hand in his own strong white hand while with the other he took up a syringe.

'Tell me, Jameson,' Rhodes said almost inaudibly, 'tell me, is this the end, Jameson?'

The doctor swallowed several times before answering: 'Not quite—but it's damned serious.'

Dr Jameson and the other two doctors who attended him could not keep Rhodes in bed. The next day he was sitting in the library with Michell, the former bank manager who was in charge of all his business and private affairs, discussing his last will and testament. It bore the date 1 July 1899 and was a voluminous document with several codicils attached. This was his sixth will and there was not much left in it of the juvenile romanticism with which he had filled the pages of his first testament written on that rainy night in Kimberley exactly twenty-five years before.

Rhodes had removed the name of W. T. Stead from the list of trustees of his estate in 1901. There remained Earl Rosebery, Earl Grey, Beit, Milner, Michell and Hawkesley, and Rhodes now directed Michell to add the name of Dr Jameson to the list.

Rhodes' friendship with Stead had lost some of its intimacy during the passionate days of the Boer War when Stead had been one of the leading Boer-sympathizers and had pleaded against the annexation of the Transvaal.

At their last meeting, in 1901, Rhodes told him: 'I would annex the planets if I could. I often think of that.' Stead shook his head and said: 'I regret that they did not send you to jail at the Inquiry in 1897.' At the end of the argument Rhodes told Stead: '. . . If in future you should unfortunately feel yourself compelled to attack me personally as vehemently as you have attacked my policy in this war, it will make no difference to our friendship. I am too grateful to you for all that I have learnt from you to allow anything you may write or say to make any change in our relations.' They parted as friends.

Rhodes thumbed through his will. He had put his house in order. Provision had been made that all his intentions should be promptly carried out after his death. The value of his property no one could express in figures since most of his money had been invested in ventures in Rhodesia and Central Africa where no immediate returns could be expected. There were millions of pounds in shares of railways, of telegraphs and of mines all over Africa—from the Cape to deep into Central Africa—and of industrial, commercial and trading companies. His trustees would find the title-deeds to the tremendous ranches in Rhodesia, to his farms in the Cape, to his property of Groote Schuur, to valuable building land in all Rhodesian towns and to mining and water rights in Rhodesia for which the Rhodesian Government, after a legal battle, which lasted for twenty years, eventually had to pay millions to Rhodes' executors. But among all these assets which represented the fruit of Rhodes' labour over a period of more than thirty years only the shares of De Beers and Goldfields were paying dividends.

All his fortune went into a trust fund to be controlled by his executors. Groote Schuur, his residence and the adjoining property, he left as an official residence for the future Prime Ministers of a united South Africa. With touching forethought he provided an amount which was to be used to keep for the future Prime Minister 'at least two carriage horses, one or more carriages and sufficient stable servants . . . keeping and maintaining in good order the flower and kitchen gardens . . . two competent men servants to be housed, kept and employed. . . .'

His Dalham Hall estate he settled on his brother Colonel Frank Rhodes and his male heirs, while the remainder went to his brother Ernest and his male heirs with a provision—in order to prevent a 'loafer' from enjoying his property—that future heirs to the estate must 'have been for at least ten consecutive years engaged in some profession or business, such profession or business'—and here Rhodes again showed his dislike for everything military—'not being that of the Army'.

His attachment to his old college at Oxford he expressed by leaving Oriel College a sum of £100,000. Remembering the poor dinners and indifferent wines which had been served to him when he was entertained by the Dons, he left a further £10,000 'by the income whereof the dignity and comfort of the High Table may be maintained by which means the dignity and comfort of the resident Fellows may be increased'.

The realities of life had taught a maturing Rhodes that the ideas and ideals which he had cherished in his enthusiasm for British Imperialism *à la* Ruskin in his youth would find no understanding among the new generation of a new era. For his Secret Society there was no hope in the future of introducing a *Pax Britannica*. Britain had finally established herself as the predominant world power and all that was needed was a consolidation of her position which could only be brought about, as Stead had taught him, by world peace. He wanted to prepare a better form of *Pax Britannica*, based on a supra-national understanding between the nations which were linked by racial ties. If Britons, British Colonials, Americans and Germans were given an opportunity to know each other better these nations would be drawn closer together and would form a *bloc* sufficiently powerful to guarantee permanent peace.

Such was Rhodes' idea when he founded the Rhodes Scholarship at the University of Oxford by which 60 students from the British Colonies, 100 Americans and 15 Germans, selected personally by the Kaiser, were to receive £250 p.a. (the amount being later augmented by the Trustees) for a period of three years. Rhodes stipulated that qualification for the scholarship should be independent of race or religious opinion.

For the selection of the students by the Trustees Rhodes gave the following qualifications 'as mere suggestions for the guidance of those who will have the choice of students . . . who shall not be merely bookworms':

I his literary and scholastic attainments.

II his fondness of and success in manly outdoor sport such as cricket, football and the like.

III his qualities of manhood, truth, courage, devotion to duty, sympathy for the protection of the weak, kindliness, unselfishness and fellowship.

IV his exhibition during school days of moral force and character and of instincts to lead and to take an interest in his schoolmates. . . .

Rhodes had discussed these qualifications thoroughly with various people and before he made his final stipulations he had explained his point of view to Stead and Hawkesley:

'First there are the three qualities. You know I am all against letting the scholarships merely to people who swot over books, who have spent all their time over Latin and Greek. But you must allow for the element which I call "smug" and which means scholarship. That is to stand for four-tenths. Then there is "brutality", which stands for two-tenths. Then there is tact and leadership, again two-tenths, and then there is "unctuous rectitude", two-tenths. . . .'

With trembling hands he put his signature to the last codicil. He was exhausted. Another attack followed within the next few weeks. Again he could not lie in bed as the doctors had prescribed. Listlessly he dragged himself from one room to another, resting on a couch for a few minutes, changing over to a chair and then wandering through the rooms of Groote Schuur gasping for breath, 'like a caged animal', as one of his secretaries said. A windless heat-wave made it impossible for him to sit outside. Even in the darkened rooms the heat was becoming unbearable. His whole body was bathed in perspiration. Every piece of clothing was too much; even the lightest pyjamas he tore open.

Sometimes, towards evening, he would ride in his motor-car. He took a childish delight in whizzing along the road at the devilish speed of 20 m.p.h. It made him feel better.

The doctors, hoping that he would find some relief at the seaside, sent him to Muizenberg, an idyllic fishing village on False Bay, where he had recently bought a simple cottage in preparation for building a house there. The cooling sea breeze allowed him to breathe more freely. The spasms in his chest became less painful. For hours he would sit in front of his cottage looking at the rollers breaking into bubbling foam against the rocks below. But then there followed nights of agony, with the terrifying feeling that the poor labouring heart had come to a stop. He moaned and groaned and wanted to cry out. He would not have a nurse. One of his secretaries always sat beside him. Sometimes, in his dreadful struggle, Rhodes would ask him to hold his hand or to cool his hot head by putting his hand on his forehead.

A specially large window was knocked out of the front wall of the three-roomed cottage to give him as much fresh sea air as possible. The thatched roof was opened in various places and buckets of ice placed there, and a fan was installed over his bed.

He could no longer get out of bed. His legs had become dropsical. Silver tubes had to be inserted to drain the fluid from his body. For a day or two he would feel slightly relieved. He was propped up in bed so that he could watch the road and the little fleet of fishing-boats in the bay. His breathing was easier when he sat up, but the efforts to raise himself were so strenuous that often his head would drop back.

One day he asked Toni to bring him a file out of his desk. The doctors were afraid that he would start working again and thus cause a new, perhaps the final, attack. Out of an envelope, however, Rhodes took several small amateur photographs. For some minutes he stared at them, until they dropped to the floor. Dr Jameson picked them up: they were snapshots of his eldest brother's grave: 'A great, a very great gentleman, Herbert was,' came Rhodes' soft hoarse voice. Toni was called again at midnight: 'I am sick of the damn jellies, beef teas and custards, Toni, these damn doctors force me to swallow. Grill me a couple of nice chops—on an open fire as we had them on the veld. And bring me with it a tankard of iced champagne and stout—the old Kimberley mixture.'

Toni, afraid to let his master break the prescribed strict diet, reported Rhodes' request to Dr Jameson. The doctors knew that he had only a few more days to live at the most and that up to now death had been delayed only by his iron constitution. Dr Jameson therefore replied: 'Let him have it. Nothing will hurt him any longer.'

It gave the doctor and the servant great pleasure to see the patient finish his meal with a ferocious appetite, while he poured down the cooling drink in quick large gulps, sighing: 'Ah, that makes a man of one!' A few days later, also at midnight, he felt inclined for a guinea fowl and a bottle of Hock. Soon afterwards, however, he was again plagued by the agony of a choking attack. In spite of being convulsed with piercing pains he no longer complained or groaned. Though his face was contorted, only a soft sigh escaped his lips. When the attack had lessened and he was again alone, Toni and one of the doctors in attendance in the next room heard the dying man talk. They thought that he might be delirious or talking in his sleep. Rhodes, however, was wide awake. From the daily Bible lessons which the children of the Vicarage had had to endure before they were allowed to play, much had remained in his memory. Now, on the verge of death, he wanted to draw up the balance-sheet of his life. When Rhodes had wished to reason with someone he had always put his arguments in the form of questions to which he supplied his own answers: 'You'll ask—and I answer you fairly——' In a colloquy with God he now put the questions and gave the answers, counting up frankly and ruthlessly all his shortcomings, faults, sins and crimes.

Did the ghost of Grobler, the Transvaal envoy in Matabeleland who had been killed in ambush, appear to him? Did he see the regal figure of Lobengula, dying on his flight, robbed of his country? Did he remember the masses of black corpses mown down by machine-gun fire in Mashonaland and Matabeleland? Could he hear the piercing shrieks emanating from the caves in the Matopos where women and children had been dynamited to force their men to surrender? Was he disturbed by the tears of the numerous mothers, wives and sweethearts who longed for the young soldiers buried under a wooden cross in South Africa? Did he recall the burnt homesteads of thousands of Boers, the women and children who had died in concentration camps? Was his conscience troubled by the thousands of pensioners and widows, the little folk who had lost the savings of a lifetime through Chartered shares and were now paupers? Did he think of the thousands of strong healthy Natives who had come to work in the mines of Kimberley and the Rand and went back to their kraals with maimed limbs or their lungs eaten away by phthisis, or of those, more fortunate, who were killed instantly by a rock, a fall or a machine? Perhaps he compared his own fate with that of the man to destroy whom he had devoted almost thirty years of his life. Did he visualize, now, in the struggle with death, this venerable old man Paul Kruger, almost an octogenarian, sitting in a villa in Switzerland, a homeless lonely refugee, his small wise elephant-eyes reddened by tears, his voice hoarse from praying, his once imposing body bent by sorrow, longing for his land, his family, and the blessed soil of the Transvaal?

Cecil Rhodes could not have been fully satisfied with his achievements. In this hour of departure he recited Job's lament that he had not died in infancy:

> For now should I have lain still and been quiet, I should have slept; then had I been at rest with kings and counsellors of the earth, which built desolate places for themselves. . . .

Yes, he had done his job. He had painted the map of southern Africa red, British red. For his 'dreams' he had sacrificed his health, his life and all that he had gained from gold and diamonds. And the result? He had not intended that the Imperial Factor should step in and take over so that the military gentlemen and civil servants and politicians, from 6,000 miles away, should rule half a continent blindfold by a policy of vengeance. Cecil Rhodes had to learn that, after all, he had only been a pawn on the chess-board of British Imperialism. In Whitehall South Africa had lost her significance as an individual unit. For the urgency of British imperial global strategy, for Britain's economic life, South Africa bore value only as a link in the British Empire. In helping to forge this link Rhodes had been welcomed, but if he had dared to separate the link and hammer it into an independent ring he would have been stopped.

A deep sigh escaped Rhodes' tortured chest. A stanza from Tennyson's *In Memoriam* came to his mind and he spoke it slowly like a prayer:

> So many worlds, so much to do,
> So little done, such things to be. . . .

To the astonishment of Dr Jameson who had just entered the room he muttered over and over again: 'So much to do—— So little done—— So much to do. . . .'

As he had so often done in discussions with his friend Stead, he mused on the sense of Life: 'From the cradle to the grave—what is it? Three days at the seaside. Just that and nothing more. But although it is only three days, we must be doing something. I cannot spend my time throwing stones into the water. But what is worth while doing?'

He became quite upset when he was told that the Archbishop intended to come and see him. No, he did not want him. He had his own religion which did not need a church or a priest. He asked his secretary to pass him a little book. The worn binding and soiled pages with numerous pencil marks indicated that the owner must have carried it with him for many years and made use of it constantly and intensely. It was a pocket edition of Marcus Aurelius' *Meditations*. His 'pocket bible', Rhodes used to call it. Wherever he went the little book always had to be handy and in his bedroom it was kept on his night-table. He pointed to a passage, heavily underlined, and asked that it be read to him. As the secretary, his voice almost choking, began to read how the Roman Emperor consoled those who feared the approach of death, the dying man's lips moved as though pronouncing each word:

> You have been a citizen of the great world-city. Five years or fifty, what matters it? To every man his due as law allots. Why then protest? No tyrant gives you your dismissal, no unjust judge, but nature, who gave you the admission. It is like the praetor discharging some player whom he has engaged—'But the five acts are not complete; I have played but three.' Good: Life's drama, look you, is complete in three. The completeness is in his hands who first authorized your composition, and now your dissolution. Neither was your work. Serenely take your leave; serene as he who gives you the discharge.

He rested for a while. Toni was called: 'Bring me the *Argus* that I can see what they write about my illness—These damn medicos never tell one the real truth.' When the doctors had seen that he would last only a few more days, his friends, knowing that the published bulletins would only upset him, had had a special copy printed daily which stated that he was making good progress and that a quick recovery could be expected. To cheer him up they had also altered the quotations of his shares—which had dropped considerably after the news of his illness—to show a rising tendency.

The equinoctial storms which usually bring cooling north-westerly winds and often rain had not arrived towards the end of March. The heat-wave over Cape Town and its suburbs continued with unabated intensity. Gasping for air, his face puffy and purple, his clammy hands holding his aching chest, he lay motionless as though waiting for death. Suddenly Jameson noticed that he was trying to turn his face away from the window, while muttering almost inaudibly: 'Damn that woman! Why can't she leave one alone?' Jameson instinctively looked out of the window. There indeed he saw the heavy figure of Princess Radziwill, decked out in her usual shabby finery, about to pass Rhodes' cottage again in her peculiar gliding gait.

He was still fully aware of what was going on around him. Once, when he heard that his servant George, a Coloured 'boy', had been rude to someone at the gate, he scolded him and punished him by making him sit up with him the whole night. He ordered him to sit up straight in a chair opposite him. The tired servant, when he thought his master had fallen asleep, began to make himself more comfortable, but Rhodes had noticed the movement and told him, shaking his fist at him jokingly: 'Sit there—you just sit there!'

Besides Toni, all three of his secretaries were constantly in attendance, together with three doctors and his brother Elmhirst who had just arrived from England on holiday. A few of his friends were admitted to the sickroom for a few minutes at a time. Molteno was so touched by the 'tragical and pitiful sight' that he could not speak. Afterwards he said: 'I can compare Rhodes now to a great setting sun, low down in the west, and the consuming fire within was burning him up.'

Garrett came to see him and also had to hide his emotions when he saw Rhodes 'very stoical and noble about it after the end was in sight, only sometimes there was a caged-soul look in his eyes'.

On about 22 March the doctors noticed that their patient was slowly sinking. He had to be kept almost permanently under oxygen. The news was flashed over the whole world. Editors sent instructions to their 'morgues' to prepare the necrologues of Cecil Rhodes.

Neither the contemporary writers sitting in judgment over him, nor later biographers, could do Cecil Rhodes full justice. The former were too close to a period of transition, with its birth of Britain's African colonies and all the ugly labour connected with the consolidation of the British Empire. Thus, no matter whether the opinions on Rhodes were favourable or condemning, they were all slanted in accordance with the events of the time. Men of the twentieth century, on the other hand, can have less understanding of a 'man of action' like Rhodes, the typical product of a time of forceful expansion in political, economic and social spheres. The political morality of our times has changed. The nineteenth century had a different moral code, especially in colonial matters, from what we pretend to have today. Some of his contemporary judges could thus come nearer to what is probably an unbiased opinion of Rhodes than we can arrive at today.

J. C. Molteno, in his memoirs, came to the following conclusion:

> The ordinary man cannot judge Rhodes, for he cannot understand him. The world can tolerate few men like Rhodes, and certainly only one at a time. Some think and say he was the last great Englishman. One may not say it aloud, but think it, thank God, and Rhodes was man enough not to think but to say it. His ambition and his knowledge of his bad health were his only excuses.

No one loved him more than W. T. Stead. Thus his final judgment may be accepted as a fairly just one:

> For with all his faults, the man was great, almost immeasurably great, when contrasted with the pigmies who pecked and twittered in his shade. It is seldom in the annals of the empire that one man has been permitted in his brief career to illustrate both the qualities which build up empires and faults which destroy them. . . .

Garrett called Rhodes an 'historical necessity'. Ex-President Cleveland, on hearing about Rhodes' illness, remarked to a South African parliamentarian visiting Washington: 'America would pay three hundred million dollars for Cecil Rhodes. You have got him for nothing; make the most of him!'

During his lifetime two novels were published in which Rhodes, in very transparent disguise, was the main figure: Anthony Hope's *The God in the Car* and Morley Roberts' *The Colossus*. In the latter work the author describes Loder (Rhodes) as 'the concentrated essence of England':

> He was a representative, and not an individual; his passions, thoughts, plans, and desires had the force and vagueness characteristic of all Britons, not of one. . . . He is not ordinary: he is a microcosm; you ask absurdities when you ask him to be moral with

> the morality of Brixton. You might as well require geography to be moral or electricity or a steam engine. . . . He is not a man; he is a kind of floating island, a movable England, the colonizing, grabbing instinct made concrete. . . . Behind his nature was the sombre and powerful genius of the English nation. It worked, as he worked; it was strong and it was petty; it was cruel, it was kind; it knew no scruples, yet sometimes shied at very shadows; it was inexorable as death, energetic as the sun itself, as cruel as hate, as childlike as mere folly—bland, blatant, inevitable, humorous. . . .

An old enemy, Wilfrid S. Blunt, could not even let this sad occasion go by without some biting remarks:

> . . . Rhodes was one of those of whom one always had to ask oneself: '*Quel intérêt peut-il avoir en mourant?*' . . . I think he really blundered and blustered and pretended to be wise to people who looked upon him, on account of his first successes, as an oracle. I have seen just the same thing at Homburg in the old gambling days, when a man who had broken the bank once was followed by admiring crowds, who credited him with supernatural intelligence, and went on believing in him till the day he lost all and disappeared. . .

The newspaper men, anxiously waiting for the news of Rhodes' death, were surprised to learn on 23 March that Rhodes would sail for England in three days' time.

The news was a fact. On Sunday afternoon, 23 March, Rhodes thought that he felt better, a symptom known as *euphoria* which clearly indicated that the end was near. Rhodes declared that he wanted to go to England. He was like a lion wanting to go to his old den to die. It was no use arguing with him. It would only have distressed him and caused a new attack. Dr Jameson only told him that transport over the bad roads might kill him before he reached the ship. Rhodes remained adamant. Workmen had to work day and night to install electric fans, a refrigerating plant and an oxygen tent in the cabins reserved for Rhodes in the mailship *Saxon*.

Even on the morning of Wednesday, 26 March, Rhodes hoped that he would be able to sail in the afternoon. Towards midday he became unconscious. While Rhodes was fighting his last battle for his life a telegram arrived from Naples: 'God be with you. Jan Hofmeyr.' Rhodes was no longer able to grasp this token of reconciliation from an old friend who had not spoken to him for more than six years.

Rhodes awoke from his stupor in the afternoon, but he soon became restless and his distorted face showed that he was in pain. His eyes were wide open. In a soft voice he sang to himself. It sounded like a hymn. Dr Jameson had just gone out of the room for a smoke. In a clear voice Rhodes asked for Jameson. He took his friend's hand and held it in a weak grip. His voice was hoarse as he muttered to Jameson: 'So little done, so much to do.'

A few minutes before six o'clock he turned his head slightly and closed his eyes. Dr Jameson did not need to feel his pulse: he knew that Cecil J. Rhodes was dead.

INDEX

INDEX

A

Abercorn, Duke of, 175, 200
Aborigines Protection Society, 91, 92, 96, 102, 180, 268
Afrikaans, 74
Afrikaner Bond, 74–6, 80, 94, 195, 197–8, 205, 363
Alcock, Sir Rutherford, 43–4
Allen, James Lane, *The Choir Invisible*, 249
Amalgamated Gold Fields of South Africa; *see* Gold Fields of South Africa
Arnold, Sir Edwin, 44, 172

B

Babyaan, 137, 158, 183, 334
Bailey, Abe, 281, 297
Baines, Tom, 139, 140, 179
Baker, Herbert, 243–4, 246
Balfour, Arthur, 170, 220
Barkly West, 69–70, 195–6
Barnato, Barney, 106–23, 128, 281, 297, 360–2
Barnato, Harry, 107–9
Barotseland, 207, 209
Bechuanaland, 27, 84–7, 89–92, 95, 102, 104, 231, 267–70, 369; *see* Bechuanaland police, Goshenland, Stellaland
Bechuanaland Exploration Company, 168–9
Bechuanaland police, 155, 186, 188, 191, 198–9, 201, 210, 227, 236–9, 268, 288, 299
Beira, 223–7
Beit, Alfred, 56–9, 126–8, 149, 168, 179, 222, 297; Barnato transactions, 110, 114–17, 120–122; friendship with Rhodes, 58–60, 68, 277, 402, 403, 408; in British S. A. Company, 169, 170, 175, 226, 266, 324; Johannesburg rising, 278, 285, 300, 323, 341, 349
Belgium, 77, 89, 198, 205
Bell, Moberly, 163
Berlin, congress on colonies, 89
Berliner National Zeitung, 356
Bishop's Stortford, 3
Bismarck, Prince, 43, 87–8, 91, 170, 171, 206, 250–1, 305
Bloemfontein, Bishop of, 150
Blue ground, 50, 109
Blunt, W. S., 418
Boers, 13, 19, 26–7, 77, 78, 84, 91, 99, 100, 139; *see* Kruger, Pretoria Convention, Transvaal
Booth, General, 220
Bosungwana, 239–40
Bower, Sir Graham, 144, 155, 158, 185, 242, 269, 284, 286, 289, 290, 293, 351, 353
Brand, President, 132
British South Africa Company: forming of, 169, 179, 196; Charter, 177, 178, 180–1,

British South Africa Company —*contd.* 185, 190–1, 304, 315, 318, 320, 324–5, 351, 353; support for, 175, 181; opposition to, 177, 189; police force, 202, 208, 223, 226; financial fluctuations, 222, 229, 230, 253, 266, 320, 328, 330, 364; acquisitions, 208, 209, 235, 240
Buller, General Sir Redvers, 381
Bullingdon Club, 36
Bülow, Baron Bernhard von, 373, 375, 376
Burdett-Coutts, Baroness, 174
Burgers, President, 77
Burns, Robert, 250
Butler, Sir William, 377

C

Cambridge, Duke of, 339
Cambridge University, 4
Cameroons, 89
Cape Colony, 5, 70–1, 73, 76, 87, 214, 298
Cape Parliament, 69, 324; *see* Progressive Party; *see also under* Rhodes
Cape Times, 66, 265, 365
'Cape to Cairo', 44–5, 171–2, 174, 175, 178, 181, 205, 213, 253
Cape Town, 72
Cape Town, Archbishop of, 313–14
'Caprivi Zipfel', 206
Carrington, General Sir Frederick, 332
Cawston, George, 165, 168–70, 175, 179
Central Search Association, 168
Cetywayo, 24
Chaka, 138–9, 239
Chamberlain, Joseph, 41, 95, 164–5, 167, 173, 189, 267–9, 296–305, 317–18, 321–2, 327, 343–4, 348, 350–1, 353–6, 366, 370, 378–9
Churchill, Lord Randolph, 96
Churchill, W. S., 402
Coal, 193, 370
Cohen, Louis, 108
Coillard, François, 256–7
Colenbrander, Johann, 334–5, 336
Colesberg Kopje, 21
Colquhoun, Archibald, 208
Committee of Inquiry; *see* Jameson's Raid
Copper, 370
Cotton planting, 9, 11–14
Cronje, General, 307
Cronwright, Samuel, 257–8, 396
Currie, Sir Donald, 115–16

D

Daily Chronicle, 209
Daily Mail, 378
Daily News, 320
Daily Telegraph, 42–4
Dalham Hall, 405, 409
Dalston, 175
Damaraland, 88
Dawson, James, 147
De Beers Central Company, 110
De Beers Consolidated Mines, 122, 124, 125, 168, 181, 193, 222, 254, 280
De Beers Diamond Mining Company, 50, 64, 83, 121, 123
De Beers Mine, 28–9, 49, 64, 68, 110, 111, 116, 121

Delagoa Bay, 12, 211–12, 306–7
de la Rey, 93, 105
d'Erlanger, Baron, 175
de Souza, Manuel Antonio, 208
De Villiers, Lord, 259
de Wet, Sir Jacobus, 228
de Worms, Baron, 167
de Worms, G. & A., 175
Diamond Syndicate, 124
Diamonds, 9–10, 12–13, 16–22, 28, 32, 33, 47–9, 51, 65, 71, 111, 112, 137–8, 255–6; *see* Blue ground, De Beers, Diamond Syndicate, French Diamond Mining Company, Illicit Diamond Buying, Kimberley
Dingaan, 239
Disraeli, Benjamin, 39, 40, 45
Dunn, John, 24
Dunvegan Castle, 341
Durban, 29
Dutch, 70–1, 74; *see* Afrikaners
Dutch East India Company, 26
Du Toit, Reverend S. J., 74, 75, 90, 94, 98, 102, 228

E

Edward, Prince of Wales, 174–5, 253, 345, 362, 376
Ellis, Havelock, 392
England: expansion in Africa, 19, 44, 91–2, 143–6, 151, 152, 166–7, 171–3, 226, 238, 298; policy in Cape Colony, 70, 71, 74, 76; prestige, 356; relations with Transvaal, 40–1, 78, 79, 90, 194, 267, 274, 300, 377–85; treaties with Germany and Portugal, 206–8
Eton, 4
Exeter Hall; *see* Aborigines Protection Society
Exploring Company, 149, 158, 165, 166, 168; *see* Maund, E. A.

F

Fairfield, E., 300, 301, 318
Farquhar, Sir Horace B., 175
Ferreira, Colonel Ignatius, 229
Fife, Duke of, 175
Fort Charter, 203
Fort Macloutsie, 210
Fort Salisbury, 203, 209, 234
Fort Victoria, 203, 233–4
Fortnightly Review, 163, 173
France, 89, 205
Freemasonry, 36
Free State Express, 219
French Diamond Mining Company, 110, 117–19
Fry, John, 148

G

Garrett, Edmund, 265, 277, 292, 293, 331, 343, 345, 365, 416, 417
Gaulois, 302
Gaza concession, 224
Gazaland, 223, 224, 227
Germany, 40, 42, 77, 87–91, 141, 143, 170, 173, 187, 198, 205–7, 302, 305–9, 375–6; *see* Bismarck, Wilhelm II
Gibbon, Edward, 249–52
Gifford, Lord, 165, 168–70, 175, 179

Gladstone, W. E., 19, 41, 43–5, 78, 79, 88–90, 95, 171–2
Gold: concessions, 137–59; discoveries of, 27, 39, 40, 84, 126–8, 139, 209; methods of mining, 126, 193–4, 264, 280; prices, 193, 265, 360–1; prospects, 181, 221–3, 229–30, 253, 266, 298, 328, 364; *see* Gold Fields of South Africa, Ophir, Witwatersrand
Gold Fields of South Africa, 130, 131, 169, 181, 193, 195, 223, 254
Goold-Adams, Colonel H., 236–9
Gordon, General, 81–2, 334
Goschen, Lord, 171
Goshenland, 85, 92–4, 97, 102
Greater Britain, 401
Grey, Earl, 300, 408
Grey, Lord, 175, 303, 319, 325–7, 330, 333, 365, 368
Griqualand, 13, 19, 42, 69
Grobler, Pieter, 142, 146–7
Grobler Treaty, 142, 145
Grootboom, John, 334, 338–9
Groote Schuur, 243–5, 247, 259, 276, 326, 364, 409
Gun-running, 12–13

H

Hamilton, Frederic, 277, 284
Hammond, J. H., 283, 315, 323
Harcourt, Sir William, 217, 231, 321, 326, 327, 346–50, 352–5, 371
Harris, Frank, 256
Harris, Dr Rutherford, 260–1, 268, 277–8, 281–5, 295, 300–1, 303–4, 319, 341, 343, 350, 351
Harrow, 4
Hatchards Ltd., 251
Hatzfeldt, Count, 306
Hawkesley, Bourchier, 318–19, 324, 327, 352–4, 408, 411
Heany, Major, 283, 284, 289
Heligoland, 206
Helm, Reverend C. D., 152–3, 156–8, 174
Hicks-Beach, M., 370, 371
Hofmeyr, Jan Hendrik, 74–6, 80–1, 89, 92, 95, 195, 197–8, 203–4, 217, 289, 293–5, 313–15, 317, 418
Hohenlohe, Prince, 306–8
Holden, Captain, 283
Holstein, Baron von, 305–8, 373
Hope, Anthony, *The God in the Car*, 417

I

Ice-machine, 29
Illicit Diamond Buying, 58, 110, 124, 125
Investor's Review, 357

J

Jameson, Leander Starr: early history, 53–5; friendship with Rhodes, 54–6, 58, 68, 129, 241, 253, 261, 262, 344–5, 367–8, 402–6, 408, 412, 418–19; Barnato transactions, 110, 112, 114, 123; relations with Lobengula, 158–9, 187, 189–92, 201, 233–41; part in British S. A. Company, 169, 223, 227–9,

232; part in expansion of gold territories, 202, 208, 222, 224; smallpox, 85, 239; *see* Jameson's Raid
Jameson's Raid, 277–8, 281–3, 285–90, 293–5, 304–7, 309, 310, 314, 317, 321, 323, 326, 389, 397; Inquiry into, 327, 343–58
Joel, S. B., 114, 122, 281, 314, 361
Johannesburg, 126, 130, 132, 193–4, 264
Johannesburg rising, 265–79, 281–95, 299–303, 314; *see also* Jameson's Raid
Johannesburg Star, 293
Johnson, Frank, 201, 203
Johnston, Harry Hamilton, 171–3
Joubert, Pieter, 94, 140, 212, 227, 232

K

Kaiser; *see* Wilhelm II
Katanga basin, 370, 373
Kekewich, Colonel R. G., 381, 383, 384
Khama, 146–7, 238
Kimberley, 16–18, 21, 22, 24, 34, 51, 58, 67, 69, 380–3
Kimberley Central Company, 107, 110, 111, 113, 115–17, 119–21, 123
Kimberley Club, 107, 121, 122, 201, 382
Kimberley Literary Society, 257
Kimberley Mine, 21, 28, 106, 109–11, 113, 115, 117
Kipling, Rudyard, 247
Kitchener, Lord, 371, 372, 376, 383, 384
Knorr, Admiral, 308
Knutsford, Lord, 154, 165–8, 170, 177, 178
Koopmans-De Wet, Mrs, 388–90
Kruger, Paul: leadership of Boers, 78, 98–100, 232, 368, 413–14; expansion of Transvaal, 86, 94, 97, 100–2, 142, 171; relations with Europe, 91, 146, 296, 299, 306, 308, 375; relations with Rhodes, 102, 105, 131, 194–5, 211–12, 220, 227–8, 265–70, 376, 377, 379; distrust of foreigners, 132–4; Johannesburg conspiracy, 292–4, 323, 361; *see* Boers, Transvaal

L

Labouchere, Henry du Pré, 167, 176, 241, 320, 324, 326, 327, 346, 348, 349, 353
Lawson, Sir Wilfred, 344
Lendy, Captain, 233–4
Leonard, Charles, 277, 281–6, 288
Leopold II of the Belgians, 43, 90, 372–3
Leslie, David, 40
'Letter of Invitation', 287–8, 304, 378
Lewanika, 209
Leyds, Dr, 105, 301, 306, 375, 380
Lippert concession, 189, 232
Lippert, Edward A., 57, 149, 187–9
Lloyd George, 378

Lobengula: negotiations with concession hunters, 137, 139–142, 144–6, 148–51, 165, 168, 169, 171, 182–4, 188, 189; Rudd concession, 152–9, 167, 178, 186; letters to Queen Victoria, 165–6, 185–6, 235; resistance to British S. A. Company, 190–2; 202, 220; elimination of, 232–42; treasure of, 138, 183, 232, 236, 239, 240; *see also under* Jameson
Loch, Sir Henry Brougham, 199–201, 209–13, 226–8, 231, 234, 236, 237, 240, 269, 299, 300
Lodge, Senator Henry Cabot, 255
London Convention, 1884, 142, 143, 171, 267
London Missionary Society, 152, 268
Lotje, 137, 157, 183
Low, Sir Sidney, 163

M

Mackenzie, Reverend John, 91–3, 96, 97, 102, 176
MacMahon, General, 43
MacNeill, Swift, 160–1
Maguire, T. R., 34, 149, 150, 156, 175, 184, 302, 319, 354, 402
Majuba Hill, 78, 142
Manicaland, 207–8, 224–7
Marcus Aurelius, 252, 415
Marks, Sammy, 376
Martin, Sir George, 247
Martin, Sir Richard, 329, 338
Marx, Karl, 37
Mashonaland, 141, 158, 165, 190, 192, 198–203, 206, 209–11, 220–2, 227–30, 232–4
Matabele, 139, 236–9, 328–38
Matabeleland, 27, 138, 139, 141, 160, 162; *see* Lobengula
Matabeleland Scandal, The, 241
Mauch, Karl, 27
Maund, E. A., 149, 152, 156–8, 165, 166
Maund concession, 179
Meade, Sir Robert, 300, 351
Merriman, John Xavier, 25, 197, 203, 292, 317, 324, 363
Metcalfe, Charles, 34–5, 169, 173, 403
Methuen, Lord, 383
Michell, Sir Lewis, 362, 408
Milner, Sir Alfred, 366–9, 377, 378, 381, 384, 385, 407, 408
Milner, Lord, 220
Missionary Road, 27, 83, 84, 86, 87
Moffat, Reverend J. S., 145–7, 151, 152, 154, 157, 158, 183, 185, 186, 232, 235; *see* Moffat Treaty
Moffat, Robert, 139, 145
Moffat Treaty, 171
Molteno, J. C., 197, 363, 366, 416, 417
Morning Leader, 320
Moscow Gazette, 356
Mount Hampden, 203

N

Namaqualand, 88
Napoleon, 249
Natal, 5, 9
News of the World, 378

Newton, Sir Francis, 144, 155, 158, 234, 269, 351
New York World, 316–17, 380
Nineteenth Century, The, 204–5
Norris, J., 259–60
Nouvelle Revue, 379
Nyasaland, 173, 206
Nyasaland agreement, 179

O

Ophir, Gold of, 27, 84, 127, 176, 182, 210, 403
Orange Free State, 19, 170–1
Oriel College, Oxford, 31, 410
Oriental Company, 110
Oxford University, 30–45, 83, 376; *see* Oriel College, Rhodes Scholarship

P

Paarl, 197
Pall Mall Gazette, 161–3
Parnell, Charles Stuart, 160, 161, 163, 164
Peacock, Sophia, 5, 8, 9
Pfeil, Count, 150
Phillips, Lionel, 279, 299, 300, 314, 323
Pickering, N. E., 68–9, 129
Plumer, Colonel, 330
Pondoland, 240
Porges, Jules, 57
Portugal, 77, 89, 141, 143, 191, 198, 205, 207–8, 223–7, 306
Pretoria Convention, 79, 90
Progressive Party, 363, 378
Prout, Colonel, 371
Pungwe River, 224–6

R

Radziwill, Princess, 398–402, 404–7, 416
Railways, 29, 91, 132–3, 168–9, 177, 193, 195, 211, 215, 223, 253, 266–7, 359, 368–74
Rand; *see* Witwatersrand
Reade, Winwood, *The Martyrdom of Man*, 25
'Red Caps', 21, 28
Renny-Tailyour, E. R., 149, 187, 188
Review of Reviews, 254, 324, 378
Rhodes, Cecil John:
I. *General:* birth and education, 6–8, 10, 12, 15, 19, 20, 31–3, 34–6, 44, 45, 83; character, 5–8, 15, 16, 23, 33, 37, 55, 56, 63, 67, 113, 216, 244, 250, 260–1, 263, 363; health, 9, 26, 31, 46, 47, 52, 68, 215, 216, 262–3, 326, 359–60, 363, 367–8, 388, 402, 404–6, 408, 411–13, 415–16; love of talking, 24, 35, 60, 72; interests in art, literature and history, 25, 247–52; social status, 33–6, 244, 253–4, 324, 366; reputation, 67, 97, 104, 125, 248, 258, 339, 376; 'squaring', 70, 82, 161, 182, 195, 204, 254, 256–7, 367; interest in power, 112, 114, 128, 254, 365; relations with Press, 161–3, 176, 200, 204–5, 256, 326; treatment of natives, 11, 15, 250, 328–9, 335–7, 382; agricultural activites, 26–7, 218, 367, 403–4; interest in flowers, 245–6; private zoo, 246; houses and private property, 26–7, 132, 175, 243–5, 405; entertaining,

Rhodes, Cecil John—*contd.*
259–60; attitude to women, 386–402, 406–7, 275–6; private income, 254; honours and achievements, 52, 376, 414, 416–18; friendships, 24, 53–6, 58, 59, 68–9, 81–2, 129, 403; *see also* Schreiner, W. P.; death, 418–19; wills, 62–3, 69, 220, 339, 362, 408–11
II. *Business Activities:* goes to Africa to plant cotton, 9, 11–14; activities in diamonds, 12–15, 19–22, 28–9, 46–51, 64–7, 83, 107, 110–24, 255–6; interests in Bechuanaland, 27, 83, 85, 86, 89, 92–7, 101–4, 209–10, 369; activities in gold, 126–9, 130, 131, 177, 195, 222–4; activities in Matabeleland, 143–59, 184–9, 232–42, 256, 330–8; work for British S. A. Company, 160, 162–81, 220–1, 223, 230, 364
III. *Political Activities:* influence of Ruskin on, 37, 38, 60; writes to Disraeli, 39; imperialism, 60–3, 68, 333; wish to 'eliminate the imperial factor', 79, 86, 97, 105, 164, 176, 195, 205, 213, 238; plans for unity and expansion in S. Africa, 73, 104, 205, 220, 264; in Cape Parliament, 69–72, 83, 88, 197, 198, 203–4, 206–7, 214–15, 217–19, 310, 314–15, 363, 365–6; alliance with Afrikaners, 74–6, 80, 197–8, 217; belief in federation, 160–1, 205, 385; relations with Kruger, 133, 142, 187, 211–12, 232, 376–7; meets Queen Victoria, 212–13; Liberalism, 231; interest in Ireland, 160–1; relations with Chamberlain, 164–6, 296–301, 318–21, 327; northward expansion in Africa, 172, 190–3, 195–6, 198–203, 208–11, 224–7, 231–2, 240–1; resistance to Boers, 227–9, 257–8, 280; Johannesburg revolt and Jameson's Raid, 265–70, 274, 277–9, 281–95, 302, 310–13; relations with Milner, 368–9; results of Jameson's Raid, 315–18, 320, 321, 323–4, 327–8, 339–58, 360–2; activities during war, 379–85
Rhodes, Edith, 5, 6, 251, 321, 386
Rhodes, Ernest, 4, 5, 409
Rhodes, Reverend Francis William, 3, 4, 6, 7, 8, 22
Rhodes, Frank, 4, 5, 7, 16, 23, 31, 104, 278, 282, 314, 321, 323, 409
Rhodes, Herbert, 4, 5, 9, 11–14, 16, 21, 22, 26–8, 68, 412
Rhodes, Louisa, 6, 7, 22, 30
Rhodes, Samuel, 175
Rhodes family, 4, 175, 251
Rhodes Scholarship, 410–11
Rhodesia, 241
Rhodesia Railway Company, 359
Ripon, Lord, 179, 231, 234, 299, 300
Roberts, Lord, 383, 384
Roberts, Morley, *The Colossus*, 417–18
Robinson, Sir Hercules, 92, 95, 96, 104, 143–4, 154, 155, 158, 176–7, 186, 269, 274, 289, 303–4, 353
Robinson, Joseph Benjamin, 65–7, 69, 126–8, 195, 224, 278, 297

Rolleston, Captain, 9, 13
Rose-Innes, 203, 324
Rosebery, Lord, 164, 166, 231, 232, 269, 274, 300, 302, 343, 345, 349, 373, 408
Rothschild, House of, 58, 117–120, 122, 128, 130, 163, 174, 181, 193, 230
Rothschild, Nathaniel Mayer, first Baron, 117, 163, 164, 172, 220, 223, 343, 345
Royal Geographical Society, 174
Royal Horse Guards, 190–1
Rudd, Charles Dunell, 24, 26, 28, 29, 32, 49, 50, 60, 68, 127, 129–31, 148–53, 168–70, 175, 179, 193, 194
Rudd concession, 152–60, 167, 178, 179, 184, 186, 189, 199, 227, 232
Ruskin, John, 37–8, 60

S

Saint James Gazette, 163
Salisbury, Lord, 143, 160, 170–173, 175, 178, 203, 205–7, 226, 274–5, 297, 306, 309, 318 323, 344, 362, 372
Samoa concession, 376
Saturday Review, 194, 256
Sauer, Hans, 112, 126–9, 197, 203, 237, 317, 335, 337, 349, 363
Saxon, 418
Schickerling, Maria Elizabeth, 388
Scholtz, Dr, 401
Schreiner, Olive, 204, 257–8, 341–2, 390, 391, 392–7; *Trooper Peter Halket*, 341, 397–8; *Story of an African Farm*, 391, 394–5, 397
Schreiner, W. P., 197, 218, 286, 289, 291–3, 310, 313, 317, 324–5, 341–2, 362–3, 393, 397
Secoconi, 12–13
Secret society, Rhodes' plan for British expansion, 62–3, 162, 219, 220, 410
Seeadler, 307
Selborne, Lord, 300, 343
Selous, Frederick Courteney, 174, 192, 199, 200, 202, 203, 208, 234
Shangani River, 239
Shaw, Flora, 301, 303, 304, 319, 350, 351
Shepstone, T., 188–9
Shippard, Sir Sidney Godolphin, 62, 144–5, 151, 152, 154–8, 185, 188, 209
Sigcau, 240–1
Slavery, 181, 329
Smith, 'Scotty', 84
Smuts, Jan Christiaan, 60, 198, 257–8, 378
Somabulane, 336
South Africa, policies for, 39, 41, 74–6, 79, 80, 104, 264, 367
South African League, 364
South African Republic, 78, 90; *see* Transvaal
Southey, Sir Richard, 10
Spectator, *The*, 229
Sprigg, Sir Gordon, 317
Stanley, H. M., 42–4, 170, 206
Stead, W. T., 161–3, 219, 220, 241, 254, 324, 345, 349, 378, 386, 392, 395, 408, 410, 411, 417
Stellaland, 85, 92, 93, 94, 95, 96, 102
Stellenbosch, 198

Stent, V., 335, 337
Strop Bill, 217
Sutherland, Duchess of, 387
Sutherland, Dr, 9, 10, 12–14, 25, 31
Swaziland, 227
Swaziland convention, 212
Swinburne, Sir John, 177

T

Tantallon Castle, 362
Tati district, 27, 177, 179
Telegraph, 177, 193, 253
Temps, Le, 356
Thompson, Frank R., 149–51, 153, 156, 182–7, 189, 277, 285
Times, The, 27, 40, 65, 104, 126, 132, 141, 160, 163, 176, 194, 219, 304, 317
Togoland, 89
Transvaal: expansion, 19, 94, 138–42, 212; gold in, 39, 40, 127, 132, 264–5, 280; relations with Germany, 299, 307; annexation of, 40, 41, 45, 77, 165; self-government restored to, 79; alliance with Orange Free State, 170–1; Reform movement in, 277–8, 281, 287, 314, 321, 361; coal in, 193; friendship with Cape, 265; English designs on, 266, 366, 368, 377–85; *see* Boers, Jameson's Raid, Johannesburg rising, Kruger
Transvaal Naturalization Law, 279
Travellers' Club, 324
Truth, 167–8, 241, 320
Twain, Mark, 357–8

U

Uganda, 206, 231–2
Uitlanders, agitation for alien franchise, 264–5, 279, 377, 378; *see* Johannesburg rising
Umkomaas Valley, 9, 11, 13
Umsheti, 137, 158, 183
Umziligazi, 137–9
United Concessions Company, 168, 179
University College, 31

V

Van Niekirk, 92, 93, 95, 96, 102
Van Pittius, Gey, 92–4
Varzin, Bismarck's farm, 88
Verschoyle, Reverend John, 163, 172
Victoria, Queen, 70, 142, 145, 157–8, 165–6, 185–6, 191, 207, 212–13, 235, 252, 308–9, 372, 375, 386
Vincent Club, 36
Von Bieberstein, Baron Marschall, 307, 308

W

Warren, General Sir Charles, 95–7, 100–4, 141, 144
Waterboer, 16, 19
Wernher, Julius, 57–8, 121
Westminster Budget, 357
White, Hon. 'Bobby', 318
Wilde, Oscar, 36–7
Wilhelm II, Kaiser, 33, 60, 173, 206, 275, 299, 305–9, 373–5
Williams, Gardner, 128
Williams, Ralph, 144